OMNIBUS PRESS
London / New York / Sydney

The Doors

on the road
Greg Shaw

ISBN: 0.7119.6546.3
Order No: OP 48001

Book produced by Stacy Kreutzmann Quinn at

Acid Test Productions
1370 Industrial Avenue, Suite G
Petaluma, California 94952

Editor: Coco Pekelis
Book design: David Dalton & Kip Shaw

PHOTO CREDITS
Tom Shaw: Title Page
Flower Children LTD/Chuck Boyd: Pages 15, 41, 71, 77, 82, 83, 87, 109, 123, 171
Elliott Landy, Landy Vision, Inc: Pages 3,95,115,121,139
Jack Rosen: Pages 5,7,11,17,21,33,101,105,129,135,151,161, Front cover photo
Gene Anthony: Pages vi, 1, 25, 49, 55, 63, 90, 91, 187, 197, 207, Back cover photo

Reviews from *Billboard* magazine used with permission from
BPI Communications, New York, New York
Reviews from *Variety* used with permission from
Cahners Publishing Corporation, New York, New York
Reviews from *Rolling Stone* used with permission from
Wenner Media Incorporated
Reviews from *Cash Box* used with permission from *Cash Box*

Exclusive Distributors
Book Sales Limited
8/9 Frith Street
London W1V 5TZ, UK

Music Sales Corporation
257 Park Avenue South
New York, NY 10010 USA

Music Sales Pty Limited
120 Rothschild Avenue, Rosebery
NSW 2018, Australia

To the Music Trade only:
Music Sales Limited
8/9 Frith Street
London W1V 5TZ, UK

A catalogue record for this book is available from the British Library

Printed in the United States of America by
Vicks Lithograph and Printing Corporation

Visit Omnibus Press at http://www.musicsales.co.uk

CON-TENTS

Author's Preface

In *The Doors On the Road* I have attempted to catalog accurately a performance history of the Doors—a group renowed for its live performances. To classify the sequence of historical events, I sought to verify the exact date and location of each show, and to assemble whatever information I could about the performance, as well as any additional notes of interest.

I would appreciate any opportunity to expand upon the information in this book, and I welcome anyone with additional information (including rare recordings, videos, articles, etc.) to contact me at the following address.

Greg Shaw
c/o TDM, Inc.
P.O.Box Orem Utah
Orem, Utah 84059-1441
E-Mail= greg@doors.com

My aspiration is to continue to document the Doors' history, correcting any errors and adding relevant information. Any requests for confidentiality will be honored (as they have been for this book).

When I first began researching this project, I compiled a rough draft of probable shows and their approximate dates—a sketchy outline devised for research purposes only. This misinformation appears to have circulated among Doors enthusiasts unaware that it was a crude approximation never intended for publication. A number of these shows were dead leads—events that never actually occurred—and many of the dates were weeks or months off. For *The Doors On the Road* I have double-checked every date to insure its accuracy, and I have let the reader know when the date or location was uncertain. As with any book of this nature, there are bound to be a few errors and for those I offer my sincere apologies. I hope *The Doors On the Road* serves as a helpful and comprehensive retrospective for all enthusiasts of the band. Should new information continue to emerge, it may well warrant a second edition!

The music's far from over.

Greg Shaw

Enthusiastic fan drops in on
the Fantasy Faire & Magic Festival
Mt Tamalpais, Marin County,
California, June 10, 1967.

Acknowledgments

Many people have given generously of their time and knowledge. In addition to the listing below, I wish to thank two in particular for their extensive contributions.

(1) I am exceptionally grateful to Andrew Hawley for his wealth of knowledge, unrelenting encouragement, and uncompromising generosity. Mr. Hawley unquestionably maintains the well-deserved reputation of having the premier collection of posters and handbills on the Doors, and he is always seeking to expand that collection. His forte is in art pieces, especially posters, and he has a phenomenal reputation in that field.

He is currently recognized as a prominent independent distributor; locating and merchandising rare and valuable posters, flyers, photographs and memorabilia from events of the 1940s through the 1970s. He coordinates the sale and trading of rare pieces while staying abreast of this rapidly fluctuating and demanding business.

Mr. Hawley is constantly on the lookout for concert ephemera from any of the bands from these time periods, especially:
The Doors
Jimi Hendrix
Old rhythm and blues
Jazz

Anyone interested in selling or trading rare art pieces or other treasures should contact him at:
Andrew Hawley
Beverly Hills, CA 90212
Phone: (310) 552-2851
Fax: (310) 552-2857

(2) I wish to extend my special thanks to Kerry Humpherys, the founder of *The Doors Collectors Magazine*, for his continued support for this project and his invaluable contributions. His extensive knowledge of the band, especially their post-Doors activities, has helped put this whole undertaking in perspective. I am indebted to his generosity of spirit and time, as well as his exceptionally amiable disposition. *The Doors Collectors Magazine* is absolutely the finest fanzine I have ever seen on the Doors. See the Bibliography for his address and ordering information.

The author would like to extend his genuine appreciation to all the people who have so generously contributed their time and knowledge toward the compilation of information included in this book. Many "Thank You's" for all of the support, guidance, patience and enthusiasm contributed by all.

First, I would like to thank those instrumental in publishing this work. My deepest gratitude is extended to my literary agent, George Wieser, whose persistence and steadfast encouragement in this and other projects helped bring the entire endeavor to fruition. And special thanks to all those involved with Acid Test Productions, especially Stacy Kreutzmann Quinn, Nancy Reid, David Dalton and Coco Pekelis, whose generous enthusiasm and inspiration kept the ball afloat when I had lost all objectivity.

I would particularly like to extend my deepest gratitude to Ray and Dorothy Manzarek, whose contributions to this project were incalculable. After speaking with them, it comes as no surprise that such notables as producer Paul Rothchild and author Albert Goldman frequently referred to the Doors as one of the brightest rock bands to have ever emerged on the scene. The Doors — IQ Rock — Mensa caliber rock 'n' roll — may it continue to eclipse the generations.

To those who wished to remain anonymous, I offer my sincerest gratitude. Your absence in this listing is certainly no reflection on the contributions you made.

In Alphabetical Order:

Tarric Akkad	Bob Gately	Ray Manzarek	James Salzer
Bruce Botnick	Bill Gazzarri	Chip McKuen	John Scott
Dave Bourdon	Albert Goldman	Ronnie Harran Mellon	Ira Schneider
Howard Branker	Barry Gruber	Phil Mendelson	Sue Schneider
Paul Carmaratta	Paul Grushkin	Fred Mills	Barclay Shaw, Jr.
Nancy Carter	Robert Haimer	Ranier Moddeman	Mrs. Barclay Shaw
Paul Caruso	Janet W. Hendricks	Bill Moran	Neal Skok
Larry Clark	Jerry Hopkins	James Musil	Larry Skuce
Joseph Cochrane	Nick Irwin	Bill Nitobi	Tarn Stephanos
Jeannie Cromie	Jay/Psychedelic Solution	Allen Orleman	Danny Sugerman
Bob Curling	Seth Johnson	Mike Parrish	Bill Tikellis
John Densmore	Sandra Kerwath	Harlan Peacock	Vince Treanor
Dennis Dewitt	Linda Kyriazi	Jerry Pompili	John Walden
Michael Dolgushkin	Andy Leoni	Jerry Prochnicky	Mark Wannamaker
Pam Elness	Richard Linnell	"The Rev!"	Gregg Williams
Bob Embrey	Frank Lisciandro	Chip Reynolds	Mark Williams
George Feist	Katherine Lisciandro	Steve Roby	Ed Wincensten
Howard Fields	Mario Maglieri	Rick Rosen	Nina Zolten
Geoff Gans	Manny Mamzellis	Paul Rothchild	John & Sherry/The Satisfied Mind
	Dorothy Manzarek	Joe Russo & The Soft Parade	

I would also like to express my sincere gratitude to the many librarians who so graciously gave of their time in helping to research this project. Among them, special thanks are given to:

Helen Baer (San Luis Obispo), Ed Brazee (Corvallis), Doris Dysinger (Bucknell University), Bertha L. Ihnat (Columbus), Barbara Kautz (Milwaukee), Kathy Kube (Madison), Gayle D. Lynch (Providence), Dan McLaughlin (Pasadena), Irene Still Meyer (Long Beach), Carolyn Resnick (Chappaqua, NY), Marie Sapione (Pittsburgh), David Sigler (California State, L.A.), John Walden (Bakersfield).

How To Use This Book

THE DOORS ON THE ROAD is a bit like getting tickets to 600 Doors concerts—at first glance a daunting prospect! To help you make your way, we have highlighted some of the Doors' Most Outrageous (left) and Most Outstanding (right) shows—a distinction that wasn't always that clear with Jim Morrison and the Doors. Pick any one, and take your front row seat.

CANCELLED refers to shows cancelled due to the Doors infamous performance in Miami, Fla.

"indented and in quotes" entry in a set-list indicates a poem (see page 157)

(DU)(LU) indicates "date uncertain" or "location uncertain." Even for us, there are still some mysteries.

 At the end of many entries you will find a number of dingbats like the one here, each accompanied by informative notes covering such arcana as promoters, capacity, other groups playing on the bill, etc.

EARLY LIVES

Ray Manzarek

Ray Manzarek grows up in Chicago. As a youth, studies classical music at the Chicago Conservatory. Develops affinity for the blues, frequenting South Side nightclubs. In high school, plays weekend gigs with a variety of bands. Wariness of music as a profession leads him to De Paul University, from which he graduates with bachelor's degree in economics. Family relocates to California where Manzarek briefly enrolls at the UCLA law school before joining the service. After a stint in the army, enrolls as a graduate student in the UCLA film department. Becomes immersed in fanatical art scene, and befriends fellow student Jim Morrison. While at UCLA, Manzarek helps pay tuition by playing keyboards and singing (as "Screamin' Ray Daniels") in Rick and the Ravens with his brothers Rick and Jim. During that summer, Manzarek enrolls in a transcendental meditation course, and while seeking a permanent drummer for the Ravens is introduced to John Densmore. Densmore introduces Ray to Robby Krieger. During the summer Ray reunites with Jim Morrison on the beach in Venice and the stage is set for the Ravens to evolve into the Doors.

John Densmore

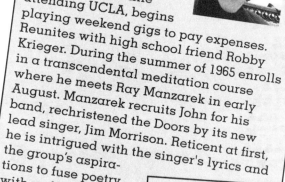

John Densmore plays percussion in high school bands. While attending UCLA, begins playing weekend gigs to pay expenses. Reunites with high school friend Robby Krieger. During the summer of 1965 enrolls in a transcendental meditation course where he meets Ray Manzarek in early August. Manzarek recruits John for his band, rechristened the Doors by its new lead singer, Jim Morrison. Reticent at first, he is intrigued with the singer's lyrics and the group's aspirations to fuse poetry with rock 'n' roll music. Densmore precedes Krieger into the Doors by a few weeks, and is involved with the group's first demo.

Robby Krieger

Robby Krieger grows up in the Los Angeles area and while attending UC Santa Barbara becomes involved in the folk and jug band music scene. Transfers to UCLA as physics major, but also attends Ravi Shankar's classes. At UCLA, teams up with John Densmore to form the Psychedelic Rangers and gets involved with another group, the Clouds. Robby, too, enrolls in the transcendental meditation courses that summer, meets Ray Manzarek, and is asked to audition for the Doors. Krieger senses the potential of the Doors and joins his old bandmate, Densmore, in the new group.

Jim Morrison

Jim Morrison graduates from George Washington High School in Alexandria Virginia in June 1961. After attending St. Petersburg Junior College and Florida State University in Tallahassee he transfers to the UCLA Theater Arts Department in January 1964, graduating with a bachelor's degree in cinematography in June 1965. Morrison, now living on the rooftop of an abandoned office building in Venice, enters a bizarre and transformative period of his life. Under starlit skies he writes incessantly. His furious scribblings and auditory memories create a vision of things to come. It is here that the very first Doors concert takes place—in Jim Morrison's mind.

RICK AND THE RAVENS

FRI., SAT. MAY 7, 8 AND
FRI., SAT. MAY 14, 15 1965 Turkey Joint West
Santa Monica, CA
Through mid-June 1965

Rick and the Ravens, the predecessor to the Doors, play regularly on the weekends through mid- to late June at this nightclub in Santa Monica. The blues-based band performs primarily to a crowd of fellow UCLA students who are regulars here. These two weekends are the only confirmed weekends the Ravens appeared, although it is presumed that they continued for several thereafter. The Turkey Joint West is a happening spot "for swingin' young people"—a boisterous clientele attracted to the club's outlandish advertising, typically headlined with "DRINK COORS—THE BREAKFAST OF CHAMPIONS."

The band consists of Ray Manzarek (aka Screamin' Ray Daniels) on keyboards and vocals, Vince Thomas on drums, and Ray's brothers Rick (guitar) and Jim (harmonica, piano). Their repertoire includes such classics as "Money," "Louie, Louie," "Hoochie Coochie Man," "Close to You," "King Bee," and "Little Red Rooster."

At one of these shows, Ray Manzarek invites Jim Morrison and several other class members from the UCLA Film School to join Rick and the Ravens onstage for a searing rendition of "Louie, Louie."

Rick and the Ravens also record three singles, a total of six songs, for Aura Records, a subsidiary of World–Pacific Records.

SINGLES

Soul Train	b/w	Geraldine
Henrietta	b/w	Just for You
Big Bucket "T"	b/w	Rampage

FRI., SAT. MAY 21, 22 1965 Royce Hall Auditorium
University Of California,
Los Angeles, CA

The UCLA Film School presents its fifth semiannual evening of student films. Among them is Ray Manczarek's (sic) *Evergreen*, and future Doors' photographer Paul Ferrara's *End Of Summer*.

FRI. JUN. 11 1965 Ports 'O Call
San Pedro Marina (Harbor), CA (DU)

Rick and the Ravens are hired as an opening act for a Los Angeles high school graduation dance headlined by the pop group Sonny and Cher. The contract somehow specifies that the band is to consist of six musicians, requiring that they find someone willing to sit in with them or forfeit the job. Ray Manzarek approaches Jim Morrison with an offer of equal pay for standing in with the band while pretending to play an unplugged guitar throughout the show. Jim graciously accepts and later remarks that it's the easiest money he ever made. Sonny and Cher never appear for their performance, so the future bandmates play together for the entire evening.

The Doors
on the road
1965

Venice Beach (DU)

After graduation from UCLA, Ray Manzarek lives on the beach in Venice, California, while Jim Morrison presumably leaves for New York to pursue film production. One summer afternoon, a week or so after the Fourth of July crowds have died down, Ray is out on the beach when he runs into Jim. The two have not seen each other since UCLA and begin to discuss what they have been doing since graduation. Jim reveals that he has been consuming a substantial amount of (the then legal) LSD, while residing on a nearby rooftop. While there, he has drafted some lyrics for a succession of melodies that seem to have arisen within him late one night as he sat on a rooftop gazing at the stars. Ray encourages him to sing one of the songs, and after some embarrassed reluctance, Jim recites "Moonlight Drive." Immediately struck by the uniqueness of the lyrics, Ray enthusiastically proposes that they work together—with Jim joining his band—and bring their creative ideas to fruition. Jim discloses that he has been seriously contemplating assembling a group, and had even considered calling it the Doors, a name abbreviated from *The Doors of Perception*, the title of Aldous Huxley's book about his experiences with hallucinogenic drugs, which in turn was based on a line from William Blake: "If the doors of perception were cleansed, everything would appear to man as it truly is, infinite."

THU. SEPT. 2 1965 World Pacific Jazz Studios
Los Angeles, CA

Moonlight Drive
Hello, I Love You
Summer's Almost Gone
My Eyes Have Seen You
The End of the Night
Go Insane (A Little Game)

This recording is often referred to as the first Doors recording, which is not technically true due to the absence of Robby Krieger. At this time, the band consisted of Jim Morrison (vocals), Ray Manzarek (piano), John Densmore (drums), Rick Manzarek (guitar), Jim Manzarek (harmonica), and a woman bass player whose identity remains undetermined. They set up and record all six songs in just three hours, and afterward press a few acetates (test records) for booking purposes.

Their studio time is obtained through a contractual exchange with Aura Records as a substitution for studio time for Rick and the Ravens, whose previous singles have not fared well. (It is interesting to note that the Doors never opted to record "Hello, I Love You" until their third album, and that was after Elektra president Jac Holzman's son remembered the song from this session and brought it to their attention.)

Around this time, Ray Manzarek's brothers express a growing uncertainty and dissatisfaction with the direction the group has taken and shortly thereafter decide to leave the band. However, Ray and Jim Morrison possess a strong vision of creating something musically that will be quite distinct from the ordinary fare of the day.

After the others have departed from the band, Manzarek quickly seeks to reconstruct it. John Densmore eagerly recommends his cohort Robby Krieger, from his Transcendental Meditation course, as a potential new guitarist. Shortly thereafter, Krieger displays his brilliance on slide guitar on "Moonlight Drive" during an audition, and the group immediately invites him to join. Manzarek's foresight and persistence bring the band members together, creating the foundation for the band.

SEPTEMBER 65

Quest for a Bass Guitarist

After this lineup for the Doors has been established, the band actively searches for a bass player with a unique style that will distinguish their evolving sound from that of the established bands of the period, such as the Rolling Stones. During this search, Ray Manzarek happens upon the Fender-Rhodes bass keyboard that will serve as substitute for bass guitar and be significant in developing the innovative sound the band is looking for. The precedent for this innovation had been observed by Manzarek in his earlier years when he admired the boogie-woogie style of keyboard playing that was grounded by a repetitive left-handed bass line, while the right hand danced across the keys.

SEPTEMBER & OCTOBER 65

Early Rehearsals

The Doors rehearse at a number of Los Angeles locations, including: the beach house where Ray Manzarek is staying, Robby Krieger's home, and their friend Hank Olguin's residence located behind the Santa Monica Greyhound bus depot in Venice. Hank Olguin (Henry Crismonde) is an actor with whom Ray had worked while producing his movies at UCLA. The band rehearses, on the average, about five days a week.

OCTOBER 65

Provisional Contract

With great anticipation, the Doors are signed to an initial contract with Columbia Records after shopping the acetate demo around to various companies. Billy James, manager of Talent Acquisition and Development for Columbia, perceives the possibilities of the band—despite the dubious sound quality of the acetate—and signs them to a six-month commitment with Columbia. James has an extensive background in the arts. He attended both CCNY Film School and Juilliard, and before being hired by Columbia was involved in many Broadway plays and television broadcasts. While at Columbia, he was present at Bob Dylan's first LP recording session, worked with John Hammond, and enthusiastically cheered as the Byrds took flight.

Since the Doors are a new and unestablished band, he can offer only a restricted contract and the lowest royalty rates. Despite these drawbacks, the Doors remain excited by the possibilities of working with the company that signed Bob Dylan.

The following February, just before the contract is to expire, Billy James receives a notice of termination from Bill Gallagher (who also has the distinction of having dismissed Lenny Bruce) stating in no uncertain terms that Columbia has no interest in discussing any future possibilities with the Doors. Having received no encouragement from the company, the band visits Billy James, who informs them that Columbia has no intentions of fulfilling the contract. Disillusioned with these circumstances, the Doors opt to terminate the six-month contract after five

months, despite the fact that the band members would have received $1,000 had they chosen to wait an additional month.

Shortly thereafter, Billy James leaves Columbia to help open the West Coast branch for Elektra. In June 1967, he strikes out on his own, providing personal management for such artists as Jackson Browne and the Peanut Butter Conspiracy.

OCT. & NOV 1965 Periodic Weekend Performances

During this time, the Doors are hired for a number of private gatherings in the Los Angeles area, including weddings, fraternity dances, and friends' parties.

FRI. NOV. 5 1965 Pioneer Club Boat Ride
Los Angeles, CA (DU)

One of the Doors' earliest bookings outside their circle of friends is for a boat party for this private club.

FRI. NOV. 19 1965 Hughes Aircraft Union Dance
Los Angeles, CA (DU)

FRI., SAT. DEC. 10, 11 1965 Royce Hall Auditorium
University Of California, Los Angeles, CA
Op, Pop & Kicky Flicks

During the weekend of the annual pre-Christmas presentation of the best of the UCLA Film School, the Doors set up offstage and perform a "live" acoustic soundtrack for the presentation of Ray Manzarek's films *Who & Where I Live* (1965) and *Induction* (1965).

The previous year, Ray had been invited to present his film *Evergreen* (1964). All three of these films feature Ray's dear friend and future wife, Dorothy Fujikawa.

The 2½-hour program, presented by the Motion Picture Division of the Department of Theater Arts, is repeated the following weekend (December 17 through 19), but it is uncertain if the Doors again provide accompaniment for Manzarek's films. Also on the program is *Les Anges Dormants* by Morrison's acquaintance Felix Venable.

This is a banner year for the UCLA film school. Their students win awards at more film festivals than all other American film schools combined.

⌘ Presented by the UCLA Committee on Fine Arts Production and the Department of Theater Arts (8:00 p.m.)

FRI. DEC. 31 1965 Private Residence
Los Angeles, CA

The band is hired to perform at a private New Year's Eve party given by friends of the Kriegers. They spend the majority of the evening honoring requests for popular songs of the day from the partygoers. As the new year is rung in and attendees celebrate with toasts to the occasion, Jim Morrison tosses a quarter in the air, catches it in his mouth and swallows it whole. A toast to the band's portrayal as a living jukebox!

JAN. 1966 Private Residence
Los Angeles, CA

Another booking for a private gathering, this time at the Louis Marvin residence.

JANUARY
20
THURSDAY

Aborted Trip to Mexico (DU)

Jim and two friends from UCLA, Phillip O'leno and Felix Venable, embark on an expedition to Mexico with the intention of discovering Indians. Inspired by the descriptions published by UCLA professor Carlos Casteneda, the three hope to be initiated in the Spirits of Peyote. In spite of their noble intentions, Jim Morrison leaps out of the car while they are stopped at a traffic light on their way to Mexico and gives a big kiss to a Mexican-American woman standing at the crosswalk. He then jumps back into the car as they speed off down the road. Jim's comedic spirit fails to arouse the humor of the woman's male companions, who hasten to their car and take off in pursuit of the depraved men. Catching up with them outside of town, the men reward Morrison's humor by giving all three of them a good thrashing. They abandon their journey and backtrack toward home. On the way, Phil parts company from the other two while Jim decides to take advantage of their disheveled appearance to fabricate a story of how he and Felix have murdered Phil and disposed of the body in a riverbed. Again, Jim's distorted sense of humor is not without its consequences.

JANUARY
23
SUNDAY

Arrested in Inglewood, CA

Phil O'leno's father is an attorney who is understandably disconcerted when he catches wind of the story Jim is circulating about Phil's death. After attempts to acquire any legitimate information about his son fail, he reluctantly decides that the only way to locate Phil is to press assault and battery charges against Jim. After proceeding with this lawsuit, the truth is rapidly divulged. Once he is assured that his son is indeed alive and well, Mr. O'leno immediately withdraws all charges against Jim.

SAT. JAN. 29 1966 Redlands Bowl
Redlands, CA (DU)

This date is a modest afternoon gathering on the edge of the desert, where the Doors are amongst a number of bands that play one weekend afternoon.

Note: This affair may have been held at Prospect Park (1670 Euclid Ave.) or another of the surrounding small parks off of Highway 60 near the eastern edge of Orange County.

FRI. FEB. 11 1966 Valley Teen Center
Van Nuys, CA (DU)

FEB.-MAY 1966 London Fog
West Hollywood, CA

This is the Doors' first real gig. They perform here from sometime in late February (possibly early March) until the beginning of May, when the club experiences serious financial troubles. The exact starting and ending dates are not known; this is a close approximation. These shows are not particularly well attended, although the club seems to attract an interesting variety of sordid characters.

The London Fog shows provide the opportunity for the band to solidify as a unit and for Jim Morrison slowly to develop his confidence and the charisma to emerge as lead singer.

The band starts with four nights a week, and later expands to six. They perform four or five sets a night that are essentially live rehearsals where they can experiment with their material, and Morrison frequently stands facing the band rather than the small audience. In addition to developing their own material, the Doors' repertoire consists of such standards of the time as "Gloria," "Who Do You Love," "Louie, Louie," "Little Red Rooster," "Get Out of My Life, Woman," "Crawlin' King Snake," "Hoochie Coochie Man," "King Bee," "Got My Mojo Workin'," "You Need Meat," "Close to You," and "Money." Their final performance at the club is on a Saturday, with their first appearance at the Whisky A Go Go the following Monday.

The London Fog had previously been the site of the Unicorn Club, which concentrated on the folk-music scene of the early 1960s. It later became Sneaky (Whisky) Pete's and is presently the location of Duke's.

Proprietor: Jesse James

SAT. APR. 23 1966 Will Rogers State Park
Los Angeles, CA

The escalating violence of the war in Vietnam is beginning to make many people increasingly sensitive to the unglamorous aspects of war. A number of organizations that oppose the glorification of violence are developing, one of which is a group of parents who oppose the continued popularity of war toys. This is just one of a number of "No War Toys" gatherings.

MAY 1966 Ford Motor Company Training Film

It is around this time, when the Doors are not under any contracts, that they are hired to provide the soundtrack for a Ford industrial training film for mechanics. The band creates a light instrumental piece for the opening sequence, which is later resurrected in a musically similar arrangement for the transitional passage in the song "The Soft Parade," which lyrically begins with "Catacombs, nursery bones." That piece, and the other "forgotten" compositions, are fashioned to convey an atmosphere of small-town America. The Doors compose the soundtrack while viewing the film on a monitor in a small studio in Los Angeles.

MAY 1966 The Trip
West Hollywood, CA

Cancelled. Andy Warhol's "Exploding Plastic Inevitable," a mixed-media show featuring some fourteen performers including the Velvet Underground and Nico, is scheduled to appear at the Trip through May 18. From the beginning of their stint at the Trip, they clash with the opening act, Frank Zappa and the Mothers of Invention. Each group seems to thrive on making derogatory comments about the talent of the other, reigniting the ancient East Coast vs. West Coast rivalry. Because of the competition between the two bands, the Doors are considered an alternative opening act and they are scheduled to perform with the Velvet Underground in early May. However, the "Exploding Plastic Inevitable" has only appeared for a few nights when the sheriff's department shuts down the Trip for suspected drug use and disturbing the peace. Warhol's entourage remains in LA for a while before leaving to appear at Bill Graham's Fillmore Auditorium in San Francisco on May 27. Consequently, the Doors never get the opportunity to open the show.

Zappa and the Mothers didn't just break all the boundaries of convention in rock music in the 1960s, they danced on the residual debris with diabolical glee. When their album *Freak Out* is released in August of 1966, they rise to national prominence as the foremost proponents of bizarre and outrageously amusing satirical rock.

Lou Reed formed the Velvet Underground with John Cale around 1965, with Sterling Morrison and Maureen Tucker. Their dark and disturbing music featuring uncompromising lyrics is often compared to that of the Doors. Andy Warhol approached the group about appearing in his multimedia exposition, the "Exploding Plastic Inevitable," and incorporated Nico, an actress in his films, as an additional lead vocalist.

THU. MAY 5 1966 London Fog
West Hollywood, CA (DU)

After substantial prompting on Morrison's part, the Whisky A Go Go talent agent Ronnie Harran finally comes to see the Doors perform at the London Fog, and ends up inviting them to audition at the Whisky the following Monday. Accounts vary as to the exact sequence of events, but the Doors are also informed at this time that the Fog will have to let them go after the weekend's performances.

FRI. MAY 6 1966 Warner Playhouse
Los Angeles, CA

The early morning "Night Flight" performances are after-hours shows that are scheduled between two and four a.m. The shows are put on by a local impresario and feature rock bands with exotic dancers.

The Doors were probably scheduled to perform after the London Fog show.

SAT. MAY 7 1966 (1) London Fog
West Hollywood, CA (DU)

This is the Doors' last performance at the London Fog before they are dismissed because of the club's financial difficulties. The London Fog closes shortly thereafter and is replaced by Sneaky Pete's, which opens on May 13 featuring Jesse Davis.

SAT. MAY 7 1966 (2) Warner Playhouse
Los Angeles, CA

"Night Flight" performance from 2:00 to 4:00 a.m.

MON. MAY 9 1966 Whisky A Go Go
West Hollywood, CA (DU)

Tonight's audition is the Doors' first appearance at the prominent Whisky A Go Go on the Sunset Strip in Los Angeles. After this live audition, Elmer Valentine decides to hire the Doors as the Whisky's house band, which means they open for the featured acts. However, the Doors do not start immediately because they are so difficult to locate. They are no longer employed at the London Fog and lack any permanent address. It takes Ronnie Harran a couple of weeks to track them down and get prepared for their highly acclaimed summer engagement at the Whisky A Go Go.

THU., FRI. MAY 12, 13 1966 Brave New World
Hollywood, CA (DU)

The Doors are the opening band for Love, which features Arthur Lee. The club closes shortly after their appearance.

🐾 Note: These performances may have actually taken place in April while the Doors were still performing at the London Fog.

FRI. MAY 13 1966 (2) Warner Playhouse
Los Angeles, CA

"Night Flight" performance from 2:00 to 4:00 a.m.

FRI. MAY 13 1966 (3) Royce Hall Auditorium
University Of California, Los Angeles, CA

The UCLA Motion Picture Division presents its seventh semiannual exhibition of student films. Among the headliners at this very popular event is Raymond D. Manczarek's (sic) Induction. The program is repeated on May 20, 22, 27 and 28.

SAT. MAY 14 1966 (1) Brave New World
Hollywood, CA (DU)

🜋 Also performing: Love

SAT. MAY 14 1966 (2) Warner Playhouse
Los Angeles, CA

"Night Flight" performance from 2:00 to 4:00 a.m.

THU. MAY 19 1966 Betty's Music Shop
Venice, CA (DU)

The Doors are probably researching equipment when they play a quick set of four or five songs to a small crowd around 3:00 or 4:00 in the afternoon in front of this local music store. The impromptu public practice session occurs on a weekday during the school year shortly before graduation.

MON. MAY 23 1966 Whisky A Go Go
West Hollywood, CA

The Doors begin their legendary engagement as the house band for the Whisky A Go Go. While there, they open for such acts as Them (featuring Van Morrison), Buffalo Springfield, Love, Gene Clark, the Chambers Brothers, and Captain Beefheart and the Magic Band.

Contrary to popular mythology, the Doors are not fired repeatedly by proprietor Phil Tanzini. This is essentially an embellishment of the continuous tension that existed between them. Phil Tanzini is very up-front about his conflicts with the band, and the opposing factions each have respect for what the other is doing. However, it is Phil who dismisses them in August on the night that Morrison inserts the Oedipal section into "The End."

The Doors' sets are comprised primarily of songs that will appear on their first two albums. Night after night they develop and refine their songs in front of a live audience. "The End" gradually metamorphoses from a rather transient love song of bittersweet departure into the ominous saga that evokes a descent into the dark night of the soul.

A typical set for a night at the Whisky a Go Go would be:

1st Set	2nd Set
Break on Through	My Eyes Have Seen You
Take It As It Comes	Alabama Song
Moonlight Drive	Summer's Almost Gone
20th Century Fox	Light My Fire
I Looked at You	The Crystal Ship
Money	Gloria
Little Red Rooster	The End of the Night
Unhappy Girl	Soul Kitchen
When the Music's Over	The End

In addition to the songs listed above, the Doors occasionally play other songs, usually on the slower nights such as Monday, Tuesday, or Wednesday, when fewer people are in attendance.

"Latin BS (Bullshit) #2" is an instrumental jazz piece roughly based on a Gil Evans composition from his *Out of the Cool* album. The instrumental serves primarily as a filler, which they continue to play throughout their nights at Ondine's in New York. It later evolves into "Away in India," which is featured within a medley often called the "People Get Ready Jam," which they often performed in 1970. "Summertime" is a waltz instrumental loosely styled after John Coltrane's version of "My Favorite Things," and includes chord changes somewhat similar to "Light My Fire."

These two instrumentals often serve as set openers when Jim Morrison has not yet arrived at the club.

In addition to these instrumentals, the Doors also perform:

Goin' to New York
Crawlin' King Snake
Rock Me
King Bee
Close to You

- Note: Although the Doors admire the work of the Rolling Stones, they do not perform a version of "The Last Time" as has often been rumored.
- Note: Johnny Rivers is scheduled at the Whisky A Go Go through May 22, and the Doors do not open for him at that time.
- Also performing: Captain Beefheart and the Magic Band; Buffalo Springfield

TUE. MAY 24-FRI. 27 1966 Whisky A Go Go
West Hollywood, CA

Captain Beefheart (Don Van Vliet) is a personal friend of Frank Zappa's, as well as a spiritual contemporary in that school of bizarre avant-garde rock. He formed the Magic Band in 1964 and had just returned from a successful tour of Europe before this Whisky appearance.

Buffalo Springfield, who were to later achieve legendary status as one of the 1960s Los Angeles groups, had just formed in the spring and are still relatively unknown at this point. Their rise to stardom is even faster than that of the Doors, and by July 25 they are featured at a Hollywood Bowl concert and signed to Atco Records. Their musical commentary on the Sunset Strip riots between the police and the youth culture, released in the fall as "For What It's Worth," propels them to national stardom. The diversity of musical directions within the group create enough internal dissension that they disband in early 1968 after only three albums. Featured in the band are Neil Young and Steve Stills of Crosby, Stills, Nash and Young fame, as well as Richie Furay, who went on to form Poco with Jim Messina (who joined in late 1967), Dewey Martin, and Bruce Palmer.

- Also performing: Captain Beefheart and the Magic Band; Buffalo Springfield

SAT. MAY 28-WED. JUN 1 1966 Whisky A Go Go
West Hollywood, CA

A letter to *Rolling Stone* years later reflected on these nights at the Whisky: "When they did hour sets at the Whisky, Morrison in jeans and a T-shirt, Ray being mistaken for [John] Sebastian, Robby with a slide on his guitar, and Densmore—well why would anyone want to drum for a group with a funny name like the Doors? Who was this person who turned his back to the audience 20 minutes at a time and pounded a wood block. What's this swimming to the moon and soul kitchen business? I mean, we came to see Love. But we went home singing 'Light My Fire' and in about a week we even braved the Locos to get stoned to 'The End.'" (D. P. Boller, "Correspondence, Love Letters & Advice," *Rolling Stone*, Mar. 7, 1970; used with permission: © Straight Arrow Publishers, Inc. 1996)

Love, featuring Arthur Lee, formed in 1965 and debuted their electric and jazz-influenced rock style at the Brave New World in April of that year. By 1966 they have signed with Elektra Records and released "Little Red Book," which brings them national recognition in the spring. During this time they frequently perform at the Brave New World and the Hullabaloo. With the release of "7 and 7 Is" in July, they quickly rise to national prominence as one of the new and exciting Los Angles bands.

- Also performing: Love

MON. MAY 30 1966 (2) Hullabaloo Club
West Hollywood, CA

This is another after-hours booking for the Doors. They open the show with "Light My Fire."

THU. JUN. 2 -FRI. 17 1966 Whisky A Go Go
West Hollywood, CA

The Doors open for Them (with Van Morrison) for a two-week engagement.

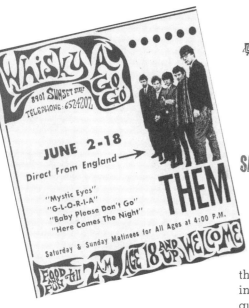

Note: In the previous year, Van Morrison founded the legendary yet ephemeral group Them and set up the R & B Club in Belfast. The band was an immediate success with the releases of "Gloria," "Baby, Please Don't Go" and "Here Comes the Night." In May 1966 they do an exhaustive West Coast tour that proves to be their only tour of the U.S. with Van Morrison. He leaves the group after their return to Europe.

SAT. JUN. 18 1966 Whisky A Go Go
West Hollywood, CA

In the Midnight Hour
Gloria

At the conclusion of the late show, the Doors appear onstage with Them for the final set of their extended booking. They set up the stage by combining all the instruments of both bands, resulting in two drum kits, two keyboards, and multiple guitars. After a few numbers, the temporary supergroup goes into a twenty-minute jam on Wilson Pickett's "In the Midnight Hour." The grand finale is an equally long version of Van Morrison's classic "Gloria," a song that the Doors regularly include in their live sets.

Ray Manzarek: "Yeah, there were some good times at the Whisky A Go Go. Boy, that's for sure. We played with Them; the first gig we played at the Whisky was Van Morrison and Jim Morrison—on the same stage. And Van Morrison was *insane.* You know how he got into just kind of standing there and singing? I haven't really seen him in a long time but when he was with Them, the guy was *all* over the stage, man. Absolutely insane. Did that thing of holding the microphone stand upside down and singing, and *smashing* the microphone stand into the ground and just . . . God, was he incredible! He was so good. Then the last night we played we had a jam. We got a couple of photographs of that somewhere, but nobody recorded it. The Doors and Them, together on stage, the two Morrisons. Mmmmh!" (Paul Lawrence, "Ray Manzarek: The Audio interview," *Audio,* Dec. 1983)

This one-night jam session is not only a high point for the Doors, but for Them as well. Van Morrison later comments that the performance with the Doors was one of the highlights of his career with Them.

Also performing: Them

Early (4:00 p.m. all-ages matinee) and late shows on Saturdays and Sundays

SUN. JUN. 19 -WED. JUL. 27 1966 Whisky A Go Go
West Hollywood, CA

Los Angeles Times reviewer Pete Johnson attends one of the shows, probably on Saturday, July 16, primarily to write a review of the headlining Turtles. At the conclusion of that review, he writes a less than enthusiastic (but enticing) response to the Doors.

Published the following Monday, this brief but memorable commentary is the earliest known review of a Doors performance, subtitled "Lost in Space": "Sharing the bill are the Doors, a hungry looking quartet with an interesting original sound but with what is possibly the worst stage appearance of any rock 'n' roll group in captivity. Their lead singer emotes with his eyes closed, the electric pianist hunches over his instrument as if reading mysteries from the keyboard, the guitarist drifts about the stage randomly and the drummer seems lost in a separate world." (Pete Johnson, "Bo Diddley, Turtles: Both ends of the rock spectrum in town," *Los Angeles Times,* Part IV, p. 22, July 18, 1966)

After the Doors' infamous New York Singer Bowl "riot show" in August 1968, they run into Pete Johnson at their hotel. He quickly tells them that he is in New York on freelance business and did not know that the band was in town. The band seems totally unconcerned with whether or not he attended their show, but Morrison is clearly elated to have run into him. As Ellen Sander relates in her book *Trips*, "Morrison whooped, almost slapping Johnson on the back. 'Man, when you wrote that we were the ugliest group in captivity, that was your finest hour!'" (Ellen Sander, *Trips,* New York: Charles Scribners Sons, 1973)

🎹 Also performing: Gene Clark and the Group; the Locos; [movies] (June 22–July 10)

🎹 Also performing: The Turtles (July 16–July 23)

🎹 Also performing: Johnny Rivers; the Chambers Brothers (July 27)

🎹 Note: Gene Clark was one of the founding members of the Byrds in 1964. He had left the group the previous April because of his personal difficulties with their touring schedule.

🎹 Note: On drums, the Turtles feature John Barbata, who later performs with Crosby, Stills, Nash and Young. He also sits in with the Doors and John Sebastian at the Felt Forum show in New York on January 18, 1970. The front line for the band includes Mark Volman and Howard Kaylan, who will later regularly open for the Doors on their final tour in 1972 as "Phlorescent Leech and Eddie." The Turtles' hit records include a cover version of Bob Dylan's "It Ain't Me, Babe."

THU. JUL. 28 1966 (1) Starlight Ballroom
Oxnard, CA

🎹 Also performing: Them; the Count Five ["Psychotic Reaction"]

🎤 Promotion: James Salzer

THU. JUL. 28 1966 (2) Earl Warren Showgrounds
Santa Barbara, CA
Mid-Summer Spectacular Show of Shows
(7:30 p.m. to midnight)

Curiously, the local newspaper's commentary on the upcoming show includes this remark: "The Doors, a controversial group in Los Angeles, is coming to Santa Barbara direct from the 'Whisky A Go Go' in Hollywood." Apparently the group has already acquired a reputation as "controversial" as far north as Santa Barbara while still just the opening act for headliners at the Whisky. ("3 Combos Schedule 'Show of Shows' at Earl Warren," *Santa Barbara News Press*, July 26, 1966)

James Salzer was one of the earliest and most commendable promoters to sponsor appearances by famous rock groups in Southern California. Concentrating on the Santa Barbara area, he frequently presented shows by such notable acts as the Jimi Hendrix Experience, Blind Faith, and the Grateful Dead at the Santa Barbara Showgrounds. James Salzer also held the distinction of being the first promoter to have presented the Doors in a larger concert venue.

🎹 Also performing: Them; the Count Five

🎤 Promotion: James Salzer

FRI. JUL. 29 - SUN. 31 1966 The Fifth Estate
Phoenix, AZ (DU)

Because of the Fifth Estate shows, the appearances at the Whisky scheduled for July 29–August 2 are probably cancelled.

🎸 Also performing: The Mile Ends

🎭 Promotion/Proprietor: James Musil, Jr.

✳ Note: These Fifth Estate shows may have actually occurred on a weekend in mid-August (Aug. 12–14, 1966)

MON. AUG. 1 - THU. 4 1966 Whisky A Go Go
West Hollywood, CA

On August 3, the Rolling Stones arrive in Hollywood for a recording session at RCA Studios that lasts through August 11. During their stay, they visit the Whisky A Go Go and hear the Doors. They are reportedly not very impressed.

It is also on this night that David Crosby (performing with the Byrds at this time) has a confrontation with Jim Morrison that he recounts in his autobiographical *Long Time Gone*. He says that on the night of Lenny Bruce's death, he went with some friends to the Whisky while well saturated with LSD. At one point, Morrison apparently leaped at Crosby while pointing to his sunglasses and shouting that he can't hide behind those shades!

🎸 Also performing: Johnny Rivers; the Chambers Brothers

FRI. AUG. 5 1966 Starlight Ballroom
Oxnard, CA

While promoter James Salzer is attempting to present musical performances in the area, the city of Oxnard is actively seeking to prevent such performances by enforcing an archaic city ordinance against dancing. The Doors make an appearance at Salzer's Arcade Record Store to lend support for the show and to sign autographs.

🎸 Also performing: The Seeds

🎭 Promotion: James Salzer Productions

SAT. AUG. 6 1966 Earl Warren Showgrounds
Santa Barbara, CA

This performance is held in the Flower Show Building. The Doors are the opening act for the Seeds, which features Sky Saxon, another Turkey Joint West alumni who played there before Rick and the Ravens.

🎸 Also performing: The Seeds

🎭 Promotion: James Salzer Productions

🏃 8:00 p.m. to midnight

SUN. AUG. 7 - TUE. 9 1966 Whisky A Go Go
West Hollywood, CA

🎸 Also performing: Johnny Rivers; the Chambers Brothers

🎭 Note: There is a possibility that the Doors played in Merced instead

WED. AUG. 10 1966 Whisky A Go Go
West Hollywood, CA

Jac Holzman, president and founder of Elektra Records, arrives at the Whisky A Go Go specifically to see the Doors perform. However, he is not immediately impressed with the band. He is encouraged to return by Arthur Lee, who fronts the Elektra group Love, and by Ronnie Harran, talent agent for the Whisky. Over the course of several visits during the next few nights, he becomes increasingly interested in the group, but they are so unusual that he is uncertain as to their commercial potential. He calls Elektra's staff producer Paul Rothchild in New York and asks him to fly out and help him make a decision. Rothchild sums up Jac's request: "Come out to LA, see what you think. Let's put our heads together and decide whether to sign this band."

🎭 Also performing: Love

🎵 Note: The exact date remains uncertain. This date, as well as the following regarding Elektra Records, are as accurate as possible based on the recollections of producer Paul Rothchild.

THU. AUG. 11 - SUN. 14 1966 Whisky A Go Go
West Hollywood, CA

🎭 Also performing: Love

MON. AUG. 15 - SAT. 20 1966 Whisky A Go Go
West Hollywood, CA

On August 15, Paul Rothchild accompanies Jac Holzman to see the Doors perform at the Whisky A Go Go for what is probably Holzman's fourth or fifth return visit. Rothchild describes the event as follows: "I came to the club and there was a small crowd, not big. The Doors opened, and I heard one of the worst sets of music I ever heard in my life. Knowing that the record company always gets to hear the bad sets, and that I had just travelled across the country to hear them, I stayed and heard one of the greatest sets of music I ever heard in my life!"

After that second set, Rothchild and Holzman approach the band. Ray Manzarek is excited and elated that Rothchild is already acquainted with the Brecht/Weill compositions they perform, and that his extensive musical knowledge encompasses the avant-garde, as well as multiple aspects of blues and rock. Rothchild has no qualms about telling the band that he is immensely impressed with their performance and that he will immediately recommend that Elektra sign them. His enthusiasm is so contagious that Jac Holzman offers them a record contract that very night.

While the Doors, too, are excited, their experience with Columbia cautions them to wait. They spend the next few days talking it over. Jac Holzman returns to New York, and the Doors seek some legal advice. On the recommendation of Robby Krieger's father, they retain the services of attorney Max Fink, who will represent them throughout their career.

At this time, Elektra is primarily a folk label and is in the position to offer individual attention to the band—an aspect that is lacking in the larger companies. Elektra has already signed the Paul Butterfield Blues Band, as well as Love featuring Arthur Lee. It is Lee who has repeatedly encouraged Jac Holzman to go see the Doors.

🎭 Also performing: Love

🎵 Note: Paul Rothchild had been in the music business for years. In the early 1960s he was intimately involved with the Cambridge folk music scene. He even joined the board of directors for Club 47. After producing one album himself (*The Charles*

> The Doors opened, and I heard one of the worst sets of music I ever heard in my life. Knowing that the record company always gets to hear the bad sets, and that I had just travelled across the country to hear them, I stayed and heard one of the greatest sets of music I ever heard in my life!

River Valley Boys), he became head of Prestige's folk division, recording the likes of Tom Rush, Dave van Ronk, and the Holy Modal Rounders. He joined Elektra in 1963, and shortly thereafter heard the astonishing Paul Butterfield Blues Band and began production on their legendary first album. Things shifted into an even higher gear when his good friend John Sebastian formed the Lovin' Spoonful. Rothchild became devoted to the new rock music. From there he did Tim Buckley's first album and Love's second LP, *Da Capo*. Then he heard the Doors.

🔄 Note: Dates are approximate.

🌀 On August 16, the Doors' attorney, Max Fink, and Jac Holzman begin their negotiations on a recording contract with Elektra Records.

🌀 On August 18, in the afternoon, the Doors sign their initial contract with Jac Holzman and Elektra records. While in New York in November they agree on a complete contract specifying seven albums and other details.

SUN. AUG. 21 1966 — WHISKY A GO GO
West Hollywood, CA

The Doors' final performance at the Whisky A Go Go for the summer of 1966.

The Doors play their first set without Jim Morrison, who is gaining notoriety for appearing late at shows. The band compensates by performing their instrumentals and their repertoire of blues standards with Ray Manzarek on vocals. During the break, the proprietors of the Whisky demand that the band members retrieve Jim from wherever he is. They locate him at a hotel (probably the Tropicana), spinning in his own orbit on a large quantity of LSD. The band's frantic entreaties convince Jim that he ought to at least appear on stage with them, perhaps even sing a song or two. He is to do much more than that.

The Doors finish their set with an ominous version of "The End." The dark and otherworldly mood of the song begins to mesmerize the crowd and soon all dancing has ceased. Morrison behaves as if he were enveloped in the great serpentine myth of the song and his trance-like state slowly begins to encompass the entire audience.

The club is deathly still by the time Morrison quietly begins to recite the Oedipal passage, building it into a crescendo as the other band members seek to drown out his lyrics—lyrics that at the time were shocking, and that the ever-provocative Jim insisted on repeating and emphasizing. The cathartic imagery sends waves of oscillating emotions through the club. The Doors quickly bring the song to a close and leave the stage.

In the aftermath of this performance, the Doors are summarily dismissed from the Whisky and the event takes on legendary proportions. Within a few days, the Doors enter the studio and create one of the most extraordinary first albums of all time.

Jim Morrison on "The End": "It didn't start out as an Oedipus thing, more of a goodbye song. We played it at the London Fog (on the Strip) where we first started. Then as we played it each night it got a little more serious. I'd make up the lyrics each night. Then one Sunday night at Whisky A Go Go—we were the second band—something clicked. I realized what the whole song was about, what it had been leading up to. It was powerful. It just happened. They fired us the next day." (Quote from "The Doors swing out Thursday," *Cleveland Plain Dealer*, Sept. 8, 1967)

🔄 Note: This performance could possibly have been on Saturday. On Monday, the Whisky presented Moby Grape and the African Blues Quartet. The Jefferson Airplane was scheduled to begin on August 24.

🎭 Also performing: Love

🤸 Early (matinee) and late shows

Sunset Sound Studios #1
Hollywood, CA

The band records their first album—*The Doors*—in the last week of August with Paul Rothchild as producer. They complete the recording in exactly six days (with a weekend break), after which Rothchild flies back to New York with the one-half-inch four-track master reels to begin some extensive editing. "Moonlight Drive," which will not be released until their second album, is among the songs recorded at this first session.

Back in New York Paul Rothchild begins editing. Perhaps the most notable edit occurs on "The End," where he switches between first and second takes right before the lyric "The killer awoke before dawn. . . ." The editing process itself requires weeks before the mixdown can even begin.

Additional musician: Larry Knechtel on bass

THU. SEPT. 15 - SUN. 18 1966 Bido Lito's
Hollywood, CA (DU)

The Doors auditioned for Bido Lito's on several occasions, but had never been given the opportunity to play there. After their summer at the Whisky A Go Go and the securing of a record deal with Elektra, they perform here over one weekend. The uncertainty around this booking is due to the fact that none of the band members recalls playing more than one show (on a Sunday), but the club usually booked for a four-day weekend.

Also performing: The Seeds

Halloween

The Doors arrive for their first engagement in New York, staying at the popular Henry Hudson Hotel on 57th Street. That night they attend an outrageously bizarre, New York-style Halloween party at Ondine's on the Upper East Side.

TUE. NOV. 1 - WED. 30 1966 Ondine Discotheque
New York, NY

This is the opening night of the Doors' first New York appearance. New York based Elektra is anxious to promote their artists in the company's hometown—a very beneficial situation for out-of-town groups like the Paul Butterfield Blues Band and the Doors. As a result the band jumps straight from Los Angeles to New York before even appearing in San Francisco.

During their one-month engagement at Ondine's, the Doors and Paul Rothchild work on mixing the first album in the afternoons. Rothchild has completed the editing and is at least halfway through the final mix into stereo when the Doors arrive. Together, they continue the mix down to stereo, and during one month are able to complete both of the mixes into stereo and mono.

Toward the end of the month, the *Break on Through* publicity film is shot at Elektra's studios. The simple but effective film is directed by Mark Abramson, and clearly captures the intensity of the band at that time. Although designated for television promotion, it is rarely aired.

During one meeting with Elektra, Jac Holzman implores the band to remove the word "high" from the lyrics "she get high" in "Break on Through."

🌀 On November 15, the Doors confirm their contract with Elektra, officially signing on as exclusive recording artists for seven albums.

🎆 Thanksgiving (November 24): no performance; dinner at Paul Rothchild's home.

DEC. 9, 10, 16, 17 1966 The Sea Witch
Hollywood, CA

After their first weekend at the Sea Witch (December 9 and 10), the Doors appear for a second weekend, most likely following the first.

SAT. DEC. 31 1966 Private Residence
Montecito, CA

This is a New Year's Eve party at a private residence.

THE DOORS
Fri.—Sat.
DEC. 9   DEC. 10
THE SEAWITCH

SUN. JAN. 1 1967 Shebang, KTLA-TV Channel 5 Los Angeles, CA (DU)

Break on Through

The Doors make their first television appearance—lip-synching to a playback of their first single, "Break on Through." The whole band looks very collegiate, and the unusual stage setup places Densmore at center stage on drums between Morrison (on stage left) and Manzarek. Krieger stands behind them, directly in front of some garden furnishings. The host is Casey Kasem, and the show is typically broadcast "live and in color" on Sundays. This is one of the final episodes of the *Shebang* show.

⌘ Note: Although another episode is broadcast on January 8, the Doors are in San Francisco. This date seems to be the most probable—coinciding with the release of the album.

✳ Production: Dick Clark and Casey Kasem Present

WED. JAN. 4 1967

The Doors
First Album Released (E-74007)

Side One (A):	Side Two (B):
Break on Through	Back Door Man**
Soul Kitchen	I Looked At You
Crystal Ship	End of the Night
Twentieth Century Fox	Take It As It Comes
Alabama Song*	The End
Light My Fire	

🎵 **Singles**
Break on Through / End of the Night (E-45611)
Light My Fire / The Crystal Ship (E-45615)

At the beginning of January, Elektra Records releases the Doors' first album, as well as their first single: "Break on Through" b/w "End of the Night." In addition, promotional arrangements are made for securing the first "Rock Signboard" on the Sunset Strip, which announces:

"THE DOORS: Break on Through with an Electrifying Album"

✳ Authors: Bertolt Brecht and Kurt Weill (1928), *The Rise and Fall of the City of Mahagonny.* Copyright is held by Weill-Brecht-Harms Company, Inc.

✳✳ Author: Willie Dixon. All other songs by the Doors.

FRI. JAN. 6 - SUN. 8 1967 Fillmore Auditorium
San Francisco, CA

First Set
When the Music's Over (opening song)
Break on Through
Take It As It Comes
Light My Fire

Second Set
Spanish Caravan
Crawlin' King Snake
The End

On their first trip to the burgeoning music scene in San Francisco, the Doors are booked for two weekends at the Fillmore Auditorium. This is the Doors' first of five weekends at the Fillmore. The Doors check in at the Swiss America Hotel, which at that time is located in the heart of an "active" neighborhood bordering San Francisco's red-light district.

- Also performing: The Young Rascals; Sopwith Camel
- This set-list is incomplete and could possibly come from one of the other nights. Whichever night it was, at least one song ("Crawlin' King Snake"), and probably more, are recorded and preserved in the archives.
- Promotion: Bill Graham Presents

FRI. JAN. 13 - SUN. 15 1967 Fillmore Auditorium
San Francisco, CA

This is the Doors' second of five weekends at Bill Graham's Fillmore Auditorium. After these two weekends, they don't return until June 9 and 10.

Friday night is probably the Fillmore show at which Jim Morrison never arrived. In *Bill Graham Presents*, Graham recalls that on that night no one had the slightest idea where Morrison was, and patrons were given the option of returning another night or receiving a refund.

The following day, Jim appears at Graham's business office and explains that he had been leaving Sacramento when he spotted *Casablanca* playing at a local movie theater. He says that he had felt compelled to stop and sit through three showings of the Humphrey Bogart classic, consequently missing the Doors' scheduled appearance at the Fillmore. Graham is exasperated, insisting that Jim should have called, but ultimately forgives him, hoping that this will be Morrison's final disappearance.

- Also performing: The Grateful Dead; Junior Wells Chicago Blues Band
- Production: Bill Graham Presents

SAT. JAN. 14 1967 (2) Polo Field
Golden Gate Park, San Francisco, CA

The Doors attend "The Great Human Be-In" event in Golden Gate Park, which includes performances by the Grateful Dead, Jefferson Airplane, Quicksilver Messenger Service, Country Joe and the Fish, Dizzy Gillespie, and the Charlatans. There are also readings and talks by such noted poets and personalities as Allen Ginsberg, Timothy Leary, Lawrence Ferlinghetti, and Michael McClure. This extraordinary gathering unquestionably serves as a catalyst for the famous rock music festivals of the 1960s, which begin six months later.

THU. JAN. 19 -SUN. 29 1967 Ondine Discotheque
New York, NY

On their second trip to New York City, the Doors return with their enthusiasm bolstered by the success of their last appearance at Ondine's and the release of their first single and album. This is the opening night of the Doors' second of three scheduled lengthy appearances at the club. Also, their first New York review appears in the local music paper *Crawdaddy* during this stint at Ondine's, extolling the band for its passionate zeal and urging readers to catch the show.

On opening night, Morrison appears on stage in faded jeans with a furious energy that keeps the whole first set moving at breakneck tempo. At the conclusion of the last song, he leaps into the air and smashes his head into the low rafters. Clearly dazed, he apparently recovers fully during the break.

- Booking agent for Ondine's: Brad Pierce
- Note: Richard Goldstein writes an exceptionally positive and upbeat review of the show for the *Village Voice*.
- Jan. 26–29 are uncertain but highly probable.

TUE. JAN. 31 - THU. FEB. 2 1967 Gazzarri's
Hollywood, CA

- Also performing: The Soul People

TUE., WED. FEB. 14, 15 1967 Whisky a Go-Go
San Francisco, CA

The Doors perform for only two nights at this venue despite the fact that the original poster has them advertised from February 4 through 19. Later advertisements have them opening on the 14th, and the fact that Jim Morrison was arrested in Los Angeles on February 11 for public intoxication supports this. The Doors are actually hired to open for the Peanut Butter Conspiracy, which is the act that most of the small number of patrons (estimate: 10 to 15) actually come to hear. Not exactly an inspiring gig, the Doors arrange to be replaced by the Wildflower.

- Also performing: The Peanut Butter Conspiracy
- Lighting: Love Conspiracy Commune
- Note: This San Francisco variation on the Los Angeles Whisky a Go Go had a different approach to presenting live entertainment. In addition to having live music at 8:00 p.m., they regularly featured "Topless luncheon fashion shows & fencing exhibitions."

"Topless luncheon fashion shows & fencing exhibitions."

SAT. FEB. 18 1967 The Hullabaloo
Hollywood, CA (DU)

The Hullabaloo location was first known as the Earl Carroll Theater, then as the Moulin Rouge, and later the Aquarius Theater.

TUE. FEB. 21 1967 Gazzarri's
Hollywood, CA

This is the grand opening night for Gazzarri's new location, a nightclub featuring up-and-coming bands that is still prominent on the Sunset Strip. Proprietor Bill Gazzarri is thrilled with the Doors' engagements there.

The Doors' contract specifies that the band perform six nights a week, at either 8:15 or 9:15 p.m. depending on the day of the week.

🎤 Also performing: The Enemys; the Quirks

WED. FEB. 22 1967 Valley Music Theater
Woodland Hills, CA
George Washington's Birthday Bash

Tonight's show is a benefit performance for CAFF, the Community Action for Fact and Freedom, a foundation established by members of the entertainment business following the Sunset Strip riots in 1966. CAFF's members actively seek to mediate some sort of resolution to the conflicting interests of people in the community. Local business owners are appalled by the massive influx of young people on the streets, and seek to remedy the situation through police arrests for loitering and similar misdemeanors.

The Doors are the opening act for the benefit, which begins at 7:30, and they are followed by Hugh Masakela.

🎤 Also performing: The Byrds; Buffalo Springfield; Peter, Paul and Mary; Hugh Masakela

THU., FRI. FEB. 23, 24 1967 Gazzarri's
Hollywood, CA

🎤 Also performing: The Enemys; the Quirks

SAT. FEB. 25 1967 (1) Griffith Park
Burbank, CA
The Second Meeting of the Tribes for a Human Be-In

The Doors attended but did not perform at the large "Human Be-In" gathering in San Francisco on January 14. There was one at Griffith Park on that day as well, although only around 500 people attend. This event is much larger, attracting approximately 5,500 people to the park just north of the Greek Theater. Jerry Hopkins, who serves as emcee for the event, takes the stage (donated by the UCLA Film Department) at three in the afternoon and proceeds to introduce the continuous stream of bands throughout the day.

🎤 Also performing: Alexander's Timeless Blooz Band; Ma's Preserve Jug Band; New World Jazz Company; the Sound Machine; City Lights; W.C. Fields Memorial String Band; UFO; with emcee Jerry Hopkins

SAT. FEB. 25 1967 (2) Gazzarri's
Hollywood, CA

SAT. FEB. 25 1967 (3) The Hullabaloo
Hollywood, CA

This is an after-hours performance following the Gazzarri's show.

SUN. FEB. 26 - THU. MAR. 2 1967 Gazzarri's
Hollywood, CA

The *Los Angeles Times* gives this enthusiastic account of a Doors performance at Gazzarri's: "The Doors wield a rock 'n' roll beat with continuous jazz improvisation to produce an intense, highly emotional sound. They call their music 'primitive and personal' and find it hard to work without audience reaction. Their numbers change constantly at live shows and new ones are written as they perform. The words build with the music into an accelerating crescendo of frenzied sound. Trying to avoid the 'hard straight sound' of many rock groups, the Doors aim for 'dramatic impact' in their music. Gazzarri's crowded dance floor proves that the Doors' lyrical freedom hasn't hurt their strong rock 'n' roll dance tempo." (Francine Grace, "Vibrant Jazz-Rock Group at Gazzarri's," *Los Angeles Times*, Feb. 28, 1967)

　Note: No performance on March 1.

FRI. MAR. 3 1967 Avalon Ballroom
San Francisco, CA

Light My Fire
The End

On their second trip to San Francisco's prestigious ballrooms, the Doors appear as the headlining act at Chet Helms's Avalon Ballroom.
This is the Doors' first of four weekends at the Avalon.

　Also performing: Country Joe and the Fish; Sparrow [featuring John Kay, who soon changes their name to Steppenwolf]

　Set-list incomplete

　Promotion: Chet Helms and the Family Dog Present

　Capacity: 1,200 to 1,300

SAT. MAR. 4 1967 Avalon Ballroom
San Francisco, CA

Moonlight Drive*
Back Door Man*

This early rendition of "Moonlight Drive" features Morrison and Manzarek collectively on vocals. After the first two stanzas, they engage in a long "call and response," until Morrison brings it back with his "You got fishes for your friends" poetry, and then comes in with the concluding verses. "Back Door Man" opens with some peculiar yelps and growls by Morrison, followed by a brief harmonica section. During the instrumental break, he brings out the harp again, playing both alongside and after Krieger's lead. Overall, it is a very unusual version of this song.

　These two songs are among the earliest known live recordings of the Doors; however, the exact date and location remain unconfirmed.

　Also performing: Country Joe and the Fish; Sparrow [pre-Steppenwolf]

　Promotion: Chet Helms and the Family Dog Present

March 7 Set-list
1st Set
(Warm-up)
Back Door Man
My Eyes Have Seen You
Soul Kitchen
Get Out of My Life, Woman
When the Music's Over »
  "Everything You Do Will Be Reported" »
  "Who Scared You?" »
When the Music's Over

2nd Set
Close to You
Crawlin' King Snake
I Can't See Your Face in My Mind
People Are Strange
Who Do You Love
Alabama Song
Crystal Ship
Twentieth Century Fox
Moonlight Drive
Summer's Almost Gone
Unhappy Girl

3rd Set
The Devil Is a Woman*»
  "Sittin' Round Thinkin'"»
Rock Me
Break on Through
Light My Fire
The End »
  "Fall Down Now, Strange Gods Are Coming" »
  "Can You Stand By, and Watch the
        Pictures Burn?" »
The End

The Matrix is a relatively small San Francisco club (seating just over 100 people) that features many of the prominent Bay Area bands from the sixties and early seventies. It is host to many other touring acts as well, attracting them with the proposition of multiple-night bookings. Opening in 1965, it features Marty Balin of the Jefferson Airplane as one of the original proprietors. The Matrix is a mainstay on the San Francisco scene until 1971.

These Matrix shows are relatively sedate compared to other Doors shows at the time. The band seems almost stoic in this intimate environment, which is quite different from the ballrooms that are attracting immense crowds. They appear content with just introducing their music with minimal fanfare, although Morrison does interject some spontaneous poetry into the longer pieces.

Of particular note is the Doors' version of "Light My Fire," which features an unusual introduction and a structure that is quite different from their regular version. The Doors frequently experiment with variations on their music, keeping the creative spirit alive even after the studio arrangement is completed. (Another instance includes the new introduction and dramatic musical passages that appear during their live performances of "The End" in 1968.)

Morrison also produces an extended intro leading into "Rock Me," paraphrasing the film title *The Devil Is a Woman*, and later incorporating some obscure and vivid poetry into "The End."

❋ *The Devil Is a Woman* is a reference to the last Josef Von Sternberg movie starring Marlene Dietritch, filmed in 1935. Von Sternberg was an instructor of film direction at UCLA during Jim's years there, and Morrison sometimes avowed that Von Sternberg's obscure *Anatahan* was his favorite film. Morrison rearranges the sequence of words ("Woman Is the Devil") for this introductory piece to "Rock Me."

✵ Also performing: Larry Vargo

FRI. MAR. 10 1967 Matrix
San Francisco, CA

2nd Set

My Eyes Have Seen You
Soul Kitchen
I Can't See Your Face in My Mind
People Are Strange
When the Music's Over
   "Confusion" »
When the Music's Over

3rd Set

Money
Who Do You Love »
Moonlight Drive
Summer's Almost Gone
I'm a King Bee
Gloria »
   "Meet Me in the Graveyard" »
Gloria
Break on Through
Summertime (instrumental)
Back Door Man
Alabama Song
The End »
   "Let's Feed Ice Cream to the Rats" »
The End

One of the highlights of this particular show is the rare performance of the instrumental "Summertime," a beautifully arranged piece that unfortunately did not appear more often in the Doors' live repertoire. The Doors also pull out old standards: "I'm a King Bee" featuring Manzarek on vocals, and the ever popular "Gloria." "The End" includes some bizarre poetry not heard in other versions— probably some spontaneous improvisation on Jim's part.

🌿 Above set-lists are probably incomplete. Sets are entitled two and three because there may be a missing first set.

🐸 Also performing: Larry Vargo

SAT. MAR. 11 1967 Matrix
San Francisco, CA

🐸 Also performing: Larry Vargo

MON. MAR. 13 - SUN. APR. 2 1967 Ondine Discotheque
New York, NY

March 13

Break on Through
Back Door Man
People Are Strange

This is the third and final scheduled group of shows at Ondine's. The Doors are booked into Steve Paul's Scene beginning in June. *Cash Box* raves about the opening night's show: "The Doors have opened . . . WIDE. Mar. 13th saw the return of the crack Elektra rock group to Manhattan's Ondine. A packed house greeted these four young purveyors of west coast psychedelia, a crowd that just stopped dancing and took in the sounds. At a cost of $4 a head to get in and a $5 minimum (each) at the tables, that's $10 a seat for a rock concert. From where this reviewer sat, no one left disappointed. They use their own material, and in so doing infuse the New York (nitery) scene with a fresh, contemporary sound from the west. Then having created their own rock bag, they play it well and are well worth seeing any time you get a chance." ("Talent On Stage," *Cash Box*, Mar. 25, 1967)

On March 23rd, music critic and enthusiast Richard Goldstein's sparkling review appears in the *Village Voice:* "First New York opening in a while. The Doors—fresh from Los Angeles with an underground album of the hour—return. This time, they are worshiped, envied, bandied about like the Real Thing. The word is out—or 'in'—'The Doors will floor you.' So not all the pretty people in New York were present at opening night, but enough to keep a few publicity agencies busy. The four musicians mounted their instruments. The organist lit a stick of incense. Vocalist and writer Jim Morrison closed his eyes to all that Arnel elegance, and the Doors opened up. Morrison twitched and pouted and a cluster of girls gathered to watch every nuance in his lips. Humiliating your audience is an old game in rock 'n' roll, but Morrison pitches spastic love with a raging insolence you can't ignore. His material—almost all original—is literate, concise, and terrifying. The Doors have the habit of improvising, so a song about being strange which I heard for the first time at Ondine may be a completely different composition by now. Whatever the words, you will discern a deep streak of violent—sometimes Oedipal—sexuality. And since sex is what hard-rock is all about, the Doors are a stunning success. You should brave all the go-go gymnastics, bring a select circle of friends for buffer, and make it up to Ondine to find out what the literature of pop is all about. The Doors are mean; and their skin is green." (Richard Goldstein, "Pop Eye," *Village Voice*, Mar. 23, 1967)

Set-list incomplete

On the 25th, *Cash Box* reports: "The Doors opened at Ondine's last week. They've been packing 'em in ever since. The Elektra group has an avid following on the coast and seems well on the way toward building one here." And a week later *Cash Box* reiterates: "The Doors are still packing 'em in at Ondine." ("Record Rambling," *Cash Box*, Mar. 25, 1967)

WED. APR. 5 1967 Fresno District Fairgrounds
Fresno, CA (DU)

THU. APR. 6 1967 Modesto Skating Rink Arena
Modesto, CA (DU)

FRI. APR. 7 1967 The Merced Legion Hall
Merced, CA

Also performing: Infinity

SAT. APR. 8 1967 The Turlock Fairgrounds
Turlock, CA

Also performing: Infinity

The Iron Butterfly
Alexander's Timeless Blooz Band
Sun, May 14, 8 P.M.
The Doors
The Daily Flash

COME DANCE WITH ME BY THE SEA

CHEETAH

HUMBLE HARVE

bonus

1 NAVY STREET P.O.P. STA. MONICA. 392-4501

SUN. APR. 9 1967 Cheetah
Santa Monica Pier, Venice, CA

Early Show
When the Music's Over
Back Door Man

The Los Angeles version of the Cheetah just opened on March 21, and is patterned after the nightclub of the same name in New York. The 3,750-capacity venue is located at the site of the old Aragon Ballroom in Santa Monica's Pacific Ocean Park and sports a 7,000-square-foot dance floor bordered by stainless steel walls.

It is at the late show that Jim Morrison unveils his "tightrope walk," where he precariously balances himself as he walks along the edge of the stage. At one point he loses his balance and falls off the eight-foot-high stage and into the crowd.

He continues to do the "tightrope walk" in other live performances until one journalist sarcastically comments on how contrived it appears. Nevertheless, Morrison maintains a well-deserved reputation for risking life and limb on his dangerous jaunts along the ledges of tall buildings.

Happening magazine comments on these shows: "Robby picked their first Cheetah appearance as their most exciting show. 'We just got back from New York and everybody was waiting for us. "Break on Through" was out and people were turning on to the album. It was our first really large crowd.' Over 3,000 persons were at the Cheetah in Venice when Jim Morrison fell a good 8 feet off the high stage during a wild rage." (Hank Zevallos, *Happening* magazine #5)

- Also performing: Jefferson Airplane
- Early Show (3:00 p.m. matinee)/Late Show (8:30 p.m.)
- Set-list incomplete
- Proprietors: Oliver Coquelin and Borden Stevenson.
- Entertainment Coordinator: Pierre Groleau

FRI., SAT. APR. 14, 15 1967 Avalon Ballroom
San Francisco, CA

This is the second of four weekends that the Doors perform at the Avalon Ballroom.
- Also performing: The Steve Miller Band; Aji Baba's Band [with his dancing girls]
- Promotion: Chet Helms and the Family Dog Present

THU. APR. 20 1967 Taft High School
Woodland Hills, CA (DU)

FRI. APR. 21 - SUN. 23 1967 The Kaleidoscope
at Ciro's
Los Angeles, CA

These shows are the first ones future Doors associate Richard Linnell attends. Linnell, who had roomed with Krieger's brother Ron in college, soon becomes an equipment handler for the band, then begins promoting them in

December (Long Beach, 12/1/67), and later will help manage the band for five years starting around the time of the sessions for *An American Prayer*. Following Miami, it is Linnell's "clean file" of reviews and favorable letters from concert hall managers that helps the band get concert dates again.

- Also performing: UFO; Kaleidoscope; the Peanut Butter Conspiracy
- Light show: New Glory
- Note: This is one of the temporary locations for the Kaleidoscope during their difficulties in finding an adequate location in Los Angeles. When the Doors play there again in April 1968, the club has relocated to the Earl Carroll Theater, having opened on March 21 with the Jefferson Airplane.
- Promotion: John Hartman, Skip Taylor and Gary Essert

SAT. APR. 29 1967 Earl Warren Showgrounds
Santa Barbara, CA

This is one of the Grateful Dead's first appearances in Southern California following the release of their first album. In the book he wrote with David Dalton, *Living with the Dead*, Grateful Dead manager Rock Scully relates how the Dead and the "Acid King" himself, Owsley Stanley, personally present Morrison with a baggie full of purple-barrel acid. For Jim, this was like Joseph of Aramathea handing him the Holy Grail. Although the two bands are from dissimilar musical paths, they share the late '60s enthusiasm for wild sojourns into inner worlds, especially when the tickets are punched by that grand conductor himself—the infamous Owsley.

- Also performing: The Grateful Dead; UFO; Captain Speed
- Promotion: James Salzer

SUN. APR. 30 1967 The Hullabaloo
Hollywood, CA
Freedom of Expression Concert

"The Freedom of Expression Committee" benefit is held to provide funds for the legal expenses surrounding the defense of performances in coffee houses, as well as for sales of the *Love Book* at the Free Press Book Store. (On November 17, 1966, police in San Francisco raided the Psychedelic Shop and Lawrence Ferlinghetti's City Lights Book Store, making arrests for the distribution of alleged pornography for the sale of the *Love Book*, a collection of poems by Lenore Kandel.) The emcee for the event is Elliot Mintz for KPFK-FM, a listener-supported station in North Hollywood operated by the Pacifica Foundation.

- Note: There is a possibility the Doors may not have performed at this show because of scheduling conflicts. The scheduling assignments for such a large number of bands would certainly have been a logistical nightmare. KPFK does not have the Doors included in their records of this performance.
- Also performing at both shows: Barry McGuire; Canned Heat; Clear Light; Taj Mahal; Hamilton Street Car; the Factory; Robert Baker; Blues Express; Hearts and Flowers; UFO; Ladybirds; Jay Walker and the Pedestrians; New Generation; Yellow Brick Road; the Rain; Lovin' One; Rick Martino; Biff Rose; the Poor; and others
- Early (7:00 to 10:00 p.m.) and late (10:30 p.m. to 2:00 a.m.) shows

"Light My Fire" / "The Crystal Ship"
Second Single Released (E-46515)

The Doors second single, an edited version of the seven-minute "Light My Fire," is released after repeated requests from deejays for an AM-formatable version of the song. It begins a slow but steady climb up the charts that will peak in July.

MON. MAY 1 1967 Whisky A Go Go
West Hollywood, CA

There is a good possibility that this show did not take place. Hugh Masakela had begun a series of shows on April 25, but since Monday nights are often open, there is still the possibility that the band made an unadvertised appearance announced only with handbills.

Sunset Sound Studios #1
Hollywood, CA

The Doors begin work on their second album, with Paul Rothchild producing. After the initial sessions, they don't reconvene in the studio until August, by which time the studio has upgraded from four- to eight-track recording equipment.

SAT. MAY 6 1967 Hi-Corbett Field Baseball Stadium
Randolph Park, Tucson, Az (DU)
Happening #1

 Capacity: 9,600

SUN. MAY 7 1967 Valley Music Theater
Woodland Hills, CA

There is a distinct possibility that this show did not take place. The show is apparently intended as a means of acknowledging deejay Dave Diamond, who has enthusiastically supported the Doors' music on the air. Diamond is scheduled to appear today at the Reseda Park Be-In with Canned Heat, Rainy Daze, and other bands.

FRI., SAT. MAY 12, 13 1967 Avalon Ballroom
San Francisco, CA

This is the Doors' third of four weekends at the Avalon Ballroom. Bill Siddons, who had been assisting the band with road work, is offered the position of the Doors' road manager at this engagement. He will officially start in that capacity on June 11 in New York.

Also performing: Sparrow [pre-Steppenwolf]

Promotion: Chet Helms and the Family Dog Present

SUN. MAY 14 1967 Cheetah
Santa Monica Pier, Venice, CA

✹ Also performing: Daily Flash
✹ Capacity: 3,750
✹ Promotion: Humble Harve

TUE. MAY 16 - FRI. 19 1967 Whisky A Go Go
West Hollywood, CA

May 16

When the Music's Over
Back Door Man
Take It As It Comes

My Eyes Have Seen You
Break on Through
Light My Fire

Although the Byrds are also scheduled to perform at this show, they cancel at the last minute because of Roger (Jim) McGuinn's bout with the flu. However, the Whisky's proprietors are able to replace them at the last minute with Buffalo Springfield. It remains uncertain if the Byrds are able to appear for their performances later in the week.

This is the Doors' first performance at the Whisky since their infamous summer run in 1966 and it goes very well. When he isn't singing, Jim Morrison spends the evening limply slouched against his microphone stand as if it were holding him up, periodically bursting from his repose with rousing screams.

Doug Weston comments in the May 19 issue of *Open City*: "Last Tuesday's opening of the Byrds and the Doors disappointed many flower children because Jim (Roger) McGuinn dropped out with the flu. By now they should be back in action. Club owner Elmer Valentine used good taste is substituting the sensitive Buffalo Springfield. But of course, they don't sing "Mr. Tambourine Man," and their song "For What It's Worth" makes me remember that this opening marks the return of long haired folk rock music to the Sunset Strip. I wonder if last year's Strip problems are going to develop again by summer; hopefully long and short hairs should be able to live more peacefully together this time around." (Doug Weston, "A New Column," *Open City*, May 19, 1967)

✹ Note: There is a chance that the Doors made one unscheduled appearance at the club on May 1.

✹ Note: By 1967, the Byrds had achieved mythic status among L.A. bands. Following the release of their first single, "Mr. Tambourine Man," and their legendary appearances at Ciro's on the Sunset Strip in March and April 1965, they went on to become one of the foremost purveyors of the new rock music of the 1960s. Through the second half of 1966 and most of 1967, the band consisted of Roger (Jim) McGuinn, David Crosby (later of Crosby, Stills, Nash and Young), Chris Hillman, Michael Clarke, and periodically Gene Clark. In early 1968, Gram Parsons is added to the roster and makes a significant contribution to the group before leaving with Chris Hillman to start the Flying Burrito Brothers. Billy James, the West Coast public relations director for Columbia Records who unsuccessfully tried to secure the Doors on contract with Columbia, is also an ardent supporter of the Byrds and later assumes a management position with them.

✹ Also performing (May 16): Buffalo Springfield

✹ Set-list incomplete

✹ Also performing (May 17–19): either the Byrds or Buffalo Springfield

SAT. MAY 20 1967 (1) Birmingham Stadium
Van Nuys, CA

This is the Doors' first major outdoor appearance in Los Angeles, sharing the billing with San Francisco's Jefferson Airplane. The event is scheduled by the Birmingham High School Committee as a fund-raiser to provide an additional 6,500 seats to this 10,200-capacity football stadium. Among the members of the committee are prominent entertainment personalities such as Dick Van Dyke and Dennis Weaver, who also plans to attend the performance.

🎤 Also performing: Jefferson Airplane; the Nitty Gritty Dirt Band; the Great Peanut Butter Conspiracy; Merry Go Round; and the "Pepsi Boss Battle of the Bands," which included the local Distortions

🕕 6:00 p.m. show

🎟 Promoters: Birmingham Stadium Committee and the Dads Club

SAT. MAY 20 1967 (2) Whisky A Go Go
West Hollywood, CA

🎤 Also performing: Either the Byrds or Buffalo Springfield

SUN. MAY 21 1967 Whisky A Go Go
West Hollywood, CA

This is the Doors final appearance at the famous Whisky. Although Morrison will sit in with other bands later, it is the band's last official performance there.

🎤 Also performing: Either the Byrds or Buffalo Springfield

SAT. MAY 27 1967 Earl Warren Showgrounds
Santa Barbara, CA

🎤 Also performing: Country Joe and the Fish

🎟 Promotion: James Salzer

FRI. JUN. 2 1967 Victoria Memorial Arena
Victoria, British Columbia

Advertised primarily by flyers, this performance is apparently scheduled shortly before the date of the show. The Avalon Ballroom shows are usually set for Friday and Saturday nights, and are apparently moved to Saturday and Sunday to accommodate this performance.

🎤 Also performing: Collectors; Blues By 5

FRI. JUN. 2 1967 Pasadena Civic Auditorium
Pasadena, CA

Cancelled. This performance is apparently cancelled because of extensive renovations that are being completed to the auditorium. The venue reopens the following night with a show featuring the Seeds.

- Also scheduled to perform: Love; Canned Heat
- 8:00 p.m. show
- Poster artist: Gary Weisser
- Capacity: 2000

SAT. JUN. 3 -SUN. 4 1967 Avalon Ballroom
San Francisco, CA

This is the Doors' fourth and final weekend at the Avalon Ballroom.

- Also performing: The Steve Miller Band
- Promotion: Chet Helms and the Family Dog Present

WED. JUN. 7 1967 Beverly Hills High School
Peters Auditorium
Beverly Hills CA (DU)

- Also performing: The Coasters; [and possibly] Three Dog Night

THU. JUN. 8 1967 The Hullabaloo
Hollywood, CA

These unadvertised shows are a last-minute addition before the band is to leave for San Francisco and New York.

Commenting on the show, *Happening* magazine reports: "Soon the Doors are making music, Morrison slouches over the rigid microphone and the Hullabaloo's turntable stage slowly begins to spin them towards a wildly screaming audience as the curtains pull back. A wild strobe of Instamatic flash bulbs silhouettes frantically waving hands in a lightning sky. Girls press forward against the stage. Morrison grunts, begins squirming, singing, and there's another wild barrage of flash bulbs and press towards the stage. The music weaves and screams into one climax after another. Morrison is literally raping the microphone between his quivering thighs, advancing toward the hungry girls pressing against the stage. And then he trips on the microphone and falls. It happens along with a musical peak and the girls scream, thinking this is the way it should be. Morrison picks himself off the floor. He shouts the lyrics. Picks up the microphone stand and throws it hard. The girls can't believe it. Few are frightened, most of them have eyes that mirror an erotic spell. And Morrison jumps hard upon the fallen stand. Picks it up again and throws it hard once more. Shouting the lyrics. Screaming. You look at the girls and you'd swear they're having orgasm. Morrison destroys the mike and its stand." (Hank Zavellos, "The Doors," *Happening* magazine #5, 1968)

- Also performing: The Sunshine Company
- Early and late shows

> Morrison grunts, begins squirming, singing ... literally raping the microphone between his quivering thighs, advancing toward the hungry girls pressing against the stage. And then he trips on the microphone and falls.

FRI. JUN. 9 1967 Fillmore Auditorium
San Francisco, CA

This is the third of five weekends for the Doors at the legendary Fillmore Auditorium, and the first time they receive top billing there. Morrison is typically late and typically intoxicated, and he exchanges some heated words with Bill Graham before the show begins. In *Bill Graham Presents*, Graham tells the story of standing in the rear of the Fillmore when he sees Morrison perilously twirling his microphone like a lasso over the heads of people in the audience. He hastily makes his way through the crowd toward the stage to tell him to stop. When he is less than a dozen feet from the stage, Morrison's microphone somehow zips past everyone else in the audience to strike Bill Graham square in the head. Graham is outraged and tracks down Morrison immediately after the show. First he clears everyone out of the dressing room and then turns to Morrison and barks, "Are you out of your fucking mind!?" He explains that Jim would be liable if there was ever an injury resulting from his antics on stage. Jim promises to be more careful in the future.

This is also probably the night that some of the band members go over to the Avalon Ballroom between sets to see Janis Joplin performing with Big Brother and the Holding Company (on a bill with Canned Heat).

Also performing: Richie Havens; Jim Kweskin Jug Band

SAT. JUN. 10 1967 (1) Mt. Tamalpais Outdoor Theater
Marin County, CA
The Fantasy Faire & Magic Festival (KRFC presents)

This festival is actually the very first of its kind featuring a multitude of high-profile bands, and helps to usher in the dawn of the 1960s rock festivals. Despite this, the Monterey Pop Festival the following weekend is an international and more significant affair, and its attendant publicity far outshines this comparably modest, though historic, benefit.

More than 15,000 music enthusiasts make the trek to the sold-out event (via appointed buses) at the Sydney B. Cushing Memorial Theater situated near the peak of this mountain, with panoramic views of San Francisco and the northern California coastline. The colorful crowd is greeted by warm sun and clear skies for a vibrant and peaceful festival where hippies successfully intermingle with such characters as the Hell's Angels. The *San Francisco Chronicle* applauds it as a two-day relocation of the Haight-Ashbury and Fillmore Auditorium scenes to the top of Mt. Tamalpais.

Says the *Chronicle*: "It was the weekend of the Big Blast on Mt. Tam. It was wild sounds and wild colors, skydivers and side-shows, bizarre hippies from the Haight-Ashbury and T-shirted fraternity boys from Cal., young people necking on the sun-burnt slopes and children sitting wide-eyed in a real tepee, Hell's Angels munching peanut butter sandwiches at a health food bar. . . . There was something for everybody." (Maitland Zane, "Bash on Mt. Tam," *San Francisco Chronicle*, June 12, 1967)

The Doors put on a smooth, well-executed performance despite the somewhat hectic atmosphere of the afternoon. Morrison frequently swings on the flagpoles on either side of the stage and emulates shamanistic movements during instrumental passages in the music. Densmore works diligently to bring the small stage to life with theatrical percussion movements.

Note: The "Fantasy Faire" was originally scheduled for June 3 and 4 as a benefit for the Hunters Point Child Care Center, but is delayed by inclement weather. Performances are scheduled on Saturday and Sunday from 10 a.m. to 6 p.m. The event is filmed by an independent producer.

Also performing on Saturday: The Fifth Dimension; Dionne Warwick; Canned Heat; Jim Kweskin Jug Band; Moby Grape; 13th Floor Elevators; Spanky and Our

> Bizarre hippies ... T-shirted fraternity boys ... children sitting wide-eyed in a real tepee, Hell's Angels munching peanut butter sandwiches at a health food bar.

Gang; Roger Collins; Blackburn and Snow; Sparrow; Every Mother's Son; Kaleido-scope; Chocolate Watch Band; Mojo Men; Merry Go Round—at least eleven bands in total

🎜 Also performing on Sunday: Jefferson Airplane; the Byrds; P.F. Sloan; the Seeds; the (New) Grass Roots; the Loading Zone; Tim Buckley; Every Mother's Son; Hugh Masakela; Steve Miller Blues Band; the Seeds; Country Joe and the Fish; Smokey Robinson and the Miracles; Captain Beefheart and the Magic Band; Sons of Champlin; Lamp of Childhood; Mystery Trend; Penny Nichols; Merry Go Round; New Salvation Army Band

🎜 Other possible appearances are made by: The Blues Magoos; Tim Hardin; Mojo Men; and Kim Weston. Due to rescheduling, Wilson Pickett and other acts are unable to appear

SAT. JUN. 10 1967 (2) Fillmore Auditorium
San Francisco, CA

🎜 Also performing: Richie Havens; Jim Kweskin Jug Band

SUN. JUN. 11 1967 Village Theater
New York, NY
WOR-FM's First Anniversary Show

The Doors arrive in New York for their first major performance at the Village Theater for WOR-FM's first anniversary. In 1967, WOR-FM (98.7) is in the vanguard of providing alternative music in contrast to the stagnation that permeates "top 40" AM stations. The two most prominent deejays, Rosko Mercer and Murray the K Kaufman, break with all conventional formats and help pioneer the intriguing free-form FM radio of the late 1960s, playing such heretofore unknown artists as Jimi Hendrix and the Doors. Popular journalist and deejay Rosko entertains the audi-ence with his humor during the set changes, and two years later he will be among the panelists discussing the Doors' music on the PBS special *Critique*.

Variety recounts the event: "Teenyhippies, elderboppers, rattles and rogues pushed the turnstile to capacity biz at WOR-FM's first 'birthday party' Sunday night at the Village Theater in New York's lower east side. The vent, actually a concert, proved a "hip"–penning of the month for a 5,400 person segment of the station's rock 'in stereo' listenership. The 2,700 seat house is filled in duplicate, with more tribe members turned away, for the double showing." (Bent, "WOR-FM's 1st birthday party grosses 18G as 'Hip'–penning of month," *Variety* June 14, 1967; reprinted with permission of © Variety, Inc. 1996)

Scheduled between other popular groups of the period, the Doors become the highlight of both shows when they explode into two dynamic and forceful perfor-mances that literally shake the theater with their intimidating volume. Particu-larly captivating is their commanding execution of "Alabama Song," which captures the essence of Brecht and Weill's *The Rise and Fall of the City of Mahagonny*.

The opera, which premiered in Berlin in 1930, details the rise of a city of par-adise called Mahagonny, born from the ashes of a world destitute of faith, and so permeated with evil that no peace is possible. The original settlers of the city are called the "Sharks." As the main women figures arrive in Mahagonny, they break into the "Alabama Song," which expresses the central theme of a world governed by leaders so alarmingly disconnected from their own fundamental humanity that even prostitution seems virtuous in comparison. Because the lyrics are from the women's perspective, the Doors have to rearrange some of them concerning men and money, but the essential theme remains intact.

Jim Morrison is never far from the sexual shaman Mick Jagger represents, but his is a darker, bleaker war dance. His hand cupped pillowlike over his ear, Morrison's pudgy cherub face curls into a bristling lip.

Richard Goldstein of the *Village Voice* comments: "When the Doors appeared, backed by a skyscraper of amplifiers, the crowd sat through some stunning improvisation, and someone actually shouted "Bravo"—when it was over. The Doors begin where the Rolling Stones leave off. Lead singer Jim Morrison is never far from the sexual shaman Mick Jagger represents, but his is a darker, bleaker war dance. His hand cupped pillowlike over his ear, Morrison's pudgy cherub face curls into a bristling lip. He stands like a creature out of Kenneth Anger, then sidles up to the mike, curls around its head, and belts—what he says has been called 'Artaud Rock' by the UCLA Bruin, and I think the definition fits. It is cruel cool. The organ and guitar chatter in the background, and when they race through a bridge together, the urgent harmony between them is stunning. When the P.A. system begins to fight back, Morrison twists the neck of the microphone until the feedback itself becomes percussion. And so naturally, the only thing to say is 'Bravo.' (Richard Goldstein, "Pop Eye" column, *Village Voice*, June 22, 1967)

This is the first of two Doors appearances at the Village Theater; the other is on September 9.

Note: The Village Theater was purchased by Bill Graham Presents, and reopened as the Fillmore East on March 3, 1968 with Big Brother and the Holding Company featuring Janis Joplin.

Also performing: Janis Ian; the Blues Project; the Chambers Brothers; Richie Havens; Jeremy and the Satyrs; emcees include Rosko Mercer, Scott Muni, Johnny Michaels, Jim Lounsbury, and Murray the K

Production: Sid Bernstein and Fred Weintraub

Early and late shows

MON. JUN. 12 -THU. 15 1967 Steve Paul's Scene
New York, NY

The Scene is a popular westside midtown nightclub at 46th St. and 8th Ave. with a labyrinthine floor plan that extends through a bizarre network of brick-walled cellar rooms and passageways. While the club caters primarily to the jet set, it also attracts a congenial intermingling with the growing hippie community. Steve Paul once described the purpose of the club as "to use music as a common denominator for the fusion between music, musicians, people who like music, and people who are music in their very being." This is the Doors' first engagement at the Scene; the second is in October of this year. (The Doors stayed at the Great Northern Hotel on 57th St.)

Steve Paul, who had an uncanny eye for spotting future stars, would often feature new talent at his club long before word of them had gone out. Among the wide variety of performers and artists featured are the Velvet Underground, Pink Floyd, Jeff Beck, Traffic, the Rascals, Fleetwood Mac (original band), and the Chambers Brothers. The Scene also became one of Jimi Hendrix's favorite locations for his impromptu jam sessions when hanging out in New York City.

The Doors' performances here are notoriously fast, furious, and excessively loud—quite distinct from the soundtrack of the "Summer of Love" that is beginning to flourish on the West Coast. Jim Morrison continues to experiment with improvised lyrics during longer songs. Writer John Kreidl recounts one of these streams of inner consciousness (during a version of "The End" at the Scene) in *Vibrations* magazine, citing some of the lyrics as follows:

```
We want the world and
We want it now
I love my baby,
Come on now

I'm a man *
I'm no boy child
I'm twenty-one
Society's got to have it's fun
```

She took me home **
After school
She was my queen
And I was her fool
Her father was at work
Her mother was shopping
I didn't want to do it
She took me home in her car
It was in Florida ...

I want to tell you about
The world and the wagon wheel
turning all the time
You got to try harder
I want you to see where I'm at
I want you to know
How I feel
With the wagon wheel

❋ Reference to the song "Mannish Boy"
❋❋ Reference to Jim's "Coda Queen"

Also appearing nightly with the Doors is Tiny Tim, who was one of the most bizarre figures to appear on the pop music scene during the late 1960s. He could frequently be spotted slinking around carting his beloved ukulele in a brown paper shopping bag held in one hand and a New Testament in the other. Tiny Tim would unabashedly skip onto the stage in his bright orange socks, fluttering his eyelids and blowing kisses to the audience. His frolicking rendition of "Tiptoe Through the Tulips" was just a natural extension of his demonstrated personality, which led to some memorable appearances on television's acclaimed *Laugh In*.

After one of Tiny Tim's opening performances for the Doors, Jim Morrison half seriously offers him one of his new songs entitled "People Are Strange." However, before Tim can respond, "Light My Fire" is hitting the top of the charts and the discussion is never continued.

Happening magazine includes this commentary about one evening at the Scene: "A concert promoter laughed as he told the story of Morrison madly swinging the microphone at an audience at the Scene in New York. 'Tiny Tim is scared stiff. Morrison just missed his head.' Asher Dann, former Doors manager, tried to stop Morrison, resulting in a bloody fist fight on stage." (Hank Zavellos, "The Doors," *Happening* magazine #5, Summer 1967)

On the June 14, Jimi Hendrix attends the Doors' performance while en route to the Monterey Pop Festival.

🐸 Also performing: The Free Spirits featuring Larry Coryell

FRI. JUN. 16 1967 The Action House
Long Beach, NY

One of the infamous oversights by the producers of the Monterey Pop Festival are the Doors; others include Cream and Traffic. Although the festival is often regarded as a catapult for the definitive bands of the sixties, many of the great artists were not in attendance. The enormous publicity that escalated just prior to the festival led to the decision to close the Scene over that weekend, and the Doors needed to secure other bookings for those nights. It is curious that one of the most influential bands in the United States did not appear at either Monterey or Woodstock.

Before the first Action House show, Jim Morrison reportedly instructs the bartender to line up fifteen shots of Jack Daniel's, and then drinks them all, one after another, just prior to taking the stage. As the show progresses, he consumes an additional fifteen shots and clearly exhibits the consequences. The club is exceptionally hot before the band begins, and the stage continues to heat up as the show wears on. Finally, as if in premonition of events to come, Jim begins to disrobe during one song, but is interrupted before he can achieve his ultimate goal.

🐸 Also performing: The Side Kicks

"A concert promoter laughed as he told the story of Morrison madly swinging the microphone at an audience at the Scene in New York. 'Tiny Tim is scared stiff. Morrison just missed his head.' Asher Dann, former Doors manager, tried to stop Morrison, resulting in a bloody fist fight on stage."

Probably the shortest Doors show ever. At the start of the show, Jim Morrison places the microphone in his mouth and begins to create "unearthly sounds" until the other band members help him off stage. Because it is primarily a dance club, the abbreviated show causes little disturbance.

Also performing: The Side Kicks

SUN. JUN. **18** 1967 The Town Hall
Philadelphia, PA

Alabama Song
The End

The Doors' cancellation at the Scene this weekend turns out to be a rock 'n' roll blessing for Philadelphia. The Doors put on a magnificent show that culminates in an astonishing version of "The End," leaving people exhausted and slumped in their chairs.

Also performing: The Nazz
Promotion: Batoff & Warfield Presents
Set-list incomplete
One show at 7:30 p.m.

MON. JUN. **19** -FRI. **30** 1967 Steve Paul's Scene
New York, NY

The Scene is host to a series of WOR-FM's "Rock in Stereo" gatherings designed to attract their listenership to live performances of artists from their playlists. On June 25, the Doors put on a hard-driving, earthy show, and Morrison's subtle movements sway rhythmically to the dynamics of the music. *Variety* comments: "Lead singer of the foursome, Jim Morrison, is an attraction in himself as his understated gestures perpetuate the verbal themes of the Californian's songs." (Bent, *Variety*, June 1967; reprinted with permission of © Variety, Inc. 1996)

June 25

People Are Strange	Soul Kitchen
Strange Days	The End
When the Music's Over	Light My Fire

Before their shows at the Scene on June 30, the Doors catch the 8:00 p.m. performances by the Paul Butterfield Blues Band and Charles Lloyd Quartet at Wollman Rink's Central Park Music Festival.

FRI. JUN. 23 1967 (2) Greenwich High School Auditorium
Greenwich, CT (DU)

Note: Although references to a Doors performance at Greenwich High School is made in some publications, there is a good chance that this show never occurred. A local rumor has it that they appeared around the time of graduation with little or no advertising, but Greenwich High School has no record of such an event, nor is there any mention in the local papers. Greenwich has most likely been confused with Danbury, where the Doors did perform in October.

SAT. JUL. 1 1967 Steve Paul's Scene
New York, NY

Toward the conclusion of the Doors' summer appearance at the Scene, *Cash Box* gives a glowing review of their sets: "Elektra's crack rock act the Doors has been filling Steve Paul's west side nitery, the Scene. Their act is every bit as strong as it sounds on the first LP, "Break on Through." Jim Morrison's strong, powerful vocals working in front of a guitar, drum, organ back ground, set the pace and drive each point home. The Doors have a funky, wailing, west coast type of sound not often heard live in these parts and it seems to be just what the kids want. The Doors' material hits high spots with 'Break on Through' and 'Light My Fire,' their two singles to date. They occasionally slide into a Blues bag as well as doing things like Kurt Weill's 'Alabama Song' from *Mahagonny*. The Doors are a particularly good live act and should be seen to be fully believed." ("Talent On Stage," *Cash Box*, July 8, 1967)

In the same issue, they announce: "The Doors have just completed a record-shattering gig at Steve Paul's Scene." ("Record Ramblings," *Cash Box*, July 8, 1967)

After the performances tonight, Steve Paul celebrates the Doors' phenomenally successful run of shows at the club with a private party for the band.

Early and late shows

MON. JUL. 3 1967 Santa Monica Civic Center
Santa Monica, CA

Also performing: Iron Butterfly; Rubber Maze

8:30 p.m. show

Capacity: 3,000

TUE. JUL. 4 1967 Unicorn Coffee House
Boston, MA

Cancelled. The Doors are originally booked at this club from July 4 through 13. The Grateful Dead, scheduled for the previous two weeks, are cancelled as well.

WED. JUL. 5 1967 Lowell High School Auditorium
La Habra, CA

Also performing: The Coasters; the Standells

SAT. JUL. 8 1967 Balboa Stadium Horseshoe
San Diego, CA

Light My Fire
The End (finale)

The Doors present a superb 45-minute set consisting of five songs and climaxing with a driving version of "The End." The stage is set up at the "horseshoe" end of Balboa Stadium, and although the restricted field separates the audience from the stage, the sound is clear and well defined throughout the show. During "Light My Fire," two women leap over the railing partitioning the field and race to the stage, briefly clutching Morrison's feet before being briskly escorted off by the police. The Doors' energetic and inspiring version of "The End" brings half the crowd to its feet, cheering wildly as the band drives the song to its climatic ending. Afterward, in an unusual "Beatlesque" scenario, dozens of fans begin pursuing the Doors' car out of the stadium while the police try to blockade the exuberant ambush.

> Note: The Jimi Hendrix Experience was thought at one time to have appeared as one of the opening bands; however, they had already returned to New York City.

> Also performing: Marsha and the Esquires; the Lyrics; and two other bands; emcee: Les Turpin

> 8:30 p.m. show

> Capacity: 4,324

> Promotion: Pagni Productions

> Two women leap over the railing partitioning the field and race to the stage, briefly clutching Morrison's feet before being briskly escorted off by the police.

SUN. JUL. 9 1967 Continental Ballroom
Santa Clara, CA (DU)

Soul Kitchen
Break on Through »
    "There You Sit" »
Break on Through
Alabama Song »
Back Door Man »
    "We Came Down the Rivers and Highways" (Names of the Kingdom) »
    "Lost in a Roman Wilderness of Pain" (from "The End") »
Back Door Man*
Light My Fire
The End »
    "Stop the Car, I'm Getting Out!" »
The End

The Doors perform a standard although somewhat sedate set, with Morrison injecting some additional lyrics into the songs. During the "There you sit" phrases in the middle of "Break on Through," his voice is fierce, as if he were berating the audience, which he quite possibly is. The crowd is unusually quiet during the show and seems thoroughly unfamiliar with the songs. "Back Door Man" yields some demented laughter and groans from Morrison, who then extends the song with some supplementary poetry adopted from the evolving "Celebration of the Lizard" and "The End." Of additional note is that Jim inserts lyrics from the emerging "Five to One" ("Get together, one more time") just before the concluding stanza of "The End."

> Note: The date and location for this show are uncertain, but the Doors did play in San Jose while on a joint tour with the Lyrics. The Lyrics manager, Harlan Peacock, who was a good friend of the Doors as well, says that to the best of his recollections they did San Jose right after the Balboa Stadium show. It was a hot summer day and the Lyrics had flown in to San Jose when a weary looking Doors entourage arrived having travelled north by car. Since there is no mention of this

show in any of the local papers, someone will hopefully unearth a rare flyer to confirm the date.

Also performing: The Lyrics

Above set-list may be incomplete. There were probably additional songs between "Back Door Man" and "The End."

THU. JUL. 13 1967 Oakland Auditorium Arena
Oakland, CA

This sweltering July weekend is still remembered as one of the most demanding and exhausting runs that the band and road crew ever endured. There are precious few, if any, moments for anyone to relax as they run up to Oakland from LA on Thursday, over to Sacramento on Friday, back down to Anaheim for an afternoon and evening show Saturday, and finally over to Devonshire Meadows for an afternoon show on Sunday.

Also performing: Chocolate Watch Band; Peter Wheat and the Bread Men

Promotion: William Quary Productions/White Star Tuna

Note: This performance was originally scheduled at the Coliseum, but was moved to the Auditorium just days prior to the show. Acoustic tiles had begun to fall from the ceiling and the Coliseum was temporarily closed for repairs.

FRI. JUL. 14 1967 California State Fairgrounds Grandstand
Sacramento, CA
Crepuscular Happening at the State Fair Grandstand

Also performing: The Parrish Hall Blues Band; the Working Class; the Public Nuisance; emcee: Buck Herring of KROY

8:30 p.m. show

SAT. JUL. 15 1967 Anaheim Convention Center
Anaheim, CA

Late Show

When the Music's Over	Alabama Song
Break on Through	The Crystal Ship
Light My Fire	The End

Both the Doors and the Jefferson Airplane perform superb sets. At the late show, Jim Morrison is in high and mischievous spirits. Although his voice is hoarse and his singing occasionally off pitch, he seems intent on delivering a powerful show. Morrison is characteristically intent on pulling out all the stops, frequently engaging in peppery interactions with the audience and provocatively flicking his lit cigarette butts at the crowd.

Also performing: Jefferson Airplane; the Merry Go Round

Set-list incomplete

Early (3:00 p.m.) and late (8:30 p.m.) shows

Promotion: Tommy Walker/KFWB

Capacity: 8,500

Although his singing is occasionally off pitch, he seems intent on delivering a powerful show…frequently engaging in peppery interactions with the audience and provocatively flicking his lit cigarette butts at the crowd.

SUN. JUL. 16 1967 Devonshire Meadows Raceway
Cal. State, Northridge, CA
Fantasy Faire & Magic Music Festival

Also performing: Jefferson Airplane; Country Joe and the Fish; Butterfield Blues Band; the Mothers; Canned Heat; Iron Butterfly; Grassroots; Kaleidoscope; New Delhi River Band; Sunshine Company; Powers of Evil; Solid State; Morning Glory; Second Coming; Rubber Maze; New Breed; Trans-Atlantic Flash; and more

Saturday and Sunday, 10:00 a.m. to 6:00 p.m.

THU. JUL. 20 1967 Victoria Memorial Arena
Victoria, Canada

Also performing: The Collectors; Painted Ship

FRI., SAT. JUL. 21, 22 1967 Dante's Inferno
Vancouver, Canada

Also performing: The Collectors; Painted Ship

SAT. JUL. 22 1967 (2) American Bandstand
ABC Studios, Hollywood, CA

The Crystal Ship
Light My Fire

This special midsummer edition of *American Bandstand* runs through the countdown of the top-10 hit songs for July. "Light My Fire" will soon be number one, but tonight the Doors are sandwiched between Jefferson Airplane's "White Rabbit" (number three) and Procul Harum's "Whiter Shade of Pale" (number one). After the countdown, host Dick Clark sits next to a member of the studio audience and asks him what his favorite tune is. He replies "Crystal Ship" upon which Clark introduces the Doors. They run through a lip-synched version of the song and then Clark does the traditional band interview between songs. He begins by asking Manzarek about how the band characterizes their music, and then moves on to Morrison.

Dick Clark: "A lot of people seem to think you come from San Francisco. Is that true?"

Morrison: "No. We actually got together in LA. We do play in San Francisco a lot."

Dick Clark: "That's the explanation of why you have that association. Why is so much happening in San Francisco? You figured it out yet?"

Morrison: "The West is the best!" (A quote from "The End")

Dick Clark: (chuckling) "All right! Fair enough!"

Clark then moves to Densmore with questions about recording their first and second albums, and then asks Krieger about their future plans. He concludes the interview by returning to Morrison.

Dick Clark: "Have you selected a name for the new album yet Jim?"

Morrison: "I think it's 'Strange Days.'"

Dick Clark: "All right. Fair enough. We'll do the thing that set the whole music business on fire. Ladies and gentlemen, again, the Doors!"

The Doors then run through a lip-synched version of "Light My Fire," complete with the appropriate audience hysterics. On both songs, the band does a reasonably good job miming the songs, which are shot with plenty of close-ups on Morrison. Manzarek is convincing with his performance, but Krieger and Densmore are clearly not overjoyed with the circumstances. In fact, during a couple of brief moments they look as if they're about to start laughing at their situation.

Note: Broadcast in New York on Channel 7 (ABC) at 1:30 p.m.

Dick Clark: "Why is so much happening in San Francisco? You figured it out yet?"

SUN., MON. JUL. 23, 24 1967 Eagles Auditorium
Seattle, WA

These first shows at Eagles are extraordinarily intense, praised at the time as being two of the most dramatic and vividly cathartic rock performances to have ever hit Seattle—so much so that even the tuning up between songs conveys a dark and foreboding air. Before the Doors' set, Jim Morrison joins the P. H. Phactor Jug Band onstage for several songs.

Tom Robbins makes these observations for *Helix* magazine in Seattle: "The intensity begins the moment they stalk on stage and it doesn't let up until the purge is over, the catharsis is complete. Even between numbers, there is no relaxation—no chit-chat, no horsing around. Like the great actors of Japan, the Doors project all the more intensity when they are silent. The Doors are carnivores in a land of musical vegetarians. Their craftsmanship is all the more astonishing in light of their savagery. They have the ensemble tightness of the Juilliard String Quartet—but their grandeur is not of the intellect but of warm red blood. Their talons, fangs and folded wings are seldom out of view, but if they leave us crotch-raw and exhausted, at least they leave us aware of our aliveness. And of our destiny. The Doors scream into the darkened auditorium what all of us in the underground are whispering more softly in our hearts: We want the world and we want it .... NOW!" (Tom Robbins, *Helix*, member of the Underground Press Syndicate, July 1967)

> *The Doors are carnivores in a land of musical vegetarians.*

⚏ Note: While the Doors are in Seattle performing these two highly anticipated and well-received shows, the Los Angeles "freak scene" holds another "Love-In" at Griffith Park that erupts into violence. Dubbed the Crystal Springs "Hate-In," the incident begins with a confrontation between the police and two Hell's Angels, and quickly develops into a full-blown riot with hippies hurling soda cans at undercover police.

🜲 Also performing: Chrome Syrcus; P.H. Phactor Jug Band

🜲 Promotion and booking: Boyd Grafmyre & Pat Eagle

🜲 Lighting: Union Light Co.

🜲 Art: Gebaroff Sign

"Light My Fire" Hits Number One on the Charts

In anticipation of the occasion, Morrison purchases his infamous black leather suit. The Doors album itself goes gold in September.

WED. JUL. 26 1967 Masonic Temple
Portland, OR

🜲 Promotion: Diamond Productions & KGAR

FRI. JUL. 28 - SUN. 30 1967 Fillmore Auditorium
San Francisco, CA

Light My Fire (an extended version)

This is the Doors fourth of five weekends at the Fillmore Auditorium. They don't return again until November.

Before the first show, Jim Morrison presents Bill Graham with a cleverly appropriate gift. It is a pith helmet, adorned in a variety of brilliant psychedelic colors, with "The Morrison Special" inscribed across the front. It is a humorous apology to Bill for his having mistakenly bashed him on the head with an airborne microphone during their last appearance.

Tonight's show is a solid top-notch presentation by the Doors, who execute a very dynamic and moving performance. Of particular note is a sensational version of "Light My Fire" during which the entire band steadily drives the song to a fiery, intense, yet "other worldly" conclusion. The *San Francisco Chronicle* describes it: "The best of all this was their hit 'Light My Fire.' Friday night they did [it for] about ten minutes and it still seemed too short. Organist Manzarek begins doodling around after the initial chorus, like he was tuning up, slowly begins developing intensity with rolling, sweeping lines punched in the middle by angry chords and stutters, then gave way to Krieger, who wailed with more Eastern feeling than on the recording—bending notes, sharps, flats and quarter tones." (John L. Wasserman, "Exciting Instrumentalists," *San Francisco Chronicle*, July 31, 1967)

🐾 Also performing: James Cotton; Richie Havens

🦎 Promotion: Bill Graham Presents

📋 Note: The Doors are originally scheduled to appear at the Malibu Shore Club, Long Island, New York, on July 28, but cancel for the Fillmore show.

SAT. AUG. 5 1967 Earl Warren Showgrounds
Santa Barbara, CA

🐾 Also performing: Lavender Hill Mob; Joint Effort; Captain Speed

🦎 Promotion: James Salzer

☿ 8:00 p.m. show

WED. AUG. 9 1967 Hampton Beach Casino
Hampton Beach, NH

THU., FRI. AUG. 10, 11 1967 Crosstown Bus Club
Brighton, MA

🐾 Also performing: The Ragamuffins

☿ Early (8:00 p.m.) and late (10:30 p.m.) shows

SAT. AUG. 12 1967 Forest Hills Tennis Stadium
Forest Hills, Queens, NY
The Forest Hills Music Festival

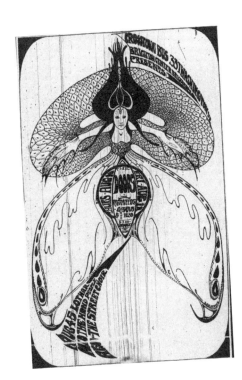

Break on Through
Back Door Man
Light My Fire
The End

Simon and Garfunkel headline the performance this evening, and the choice of the Doors as the opening act is a musical mismatch. Their dark and foreboding music makes a poor contrast to the more folk and harmony-oriented duo. Simon and Garfunkel are enthusiastically welcomed as local heroes, a "homegrown" success story, with the duo having originally met and graduated from Forest Hill's P.S. 164. This is a Simon and Garfunkel audience, and they have no qualms about expressing their displeasure with the opening band.

The night is off to a difficult start when the Doors' equipment flight fails to arrive on time, and the band has to hustle to borrow instruments. After an awkward delay, the Doors hit the stage to substantial applause, which rapidly declines into a pervasive silence. As the show begins, Morrison stands staring out at the crowd, then hoarsely growls "This is the end!" and the band launches into their first number. The band plays exceptionally well, especially considering the circumstances, but the audience response is nominal. They perform an abbreviated set of four songs, concluding with a striking version of "The End," and abruptly leave the stage after about a half hour.

Paul Simon is so disturbed by the harsh reaction to the Doors that he takes the stage and reprimands the audience for their animosity, describing how difficult the music business can be for new groups. In the meantime, the Doors have already left the scene, deeply distressed by how callous the audience has been. Later, they will refer to this show as one of the all-time lows in their career. Ray Manzarek recalls, "I don't think I ever felt worse on a stage than I did at the Forest Hills Tennis Stadium. I didn't know whether I was playing Forest Hills or Forest Lawn Cemetery. We were in hell. What an awful gig. That was one of the all-time lows." (Richard Hogan, "The Doors Tapes," *Circus*, January 31,1981)

New York's *Variety* reveals a subtle animosity toward the Doors in a review of the Simon and Garfunkel show: "The opening slot on the show was held down by the Doors, an electronically rigged combo with a lead singer who goes into paroxysms of caterwauling every other number. Is it for real or is he doing it for the money?" (Herm, "Simon and Garfunkel hit 71,000 capacity gross at Forest Hills fete," *Variety*, Aug., 1967; reprinted with permission of © Variety, Inc. 1996)

However, the *Cash Box* review is substantially more generous in its appraisal of the band: "Not only was there a vibrant show for the ears due to the majestic artistry of each member of the Doors; but the eyes were given an antic performance by Morrison and others who were spotlighted in lengthy solos during 'Light My Fire,' in an extended playing of the team's number one outing. In spite of the overwhelming reception of 'Fire,' the team achieved new heights in their follow up number that closed the act, 'The End.' Licks by the organist, drummer, guitarist and lead showed the throng that there is tremendous individual talent as well as a mighty group sound behind the Doors." ("Talent On Stage." *Cash Box*, Aug. 26, 1967)

Forest Hills bears the dubious distinction of having provided some of the most antagonistic audiences for rock performers in the 1960s. Bob Dylan's second performance with an "electric" band there on August 28, 1965 was met with such raucous hostility that even his infamous appearance at the Newport Folk Festival three days earlier pales in comparison. When the Jimi Hendrix Experience appeared there as the opening act for the Monkees just two months before the Doors show, the booing was so relentless that it prompted the Experience to abandon the tour.

🦋 Also performing: Simon and Garfunkel

🦋 Above set-list may be missing one song

🦋 Promotion: Leonard Ruskin

🦋 Capacity: 13,000

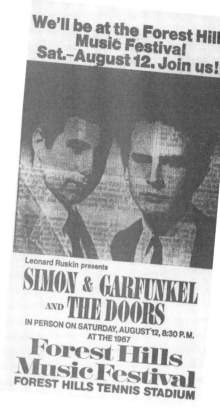

... an electronically rigged combo with a lead singer who goes into paroxysms of caterwauling every other number. Is it for real or is he doing it for the money?

AUG. 13 OR 23 1967

🔥 Note: Although some recollections have suggested that the Doors performed in Philadelphia around this time (at either the Town Hall or Philadelphia Arena) the likelihood it that these dates were confused with their Town Hall appearance on June 18.

Delmonico Hotel, New York, NY (DU)

The Doors are the recipients of the Billboard Award Presentation after "Light My Fire" becomes the number one single on July 25.

FRI. AUG. 18 1967 (1) **Annapolis National Guard Armory**

Annapolis, MD

In a rare occurrence of double booking, the Doors are scheduled for this and the following later performance in the Washington, D.C. area on the same night.

FRI. AUG. 18 1967 (2) **Alexandria Roller Rink Arena**

Alexandria, VA

Jack Alix's Flower Power Show

Light My Fire
The End (finale)

This concert marks Jim Morrison's return to the town where he had completed his teenage years at George Washington High School. During that time, he developed a taste for the blues and frequented the rough-and-tumble blues clubs and roadhouses in the surrounding environs. It was also here that his literary interests began to expand. In addition to his voracious appetite for the written word, Morrison begins composing his own poems, among them "Horse Latitudes."

- Also performing: Blades of Grass ("Happy"); Gary Scott and the Classics; McCormick Tool Co.; December's Children; the Warlox; Hounds of Baskerville; Plastic Fantastic; Corporation; Shades; Tornadoes; Essex; NY Public Library; Brotherhood; all of the bands are competing for an audition with Columbia Records
- Promotion: Jack Alix (WPGC) Presents
- Production: Bud Becker of Domestic Sound Productions; the Sound Center and the Doors rented an additional $1,000 worth of speakers
- Capacity: 2,500 to 4,000

Sunset Sound Studios #1
Hollywood, CA (DU)

The Doors recommence work on their second album, this time using Sunset Sound's newly installed eight-track recording equipment. The first compositions they focus on are "Strange Days" and "When the Music's Over."

FRI. AUG. 25 1967 (1) **Las Vegas Convention Center**

Las Vegas, NV

Jim Morrison's voice is rough, almost hoarse, but that doesn't seem to faze the enthusiastic crowd. The Doors open the show with "Soul Kitchen."

On a peculiar note, the Convention Center officials' major grievance with the concert is the profusion of shoes left behind after the show. Apparently, strolling barefoot was fashionable at that time in Las Vegas, and the officials determined that footwear would be required for admission. Upon entering the premises, patrons quickly abandoned their shoes and neglected to retrieve them on the way out, leaving behind a mountain of footwear.

- Also performing: Hamilton Street Car; Gross National Product, Scatter Blues
- 8:00 p.m. show

FRI. AUG. 25 1967 (2) Malibu U. (ABC-TV)
Leo Carrillo State Beach,
Los Angeles, CA

Light My Fire

The Doors spend two days in late July or early August filming a video for "Light My Fire" while standing around a 1940s fire engine on Leo Carrillo State Beach north of Malibu, California. The shooting goes as scheduled; however, unbeknownst to the directors, Morrison never even shows up. Jim has become so disgusted with lip-synched television presentations that he simply disappears for this one. The Doors convince Robby Krieger's brother Ron to stand in for Morrison, and never allude to Jim's absence.

Malibu U. is a summer special hosted by Rick Nelson (on Fridays at 8:30 p.m.). It operates under the ludicrous premise that Malibu U. is a mythical beachside university with Nelson as the dean of students. Its quaint "Gidget-goes-groovy" style of contrived spontaneity fails to capture the hearts of the next generation of Stri-Dex Medicated Acne Pad users, and the show is discontinued after a few weeks.

Variety comments: "Aside from the serious synch problem, the show was photographed handsomely and 'staged' well amid the sand and surf. Ultimately, however, it was a 'cutesy' show—the gospel of young Americans according to Gidget." (Mor, *Variety,* July 26, 1967; reprinted with permission of © Variety, Inc. 1996)

This segment also featured the Buffalo Springfield performing "Bluebird" at Griffith Park; Marvin Gaye performing "Ain't That Peculiar"; Chad and Jeremy performing "Distant Shores"; Lou Christie performing "Something to Remind Me"; Robbie Porter performing "Sure Good Loving You"; Sandy Posey; and Captain Beefheart and the Magic Band.

Produced by Robert E. Petersen Productions, Inc.

Note: This special is broadcast again the following night at 7:00 p.m. This short-lived summer variety show broadcasts its final episode on September 1.

SUN. AUG. 27 1967 Cheetah
Santa Monica Pier, Venice, CA

Also performing: The Nazz; Watts 103rd St. Rhythm Band

Art: Penelope Brokenshire

Early all-ages matinee (3:30 p.m.) and two late shows (7:30 p.m. and 11:00 p.m.)

Capacity: 3,750

SAT. SEPT. 2 1967 Asbury Park Convention Center
Asbury Park, NJ

Soul Kitchen (opening song)
Break on Through
Alabama Song
Light My Fire
The End

The Doors are in high form tonight, with Morrison fronting the band in his head-to-toe leather, savagely strangling the microphone as he sings with a particularly harsh edge. During "Light My Fire," Manzarek's organ becomes temporarily unplugged, which is compensated for by a spontaneous drum solo and an impromptu early rendition of "Wake Up!" by Morrison.

The Doors are scheduled to perform one show at 8:00, and then Lou Rawls's "All Star Show" performs an entirely different show at 10:30.

SUN. SEPT. 3 1967 Will Rogers Exhibit Building
Fort Worth, TX
Ft. Worth Teen Fair & Mardi Gras Festival

This festival runs from August 26 through September 4.

🏃 Also performing during the music festival: The Seeds; the Standells; the Box Tops; the Grass Roots; the McCoys; Electric Prunes; Every Mother's Son; [and tentatively] Sonny and Cher

"People Are Strange"/ "Unhappy Girl"
Third Single Released (E-45624)

The Doors' third single, pulled from their second album, is released this week, several weeks prior to the album's appearance.

FRI. SEPT. 8 1967 Lagoon Park Patio Gardens
Farmington, Salt Lake City, UT

SAT. SEPT. 9 1967 Village Theater
New York, NY

Early Show (8:00 p.m.)	Late Show (10:30 p.m.)
Break on Through	When the Music's Over (opening song)
Alabama Song »	Horse Latitudes
Back Door Man	The End
Light My Fire (finale)	Light My Fire

At this second appearance at the Village Theater, the Doors return as rising stars. They are acclaimed as one of the most brilliant, innovative, and intriguing bands on the scene.

As the second show opens, Morrison runs out on the stage and catches the rising curtain to the opening strains of "When the Music's Over." As the introduction winds up to Morrison's part, he plunges to the stage and bursts into a savage, blood-curdling scream that sets the tempo for the entire show, and evaporates any of the audience's doubts about the Doors' primal ferocity. Appropriately, the band brings the show to its conclusion with "The End" followed by "Light My Fire." During "The End," the band goes dead silent as Morrison falls to his knees during the Oedipal portion, and menacingly recites the passage in almost a whisper. At his concluding lyrics, the musicians burst into the climatic instrumental just as Morrison vaults high into the air. Then, as the instrumental intensifies, he menacingly swings his microphone in an increasingly large radius looking as if he might just let it fly into the audience at any moment, until finally retrieving it into his grip for the final verse.

🏯 This is the Doors' final show at the Village Theater before it is purchased by Bill Graham Presents and rechristened the Fillmore East.

🏯 Atlantic recording artists the Vagrants featured Leslie West and was produced by Felix Pappalardi who also did extensive studio work with Cream. Later, West and Pappalardi went on to found the early-1970s power rock group Mountain.

🏃 Also performing: The Vagrants; the Chambers Brothers

🖐 Set-lists incomplete

🎧 Promoter: Dynasty Presents

MON. SEPT. 11 1967 State University at Oswego, Lee Hall Gym
Oswego, NY

Despite the restrictions imposed on the student body by the university's activities board, the Doors present a solid, if somewhat tempered, show. Advertised three days before their performance, the show is open only to freshmen and transfer students, thereby eliminating virtually all upperclassmen. The result is a gym full of well-groomed freshmen and orientation leaders parading about in their penny loafers and white socks, who later complain that the group looked "scuzzy," and who are shocked and disgusted by the lead singer's suggestive mannerisms.

THU. SEPT. 14 1967 (1) CBC Television Studios
Toronto, Canada
The Rock Scene: Like It Is
(Part one of six-part "O'Keefe Centre Presents")

Wake Up! »
The End (with Oedipal section omitted)

The Doors are among the musicians selected to appear on this CBC-TV showcase on contemporary music that is recorded this weekend and broadcast a month later. The Jefferson Airplane and the Doors are scheduled to tape their segments first in order to maintain their prior commitments. Actor Noel Harrison (who replaced the late Brian Epstein) enthusiastically introduces all of the acts, convinced that this is the finest media special on popular music ever produced, and promises that the "show will travel into the canyons of the young mind." Harrison elaborates to Toronto's *Globe and Mail:* "I think this is going to be the best popular music program ever produced on TV. It's honest; isn't trying to feed anybody any lines. The English have no money to do this type of thing; the Americans get panicky. Yeah, Canadian TV seems much more open. The media in the States are worried only about creating the effect. Up here, they give us enough time to record." (Peter Goddard, "CBC-TV records The Rock Scene," *Toronto Globe and Mail,* Sept. 15, 1967)

The production on the show is outstanding, featuring superb camera technique and excellent sound. *Variety* gives this very positive review: "'The Rock Scene—Like It Is' was a brilliant production and stood out as the best that the Canadian Broadcasting Corp. has attempted in the musical field. It turned the staid variety format upside down and inside out with innumerable lighting effects, top notch camera work and the finest technical effects yet seen under the CBC's name. It intricately meshed today's musical sound with technique—lights and camerawork, yet even the viewer who was not orientated to rock was captivated." (*Variety,* Oct. 18, 1967; reprinted with permission of © Variety, Inc. 1996)

The Doors perform a noteworthy abridged version of "The End," with the Oedipal section delicately omitted. This is a remarkable song selection considering the norm for television broadcasts at that time, and is reportedly one of the few times the band is ever truly satisfied with a performance designated for television broadcast. Jefferson Airplane performs "White Rabbit."

Commenting on the Doors segment, *Variety* says: "By all the rules of variety shows, the program was imbalanced with the first part relatively quiet, but always lush, and then with the two rock groups taking over one after the other. The imbalance in this case was a decided asset. It took the viewer by the hand and gradually led him into the scene without hammering him over the head with the essence of the new music. By the time the Doors came on, the viewer was totally acclimated. In their sequence, the Doors did one number 'The End' with the audience standing, dancing, lying on the floor and hugging the stage. Shots of the group were super-imposed on the audience and into it giving the effect of confluence. There were many visual treats in this number and some superb musicianship was demonstrated particularly by the group's drummer." (*Variety*, Oct. 18, 1967; reprinted with permission of © Variety, Inc. 1996)

After these recordings are finished, the session goes on to tape Dionne Warwick ("Don't Make Me Over"), Eric Anderson, and Sergio Mendez with Brazil '66 ("Day Tripper"). Those acts return on Friday and Saturday for lip-synchronization. The Doors do not return for any overdub work.

This special is broadcast on CBC-TV on October 16. The Doors' segment is later broadcast in the United States on August 1, 1970, on a special summer series by New York's WPIX called the *Now Explosion*.

🎵 Producer-director: Bob Jarvis

🎵 Musical director: Don Thompson

🎵 Writer: Chris Beard

THU. SEPT. 14 1967 (2) Music Carnival
Warrensville Heights, Cleveland, OH

Soul Kitchen (opening song)
When the Music's Over
Alabama Song »
Back Door Man
Light My Fire

In a preconcert interview with the *Cleveland Plain Dealer* regarding their upcoming appearance, Jim Morrison states that "We've never been to the Midwest before. We don't know what to expect." The public relations director for the Music Carnival (Pat Rizzolo) later informs the same newspaper that he knew they were in for a "different kind of an evening" when he observed Morrison, who had been strolling nonchalantly toward the dressing room, abruptly collapse onto his hands and knees and crawl the remainder of the way into the room. (Quote from Jane Scott, "'Doors' Swing Out in Wild Tent Show," *Cleveland Plain Dealer*, Sept. 15, 1967)

Although welcomed by a somewhat sparse crowd, the Doors put on a superb show. Morrison casually walks onstage, fusses around a bit, then takes up his mike and queries, "This is one of the finest tents I've ever belonged to, but, where is everybody, man?" The 2,300-capacity venue is pitifully occupied by about 700. He then half-jokingly reflects: "Well, since there are no requests!" and the band jumps into a terrific version of "Soul Kitchen." Morrison is in fine form, cavorting on the stage with a vitality that increases throughout the show, and the musicians play so well in unison that they deliver a continuous "wall of sound."

Billboard reviews the performance: "Suddenly lead singer Jim Morrison— tall, casual, stovepipe slim—walked to the stage. He wandered around like a lost poet, twirled the mike cord like a cowboy, stepped up to the microphone, and burped. And then it begins. The wild singing, dancing, laughing, jumping. Morrison cupped the microphone, looked like a scruffier Mike Jagger, but his voice is excellent with fine control and excitement. It was hard to believe that so much original sound came from so few. . . . The audience was small—the tent was only one-third full—but they were Doors devotees all the way through." (Jane Scott, *Billboard*, Sept. 30, 1967)

🐸 Also performing: Wild Life; emcee: Bob Friend

🖐 Set-list incomplete

FRI., SAT. SEPT. 15, 16 1967 Ambassador Theater
Washington, D.C.

📖 Note: There is a possibility that these two performances at the Ambassador were cancelled.

SUN. SEPT. 17 1967 Ed Sullivan Theater
CBS, W. 54th St., New York, NY

People Are Strange
Light My Fire

The Ed Sullivan Show (*The Toast of the Town*), debuted in 1948 and was one of the most successful television shows in history. Ed Sullivan personally booked all of the performers himself, although he seldom met them until the afternoon dress rehearsal, where he painstakingly surveyed the acts with a somewhat dictatorial approach and requested that any questionable material be deleted. During the Rolling Stones' appearance in 1965, they obliged Sullivan by altering the lyrics of their song "Let's spend the night together" to "Let's spend some time together."

Sullivan's producer, Bob Precht, requests that the Doors modify "Light My Fire" by substituting "higher" with another adjective. The band had acquiesced to a similar request previously when they were asked to delete the word "high" from their studio release of "Break on Through." At the rehearsal, the Doors indicate they will oblige but instead keep the original lyrics intact during the critical live broadcast that night. One account from New York's *Village Voice* reports that while backstage just prior to going on, Morrison is so incensed with the censorship that he threatens to substitute "Let's spend the night together!" or "fuck, fuck, fuck, fuck!" in place of the offending word.

The Doors perform a straight-ahead version of "People Are Strange," shot with a significant portion focusing on a heavy-lidded Morrison, and interspersed with solemn shots of the band members' faces. Later in the show, they come back on with a terrific "Light My Fire," and the camera angle incorporates wide-angle stage shots with the close-ups. Morrison's vocals on the concluding stanza of the song are particularly forceful, including a fierce closing shout on "Fire!" where the camera successfully captures the savage fire in his eyes.

Some accounts of the broadcast indicate that Morrison exaggerated "higher!" during the broadcast, but such is not really the case. The song is presented in its standard, albeit shortened, form. Producer Bob Precht is reportedly enraged and tells the band they will never appear on the show again. Despite Sullivan's reputation as a man who doesn't hold a grudge, the Doors were never invited back.

Also performing on the show: Yul Brynner; Flip Wilson and Rodney Dangerfield; Steve Lawrence and his wife Eydie Gorme; Kessler Twins; the Skating Bredos

TUE. SEPT. 19 1967 Cafe Au Go Go
New York, NY (DU)

While the Doors are staying in the New York area, they go to see fellow Los Angeles musicians Canned Heat perform at the Cafe Au Go Go in Greenwich Village. Because of Canned Heat's deep commitment to the blues, they are one of the Doors' favorite Southern California bands. When both groups tour Europe at the same time in the fall of 1968, the Doors arrange for a double billing with them whenever possible. Canned Heat is one of the few groups Jim Morrison ever sat in with during a live show. He did so during his trial in Miami in August 1970.

Note: Canned Heat performs at the Cafe from September 12 through 24.

WED. SEPT. 20 1967 Union Catholic High School
Scotch Plains, NJ (DU)

This unusual booking at a Catholic high school apparently comes about because of the administration's broad-minded attitudes toward the popular music of the time. Although they are probably expecting a band more along the lines of the Beach Boys or Herman's Hermits, they schedule the Doors. Apparently the concert transpires without incident; the Who are presented soon thereafter.

THU. SEPT. 21 1967 Staples High School Auditorium
Westport, CT

People Are Strange
Light My Fire

After arriving at 5:45 p.m., the Doors leave for dinner and return just as the opening bands are starting at 7:15 p.m. They discreetly vanish backstage to the music department's rehearsal rooms, which are substituting as dressing rooms, and don't reappear until it is time to go on. The Doors present a compelling show, which features a suitable blend of material from their first two albums.

Their memorable appearance at Staples High School is one of numerous concerts presented around this time in this artistic township's high school auditorium. Others include the Animals, Cream, Frank Sinatra, the Rascals, Louis Armstrong, Phil Ochs, and Sly and the Family Stone.

✇ Also performing: The Coming Storm; the Mandrake Root; Strawberry Fun Band
✇ Promotion: Staples Student Council

FRI. SEPT. 22 1967 (1) Brown University Meehan Auditorium
Providence, RI

Light My Fire
The End

The Doors' appearance at Brown University is a memorable one. They do two exceptionally well-received sets (with a brief intermission) and conclude with a lively version of "The End." During that piece, Morrison demolishes the screen for a "writhing bacteria-like" light show that has been immersing the acts in psychedelic swirls throughout the show. Brown's *Daily Herald* applauds their performance: "The Doors came fourth to put on a brilliant show. Their music was incredibly powerful, marked by a churning, shifting rhythmic underpinning, frenzied builds to great heights of volume, and the brooding, sinister lyrics of singer Jim Morrison. Morrison, who arrived in black motorcycle leathers, put on an exceptional show, screaming and contorting his gaunt frame to the chaotic rhythms of the music. The Doors demonstrated the qualities of cohesiveness and musical interplay which set them apart as one of the nation's finest acts." (Alan Musgrave, "Review: The Doors," *Brown Daily Herald*, Sept. 25, 1967)

✇ Also performing: Tim Rose; the Night People
✇ Capacity: 3,000

> Morrison demolishes the screen for a "writhing bacteria-like" light show that has been immersing the acts in psychedelic swirls throughout the show.

FRI. SEPT. 22 1967 (2) Murray the K in New York
WPIX-TV, New York, NY

People Are Strange
  (skit)
Light My Fire

For this special, the Doors are filmed at Battery Park in New York City (probably earlier in the same month) and rather than lip-synching, Jim Morrison is given a live microphone to use over prerecorded music. He is in a mischievous mood, and it requires numerous takes to get a complete take of "People Are Strange." For that number, the band members alternately sit and stand around some large planters on a very windy afternoon without their instruments, and remain relatively motionless throughout the filming. The clip itself is interspersed with a succession of "strange" faces in an attempt to give visual impact to the song.

Following this is a bizarre chase scene with Morrison dressed in black while the others wear white. It parodies the secret agent fervor of the time. This leads into "Light My Fire," which is primarily portrayed through a collage of shots featuring the band members and models hired for the occasion.

This particular show receives a good deal of criticism for being disjointed and humorless. The fast-paced editing leaps from locations as diverse as Wall Street to the Bronx Zoo, and relentlessly portrays Murray the K as the foremost champion of the rock generation. Credit must be given for the technical achievements of the program, as the "live" vocals with music are mixed directly onto the film without the usual safety net of post-production work. The "People Are Strange" segment is released on a Murray the K promotional record. (WPIX Television, Channel 11, New York; color 90 minutes).

Variety comments: "If the show seemed at times over-ambitious, it still had a technical excellence in the dubbing, etc. Kaufman's prime talent remains his judgment and taste in pop music and the show's performers and score clearly reflected this." (Bill, *Variety*, Sept. 1967; reprinted with permission of © Variety, Inc. 1996)

> Other performers featured in the 90-minute special were the Association, the Young Rascals, Otis Redding, Richie Havens, Aretha Franklin, and others, including Mayor Lindsay.

> The program is rebroadcast on October 9, and again on November 4.

SAT. SEPT. 23 1967 Stony Brook University Men's Gym
Stony Brook, NY

People Are Strange
Light My Fire
The End

The Doors are the first concert of the State University at Stony Brook's academic year and the unanticipated crowd fills the Long Island gymnasium well beyond capacity. The security force is severely overtaxed by the large turnout.

The Doors have begun to introduce long passages of silence at select points in songs to step up the dramatic tension. They maintain the suspense to the breaking point—until the room seems ready to explode. And just at the point when the tension becomes unbearable, the band breaks back into the song. This is what happens during their performance of "The End" at tonight's show. The band suddenly goes silent and remains motionless for a full three or four minutes as the confused crowd becomes increasingly restless and then—right at the flashpoint—the band bursts back into the number. This was one of the most effective and stunning of the band's theatrical devices.

The university's *Statesman* publishes this review of the show: "During the Doors' 'People Are Strange,' some California prototypes mimed the whole song in the front aisle. Nobody was pulled off the stage this time, but at least one bemused spectator was shoved around by an uptight kid Executive for trying to listen to the music. Perhaps it was in time to the music—the Doors, with their Viet Cong rock, seemed to orchestrate all the latent psychosis around them. During 'The End,' that forest of electronic nerve-endings, they stopped. The pause was meant to serve as brackets around some tremendously potent imagistic assaults but people got angry, walked out—the clever ones shouted 'Louder.' Eventually cooler heads prevailed, as they say, and for those who could stop with them the group conducted their broken Black Mass. The strength of the Doors' performance can be synthesized from the potency of their fragments. The story-book instrumental in 'Light My Fire,' and the narrative of 'The End,' for example, entranced as always, and the only obstacle to full catharsis was a nagging desire to see how Frankie Valli fans were holding up." (John Eskow, "Doors Orchestrate Latent Psychoses of Audience," *The Statesman*, Sept. 27, 1967)

Michael Horowitz quotes Gloria Stavers's (editor of *Sixteen* magazine) commentary on the show for *Crawdaddy* magazine: "I remember one concert in Stony Brook,

The band members alternately sit and stand around some large planters on a very windy afternoon without their instruments, and remain relatively motionless throughout the filming.

He just stopped. Cold. You could just feel the tension building up. I thought there was gonna be an ex-ploh-sion! And then, when it was totally silent, he made that sound ... from the abyss, it's just a shriek! Later, he told me, You have to have them. They can't have you. And if you don't have them, you have to stop and get them.

he was really going to jive their heads. The audience was just too enthusiastic, you know what I mean? They were just too clapping. So in the middle of one number—I think it was 'The End'—he just stopped. Cold. You could just feel the tension building up. I thought there was gonna be an ex-ploh-sion! And then, when it was totally silent, he made that sound—I don't know the sound he makes, a sound from the abyss, it's just a shriek! Later, he told me, 'You have to have them. They can't have you. And if you don't have them, you have to stop and get them.'" (Michael Horowitz, "The Morrison Mirage," *Crawdaddy* magazine, 1968)

- Also performing: Tim Buckley
- Set-list incomplete
- Capacity: 3,094
- Note: The Doors are sometimes mistakenly credited with playing at Boise State Stadium at the University of Idaho tonight. That cancelled performance was scheduled for 1972, not 1967. The Doors had quit touring by then and were replaced by Poco headlining over Canned Heat and Cold Blood.

SUN. SEPT. 24 1967 Oakdale Musical Theater
Wallingford, CT

Soul Kitchen (opening song)
The End (finale)

The Doors play a total of nine songs tonight, and by many accounts it is a terrific show. However, during lighting adjustments for their finale of "The End," several people in the crowd begin deriding the group, and Morrison retaliates with some heated remarks. Apparently that altercation provokes an incredible version of "The End" that escalates in volume and intensity as Morrison assaults the audience with deafening screams and dramatic movements that bring the show to a formidable conclusion.

The Oakdale Musical Theater is one of the original theaters-in-the-round that cropped up during the 1950s as alternative venues for musicals previously confined to prominent cities. In the second half of the 1960s, proprietor Ben Siegel began presenting shows by such exemplary rock performers as Cream, the Byrds, Led Zeppelin, and the Doors.

- Also performing: The Wildweeds
- One performance at 7:30 p.m.
- Capacity: 3,178

Strange Days
Second Album Released (E-74014)

Side One (A)
Strange Days
You're Lost Little Girl
Love Me Two Times
Unhappy Girl
Horse Latitudes
Moonlight Drive

Singles
People Are Strange / Unhappy Girl (E-45621)
Love Me Two Times / Moonlight Drive (E-45624)

Side Two (B)
People Are Strange
My Eyes Have Seen You
I Can't See Your Face in My Mind
When the Music's Over

- Production: Paul Rothchild; Engineer: Bruce Botnick; additional bass guitar: Douglas Lubahn; moog synthesizer: Paul Beaver
- Note: The release of this album may have been delayed a couple of weeks after this release date.

WED. SEPT. 27 1967 KRNT Theater
Des Moines, IA

FRI. SEPT. 29 1967 Denver University Student Union
Denver, CO

Light My Fire

This Denver performance is filmed by an independent producer for the ABC-TV special *Bruce Morrow's Music Power,* which airs on November 8. The Doors return to the University of Denver on April 12, 1970.

- 8:00 p.m. show
- Promotion: Barry Fey, Chet Helms and the Family Dog Present

SAT. SEPT. 30 1967 The Family Dog
Denver, CO

The End
Light My Fire (finale)

Denver's version of San Francisco's Avalon Ballroom just opened on September 8 with Big Brother and the Holding Company, and is operated by the same personnel responsible for the Avalon in conjunction with local promoter Barry Fey. At the conclusion of the show, Morrison performs a segment of "The End" while hanging upside down from the stage railing in a fashion that appears to make him look thoroughly deceased.

- Also performing: Captain Beefheart; Lothar and the Hand People
- Set-list incomplete
- Note: There is a possibility that the recording attributed to tonight may actually be from the December performances.
- Promotion: Barry Fey, Chet Helms and the Family Dog Present

SUN. OCT. 1 - THU. 5 1967 Steve Paul's Scene
New York, NY

This is the second and final series of Doors shows at the Scene, the first being in June. These were to be the final set of shows the Doors would play at the smaller clubs like the Scene, the Whisky, or Ondine's. Their rise in popularity is rapidly moving them into larger venues. Within six months, the Doors will help open the Fillmore East, and by early 1969 they will be one of the first rock groups to play the cavernous Madison Square Garden.

Backstage at the Scene, the Doors give a brief interview describing their views on performing live:

Jim Morrison: "We're MUCH better in person. Our record album is only a map of our work."

Ray Manzarek: "Yes, people become familiar with us through the album, but it's when they see us that it all happens. Our music short-circuits the conscious mind and allows the subconscious to flow free."

Jim Morrison: "I'd like to play in a club where we could be with other people. Maybe we wouldn't even play. It would be great to sit down and talk with the audience, get rid of all the separate tables and have one big table."

The reviewer goes on to describe the show: "Drama, the kind that grabs your lapels and shoves you against a wall, is being reborn in a thousand clubs, discotheques and halls across America. It doesn't use sets, lighting and actors in the usual sense. It does use the rawhide-thong vocal cords of people like Jim Morrison, lead singer for the Doors. Morrison floats to the microphone, hangs limply on it, looking aside and down. Then his butterfly hand raises the microphone up, his body goes taut, his eyes look wildly into a personal darkness, and he forces his wild voice into the mike. It emerges from the amplifiers turning the room blue with hot, electric thunder. Then quietly, one hand cupped over his right ear, he begins to sing. It's theater." ("The New Generation: Theater with a Beat," *San Francisco Chronicle* via the *Chicago Tribune*. September 28, 1967)

FRI. OCT. 6 1967 California State Gymnasium
Los Angeles, CA

Soul Kitchen
Break on Through
Crystal Ship
People Are Strange
Light My Fire

In the midst of their predominantly East Coast tour in the early fall, the Doors, teeming with energy and animation, return to LA for this lone show at Cal State. The show goes exceptionally well and the audience clearly loves it. Morrison frequently lets loose with his legendary screams and makes suggestive inferences like asking Manzarek if the organ has lit his fire? The performance concludes with Morrison collapsed on his back, screaming out the final verses, while those in the rear of the gym strain to see past the excitement in the front lines. The imminent surge toward the stage prompts the promoters to encircle the band as they finish their set and assemble a human barricade against the wave of fans advancing toward the stage.

Describing Morrison's performance tonight, UCLA's *Daily Bruin* remarks: "At times during the brilliant improvisational sections to numbers, Morrison was like a conductor/dictator gone berserk. He would thrash about attempting to zap the potent energy so abundant within him to each individual member of the group. He screamed at them, urging them on to more volume, more notes, more intricacies, more, More, More. He thundered back to his life-line microphone in time to reinstate pure human horror in the black air of the auditorium." (Jan Edward Vogels, "Horror . . . the 20th century . . . the drugs . . . horror . . . the Doors," *UCLA Daily Bruin*, Oct. 12, 1967)

- Note: This is future Doors' manager Danny Sugerman's first show.
- Set-list incomplete
- Also performing: Nitty Gritty Dirt Band; the Sunshine Company
- Promotion: Kappa Sigma fraternity presents in concert. . . .

> He screamed at them, urging them on to more volume, more notes, more intricacies, more, More, More. He thundered back to his life-line microphone in time to reinstate pure human horror in the black air of the auditorium.

SUN. OCT. 8 1967 Tulsa Civic Assembly Center Auditorium
Tulsa, OK

Soul Kitchen (opening song)	Wake Up! »
Back Door Man	Light My Fire
People Are Strange	The End (finale)

The Doors' appearance is exceptionally well received on this closing night of the Oklahoma State Fair. The one-hour performance is a well-paced excursion into the dark and intense mood of their music augmented solely by red, amber and blue lighting. Morrison is quite animated throughout the show, and seemed particularly vital when "Light My Fire" is preceded by a dramatic early rendition of "Wake Up!"

- ☸ Also performing: The Rouges Five
- ☙ Set-list incomplete
- ☥ Attendance: 1,000
- ☭ Poster artist: Steve Fadem
- ☗ Note: This performance was originally scheduled for September 21

MON., TUE. OCT. 9, 10 1967 Steve Paul's Scene
New York, NY

On October 9, WPIX-TV in New York rebroadcasts the *Murray the K Special* that was originally shown on September 22.

WED. OCT. 11 1967 Danbury High School Auditorium
Danbury, CT

Moonlight Drive »	Crystal Ship
"Horse Latitudes" »	Wake Up! »
Moonlight Drive »	Light My Fire
Money	The End »
Break on Through »	"Names of the Kingdom" »
"There You Sit!" »	"Who Scared You?" »
Break on Through	"Stop the Car, I'm Getting Out!" »
Back Door Man	"Who Scared You" »
People Are Strange	The End

Western Connecticut State College opens their annual Fall Weekend by sponsoring this appearance by the Doors. It is attended mainly by students of the college and Danbury residents.

Jim Morrison spends a good portion of the day drinking with his friend Tom Baker, who incidentally gives a brief introduction to the Doors at the outset of the show. The Doors bring a good deal of energy to this show despite the somewhat awkward conditions. The show commences with a thoroughly repellent female announcer who warns the audience to stay in their seats or risk being escorted out of the auditorium. Despite this dictatorial atmosphere and the mediocre acoustics, the Doors put on an energetic and lively show, probably fueled by all their previous nights in New York City. Unfortunately, one segment of the audience is clearly disappointed that the Four Seasons haven't been rescheduled from the previous year. The school attendants gawk at the band in astonishment and are heard chattering away about how scruffy the band looks.

Morrison's stage movements seemed uncustomarily sedate until the conclusion of "The End," when he abruptly leaps from the stage toward the startled audience. He then spins around, jumps back on the stage, and continuously smashes the microphone stand against the floor until the stand breaks and he exits the stage with no encore. The dents in the floor are still clearly visible on the auditorium stage.

Danbury's *News-Times* report is not thrilled with the performance: "The first impression of the group of four males as the curtain opened was 'If seen on Main St., they would have been picked up as vagrants.' Faroutsville. As they wildly ripped into each number, they seemed to work themselves into a psychedelic trance. Their biggest claim seemed to be their ability to drag a song out for 15 minutes. However, this was what the house was clamoring for—this was what they paid for. The music was loud, had a fast beat and the psychedelic theme was emphasized even more by the lighting effects." (Kevin N. Barry, "The Doors swing at Danbury High; And so . . . luckily . . . do the doors," *Danbury News-Times*, Oct. 12, 1967)

> The first impression of the group of four males as the curtain opened was: 'If seen on Main St., they would have been picked up as vagrants.' Faroutsville.

That review prompted this response in letters to the editor: "Those of us who were fortunate enough to see the Doors' concert at Danbury High School will know better than to take the *News-Times* review of the concert with any measure of seriousness. Your intrepid, neatly clipped short haired authority on popular music was obviously completely out of touch with the performers, their music or the audience. His painfully cute remarks about them looking like Main St. vagrants, reflects accurately the feelings of amorphous, middle-aged Mr. Danbury who knows that anyone with long hair is a communist, a homosexual and has fleas. Cracks about long hair have been a tried and untrue device since the Beatles first appeared five years ago. Worst of all, the review ignores the musicianship of the Doors. Describing the music as 'loud' and with a 'fast beat' tells nothing, nor does sprinkling of the ingroupy sounding catch-all 'psychedelic.' The pieces were definitely not dragged out to 15 minutes. There is a difference between dragging a piece out and clever improvisation, which obviously your reviewer missed." (P. Gordon, "Letters to the Editor," *Danbury News-Times*, Oct. 16, 1967)

🐿 Note: The date of this performance is often incorrectly cited as occurring on October 17. There is only one show, at 9:00 p.m.

🐸 Also performing: The Newfield Patch Band

THU. OCT. 12 1967 The Surf Club
Nantasket Beach, MA

The Doors are originally scheduled for two shows (at 4:00 p.m. and 8:00 p.m.) at this club just outside of Boston, but arrive in time only for the second one. They perform superbly for a tightly packed house.

🐸 Also performing: Ultimate Spinach were the probable opening act

🐢 Poster art: Ronn Rampis

FRI. OCT. 13 1967 The Lyric Theater
Baltimore, MD

The Doors perform their entire first album, finishing their set with a startling version of "The End," during which Morrison slams himself to the floor and remains motionless for a long time. Then he rises, with his back to the audience, before abruptly spinning around, releasing a red scarf that covers his face, and screaming out the vocals to the Oedipal section of the song with such ferocity that it produces an audible gasp in the audience. After this finale, they return to encore with "When the Music's Over."

🐸 Also performing: Tim Rose

🐞 Promotion: Stanley-Williams Presents

🧍 One show at 8:30 p.m.

SAT. OCT. 14 1967 Susquehanna University Field House
Selinsgrove, PA

Who Do You Love
Light My Fire (finale)

The Doors perform material from their first album as well as some unidentified blues songs, "Who Do You Love," and a finale of "Light My Fire." Accounts from those present at the show say that tonight's performance is fantastic and that the audience of "Patty Duke types" seem shocked and unable to respond. The minimal applause provides Morrison with ample opportunity to heckle the audience, and reviews of the show focus on the band's long hair and shaggy appearance.

Susquehanna University's *Crusader* has these uncomplimentary comments on the show: "Slam the Doors. The Doors were heard to remark that if everyone had walked out on their performance they would have achieved their purpose. It is obvious their purpose and our purpose (providing big-name entertainment) do not coincide." (Sam Clapper, editor-in-chief, *The Crusader*, Oct. 19, 1967)

Another review assaults the performance with both barrels firing: "Prophets of doom have decried the decadence of American life for quite a few years now. One of the signs they use in their prediction is a lowering in the quality and form of the arts. With this in mind the Saturday night performance of the Doors envisions a quick end for us all. 'The Doors' gave us no music, no professionalism, and no entertainment, but they did present a picture of warped obscenity, both visually and vocally. The show, predictably, followed in the same vein. It varied between electronic sounds of the 'Chiller Theater' variety and the howling, screeching, groaning effusions of our boy Jim. It was pointed out by someone that he wasn't trying to sing and they weren't trying to play music, but rather were trying to create a mood. Create a mood they did; a mood where dirt, cruddy clothes, drug-laden air and sick people all mix together in order to hide from reality. This mood didn't seem to fit the spacious auditorium, the suits and ties or the hose and heels of the audience. Visually, the scene wasn't much better. Most obvious, other than what our boy Jim looked like, was the attempt of the same lead singer to use the microphone as a cross between a hot dog and dental floss. The whole picture was completed by the way he caressed the microphone stand, did a fertility dance around it and eventually made love to this simplest of all phallic symbols. The whole show should have been a required abnormal psychology exhibition, not a $3.00 or more per person, entertaining concert." (Richard Poinsett, "15-4," *The Crusader*, Oct. 19, 1967)

> They did present a picture of warped obscenity … a mood where dirt, cruddy clothes, drug-laden air and sick people all mix together in order to hide from reality … the attempt of the lead singer to use the microphone as a cross between a hot dog and dental floss.

SUN. OCT. 15 1967 Berkeley Community Theater
Berkeley, CA

KMPX deejay Tom Donahue introduces the Doors as a rising stage brings the band into sight and the applause begins. Just moments after the Doors start their first number, Robby Krieger's amplifier blows and the show comes to an abrupt halt. Although the technical difficulties are quickly remedied, the aborted introduction, which usually serves as a catalyst for the rest of the show, leaves the audience in a strange and pensive mood. After performing "People Are Strange" early in the set, Jim Morrison pauses to comment that they are the quietest crowd the Doors have ever played to and that "it must be the climate." After that, the show seems to liven up and the rest of the one hour performance goes quite well.

❦ Also performing: Notes From The Underground; the Generation; emcee: KMPX deejay Tom Donahue

♀ Early (3:00 p.m.) and late (7:30 p.m.) shows

♟ Capacity: 3,691

MON. OCT. 16 1967 (1) Steve Paul's Scene
New York, NY

MON. OCT. 16 1967 (2) The Rock Scene: Like It Is
Toronto, Ontario, Canada

This is the broadcast date for the CBC-TV special on contemporary music taped on September 14.

TUE. OCT. 17 - THU. 19 1967 Steve Paul's Scene
New York, NY

The final show at Steve Paul's Scene is also the last at the smaller New York clubs. In the months following this show, the Doors return to perform at Hunter College and the Fillmore East. In March, Morrison sits in with Jimi Hendrix during one of his numerous after-hours jam sessions at the Scene.

> Note: The final performance at the Scene may have occurred on Wednesday instead of Thursday, because there is a remote chance that the Doors appearance at Williams College, listed here as October 22, actually occured on October 19.

FRI. OCT. 20 1967 UNIVERSITY OF MICHIGAN I.M. BUILDING
Ann Arbor, MI Doors to the Wizard's Lab - University Homecoming Weekend

This entire performance is erratic and conflicts develop onstage over Jim's excessive drinking. As the musicians tune up, an intoxicated Morrison begins cursing the crowd. Jim is in a sour mood, having perhaps become disgusted when he realizes that the band has been booked into what is essentially a frat scene. He sarcastically begins asking them what they want to hear, and contemptuously suggests "Louie, Louie" or other commonly covered songs of the era. Finally, one of the band members discreetly asks if someone would help Jim out of the hall and promises that the band will return later. Two men sandwich Morrison between them and essentially carry him down to the basement dressing room. Once there, Jim immediately snaps out of his intoxication, lights up a large cigar, and leans against one wall looking clearly displeased. The other band members slowly file in and line up against the opposite wall facing Morrison. No one speaks. Meanwhile, the local band that opened the show on an adjacent stage returns and does an additional half-hour set while Morrison supposedly recuperates. When Morrison again takes the stage, he begins to chant in a contemptuous falsetto comically described as a "Betty Boop" voice by Iggy Pop in *The Oral History Of Punk*. Even the band is initially confused by what Morrison is doing. The startled audience doesn't know how to respond. When the Doors began their second number and Morrison spitefully continues to sing in his contorted falsetto, there is no longer any doubt that he is antagonistically mocking them.

As the show wears on, Morrison purposely concentrates on obscure material unfamiliar to top-forty devotees. The large crowd of straitlaced homecoming attendees becomes increasingly restless and actually begins booing during the songs. The band reacts with belittling insults and by telling them to "go fuck themselves." The crowd leaves in droves. Toward the end of the show, Densmore and Krieger leave the stage, and the show concludes with Jim Morrison and Ray Manzarek performing an early version of "Maggie M'Gill."

This show has become somewhat legendary as one of the Doors' most calamitous performances. It succeeded in enraging many and inspiring a few—such as Iggy Pop, who promptly set out to formulate the Psychedelic Stooges after seeing the show.

> Also performing: The Long Island Sound

> Note: I.M. = Intramural

SAT. OCT. 21 1967 Breadmoor Hotel Ballroom
Colorado Springs, CO
The Colorado College Homecoming Dance

SUN. OCT. 22 1967 Williams College Gym
Williamstown, MA (DU)

Break on Through (opening song)
Light My Fire
The End

Describing Morrison's performance, John Stickney of the *Williams Record* reports: "He screamed and reeled, throttling the microphone and gazing at a sea of blank faces. He shouted a strung out, distorted and violated stream of word-images which twisted the faces into expressions of shock and yet fascination." And reflecting on their finale of "The End," he goes on to say: "Morrison is at his best in this song, doing his own thing while the organist bends low and presses hard on the keys and the guitarist walks unconcernedly in and out of the spotlight. Morrison dislodged the microphone and staggered blindly across the stage as the lyrics and screams which are 'The End' poured out of his mouth, malevolent, satanic, electric and on fire. He stumbled and fell in front of a towering amplifier and sobbed to himself. The guitarist nudged him with the neck of his guitar. He sat up on his knees and stretched out his arms in an attitude of worship toward the cold amplifier, the impartial mediator between the virtues and absurdity of a music dependent upon circuits and ohms. The audience did not know whether to applaud or not. The guitarist unplugged the electric chord which makes his instrument play, the organist stepped off left, the drummer threw his sticks to the ground in contempt and disgust, and Morrison had disappeared through the velvet curtain without a wave or a smile." (John Stickney, "Four Doors to the future: Gothic rock is their thing," *The Williams Record*, Oct. 24, 1967)

🐦 Set-list incomplete

📷 Note: This performance may have actually been on the previous Thursday.

> He screamed and reeled, throttling the microphone and gazing at a sea of blank faces. He shouted a strung out, distorted and violated stream of word-images which twisted the faces into expressions of shock and yet fascination. Morrison dislodged the microphone and staggered blindly across the stage as the lyrics and screams which are 'The End' poured out of his mouth, malevolent, satanic, electric and on fire. He stumbled and fell in front of a towering amplifier and sobbed to himself.

FRI. OCT. 27 1967 California Polytechnic State University Men's Gym
San Luis Obispo, CA

When the Music's Over
Light My Fire (finale)

After a brief intermission following the opening bands, the chairman for the committee promoting the show appears on stage and announces "This is what Cal Poly is coming to." The milling crowd suddenly becomes very quiet as the musicians silently take their positions on stage, followed by Morrison who slowly and methodically paces his way up to the center microphone. Without a word, the band abruptly launches into their first song and are off into an exciting, although unusually brief, set. Morrison is remarkably animated, embracing the microphone with a passion usually reserved for lovers, his entire body twisted and tremored in response to the fierce pulse of the music.

The *Mustang Daily* describes the crowd: "Some brought mattresses, others pillows, others filled out the bleachers while they grooved out to the pulsating amoebas and the pounding music. The air was warm and hazy with the warring aromas of incense. They reacted to the throbbing music by dancing, clapping their hands, stamping their feet, shaking bells and tambourines, or just swaying in time to the beat." The Doors conclude their opening 25-minute set with "Light My Fire," and have every intention of returning for a second one. However, this fact has apparently not been communicated to the audience who immediately begin to exit after "Light My Fire," and the band is never requested to return for their second set.

Afterward, there is a bonfire rally and the band's participation in the event goes, for the most part, unnoticed. One of the few who does recognize them is a campus reporter who takes the opportunity to casually visit with the band members. When asked about their plans for the future, Jim Morrison replies, "I think we will be together for quite a while—as long as the music keeps growing in complexity." (Quotes from the *Mustang Daily*, "The Doors swing open; Homecoming festivities," Nov. 1, 1967)

🪶 Also performing: The Lyrics; the Thundermugs [a local band])

🖐 Set-list incomplete

🖐 Promotion: College Union Assemblies committee presents . . . with a complete psychedelic light show

🕊 Attendance: 4154

SAT. OCT. 28 1967 Univ. of Cal., Santa Barbara, Robertson Gym

Goleta, CA

When the Music's Over	Break on Through
Back Door Man	Light My Fire
People Are Strange	The End
Alabama Song	

At this show, the Doors and equipment crew make a transition from Jordan to Acoustic amplifiers. Since there is no time for an adequate soundcheck, there are a few tense moments at the outset of the show while everyone hopes there will be no equipment trouble. There isn't, and the show proceeds smoothly.

After the opening sets, the Doors take the stage without Morrison and begin an extended introduction to "When the Music's Over." After a lengthy few minutes Morrison appears at the edge of the stage. The crowd grows silent as he ominously walks up to the mike and stands mutely for another minute, starring mysteriously into the space above the crowd. Without the introductory howl characteristic of the song, he begins to methodically pronounce the lyrics with a formidable concentration. As the song progresses, Morrison becomes more animated and it becomes clear that the Doors are off to another memorable night. Morrison leaps, screams and shouts throughout the set and concludes with a cathartic 17-minute version of "The End."

As a somewhat regrettable addendum, the sponsors for the event then request that the opening Alexander's Timeless Blooze Band do an additional 20-minute set following the Doors. To follow on the heels of "The End" would have been a difficult situation for any band.

In all, it is a powerful night for the Doors; one that will be remembered at the the University for a long time to come. The campus newspaper comments on the event: "Paranoia, incest, death, and fate are a few of the things that got people freaked Saturday night; they are implicit on the albums, but they are explicit in person. In some ways they are like a Gothic horror story. Not the kind of story that depends on plastic monsters for effect, but the kind that depends on terror and alienation to produce an emotional experience. With the light show provided by Dry Paint, not one of the senses was left empty to sensation — the effect was so total that you could feel, taste, and touch the experience." (Jim Bettinger, "Doors Are Strange: 'A Gothic Horror Story'," *El Gaucho*, Oct. 31, 1967)

🪶 Also performing: The Lyrics; Alexander's Timeless Blooze Band

SAT. NOV. 4 1967 Community Concourse, Convention Hall
San Diego, CA

- Also performing: The Lyrics; Sandi and the Classics; Marsha and the Esquires
- Promotion: James C. Pagni Co.
- 8:00 p.m. show
- Capacity: 4,337

WED. NOV. 8 1967 Bruce Morrow's Music Power
ABC Studios, NY

Light My Fire

This one-hour color television special is broadcast from Bruce Morrow's New York radio studio and features film clips from performances around the country. It presents a portion of the Doors' show from the Denver University Student Union on September 29. Other performances include Jefferson Airplane ("Somebody To Love") performing at the Fillmore in San Francisco, the Blues Magoos ("Love Seems Doomed") from the Electric Circus in New York City, and Stevie Wonder ("Alfie"), Buffy St. Marie ("Los Pescadores"), and the Children of Paradise from New York. Broadcast in New York on Channel 7 at 7:30 p.m.

FRI. NOV. 10 1967 Eagles Auditorium
Seattle, WA

The Doors are originally scheduled to perform on both Friday and Saturday, but opt for the following performance at the University of Oregon at Corvallis instead. Since the distance between Seattle and Corvallis is over two hundred miles they aren't able to do both shows in the same evening.

- Note: Local papers listed only Friday's performance.
- Also performing: Magic Fern; Chrome Syrcus
- 8:00–12:00 p.m.
- Lighting: Retina Circus

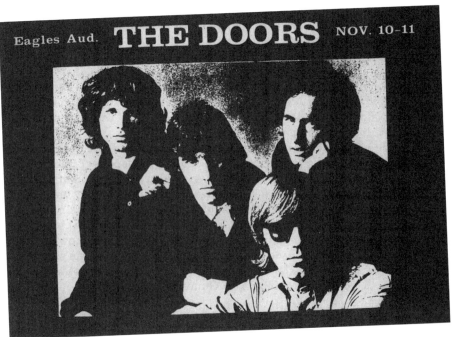

SAT. NOV. 11 1967 Gill Coliseum
Oregon State Univ., Corvallis, OR

Back Door Man
People Are Strange

The Doors open with "Back Door Man," and Morrison makes a delayed entrance to the stage. Despite being a pretty solid night for the band, a good number of people walk out during the performance, and the local paper calls it "A 'Strange' Concert."

🕴 Also performing: Red Coatsmen
👤 8:00 p.m. show
🚌 Promotion: Encore Presents
🚗 Art: John Moring

SUN. NOV. 12 1967 Univ. of Oregon Gym
Eugene, OR (DU)

Performance possibly held at the EMU Ballroom.

THU. NOV. 16 1967 Fillmore Auditorium
San Francisco, CA

This is the Doors' fifth and final weekend at the legendary Fillmore Auditorium. The Doors' performance of "The Unknown Soldier" at this show is probably their live debut of this controversial song.

Co-billing the Doors with England's ominous Procul Harum is a particularly suitable combination. Procul Harum is best known for its hit from the previous summer, "A Whiter Shade of Pale," and their entire first album has a shadowy and mystical ambience that blends well with a Doors performance.

🕴 Also performing: Procul Harum; Mt. Rushmore
🚌 Promotion: Bill Graham Presents

FRI., SAT. NOV. 17, 18 1967 Winterland Arena
San Francisco, CA

NOV. 17
Soul Kitchen
People Are Strange
Light My Fire

NOV. 18
Alabama Song
Light My Fire

During Procul Harum's set on November 18, the audience becomes extremely animated and spontaneous and dancing breaks out throughout the arena. However, when the Doors come on, the mood rapidly changes. The hypnotic effect of the Doors' music is especially powerful tonight and the audience seems to be mesmerized by the performance.

Commenting on the beginning of the show, the *New York Times* says, "When the Doors came on to do their thing, there was sudden silence and the crowd sat as if were about to hear a chamber music concert. But more important, they sat in rapt attention to every visual and vocal gyration of the Doors' lead singer, Jim Morrison, as if in homage to some primitive ritual. It is precisely this total attention that Doors audiences seek and the Doors exploit. 'For me it's a religious involvement,' said Ray Manzarek, the group's organist. 'For the public it's a total submersion into our music.'" (Robert Windeler, "Doors, a way in and a way out, rock on coast," *New York Times*, Nov. 20, 1967)

A writer for the *Stanford Daily Magazine* described the atmosphere of Winterland and its environs during the Doors appearances there this weekend: "It is oddly symbolic that one approaches Winterland through the Fillmore district. On the way one sees open evidence of the sickness which underlies our supposedly thriving civilization. Inside the pavilion, one sees and hears painful warnings that the sickness is growing. Last weekend, while the dead of Fillmore squandered away another night in what is one long night, Winterland, the center of the trans-Geary, trans-reality Hades, throbbed to the sound of the Doors. The one positive force in the group is Jim Morrison, the lead singer. Morrison has a powerful smooth voice with unusually wide range. His stage personality is nothing short of incredible: he goes through slow, sensuous contortions and seems to wrap himself around the microphone stand as he sings. The cozy quarters at Winterland are ideal for groups like the Doors. Morrison's ecstasies are shared by countless teenage girls, who throw themselves hysterically at whoever is unlucky enough to be near them. Dancing is out of the question, and the driving beat of the music creates a sense of frustration which comes out in great screams and cheers for the performers, whether they deserve praise or not. In the false discretionless world of bodies seeking souls somewhere in the spiritual void of screeching amplifiers, sexual fantasies, and perversions of love, there are few standards and things of value. Perhaps this is why the Doors have been so successful." (Jerry Fogel, "The false world behind the Doors," *Stanford Daily Magazine*, Nov. 22, 1967)

- Also performing: Procul Harum; Mt. Rushmore
- Set-lists incomplete
- Promotion: Bill Graham Presents
- Capacity: 4,500

FRI. NOV. 24 1967 Hunter College Playhouse
New York, NY

EARLY SHOW
When the Music's Over
Crystal Ship
The Unknown Soldier
The End

Tonight's performances are quite unusual for the Doors, especially Jim Morrison, who seems so fatigued that he rarely moves from his position of clasping the microphone. He seems almost oblivious to the audience, intentionally ignoring all attempts to capture his attention. The music is exceptionally loud and intense, so much so that Morrison's lyrics are periodically obscured by the unbridled instrumentation. Once again, when the Doors' intoxicating ferocity approaches a vital crescendo, the stage goes dead silent in the midst of one song, provoking enormous turbulence in the audience until Morrison breaks the silence with a scream. Audience reaction to the shows is mixed. Some praise the band's concentration on the music, while others are dismayed by the noticeable absence of Morrison's usual theatrics.

Alfred G. Aronowitz describes Jim Morrison's entry in the *New York Times*: "At Hunter College Auditorium last night, he came out in a black leather jacket and skin-tight black vinyl pants. He walked languidly to the microphone, the way Marlon Brando might have if he had started out in rock 'n' roll. He grabbed the microphone with both hands and put one boot on the base. He closed his eyes and tugged on the microphone. First it was too high. Then it was too low. Then he opened his mouth as if he was about to sing. Then he changed his mind and closed his mouth again." (Alfred G. Aronowitz, "The Doors Seek Nirvana Vote Here," *New York Times*, Nov. 25, 1967)

The Doors hold a press conference at the Delmonico Hotel in New York earlier in the day.

- Also performing: The Nitty Gritty Dirt Band
- Set-list incomplete
- Early and late (10:00 p.m.) shows

He walked languidly to the microphone, the way Marlon Brando might have if he had started out in rock n' roll... He opened his mouth as if he was about to sing. Then he changed his mind and closed his mouth again.

SAT. NOV. 25 1967 Hilton Hotel International Ballroom
Washington, D.C.

The End

Tonight's show is attended by both Jim Morrison's mother and his brother Andy.

- Also performing: The Nitty Gritty Dirt Band
- Set-list incomplete
- 8:00 p.m. show
- Poster art: Dale Beegly

SUN. NOV. 26 1967 Bushnell Auditorium
Hartford, CT

Soul Kitchen (w/extended intro)	Back Door Man
Break on Through	Alabama Song
Love Me Two Times	Light My Fire
The Unknown Soldier	People Are Strange (encore)

The Bushnell is absolutely packed for this performance, and the audience is presented with a superb and professional show that is absolutely mesmerizing. In fact, one local review likens it to a "Spiritual Happening."

The introductory passage to "Soul Kitchen" goes on for so long that some fear Morrison might not even show up. The cheering that greets his appearance quickly subsides when Morrison asks for quiet and then steadily begins the lyrics to "Soul Kitchen."

Jim possesses a formidable and commanding presence, and when the audience periodically rises above the hush that permeates the evening's performance, his mute stare is sufficient to quiet the place down. Ray Manzarek's playing dominates the night's performance. The conclusion of every song is met with long sincere applause and the entire evening is an unequivocal success, making the debacle that will occur in nearby New Haven within two weeks all the more ironic.

The *Hartford Times* reports: "Even the garish backdrop glaring blue, then green, then orange, then yellow could not divert the packed Bushnell audience which was mesmerized by the Doors Sunday night. Jim Morrison ... newest cool Paul Newman type, walked with easy confidence onto the stage. Roars, cheers, screams greeted his entrance. Morrison was shooting high for musical achievement. He was working hard with all his soul and heart. The audience continued to love all that the Doors were singing and giving out. A quiet hush had captured the entire Bushnell. It was like a spiritual happening. Morrison continued to sing as the audience remained under his spell. As the lighting continued to change and Morrison got deeper into his songs, he seemed to be in his own world, doing his own thing while listeners were just allowed to sit and keep the good thing going. If nothing else survives the rock 'n' roll epoch, the Doors shall most assuredly have their place in the annals of today's music with their originality and style." (R.B., "Doors Stage 'Spiritual Happening,'" *Hartford Times*, Dec. 1, 1967)

The *Hartford Courant* prints an interesting quote from Ralphy Barr of the Nitty Gritty Dirt Band, which had opened for the Doors on numerous occasions: "They're good, but there are a lot of groups better. The Doors like to play games with their East Coast audiences, like seeing how late they can show up to a gig and still have an audience. It's scary." The *Courant* then goes on to comment: "At last the Doors showed up and did their thing. Exactly what that was depended on what state of mind you were in. If you were in a California state, or otherwise turned on, it was 'beautiful, beautiful.' If you were a Connecticut teenybopper, it was 'cool.' If you were a Bushnell ticket seller, it was primitive, grotesque, and blatantly sexual.

> He seemed to be in his own world, doing his own thing while listeners were just allowed to sit and keep the good thing going.... His attempts to become one with the microphone were distracting, although definitely adding to the sexual imagery of the songs, and it is doubtful if he got into his skin-tight leather pants without the aid of a shoehorn.

Ray Manzarek is incredible on the organ, and if the Doors' sound could be isolated, it would reside in his talent alone. Jim Morrison is controversial. He has a unique voice that determines and communicates the songs of the group. However, his attempts to become one with the microphone were distracting, although definitely adding to the sexual imagery of the songs, and it is doubtful if he got into his skintight leather pants without the aid of a shoehorn." (James Petersen, "The Music Was Primitive," *Hartford Courant*, Dec. 2, 1967)

🐸 Also performing: The Nitty Gritty Dirt Band

FRI. DEC. 1 1967 California State Long Beach Men's Gym Long Beach, CA

LATE SHOW
Light My Fire
The End

Both of tonight's shows go extremely well despite some initial difficulties with the organ. After Canned Heat's opening set, it is discovered that the organ isn't operational and a backstage plea goes out for a substitute instrument. Although two organs are located in neighboring communities, the Doors' equipment is finally repaired and after an hour delay the band hits the stage. Although Morrison is not nearly as animated as he is at the second show, the performance is exciting and very intense.

The second show is also somewhat delayed, this time because many of those attending the first show purchased tickets for both performances and it takes the ushers a while to verify their tickets. Canned Heat comes on around midnight and gives a fun-loving set that opens with Bear tossing Mounds candy into the audience. The Doors come on for a lively show that doesn't conclude until 2:00 a.m. and is full of Morrison's legendary antics.

By the time the Doors begin to perform "The End," a small crowd has gathered under the stage and Morrison spends the first part of the song trying to convince them to leave. After they do so, Jim drapes himself over his microphone and focuses on the song. At the Oedipal climax, Morrison flicks his head back and then falls forward right off the stage. His plunge into the audience creates a great deal of commotion and applause. He disappears under the stage and doesn't reappear until the instrumental passage is over and it is time for the concluding vocals to the song. The *Open City* review of the concert expresses skepticism, saying the fall looked contrived, and perhaps because of that, Jim never repeats that particular tumble again.

> At the Oedipal climax, Morrison flicks his head back and then falls forward right off the stage.

🐸 Also performing: Canned Heat; Bridging Blue

🎪 Promotion: Richard Linnell

🚗 Art: J. Sage

🕴 Early (7:30 p.m.) and late (10:00 p.m.) shows

SAT. DEC. 2 1967 Portland Memorial Coliseum Portland, OR

Back Door Man	Unhappy Girl
Soul Kitchen	People Are Strange
Gloria	Light My Fire

The Doors performance goes reasonably well. Toward the conclusion of a somewhat routine set, Morrison pauses to ask people what they want to hear. As calls for "Light My Fire" echo through the auditorium, Morrison facetiously states, "We're going to play a new song now. We don't know it too well, but here goes...."

and then the band launches into an excellent version of "Light My Fire." During the song, Morrison leaps off the nearly ten-foot-high stage with his microphone and shouts "The blueberries [cops] have the guns, but we have the power. Yeah!" As the fans swarm toward the front of the stage, the police clearly indicate that Morrison had better return to the stage or they'll halt the concert. Morrison ignores them and begins eliciting responses from the audience with his outstretched microphone. Finally, when the instrumental portion of the song is concluding, Jim bounds back onstage and finishes the song. The police are not amused by Morrison's leisurely response and halt the show. Morrison later comments that he had hoped to encore with "The End" but was unable to. (Quote from "Teens interview the Doors: Here we go 'round the blueberry bush!" Unknown source, circa 1967)

Doors' drummer John Densmore is exhausted form touring and asks the band to find a replacement drummer for their Northwest shows. John Kilor from the Daily Flash fills in for the Portland show, as well as the Seattle one (see next entry).

🕺 Also performing: Glen Campbell

🎤 One show at 8:00 p.m.

SUN. DEC. 3 1967 (?) Eagles Auditorium
Seattle, WA

🔳 Note: Performance probably never occurred. This date has been cited as a possibility based on John Densmore's recollections of being replaced by John Kilor for shows in Seattle and Portland. However, that substitution may have actually occurred a month earlier during the Doors' performances at Eagles (on November 10) and Corvallis (on November 11). Speculation that they might have appeared at the Seattle Center Arena is unfounded because tonight the Seattle Center Arena featured a "Motown Revue" with Marvin Gaye and the Four Tops.

🎭 Promoter: Boyd Grafmyre

👥 Capacity: 6,000

FRI. DEC. 8 1967 Rensselaer Polytechnic Institute Field House
Troy, NY

Break on Through
Alabama Song »
Back Door Man »
  Five to One* (poetry) »
Back Door Man
People Are Strange
When the Music's Over
Light My Fire

The audience tonight consists predominantly of fraternity brothers and their dates who come to celebrate the tenth anniversary of the fraternity's founding on campus. They cover the floor at their "blanket concert" as if they were expecting the Beach Boys to appear at their beach party. They rudely ignore the opening act Tim Rose as they concentrate on various card games, and the Doors don't fare much better. Their music doesn't provide a soundtrack for the crowd's "Beach Blanket Bingo" illusions. (Doors fans are stationed around the perimeter of the fraternity crowd, so the band's fundamental impressions are influenced by the bewildered crowd directly in front of them.)

As they progress through the show, Morrison becomes more and more animated in his attempts to capture the audience. Despite these efforts, the crowd in front continues to be quite unresponsive, staring blankly at the stage with bewildered expressions.

The Doors curtail their show after 45 minutes with no intention of an encore; they just can't connect with the audience. Morrison is visibly disgusted with the whole scene, and toward the end of the show he berates the audience: "If this is Troy, I'm with the Greeks!" Members of the audience later actually have the gall to protest that the show has been too short.

Jim is reportedly deeply disturbed by the audience's apathy. The following night will ignite the start of the legal difficulties that will follow him throughout the rest of his troubled career. (Morrison quote from Bob Cunningham, "Doors in concert, dance, highlight frosh weekend," *The Polytechnic*, Dec. 13, 1967)

- Also performing: Tim Rose
- Promotion: Tau Epsilon Phi
- Attendance: over 2,000
- The lyrics from "Five to One" were definitely sung tonight, most likely during "Back Door Man."
- The Doors may have included some new material in addition to this setlist

SAT. DEC. 9 1967 New Haven Arena
New Haven, CT

Five to One
Unhappy Girl
People Are Strange
Back Door Man
When the Music's Over »
　[Jim's description of being maced backstage] »
When the Music's Over

This is the legendary performance at which Jim Morrison is arrested onstage for breach of peace. In addition, it is at this time that the New Haven Police are being deluged with complaints and hostile newspaper articles citing excessive force during an antiwar demonstration just days earlier, when they had apparently used strong-arm tactics in controlling the demonstrators and making arrests.

Before the show begins, Jim Morrison gets into an altercation with a police officer that results in him being Maced just prior to the show. The officer happens upon (or responds to a complaint, according to a different report) Morrison and a girlfriend in a shower room backstage at the ice arena and orders them to leave. Morrison is apparently quite incensed at the interruption and his responses are abrupt and insolent. Because of his presumed recalcitrance, the officer subdues Morrison with a canister of Mace. During the ensuing commotion, Morrison's agent (Richard Loren) pleads that he not be arrested because the show cannot go on without him, and this is, after all, a benefit for New Haven College. Apologies are then expressed and the Doors take the stage.

After a few songs, Morrison, still red-eyed from the Mace, launches into a diatribe about the cop's behavior just before the climax of "When the Music's Over" (see note below). Very methodically he announces, "I want to tell you a story. It happened . . . just a few minutes ago, right here in New Haven, Connecticut!" With exacting detail, he goes on to recount going out for dinner, meeting a woman who wanted his autograph, and coming back to the shower room where he proceeds to get "acquainted" with the local coed. As he tells of the policeman's entrance, Jim divides his discourse into two personas: himself and that of a backward, uneducated, and somewhat slow-minded cop. The police located around the perimeter of the stage are visibly offended at this depiction, and it is presumably this denigrating portrayal that leads to Jim's arrest minutes later. At the conclusion of his narration of backstage events, Jim brings the song to its insistent climax shouting, "We want the whole fucking world and we want it . . . NOW!"

As the Doors finish the song and as the audience somewhat hesitantly begins to applaud, the stage manager is ordered by the police to turn the house lights on.

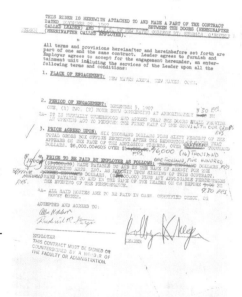

Assuming that the show is over, many people actually begin to leave. Ray Manzarek walks over to Jim and whispers something in his ear, and then Morrison announces, "Do you want to hear one more?" He follows with repeated demands that the house lights be turned off, and each request becomes increasingly peppered with obscenities.

Lieutenant Kelley then appears onstage, walking indignantly toward Morrison, while additional police appear on either side of the platform. Jim somewhat contentiously points his microphone at Lieutenant Kelley for a response, but after a brief pause during which the lieutenant stands hands on hips while disgustedly frowning at Morrison, they arrest him right onstage. Kelley announces that the show is over, and Morrison is hauled off toward a patrol car. Once they are concealed by the huge curtains behind the stage, the police begin to punch Morrison, and even land a few gratuitous kicks at vulnerable portions of his body. One account asserts that he is again assaulted with Mace after the arrest.

Morrison is taken to the precinct and charged with a lewd and obscene performance, breach of peace, and resisting arrest.

Meanwhile, the reaction from the audience becomes increasingly chaotic. The police seem unprepared to deal with the shouts and screams from the audience, as well as the large volume of people surging toward the stage, and have to call in reinforcements from headquarters. During the ensuing commotion, the police also arrest three journalists doing a feature on rock music for *Life* magazine: Michael Zwerin, jazz critic for the *Village Voice*, Tim Page, a photographer for *Life*

The officer happens upon Morrison and a girlfriend in a shower room backstage at the ice arena and orders them to leave. Morrison is apparently quite incensed at the interruption

magazine who had just returned from Vietnam, and Yvonne Chabrier, a researcher for *Life* magazine. These arrests attract national publicity, including a substantial pictorial essay in *Life* magazine's April 12, 1968 issue. All of the journalists are eventually acquitted.

Afterward, over three dozen people march on police headquarters on Court Street, and several are arrested when they refuse to disperse. Witnesses of the episode protest that the police have been inordinately rough with those arrested and have employed the use of nightsticks and mace without provocation. The chief of police indignantly responds to the accusations with, "That's silly, there must have been provocation. Do you think police go around arresting or hitting and spraying people without reason, without cause? Not in New Haven they don't." (Quote from Hugh Spitzer, "Scuffle, Arrests, End 'Doors' Show," *Yale Daily News*, Dec. 11, 1967)

One faculty member from Yale's History of Art Department responds in print that it is clearly evident that there had been "no disturbance until the police provided one," that the charges filed against Morrison concealed the real motive behind the arrest (which is that the police were acting vindictively), and that they were totally unprepared to deal with the consequences of the situation that they had created. He further accuses them of exploiting their authority to enforce their own personal moralities rather than enforcing the laws of the state.

Jim Morrison is released on $1,500 bond and the charges against him are dropped soon thereafter, but other arrestees do not fare so well. The resulting

"Do you think police go around arresting or hitting and spraying people without reason, without cause? Not in New Haven they don't."

fanfare blemishes not only the New Haven Police Department, but becomes the first notorious incident in the Doors' reputation as well.

🕴 Also performing: Tommy & the Riviera; Lochsley Hall Assembly

🏮 Note: Some accounts place Morrison's description of being Maced as occurring during "Back Door Man," but it is quite possibly during "When the Music's Over," which is the song recalled by writer Michael Zwerin in his account of the show (*The Silent Sound of Needles*), as well as photographer Tim Page's reflections on the event (*Page After Page: Memoirs of a War-torn Photographer*). However, Fred Powledge's account in *Life* on April 12, 1968, clearly has Morrison's dialogue occurring during "Back Door Man." To date, no recordings of the performance have surfaced. However, one member of the audience successfully captured almost two extraordinary minutes of the arrest on an 8 mm Polaroid home-movie camera, and that segment is featured in the Doors "Roadhouse Blues" video.

🐞 Promotion: New Haven College Interfraternity Scholarship Fund presents

🐾 Attendance: circa 2,000

DEC. **10** 1967

🏮 Note: Although some recollections have suggested that the Doors perform in Philadelphia tonight (at the Town Hall) the likelihood is that this date is confused with their Town Hall appearance on June 18. There is no indication that the band ever returned to Philadelphia after the Town Hall performance until their Arena show on August 4, 1968.

FRI. DEC. **15** 1967 Sacramento Memorial Auditorium
Sacramento, CA

Cancelled. The Doors' first show is cancelled shortly after the concert has begun when Jim Morrison fails to arrive on his flight into Sacramento. He does not show up for the second show either. Morrison was last seen at the Los Angeles International Airport around 8:00 p.m. for a late flight to Sacramento's Metropolitan Airport. The opening bands are requested to perform extended sets while the Doors await Jim's arrival. When the flight arrives, there is no sign of Jim. There is a minor downtown disturbance as hundreds of disappointed fans restlessly stick around for ticket refunds.

🕴 Also performing: Hamilton Street Car; the Creators

🧍 Early (6:30 p.m.) and late (9:30 p.m.) shows

🐞 Promotion: Scenic Sounds/Rich Linnell

SAT. DEC. **16** 1967 Swing Auditorium
National Orange Showgrounds, San Bernardino, CA

When the Music's Over	Alabama Song
"Horse Latitudes" (spoken poetry) »	Light My Fire
Break on Through	

The Doors' set suffers from sound difficulties, and as a result their performance is hampered. "Light My Fire" leads off with some serious "break up" in Jim's microphone cable, but it turns out to be a fine version of the song, effectively similar to the LP. "When the Music's Over" features some compelling and nasty guitar work by Krieger, and a punchy "Break on Through" is introduced by a strangely disembodied version of "Horse Latitudes." Speaking through some troublesome low midrange feedback, Morrison announces that they are going to break for a few minutes and attempt to remedy the PA difficulties. According to people in attendance, the Doors never do return. Apparently the sound predicament is never resolved.

🕴 Also performing: Fly By Night Company; the Friends And Relations; the Winfield Concessions; the Electric Chairs

✴ Capacity: 7,200

City Hall, Los Angeles, CA

Ray Manzarek and Dorothy Fujikawa are married at Los Angeles City Hall. Jim Morrison serves as best man and Pamela Courson as maid of honor. Afterwards, they go to the Olvera Street restaurant for the reception and celebration.

FRI. DEC. 22 1967 Shrine Exposition Hall
Los Angeles, CA

Break on Through	(Morrison talks about his arrest in New Haven) »
Back Door Man	Light My Fire
When the Music's Over	The Unknown Soldier (finale)

The Doors' first night at the Shrine is a well-executed show full of the curious theatrical movements that Morrison begins to implement as they play larger venues. He even takes the opportunity to commandeer some lighting equipment and light up sections of the audience.

Criticisms of his performances during this awkward period lack any consensus about Morrison's stage persona and highlight the singer's quandary: If he continues to hang motionless on the mike stand, he is faulted for being lackluster, but when he incorporates more extravagant movements, he risks being labeled as pretentious. Morrison is not in an enviable position as he tries to navigate his way into the larger auditoriums.

🕴 Also performing: Iron Butterfly; Sweetwater; Blueberry Jam

✋ Set-list incomplete

📽 Promotion: Pinnacle [Marc Chase, Sepp Donohower, John Van Hamersveld]

✴ Capacity: 4,000

SAT. DEC. 23 1967 Shrine Exposition Hall
Los Angeles, CA

Break on Through (opening song)
My Eyes Have Seen You
When the Music's Over

The Doors' second night at the Shrine is cut short by a police raid because of the unruly and violent behavior of the audience. The Doors take the stage at midnight and perform for only half an hour when their set is interrupted by the arrival of the police. At the onset of the show, Morrison is noticeably hoarse, but by the time they play "When the Music's Over," the band is in fine form and Jim bellows out some horrific screams. Unfortunately, it is to be the final song of the night.

Pinnacle, which frequently promotes concerts at the Exposition Hall and the adjacent Auditorium, suffers significant losses, including extensive damage to their projection screen.

🕴 Also performing: Iron Butterfly; Sweetwater; Bluesberry Jam

📽 Promotion: Pinnacle [Marc Chase, Sepp Donohower, John Van Hamersveld]

✴ Capacity: 4,000

TUE. DEC. 26 1967 Winterland Arena
San Francisco, CA

Back Door Man	When the Music's Over
Break on Through	Close to You »
When the Music's Over »	Mannish Boy
"Poor Otis, Dead and Gone" »	Light My Fire

The Doors open with a strong version of "Back Door Man," with Morrison's gravely vocals interspersed with demonic laughter. Before the concluding stanza, Jim temporarily slows the pace as he drifts into his "Softer" passage, and emerges from it with a eerie high-pitched wail, followed by "OK! All right!" and a return to the lyrics. The introductory passage to "Break on Through" is quite different from the standard, and Morrison breaks into "Come on, baby! Be my man. You understand. Yeeeaaaah!" After that, Jim's vocals are mildly restrained throughout the song, and after the instrumental break he inserts his "There you sit" poetry, and then takes a long pause before returning to the song. While the previous number is still being applauded, the Doors jump right into "When the Music's Over." The intensity of "When the Music's Over" keeps building as the song progresses. Jim spits out the "We're getting tired . . ." line with decisive irritation in his voice, and then thunders "What have they done to the earth?" in a tone more akin to a venomous challenge than a question. In the pause following "ear down to the ground," Morrison quietly engages the audience: "Ready? Well? We do want it, don't we?" The audience softly responds "Yeah," and Morrison counters with "Oh yeah? [pause] I'm serious!" He concludes with "We want the world . . ." as the band breaks into a forceful instrumental featuring some particularly fierce organ work by Manzarek. It is after that that Morrison interjects his "Poor Otis, dead and gone" poem as a tribute to the late Otis Redding.* (This stanza later serves as the introduction to their song "Runnin' Blue.")

Ray Manzarek then takes over on lead vocals for a fleeting version of "Close to You" that comes to an abrupt standstill as Ray cries out "We lost it. Hold on." The band immediately regroups and springs right into "Mannish Boy." Just prior to "Light My Fire," the audience begins clapping rhythmically, and Morrison jumps into the tempo reciting "Get together one more time" (from the developing "Five to One"), until Densmore cracks the opening snare blow to the song. The "Light My Fire" tonight is quite atmospheric, and Morrison sounds almost breathless as he brings it to a fine conclusion.

This is also the first "official" show for equipment manager Vince Treanor, who has been actively involved with the band since seeing them at the Hampton Beach Casino shows in August.

※ Otis Redding, who died in a plane crash on December 10, was originally scheduled to appear with the Doors at these shows. He is replaced by Chuck Berry.

▣ Note: The Doors did not play Monterey on this date; that mistaken date and location was actually this Winterland show.

✵ Also performing: Chuck Berry; Salvation

✺ Promotion: Bill Graham Presents

WED. DEC. 27 1967 (1) Winterland Arena
San Francisco, CA

Summertime (opening instrumental)
Break on Through
Back Door Man

The Doors open the show with their rarely performed instrumental "Summertime," and then Morrison joins them afterward. With their performance for the

The band stops mid-song to watch themselves while the audience looks on in bewilderment—this, despite San Francisco's exposure to unpredictable and bizarre performances ... but a band interrupting their own show to watch themselves on TV is a first even for them!

debut of the Jonathan Winters show being broadcast this evening at 10:00 p.m., the Doors have Rich Linnell lug a black-and-white television on stage with them, and he angles it toward the audience. In John Densmore's book he describes how during their performance of "Back Door Man," the Winters show comes on and the band stops mid-song to watch themselves while the audience looks on in bewilderment—this, despite San Francisco's exposure to unpredictable and bizarre performances. It is, after all, the land of the Acid Tests, but a band interrupting their own show to watch themselves on TV is a first even for them! When the broadcast is over, the Doors jump right back into "Back Door Man," and later Manzarek walks over and turns the TV off.

- Also performing: Chuck Berry; Salvation
- Set-list incomplete
- Promotion: Bill Graham Presents

WED. DEC. 27 1967 (2) Jonathan Winters Show
CBS TV Studios, Los Angeles, CA

[conclusion of "Horse Latitudes" on tape] »
Moonlight Drive
Light My Fire

This is the debut of Jonathan Winters's nationally broadcast TV variety show, and the Doors do excellent versions of two of their popular songs. As "Moonlight Drive" begins, after being introduced by the album's rendition of "Horse Latitudes," Morrison appears wearing an extra large pair of shades that are discarded a short while into the song. Hidden within the drum riser is apparently some dry ice submerged in water that effectively spews a dense mist out from the drums and across the stage floor.

"Light My Fire" opens with a shadowy set filtered through some psychedelic special effects. Morrison is in fine voice for both of the songs tonight, and on the concluding stanza of "Light My Fire," he lowers his voice and sings with an air of exhaustion. He then misses his concluding shout of "Fire!" as he leaps into a wire stage-prop, and the song draws to a finish with a shot of Morrison struggling furiously to break through the material.

- Also appearing on the show: Red Skelton, Barbara Eden [I Dream of Jeannie] and Ivan Dixon [Hogan's Heroes]
- Note: Broadcast in New York and San Francisco at 10:00 p.m. on CBS.

THU. DEC. 28 1967 Winterland Arena
San Francisco, CA

Alabama Song »
Back Door Man
You're Lost Little Girl
Love Me Two Times

Wake Up! »
Light My Fire
The Unknown Soldier

Jim Morrison is in fine voice tonight, and the band does a solid but rather brief set. Of particular note is a lovely version of "You're Lost Little Girl," and a particularly animated and menacing "Wake Up!" introduction to "Light My Fire." They encore with a very spirited "Unknown Soldier."

- Also performing: Chuck Berry; Salvation
- Promotion: Bill Graham Presents

FRI. DEC. 29 - SUN. 31 1967 The Family Dog
Denver, CO

- Also performing: The Allmen Joy
- Promotion: Chet Helms and the Family Dog
- Note: This is not the Allman Joy band that preceded the Allman Brothers. The Allman Brothers were later required to adopt their current name because this band had already established itself.

The Doors
on the road
1968

JANUARY
2
TUESDAY

New Haven, CT

Jim Morrison had been scheduled to appear in court for his arrest at the New Haven Arena on December 9. However, by the time of the arraignment, all charges have been withdrawn.

FRI. JAN. 19 1968 Carousel Theatre
In The Round
West Covina, CA

Love Me Two Times
Break on Through
Light My Fire
The End

This Carousel performance is full of vitality. Morrison displays an irrepressible energy as he repeatedly crashes down onto the stage and then leaps back to the microphone to resume belting out the songs.

Also performing: The Sunshine Company
Set-list incomplete

SAT. JAN. 20 1968 Carousel Theatre
In The Round
West Covina, CA

In stark contrast to the previous evening, Morrison is extremely intoxicated and his performance suffers greatly.

Also performing: The Sunshine Company

JANUARY
29
MONDAY

The Pussy Cat A Go Go, Las Vegas, NV

Jim Morrison and friend Bob Gover, author of *The $100 Misunderstanding* and a journalist for the *New York Times*, are arrested outside of the Pussy Cat A Go Go for public intoxication, vagrancy, and failure to possess adequate identification.

THU. FEB. 1 1968 Universal International Studios
Burbank, CA

Universal Studios offers the Doors $500,000 to be featured in an undisclosed motion picture. Although they do not accept this offer, they remain open to negotiations in the future.

The Doors' office also discloses that the band is considering being featured on an upcoming ABC television special, and that the Doors are designing a satirical publication to be compiled from diverse reflections and insights from the band on contemporary American culture. However, because of time restraints (their forthcoming studio and tour schedules) none of these proposals ever comes to fruition.

SAT. FEB. 10 1968 Berkeley Community Theatre
Berkeley, CA

It is probably at this Berkeley show that mystified audience members remember Morrison scrapping the Doors' usual set list and instead reading poetry, which may have actually been an early rendition of "The Celebration of the Lizard."

🐸 Also performing: Iron Butterfly

☝ Early (7:30 p.m.) and late (10:00 p.m.) shows

SAT. FEB. 17 1968 Arizona Veterans Memorial Coliseum
Phoenix, AZ

The End (finale)

There is a bomb scare during the sound check and everyone has to exit the Coliseum. Despite this disturbance, the show goes off smoothly and it is an excellent night for the band.

🐸 Also performing: The Sunshine Company; Hamilton Street Car

🐚 Promotion: Scenic Sounds/Richard Linnell

T.T.G. Recording Studios
Hollywood, CA

MON. FEB. 19 1968

Arriving at the studio with engineer Bruce Botnick, the Doors immediately begin working on an extensive dramatic composition entitled "The Celebration of the Lizard," which is to be the centerpiece of their third album. On this first day, they appear at the studio in high spirits, ready to tackle production of this crucial arrangement. Allowing for any creative ideas that might arise during recording, they declare spontaneity to be the order of the day. Jim Morrison even pauses to interject a brief harmonica segment after "The Lizard King" introduction to the song's conclusion.

Although they are all exhilarated with the results of this initial recording, repeated listenings reveal imperfections in the overall cohesiveness of the piece, which later prove formidable.

T.T.G. Recording Studios
Hollywood, CA

The Doors record a second unabridged rendition of "The Celebration of the Lizard" and are again pleased with the result. In retrospect, however, it seems that they became so absorbed in the intricacies of this complex composition that it was difficult for them to hear the entire piece objectively. The overall result is remarkable, but the different segments lack the smooth transitions that are crucial to sustaining coherence. Producer Paul Rothchild is the first to discern that the piece's general construction lacks cohesiveness. Bearing Paul Rothchild's observations in mind, Morrison labors diligently to connect the different melodies into a complimentary unit. Despite the dynamic impact of the original configuration, the Doors are dissatisfied with its overall orchestration and reluctantly accept that it is simply not coming together.

Jim Morrison comments on the piece the following year: "The central image of 'The Celebration' is a band of youths who leave the city and venture into the desert. Each night, after eating, they tell stories and sing around a fire. Perhaps they dance. It is for pleasure and to enhance the group spirit." (Hank Zevallos interview, "Jim Morrison," *Poppin* magazine, 1969)

> ... a band of youths who leave the city and venture into the desert. Each night, after eating, they tell stories and sing around a fire. Perhaps they dance. It is for pleasure and to enhance the group spirit.

THU. MAR. 7 1968 Steve Paul's Scene
New York, NY (DU)

Red House
I'm Gonna Leave This Town »
Everything's Going To Be all Right* »
　[aka Woke Up This Morning and Found Myself Dead]* »
Bleeding Heart* »
　"Morrison's Lament"* »
Uranus Rock* »
Tomorrow Never Knows (instrumental)* »
Outside Woman Blues (instrumental) »
Sunshine of Your Love (instrumental)

The Scene was fast becoming one of the hotbeds for the evolving improvisational jam sessions developing between rock groups. These types of sessions had previously been the exclusive domain of the after-hours jazz musicians. However, by early 1968, there is a new spirit of co-operation and experimentation going on across the country. From the Fillmore East and West, to the Whiskey A Go Go in Los Angeles to the Psychedelic Supermarket in Boston, musicians from different bands are jamming together, learning from each other, and exploring new and unusual musical approaches.

When Jimi Hendrix was staying in New York to work on material for his albums, he would frequently venture out to the after-hours nightspots around the city. At these clubs, he jammed with a lot of other musicians, among them Eric Clapton, B. B. King, Mike Bloomfield, and Janis Joplin. Jimi regularly visited the Scene, where after the conclusion of the evening's scheduled show, he was often urged to jump into extended jam sessions. Usually, these improvisations would start out structured around well-known songs and go on from there, often into the early hours of the morning. During one of these renowned sessions at the Scene, Jim Morrison took the stage with Jimi Hendrix and Paul Caruso (on harmonica), who were fronting a group of (as yet) unidentified musicians accompanying them on drums, bass, and second guitar. Hendrix was well aware that the abundance of creative ideas developed during these sessions could easily be forgotten later, so he began lugging around a large portable Ampex open-reel recorder. In subsequent years, some of these recordings have become available, and are among the

highlights of many collections. However, not all were accurately labeled, and because of the continuous exchange of personnel during a typical evening, it has been difficult to determine precisely who was onstage at any given time. For this particular recording, speculations as to the identity of the second guitar player have included Johnny Winter and Rick Derringer. Johnny Winter does not seem plausible because Winter did not come to New York until December 13. And, while Derringer played with the McCoys (one of the house bands at the Scene), there is some question as to whether the McCoys had yet begun their residency at the Scene. On the other hand, it's true that the McCoys had played at the club as early as the previous November, and participated in the jam sessions during February. Around this time Jimi is frequently seen jamming with Harvey Brooks and Buddy Miles from the Electric Flag. Note: If the McCoys played, the session may have included Randy Hobbsen (bass), Randy Derringer (drums), and Rick Derringer (guitar).

On this night, Hendrix opens the set with a stirring rendition of "Red House." He is soon accompanied by an extremely intoxicated Jim Morrison, who staggers onto the stage and proceeds to wail some explicitly obscene lyrics in accompaniment to the band's progression of blues songs. As the medley continues, Morrison's condition deteriorates until he collapses into a stupor, after which he leaves the stage while the band focuses on an extended instrumental. Paul Caruso recalls watching Morrison stumble off the stage and proceed to knock over a table full of drinks into Janis Joplin's lap. She sarcastically retaliates by loudly proclaiming, in her long Texan drawl, "I wouldn't mind . . . if he could sing!" Other recollections of that evening include Morrison approaching the stage, falling forward over the edge, and wrapping his arms around Jimi's ankles. Perhaps the most outrageous rumor surrounding this performance is that Hendrix, Joplin and Morrison concluded the set in a sensational brawl! Not true, since such an incident would almost certainly be evident on the recording; instead the band continues to perform long after Morrison leaves the stage. Regardless of what exactly did occur that night, Jimi Hendrix is apparently not impressed, which is evident a few weeks later (April 4) when he rather brusquely refuses Morrison's requests to join him onstage during a show at Montreal's Sauve Arena.

- ◉ Note: Initial estimates placed the date of this show as occurring on March 13. However, on that day Paul Caruso and Jimi Hendrix were together at Sound Center Studios working late into the night. According to Caruso's best recollections, the Scene jam occurred about one week prior to his recording session with Jimi. There is a remote possibility this jam could have occurred on March 6, but the highest probability appears to place it on March 7.
- ✿ Also performing: The Beacon Street Union
- ✺ With Jim Morrison

> Morrison stumbles off the stage and proceeds to knock over a table full of drinks into Janis Joplin's lap. She sarcastically retaliates by loudly proclaiming, in her long Texan drawl, "I wouldn't mind ... if he could sing!" Other recollections of that evening include that of Morrison approaching the stage, falling forward over the edge, and wrapping his arms around Jimi's ankles.

T.T.G. Recording Studios
Hollywood, Ca

The *Los Angeles Times* mentions that the Doors plan to complete their third album by late April, and that one of the songs being considered for inclusion is "Gloria." They also comment that their newest opus, "The Celebration of the Lizard," had gone from 23 to 36 minutes in length and may sprawl over both sides of their fourth (not third) album. Apparently, the distress signals for "Celebration" are already being raised.

FRI. MAR. 15 1968 Colgate University
Starr Hockey Rink
Hamilton, NY
Fortnight of the Active Arts

Break on Through   You're Lost Little Girl
Back Door Man   Not to Touch the Earth
When the Music's Over   The Unknown Soldier

As the Doors open the show with "Break on Through," Jim Morrison stares out into the audience with a deep look of concern. It soon becomes apparent that his damaged microphone is producing a weak and distorted signal. The band continues to jam on "Back Door Man" until the mike is finally replaced and Morrison can resume singing.

Despite this unfortunate introduction, the Doors manage to build their performance to a dramatic pitch. Krieger's exemplary guitar work leads the way with sensational effects and stylish leads.

🌣 Also performing: Linda Ronstadt and the Stone Poneys

SAT. MAR. 16 1968 Eastman Theatre
Rochester, NY

Five to One
When the Music's Over

🌣 Also performing: Linda Ronstadt and the Stone Poneys

SUN. MAR. 17 1968 Back Bay Theatre
Boston, MA

Early Show (4:00 P.M.)
Break on Through (opening song)
Light My Fire

The promoters for this show are notified at the last minute that the Doors will be arriving two hours late, and in an attempt to rescue the first concert, they secure two local bands, the Organ Factory and Turtles Cry, to open the show. Following the preliminary acts, Linda Ronstadt and the Stone Poneys perform an excellent set, despite periodic interruptions for announcements confirming that the Doors are soon to arrive. After the Stone Poneys, the promoters screen two of the Doors' promotional films. The first is the Elektra Records film for their first single "Break on Through"; the second is the recently completed film for "The Unknown Soldier," which has already been banned from airplay in Boston. (This is, after all, the town where they banned the Everly Brothers hit "Wake Up Little Susie" because it contained the word "asleep.") The audience responds with wild enthusiasm and insists on an additional screening of the film. Afterward, one of the promoters proceeds through the audience carrying a live microphone, eliciting viewers' responses to the censored song and film. Meanwhile, the equipment managers have set up the stage in preparation for the band's arrival. When they finally get there, the musicians rush to the stage ahead of Jim Morrison and leap into an extended introduction to "Break on Through." Morrison, always the impassive observer, casually saunters onstage as if oblivious to the fact that the entire audience has just endured an extensive delay. He actually seems annoyed at having to do yet another concert. Throughout the show he remains conspicuously indifferent to the audience, until the conclusion when he sarcastically spits out the words to "Light My Fire" in a mock South Boston accent.

Late Show (7:30 p.m.)

When the Music's Over	Light My Fire
Back Door Man »	The End »
Five to One	"Across The Sea" »
Back Door Man	"Accident" »
Break on Through	"I Am the Holy Shay" »
Love Me Two Times	"Ensenada" »
You're Lost Little Girl	The End

Fortunately for the arrivals patiently awaiting the next concert, the second show is substantially better—even superb at times. Morrison is wild, belting out numerous penetrating screams in front of the solid instrumental work of the group. In an unusual blend of songs, Morrison incorporates portions of "Five to One" into "Back Door Man" while maintaining the latter's beat. The band concludes with an engaging version of "The End" which includes a significant amount of obscure poetry designed to entice the audience into the dark and foreboding inner voyage that is this song's mythic purpose.

Also performing: Linda Ronstadt and the Stone Poneys; the Organ Factory; Turtles Cry [last two bands: early show only]

FRI. MAR. 22 1968   FILLMORE EAST
New York, NY

Early Show

When the Music's Over	Love Me Two Times
Break on Through	[introduction to Unknown Soldier film] »
Alabama Song »	[Unknown Soldier film]
Back Door Man »	The Unknown Soldier
Five to One	The Celebration of the Lizard »
You're Lost Little Girl	Light My Fire

Late Show

When the Music's Over	The Celebration of the Lizard
Back Door Man	[Unknown Soldier film]
Break on Through	The Unknown Soldier
Light My Fire	The End

Bill Graham successfully inaugurates the Fillmore East on March 8 with performances by Janis Joplin and Big Brother and the Holding Company. After the success of his productions at the Fillmore Auditorium and Winterland Arena in San Francisco, Graham expands his empire to include New York City. He purchases the Village Theater, site of a considerable number of concerts in the preceding years. For his next major attraction, he books the Doors for two nights (four shows), and these performances are frequently revered as among the finest the band will ever give.

The Doors' performances are nothing short of astonishing, and will be talked about for years to come. The entire band seems compelled to light the Fillmore on fire. They put their hearts and souls into these shows. Morrison pulls out all the stops, even taking an unexpected plunge into the lighting pit.

Ray Manzarek: "When there were a lot of people up against a stage, he could just fall and they'd sort of catch him. He'd just sort of let himself go, and fall off into

> I'm playing and he's supposed to start singing and he didn't sing and I looked up ... and he was gone. And then sure enough, a hand, another hand, and then out he comes, crawling out of the light pit.

the audience, and invariably they'd all just sort of grab him and break his fall so nothing really happened. Except one time at the Fillmore. Fillmore East had a light pit, and I knew something was gonna happen. I thought, 'God no, he's gonna fall in the damned light pit.' And he was just really stoned, and sure enough. . . . I used to play with my head down so I really didn't see a lot of the things he did. At one point I'm playing and he's supposed to start singing and he didn't sing and I looked up . . . and he was gone. And then sure enough, a hand, another hand, and then out he comes, crawling out of the light pit. But he was fine. Couldn't hurt that guy. Nothing really hurt him. Until the end." (Paul Lawrence, "Ray Manzarek: the *Audio* interview." *Audio*, Dec. 1983)

Jim Morrison introduces the New York premiere of *The Unknown Soldier* by portraying himself as a pretentious university scholar and the audience as his students. He then informs the "class" that they are to watch a recently completed motion picture and urges them to grant it their utmost attention, because afterward there will be an examination.

When the Doors open the late show with "When the Music's Over," Morrison is conspicuously absent from the stage. Then, as the music leads up to his vocal introduction, Jim comes flying from the back of the stage, leaps right over the drum kit, and bounds up to the microphone in time for his introductory scream.

- Set-list may be incomplete
- Note: Whether or not the Doors performed the entire "Celebration of the Lizard" remains uncertain. Had they done so, it would probably have been their debut performance of the entire theatrical/musical composition.
- Note: One of the many rumors in circulation pertaining to guest appearances at the Fillmore East is that during this performance the Doors spotted the members of Cream in the audience and invited them to take the stage. This seems highly unlikely since the dissimilarity of equipment requirements for each band would have created significant complications. Also, Cream was scheduled for performances (in Indiana and Massachusetts) on both nights. Cream never played the Fillmore East.
- Also performing: Chrome Syrcus; Ars Nova
- Capacity: 2,600

SAT. MAR. 23 1968 — FILLMORE EAST
New York, NY

Early Show
When the Music's Over
Back Door Man
Break on Through
Light My Fire
[Unknown Soldier film]
The Unknown Soldier

Late Show
Five to One
When the Music's Over
Break on Through
Back Door Man
Money
Moonlight Drive »
"Horse Latitudes" »
Moonlight Drive
Celebration of the Lizard
Light My Fire
[Unknown Soldier film]
The End (encore)

Springtime in New York regularly brings a bountiful supply of daffodils, and a good number of people picked these flowers on their way to the Fillmore. Throughout the show, daffodils are flung onto the stage. At one point, Jim gathers them up and, during an instrumental passage, methodically places some on each of the instruments. During "Light My Fire," however, his mischievous side emerges as he relentlessly pokes a hefty handful of daffodils at Densmore's drumsticks and flutters them under his nose. One account has Morrison walloping him over the head with flowers!

The Doors again premiere their promotional film for "The Unknown Soldier," and follow it by performing the song live at both shows.

As the band breaks into the opening number of their final show, Jim Morrison repeats his daring acrobatics from the Village Theater days by running out and seizing the rising curtain during the beginning strains of the music, grasping it tightly as it soars toward the ceiling. After climbing to a considerable height, Morrison surrenders his grip, and dramatically plunges to the stage alongside his microphone stand. Leaping up, he cradles the microphone just in time to burst into the introductory scream that characteristically launches the band into their shows.

After the show is finished and patrons began to exit the building, Bill Graham takes the stage and makes the surprising announcement that, if the audience is up for it, the Doors want to perform an extra encore. The enthusiastic audience swiftly returns to their seats as the band breaks into an extended encore that consists of an entire additional hour of music.

- Set-list incomplete
- Note: No known recordings of these legendary shows have ever surfaced, either made from the mixing console or the audience. However, it is highly probable that someone did record one or all of them and such an item would certainly be enthusiastically welcomed.
- Also performing: Chrome Syrcus; Ars Nova (Elektra Records)

MARCH 27 WEDNESDAY

Hotel Diplomat, New York, NY

While they're in town, the Doors are invited to attend "The Group Image Show," a benefit dance every Wednesday offering "The best in lights, music and surprises." The band responds not only by attending, but by screening *The Unknown Soldier* to an enthusiastic audience.

FRI. MAR. 29 1968 Kaleidoscope
Hollywood, CA

When the Music's Over

The Kaleidoscope was one of the most ambitious and well-designed rock ballrooms to have opened in the United States. The club provided a superb state-of-the-art sound system that was virtually unsurpassed in its day. After considerable effort to secure an adequate location, the Kaleidoscope celebrates it's "Grand Opening" at this Sunset address on March 22, 1968, featuring the Jefferson Airplane and Canned Heat.

The following weekend features the Doors, and the Kaleidoscope continues its celebratory "grand opening" atmosphere. In the unpredictable rock concert market, the operating costs for the Kaleidoscope unfortunately prove prohibitive. The following year the location is sold and renamed the Aquarius Theater, becoming the residence for the Los Angeles production of *Hair*. It is at the Aquarius Theater in July 1969 that the Doors initiate their triumphant comeback after repercussions from the Miami performance had precipitated cancellation of their entire spring tour.

- Kaleidoscope notes: This location first opened as the Earl Carroll Theater, later to become the Moulin Rouge, then the *Hullabaloo* television locale, before the Kaleidoscope assumed its brief occupation
- Note: A portion of the Door's performance was filmed (silent) by an independent filmmaker
- Promotion: John Hartman, Skip Taylor and Gary Essert
- Capacity: 1,468
- Set-list incomplete

T.T.G. Recording Studios
Hollywood, CA

After it becomes evident that they will probably not be able to redesign "The Celebration of the Lizard" in time to meet the required deadline for the third album, the Doors begin searching through Jim Morrison's collection of tattered notebooks for any material from which they can construct new material.

MARCH

Feast Of Friends

In March, the Doors decide to begin production of a documentary film to be compiled from live concert footage and interspersed with behind-the-scenes footage of the band on tour. They begin shooting the documentary while touring in April 1968. It concludes with the Doors' final performances before departing on their European tour in September. Three associates of the band are employed as the production crew for the project.

1) Paul Ferrara: Director of Cinematography (Film and Design)—Paul began with 16 mm black-and-white, then switched to color

2) Babe Hill: Location Live Sound Recording—Babe Hill used a portable Nagra reel-to-reel tape recorder

3) Frank Lisciandro: Editor

APRIL

The Doors' Workshop, Hollywood, CA

The increasing demands on the Doors necessitate their finding a central location from which they can conduct expanding operations. This discreet building on Santa Monica Boulevard, previously an antiques shop, is relatively accessible to everyone, and the Doors are soon established in their own offices upstairs. The downstairs of the building also serves as a rehearsal studio.

The Doors officially hire Bill Siddons as their manager and Leon Bernard as acting assistant, and provide them with an office on the second floor. Siddons comments on the Doors' decision to revolutionize their business practices and begin working with friends: "Management was management—not friends. The Doors and I have found that as five people we can work together as one united force. We have found cohesiveness in excluding any outside force which always seems to work against our own purposes in the end." ("Doors' Manager Makes Music Think Young," *Cash Box*, May 18, 1968)

Equipment manager and electronic wizard Vince Treanor is formally promoted to the position of road manager, and will now oversee all aspects of production for the Doors' performances.

THU. APR. 11 1968 Kaleidoscope
Hollywood, CA
Superball at the Kaleidoscope

Celebration of the Lizard

This show is a benefit for the KPPC-FM (Pasadena) strike fund, with the Doors headlining. Although it is a somewhat restrained night for the band, they wind up with their highly anticipated "Celebration of the Lizard," which draws to a conclusion with several female admirers crumpled at the front of the stage.

Note: This famous strike against the administrations of KMPX in San Francisco and KPPC in Pasadena received tremendous support from the music community as the new FM rock deejays fought for their right to salaries commensurate with station profits and to continue featuring the new rock music in the successful unrestrained format fashioned by such notable program directors as Tom Donahue

🐸 Also performing: Traffic; Canned Heat; Bo Diddley; Pacific Gas & Electric; the Collectors; the Committee; Kaleidoscope; the Holy Modal Rounders

🦇 Promotion: John Hartman, Skip Taylor and Gary Essert

☥ 7:00 p.m. until 2:00 a.m.

🐒 Capacity: 1,468

FRI. APR. 12 1968 Merced Fairgrounds
Merced, CA

SAT. APR. 13 1968 Santa Rosa Fairgrounds
Santa Rosa, CA

The Doors arrive with a production crew for their first on-location shooting for the *Feast of Friends* documentary.

Originally, the Doors and the Jefferson Airplane had been scheduled tonight for their London debut at the Royal Albert Hall. Unfortunately, that particular concert (booked by Tito Burns of Harold Davison Ltd.) never happened and the bands rescheduled for a joint appearance in September.

WED. APR. 17 1968 Riverside Auditorium
Riverside, CA

FRI. APR. 19 1968 Westbury Music Fair
Westbury, NY

The afternoon performance at Westbury is only modestly attended and the Doors seem somewhat less than enthusiastic about doing such an uncommonly early show. The late show proceeds quite differently, and is by many accounts an outstanding performance. Richard Sassin describes the early show in David Dalton's *Mr. Mojo Risin'*: "Morrison wasn't on stage when the music began. Suddenly there was a confrontation on one of the downhill aisles leading to the stage. He stumbled down the steps, entangling his black leather and a mass of tangled hair with the offstage darkness. He stopped to pose, and a flash of light caught him trying to regain his balance. The taunts began immediately. He responded with forced indifference or a threat of random violence.

"The other Doors were in other rooms. They played on, almost oblivious to his ranting and raving. A familiar riff would begin, the audience would briefly come to attention, and he would leave the spotlight to inflict his boredom on them. He would fall into shadow searching for worthy opponents. There were glimpses of physical confrontations: crewcutted jocks protecting their interested girlfriends from his suggestions. Morrison's fist shooting blindly in the direction of obscene threats as a fat security guard grabs at him with a pathetic attempt to control the situation. Morrison embraces the guard and tries to pull him toward the stage while delivering a passionate plea for weight loss. The guard frees himself, runs up the aisle to derisive laughter, dropping his hat. Morrison tries to wear the hat but it is too small and suddenly he is disgusted with the whole scene and lets out a frenzied scream. Silence in the theater for the moment.

"The audience stared as though it were another horrible car crash where the spirit was maimed and the blood ran into the gutter of the soul. Morrison twitched in some kind of death throes. The concert ended abruptly. Morrison howled but it was not with ecstasy. It was more Ginsberg than Blake. The lights came up before the band could walk back up the aisles and the audience booed. Morrison stood still listening. I stared so that my eyes would forever cover him. Some people were leaving, others still booing, a few watched him as intensely as I did. Then in this haphazard atmosphere he threw back his head and began to chant and dance in place like some possessed American Indian brave consecrating a sacred land, cleaning the abuse and disdain with singular belief so powerful that shivers ran through me. And my heart froze with undeniable blessing. A girl ran at him with scissors flashing to cut his hair and he disappeared into a circle of anonymous flesh carried him away." (David Dalton. *Mr. Mojo Risin'*. New York: St. Martins Press, 1991)

- Early (3:00 p.m.) and late shows
- Both shows filmed for *Feast of Friends*

WED. APR. 24 1968 Kaleidoscope
Hollywood, CA

- Promotion: John Hartman, Skip Taylor and Gary Essert
- Capacity: 1,468

THU. MAY. 2 1968 Pittsburgh Arena
Pittsburgh, PA

FRI. MAY. 10 1968 Chicago Coliseum
Chicago, IL

Soul Kitchen »
 "Running Blue" »
Soul Kitchen
Break on Through »
 "There You Sit!" »
Break on Through
Alabama Song »

Back Door Man »
Five to One
When the Music's Over
Crystal Ship
Wake Up! »
Light My Fire

This is the band's first performance in Chicago, and Jim Morrison is determined to make it a memorable one. Pulling out all stops, he begins to provoke the audience until he succeeds in generating a near riot. He actively encourages the congested audience to move past the inadequately assembled police barricades toward the stage, while officers fight to regain control of the increasingly antagonistic crowd. After Morrison has incited the crowd to near hysteria, the Doors finally leave the stage to a standing ovation. As the house lights come on, one fan in the balcony deliberately takes a swan dive into the roving crowd below, miraculously landing uninjured. Immediately following this incident, the audience lunges toward the stage but is effectively held back by a reinforced police barrier and the assistance of the Doors' road crew. There is an odd quietness that permeates these proceedings, as if the audience had been hypnotized to advance on the stage with minimal noise. Once turned back, they return to their seats and

patiently wait to see if there will be an additional encore, before finally heading for the exits.

🐾 Also performing: The Shady Daze; the One-Eyed Jacks

✋ Set-list incomplete. Some sources claim that the Doors encored with "The Unknown Soldier."

👤 8:30 show

🏋 Capacity: 4,000

📜 Note: The Coliseum became the Syndrome on October 16, 1970.

SAT. MAY. 11 1968 Cobo Arena
Detroit, MI

🐾 Also performing: The James Cotton Blues Band; the Crazy World of Arthur Brown; Jagged Edge

📽 Filmed for *Feast of Friends*

📜 Promotion: Russ Gibb

SUN. MAY. 12 1968 Canadian National Exhibition Hall
Toronto, Canada

Break on Through
When the Music's Over

The Doors' performance is met with mixed reactions, particularly because the sound system appears to be inadequate for the occasion. Morrison's voice is periodically either inaudible or distorted, making the lyrics difficult to discern.

🐾 Also performing: Earth Opera; City Muffin Boys; the Influence

📽 Filmed for *Feast of Friends* (light for shooting was insufficient)

SUN. MAY. 19 1968 Family Park
Santa Clara County Fairgrounds, San Jose, CA
Northern California Folk-Rock Festival

The Doors are scheduled to close this two-day event with a one-hour set at 4:30 on Sunday. They take the stage (following Country Joe and the Fish) after at least ten other bands have played quick and tightly scheduled sets, and put on a good performance, although it is not received all that well by the weary crowd.

🐾 Also performing during the two-day event: The Grateful Dead; the Animals; Big Brother and the Holding Company; the Youngbloods; the Electric Flag; Jefferson Airplane; Kaleidoscope; Country Joe and the Fish; Taj Mahal; and many lesser-known bands

📜 Promotion: Bob Blodgett

📽 Filmed for *Feast of Friends*

FRI. MAY. 24 1968 Hi-Corbett Field Baseball Stadium
Randolph Park, Tucson, AZ
Happening #2

Instrumental introduction
Break on Through (cut)
   (power outage)
Soul Kitchen

Moonlight Drive
When the Music's Over
Light My Fire

After a local act concludes their set, the Doors take the stage and lead off with two songs. During the pause before their third number, Morrison sternly tells the teenyboppers in the front rows to be quiet and mumbles a request for a cigarette. The stage is immediately inundated with lit cigarettes.

With "Break on Through," the stage takes on a strobe-like effect from the quantity of instamatic flash bulbs. Then, suddenly, everything goes dead. All of the stadium's power has been lost. The only light comes from the desert stars. Densmore futilely tries to keep the rhythm going for a minute, while Morrison strolls to the edge of the stage and stares up at the stars. The power comes back on without much delay, but the lighting is now relegated to one lone spotlight from the stadium roof. The performance continues without further interruption, and soon Morrison is inviting people to leave their seats while security personnel begin to establish a human barricade in front of the stage. As the intensity of the show increases, at least one person faints and is passed over the barricade and carried off by police. Morrison begins twirling the microphone, swinging it in a circle as "When the Music's Over" climaxes, just barely missing Ray Manzarek's head. Right before the finale of "Light My Fire," Jim encourages members of the audience to join the band on stage. He goes beyond making a simple request and starts pointing directly at people, shouting "I want you, and you, and you. . . ." The security fence begins to sag as the song begins, and it is not long before the barrier comes down with a splintering crash and people flood the area surrounding the stage. The security staff restructures their blockade around the periphery of the stage, and Morrison concludes the performance sandwiched between two policemen.

The *Daily Citizen* comments on the beginning of the show: "A hushed 'Here they come' ran through the crowd and necks craned expectantly toward the small gate outside the right field foul line. The three Doors' musicians . . . mounted the stage looking all business. They positioned themselves with their instruments and immediately started playing. After a short musical introduction, singer-warlock Jim Morrison, wearing skin-tight leather pants, a pea coat and a sullen expression, leaped up the side stairs, faked a spastic stumble crossing the stage, and lurched into the lyrics in a slightly hoarse voice. It is undeniably compelling. The creative nature of the Doors' musicianship became more apparent with every song. Their versatility with the instruments and their unique rapport in the tight arrangements provided a perfect backdrop for Morrison's jolting images. The occasional electronic wails, rumbles and groans had an eerie quality that heightened the mood of a Walpurgis Night. The audience began to respond to the calculated vocal frenzy and mind numbing throb. Many of the faces had assumed trance-like masks. The whole situation began to take on an atmosphere of unreality." (Greg Robertson, "Teeners' verdict on the Doors: GROOVY," *Tucson Daily Citizen*, June 29, 1968)

This is the Doors' second appearance at Tucson's Hi-Corbett Field. This unique desert location was the site of a number of noteworthy rock productions including an outstanding appearance by the Who.

☞ Set-list incomplete

> Jim Morrison, wearing skin-tight leather pants, a pea coat and a sullen expression, leaped up the side stairs, faked a spastic stumble crossing the stage, and lurched into the lyrics.... The occasional electronic wails, rumbles and groans had an eerie quality that heightened the mood of a Walpurgis Night ... Many of the faces had assumed trance-like masks. Morrison concluded the performance sandwiched between two policemen.

Early Show
When the Music's Over
Light My Fire (finale)

Attendance for the early performance of their second appearance in the heart of Mormon country turns out to be significantly lower than the promoters expected. With just a fraction of the venue filled, even Jim Morrison pauses as he appears on stage to inquire, "Where the hell is everyone?" When the Doors finish their first number, they are met by vacant stares and minimal applause. "What's the matter?" challenges Morrison. "Are you all dead out there? What did you come here for anyway?" Again the audience is unresponsive, and continues so throughout the second song. Morrison grows infuriated with the lack of audience reaction, hurling a torrent of vicious insults at the crowd, some of whom are now rapidly making their way toward the exits. Manzarek amusedly recalls one member of the audience hollering out, "Hey Morrison! Is the West really the best or are you guys just stoned on weed?" Jim pauses to ask the crowd, "Are there any songs you would like us to play?" and after people yell out their requests, Morrison responds sarcastically, "Those are night show songs; we don't play them now!"

As if in retaliation for the conspicuous lack of enthusiasm, the Doors stage an energetic but brief performance. Jim bounds about the stage with wild abandon, and at one point genuinely frightens many in the front rows when he lofts his microphone stand high into the air and it lands just short of the first section of seats. During "When the Music's Over," he snarls the lyrics "We're getting tired of hangin' around" with an animosity clearly directed at the Salt Lake audience. The Doors conclude the show after only four songs, with a stunning rendition of "Light My Fire," and then indignantly abandon the stage.

Commenting on the first show, the *Deseret News* says: "The Doors were obviously embittered by the boredom of the crowd. Morrison perked up only once, when a long-haired and bearded fan presented him with a string of beads. Morrison smiled, spoke to the boy for a few minutes, and then leaned over into the crowd to 'borrow' a cigarette from a youthful admirer." (Bryan Gray, "Doors offend Lagoon fans," *Deseret News*, May 27, 1968)

The second show does not fare much better. These two performances turn out to be Salt Lake's final opportunity for an appearance by the Doors. The next performance is scheduled for April 1970, but is cancelled after city officials determine that the Doors are "uncontrollable, unsuitable, and objectionable to the general public."

> "Where the hell is everyone? ... Are you all dead out there?" ... "Hey Morrison! Is the West really the best or are you guys just stoned on weed?"

Early and late shows

Promotion: Robert Freed

Note: There is a good possibility that this show did not occur. The Doors' November 1971 show was probably their only appearance here.

MAY

Not To Touch The Earth

This brief black-and-white film is compiled from footage taken on March 16 and 17 when the Doors performed in Rochester and Boston. It opens with footage from the Rochester airport of the Doors en route to Boston, and then moves to a pan

of the Back Bay Theater and Morrison taking a drink of whiskey. The visual collage drifts into a series of shots both onstage and backstage at the Back Bay Theater, and then to shots of Robby Krieger engaged in conversation with Linda Ronstadt on the flight to Boston. It concludes on a curious note with Robby Krieger washing his hands in a shower room.

Bobby Neuwirth is well known as an artist in the New York area, whose personality and exuberance gained him many opportunities to work as a personal aide to musicians such as Bob Dylan and Janis Joplin.

When the Doors' management become distressed at Jim Morrison's propensity for delayed arrivals, they ask Neuwirth to assist as a "companion" to Morrison (and help insure that Jim arrive at shows on time). Neuwirth is supposedly hired under the auspices of producing a short documentary for a segment of the "Celebration of the Lizard" composition entitled "Not to Touch the Earth." Morrison immediately sees through the pretense, but lightheartedly goes along with the proposition, enticing Bobby into many of his all-night drinking bouts, an occupation for which Bobby is more than suitably prepared. Neuwirth is employed from March until the completion of the "Not to Touch the Earth" project in May. Although the film is never used promotionally by the Doors, it does serve as a catalyst for future endeavors.

MAY
1968

T.T.G. Recording Studios
Hollywood, CA

The Doors finally complete the material for their third album despite the critical upheaval created by the decision not to include the highly anticipated "Celebration of the Lizard." A section of the composition however, "Not to Touch the Earth," is included on the album.

FRI. JUN. 7 1968 Fresno District Fairgrounds
Fresno, CA

A preconcert commentary in the *Fresno Bee* asserts, "Lest there be a recurrence of the on-stage suggestiveness of the group's first concert here last summer, the management of the fair ground has pledged to hold up the purse should the Doors' behavior be any less than 'in the public interest.'"

🦎 Also performing: The Shaggs; Genetic Dryft
♀ 8:30 p.m.

Lest there be a recurrence of the on-stage suggestiveness of the group's first concert here last summer, the management of the fair ground has pledged to hold up the purse should the Doors' behavior be any less than "in the public interest."

SAT. JUN. 8 1968 Bakersfield Civic Auditorium
Bakersfield, CA

🦎 Also performing: Genetic Dryft
🎥 Filmed for *Feast of Friends*
🪲 Promotion: James Pagni

SAT. JUN. 15 1968 Sacramento Memorial Auditorium
Sacramento, CA

As the curtain rises revealing a silent Jim Morrison dressed in leather pants and a velour shirt, the auditorium gradually becomes utterly silent. Morrison stands motionless, with his head resting on the microphone and one eye open, scanning the audience. With quiet, slow, and deliberate movements he carefully cups the microphone, leans forward into his amplifying hands, and mischievously lets out a resounding belch that explodes through the auditorium's sound system and elicits a tremendous round of startled applause from the audience. With that, the Doors are off to a lively one-hour performance. One memorable moment occurs during the "ear to the ground" segment of "When the Music's Over," when Morrison abruptly hits the stage, writhing and whirling around on the floor as the audience stands up, some climbing on their seats to observe the commotion.

🕷 Also performing: The Family Tree; the Lollipop Shoppe
🚗 Artist: Sam Sadofsky

FRI. JUN. 28 1968 La Playa Stadium
Santa Barbara, CA

Accounts of this show are not very complimentary.

🕷 Also performing: The Chambers Brothers
🦂 Promotion: Scenic Sounds/Richard Linnell

SAT. JUN. 29 1968 Community Concourse Convention Hall
San Diego, CA

The Doors perform two shows, the first being somewhat short and unexceptional, while the second one is longer and substantially better.

🕷 Also performing: The Chambers Brothers
🦂 Promotion: Scenic Sounds/Richard Linnell

SUN. JUN. 30 1968 McArthur Court
Univ. Of Oregon, Eugene, OR (DU)

"Hello I Love You" / "Love Street"
Sixth Single Released (E-45635)

JUN. 1968

JULY 1968

Bliss Productions/Transcendental Publishing

Doors guitarist Robby Krieger and percussionist John Densmore establish a publishing business, Bliss Productions, and a music publishing company, Transcendental (ASCAP). For their first project, they produce the rock group Comfortable Chair after securing a contract for their record to be released by Lou Adler on Ode Records and distributed by Columbia. In addition to the album, a single by Comfortable Chair is released entitled "Be Me" backed by "Some Soon, Some Day."

In two of Comfortable Chair's infrequent appearances, they open for the Grateful Dead at the Shrine Auditorium on December 20, and for Canned Heat at the Shrine on New Year's Eve.

WED. JUL. 3 1968 Hollywood Bowl
Los Angeles, CA

Arriving two days before the Doors' scheduled performance, road manager Vince Treanor and the entire equipment crew begin to assemble and erect the immense sound system required for this highly acclaimed appearance at the Hollywood Bowl.

THU. JUL. 4 1968 Hollywood Bowl
Los Angeles, CA

At noon on the Fourth of July, Vince Treanor checks the sound system with a simulated explosion that echoes through the Hollywood Hills. He lightheartedly christens it, "The Big Bang."

Note: The Doors have often mistakenly been assumed to have appeared in San Bernardino on this date. Their only appearance in San Bernardino took place on December 16, 1967

FRI. JUL. 5 1968 Hollywood Bowl
Los Angeles, CA

When the Music's Over	Spanish Caravan
Alabama Song »	Wake Up! »
Back Door Man »	Light My Fire
Five to One	The Unknown Soldier
Hello, I Love You*	The End »
Moonlight Drive »	"Accident" »
Horse Latitudes »	"Grasshopper" »
"A Little Game" »	"Ensenada" »
"The Hill Dwellers" »	The End

This legendary performance is one of the most highly anticipated shows of the year. The Doors are preceded by Steppenwolf, who deliver a surprisingly restrained set, and then the Chambers Brothers, who bring the house down with their "Time Has Come Today."

Opening with an extended intro to "When the Music's Over," the Doors deliver a straight-ahead and tightly executed show. Uncharacteristically, Jim Morrison seems rather detached and remains stationary throughout most of the show. He is obviously determined to shift the emphasis to his vocal performance, rather than his legendary wild antics. In addition to their usual repertoire, the Doors incorporate some selections from "Celebration of the Lizard" as a prelude to "Spanish Caravan." Perhaps the highlight of the evening is an impressive rendition of "The End," which features a very dark (and often quite humorous) fusion of unreleased poetry. During the climatic instrumental, Morrison breaks into a mesmerizing shamanic dance, like a man possessed, that is more characteristic of the band's shows at the time.

The *Feast of Friends* film crew shoots the entire set in color with additional cameras (one of the cameramen is Harrison Ford), and the concert is officially released on video in 1987. The sound is recorded on eight-track using the Wally Heider remote truck.

The next time the Doors appear at the Hollywood Bowl, it will be without Jim Morrison and will mark their final performance as a group.

At this performance, Jim Morrison's vocal channel is plagued with an intermittent microphone cable. Although these audio breaks are not apparent to the audience, the lack of continuity proves fairly obvious on the master recordings. In preparation for the official release of the video, the audio tracks are taken to Sonic Solutions in San Francisco. Sonic Solutions was established by Dr. James Moorer in 1986 as a business specifically developed for the restoration of rare and valuable recordings. By using a series of corrective state-of-the-art technologies, sometimes referred to as "No Noise," Sonic Solutions developed the capacity to enhance even lackluster recordings to a brilliant clarity only hinted at on the master tapes. For this recording, Dr. Moorer and associates synthesize the missing portions of the vocal track, achieving an audibly flawless simulation of the absent segments of the material.

Note: Steppenwolf, featuring lead singer John Kay, evolved from the group Sparrow in 1967. They were another group to come out of the Venice Beach scene in the mid-1960s, and performed with the Doors on a number of occasions, both as Sparrow and Steppenwolf. Their hard-rocking "Born to Be Wild" became a virtual anthem to the rebellious spirit of the era.

"Hello, I Love You" was not included on the officially released video because of inadequate sound quality. It may have been preceded by a "Texas Radio and the Big Beat," not included on the video for the same reasons.

Also performing: The Chambers Brothers; Steppenwolf

Capacity: 17,900

SAT. JUL. 6 1968 Kaleidoscope
Hollywood, CA

This is a last-minute unadvertised benefit performance.

Promotion: John Hartman, Skip Taylor and Gary Essert

Capacity: 1,468

SUN. JUL. 7 1968 Ed Sullivan Show
New York, NY

A rebroadcast of the September 17, 1967 show featuring "Light My Fire" and "People Are Strange."

TUE. JUL. 9 1968 Dallas Memorial Auditorium
Dallas, TX

Soul Kitchen	Texas Radio and the Big Beat »
Back Door Man »	Hello, I Love You »
"Softer" »	Moonlight Drive »
Five to One	Money
Break on Through »	When the Music's Over
"There You Sit" »	Wake Up! »
Break on Through	Light My Fire
Crystal Ship	

Although they start off a bit hesitantly, the Doors are in fine form for this Dallas performance. The musicians are tight, and Morrison sings with a deliberate pacing. After "Crystal Ship," the show surges as Morrison lets loose on "When the Music's Over." During the quiet "gentle sound" portion, Jim moans like an Islamic devotee and continues to speak placidly, sounding almost exasperated, before erupting into "We want the world . . ." to the wildest cheering and applause of the evening.

During the instrumental passage of "Light My Fire," Jim nonchalantly jumps from the stage and extends his mike to various audience members who yelp appreciatively. He is met with stern silence when he offers the mike to one of the police officers stationed in front of the stage. Morrison then taunts the police by throwing his hands on the stage as if he were being frisked, and then swings around offering his lit cigarette to the cops as if it were a joint. When Jim returns to the stage, he finishes the set with his back turned derisively to the audience, and strides off the stage.

The local underground paper *Dallas Notes* comments on the show: "July 9, Jim Morrison and the Doors made their first appearance in Dallas. The show is enough to convince this reviewer that no other pop group can come near them. I say 'Jim Morrison and the Doors' because Morrison's personality totally dominated the performance as it may soon dominate the new rock scene. His dynamic fluctuations from hot to cold, his gyrations, kept the audience flowing with him, and the enthusiastic applause was a testimony to his swaying power. He is a well balanced combination of actor and accomplished singer. Although Morrison dominated the show, it is not fair to say that the other members were not great also. They were, especially drummer John Densmore. And Ray Manzarek's organ, closer to jazz than rock, gave out some of the most original sounds ever heard in Dallas. Robby Krieger's guitar also came through in marvelous fashion." (John Marken "Morrison dominates Doors performance," *Dallas Notes*, July 1968)

📽 Filmed for *Feast of Friends*.

WED. JUL. 10 1968 Sam Houston Coliseum
Houston, TX

Break on Through
Back Door Man »
  "Once I Had a Friend . . ." »
  "Can the Wind Have It All?" »
  "We Tried So Hard, Maybe We Tried Too Hard" »
  "Fall Down Now, Strange Gods Are Coming" »
Back Door Man
When the Music's Over »
  "Confusion" »
  "Winter Photography" »
  "Talking, Waiting, Smoking" »
  "Count The Dead and Wait for Morning" »
  "Feel Warm Days and Faces Come Again" »
When the Music's Over
Texas Radio and the Big Beat (spoken intro) »
Hello, I Love You
Little Red Rooster
Who Do You Love
Crystal Ship
Light My Fire

This outstanding performance by the band includes a wealth of unique improvisational poetry by Jim Morrison fueled by an intense, almost furious, instrumentation by the band. Robby Krieger brings the opening "Break on Through" to a dramatic conclusion by means of some vehement guitar playing. Morrison leads off "Back Door Man" with some gutsy, guttural vocals, which evolve into a long stream of consciousness. "Once I Had a Friend" is punctuated effectively by Ray's subtle verbal responses, and Jim follows "Can the Wind . . ." with a salty paraphrasing of his standard "Softer" narration, ending with "What do you know about my baby?" He returns to the "Softer" routine after "Fall Down Now, Strange Gods Are Coming" until he comically whispers "Touch Me!" and the crowd breaks into applause, which leads back into "Back Door Man."

Krieger opens "When the Music's Over" with some formidable guitar work, and Morrison again drifts into a sequence of poetic improvisations. At the end of the "We want the world . . ." stanza, the auditorium drifts into an elongated dead silence until Morrison erupts into "Now!" and propels the song to its conclusion.

They continue with excellent versions of "Little Red Rooster" (complete with barks and howls by Jim at the appropriate moments) and "Who Do You Love," which is kicked off by an extended percussion prelude. By the time they reach their finale of "Light My Fire," the crowd is exceptionally rowdy. Manzarek takes an extended solo that concludes with some ominous *Close Encounters of the Third Kind*–style organ passages. When Krieger begins his instrumental, Morrison dives under the stage, creating waves of commotion in the audience. Then Jim erupts into a horrendous scream and tears into the crowd, continuing to holler fiendishly as Krieger extends his instrumental to accommodate the fracas. By the time Jim returns to the stage, there is a bastion of police barricading the front of the stage, which essentially blocks the band from view. Over the PA, Morrison's voice thunders "If nobody's gonna come up here, I guess I'll have to go right through them [the police]. [pause] This is your last chance!" The police respond by intensifying their blockade, effectively creating a wedge between audience and performers until the Doors conclude their performance and leave the stage.

> Morrison's voice thunders "If nobody's gonna come up here, I guess I'll have to go right through them [the police]. [pause] This is your last chance!"

- Also performing: Moving Sidewalks
- Filmed for *Feast of Friends*.

FRI. JUL. 12 1968 (1) Seattle Center Arena
Seattle, WA

Tonight's sold-out performance at the Arena goes exceptionally well, and the entire band is in top-notch form. The Doors have previously appeared at the Eagles Auditorium, but for this show the promoter schedules them for this larger-capacity venue. Seattle's *Daily Times* offers this glowing evaluation: "A full-house audience presents an aura of high expectations, and its hopes were satisfied by one of the finest rock concerts offered in this city. Morrison presents the songs, largely social commentary, in an exciting, compelling manner. Whether he is quietly speaking free-verse poetry to the hard-rock accompaniment of the musicians or belting save-the-world lyrics at the top of his lungs, he creates the impression that he cares about and believes in what he is saying. There is no feeling of hypocrisy, no sense that he is merely offering the commodity for which the audience has paid. The Doors met the crowd's desires completely. They are a band that deserves to play to a full house." (Janine Gressel, "Full House Likes 'Doors' at Arena," *Daily Times*, July 15, 1968)

- Also performing: Chrome Syrcus; the International Brick
- Promotion: Boyd Grafmyre
- Capacity: 6,000

Waiting for the Sun
Third Album Released (E-74024)

Side One (A)
Hello, I Love You
Love Street
Not to Touch the Earth
Summer's Almost Gone
Wintertime Love
The Unknown Soldier

Side Two (B)
Spanish Caravan
My Wild Love
We Could Be So Good Together
Yes, the River Knows
Five to One

Singles
The Unknown Soldier / We Could Be So Good Together (E-45628)
Hello, I Love You / Love Street (E-4563)

The original working titles of this album include *American Nights* and *Celebration of the Lizard*.

The complete text to the "Celebration of the Lizard" is enclosed inside the gatefold cover of this album, although the only portion included on the record is "Not to Touch the Earth." The highly anticipated complete version of the "Celebration of the Lizard" will not be released until the *Absolutely Live* album two years later. "Hello, I Love You" had basically been disregarded since the original demo acetate of it was made in September 1965, but it is resuscitated because of the urgency for additional material for the album. Following the prohibitions on airplay that surround the releases of "Love Me Two Times" and "The Unknown Soldier," the Doors' management opts to release the more pop-oriented "Hello, I Love You." An unusual song for the Doors' repertoire, it soars up the charts to become the nation's number-one single by August 3, maintaining that position for two weeks. The album itself goes gold on August 8, and continued interest pushes it into the number-one sales position on September 7, where it remains throughout most of September into early October.

Additional musicians employed on bass guitar for the album are Kerry Magness and Leroy Vinegar.

> Note: For some inexplicable reason, Jim Morrison's vocals on the CD version of "Wintertime Love" are fractionally different from those on the LP. Since both were produced from the identical master reel, this is theoretically impossible. No one involved can explain this discrepancy; it resides in the ever-expanding department of unexplained mysteries surrounding the Doors.

SAT. JUL. 13 1968 P.N.E. Coliseum
Vancouver, Canada

Wake Up! »
Light My Fire
The Unknown Soldier

After two relatively composed opening songs, Jim Morrison flies into high gear, assaulting his microphone and steering the band into a fresh, dynamic, and wildly energetic show. Morrison magnetizes the capacity crowd of thirteen thousand with an engaging series of screams and chants, and leads off several songs with his improvisational poetry. During the finale, hundreds of people vault onto the stage, overwhelming security personnel who vigorously try to restrain the crowd. Their efforts at clearing the stage are futile; there are just too many people. Those who manage to squeeze through the human barricade surround Morrison in a circle of wild enthusiasm and insane dancing.

One Vancouver paper remarks: "An orgy of experience is the only way to describe the result. A great rainbow ball was thrown back and forth between the two pinnacles which the Doors use to express themselves. The first is their rather conventional if effective instrumental combination of organ, guitar, bass, piano and drums. The second can only be described as a shattered and ragged piece of glass, being used by an unknown force to gouge and scrape a peep hole through other doors which hide that which is unearthly, evil or obscene. This cutting edge takes human form in the being which is vocalist Jim Morrison. This young man retains every possible animal characteristic present before the erosion of a million years of evolution, while remaining obscure and intangible like a spirit not really of this world at all, who mocks as he reveals. Morrison laughs the hollow laugh of the insane. He burps, moans, beckons and shrieks and then as the rest of the group takes a solo, he is gone, only to reappear in a sudden, spread eagled lunge from the shadows to strangle the cold steel of the microphone. He is rebellion in perpetuity, and his spell is completely cast upon his audience." (Brian McLeod, "The Doors open upon orgy of experience," *Vancouver Sun*, July 1968)

> Also performing: Crome Syrcus; Hydroelectric Streetcar; Tom Northcott; [additional performers possibly included] the Collectors

This young man retains every possible animal characteristic present before the erosion of a million years of evolution ... a spirit not really of this world at all, who mocks as he reveals. Morrison laughs the hollow laugh of the insane.

- Promotion: Scenic Sounds/Richard Linnell
- 8:30 p.m.
- Capacity: 13,000
- Note: P.N.E. is the abbreviation of Pacific National Exhibition.

SAT. JUL. 20 1968 Honolulu International Civic Arena
Honolulu, HI
Summer Shower of Stars

Light My Fire (finale)

The Doors' Honolulu appearance is apparently one of those uncharacteristically lackluster nights, with long pauses between the songs while the band huddles together, deciding on their next number. Despite the delays, the musicianship is solid, but the usual swell of enthusiasm just doesn't materialize. Jim's exchange with the audience is so minimal that at times it seems he is unaware they are even present. Applause is appreciative but polite (without the customary screams), and apparently no one feels compelled to rush the stage.

Just before the "Light My Fire" finale, someone in the center aisle near the stage sets off a mammoth roll of firecrackers, which ignites applause from the Doors and the crowd alike as the racket subsides.

- Also performing: Silver Bicycle; Golden Days in Grandpa's Garden
- 8:00 p.m. show
- Filmed for *Feast of Friends*.
- Production: Dick Clark Enterprises and KKUA present
- Lights by Piccadilly, Ltd.

THU. AUG. 1 1968 Kennedy (JFK) Municipal Stadium
Bridgeport, CT

Break on Through (opening song)
Light My Fire
Little Red Rooster (1st encore)
The Unknown Soldier (2nd encore)

The Doors' performance tonight is stern and aggressive, and the audience responds with quiet, riveted attention. Morrison moves very little until the conclusion of the show, and behind his closed eyelids appears to be thoroughly absorbed in the lyrics. An encroaching New England midsummer thunderstorm gives the whole evening an eerie, otherworldly ambiance.

- Also performing: Pulse; Spinning Wheel; Graffiti
- Set-list incomplete
- Capacity: 5,000

FRI.
AUG.
2
1968

SINGER BOWL
Flushing Meadows, Queens, NY
The New York Rock Festival at The Singer Bowl

[introductory instrumental]
Back Door Man »
Five to One
Break on Through
When the Music's Over »
   "Vast Radiant Beach" »
   "Dawn's Highway" »
   "The Royal Sperm" »
When the Music's Over
Wild Child
Wake Up! »

Light My Fire
The End »
   "Fall Down Now; Strange Gods Are Coming" »
   "The Sea Is Green" »
   "I'm Coming; I Hear You Calling" »
   "The Creature's Nursing Its Child;
      Leave This Child Alone!" »
   "Don't Come Here! Don't Come In!" »
   "Ensenada" »
   "The Killer Awoke Before Dawn . . ." »
The End

Over the years there were numerous accounts of the Doors provoking riots at their performances. Some of these reports were elaborate embellishments perpetrated by the venues for the purpose of interfering with performances by the rock groups they wished to ban. Other bands, such as the Jimi Hendrix Experience, found themselves engaged in the same controversy. One serious consideration raised by these conflicts was how to provide adequate security without inhibiting the performers or interfering with the audience's enjoyment.

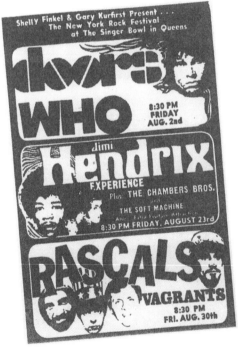

Jim Morrison, however, does not share these concerns. In fact, he is intrigued by the mob mentality he has observed at the Doors' and other bands' performances. Despite the exaggerated portraits of violence surrounding some concerts, accounts of this performance are undeniably valid. From the outset, the show on this dreadfully hot and humid New York summer night is plagued with difficulties. The Kangaroo open the show, and are poorly received by an impatient, unruly crowd. They are followed by the Who. It is a year before the Who's rock opera *Tommy* is released, and the band has yet to achieve legendary status in the States. Nevertheless, they are determined that the stage set-up specifically accommodate their presentation and are adamant that none of the Doors' equipment obstruct the stage. During the Who's performance, the rotating stage breaks down, leaving a section of the audience unable to see the band adequately. The Who put on a good, but not exceptional, show. They leave the stage visibly annoyed. After their set, there is an hour-long interim before the Doors take the stage, and the delay further aggravates the impatient audience.

As soon as the Doors appear, they are greeted with a thunderous assault of screaming fans, and segments of the crowd begin rushing the stage. A column of policemen are stationed at the front of the platform to curtail this onrush of people, while Morrison fiercely jostles his way through them to face the crowd. The chaos escalates continuously during the performance, with fights erupting throughout the Singer Bowl. Morrison sings with a very precise and articulate emphasis on the lyrics, and actually appears to be substantially more sober than the crowd he is facing.

Ellen Sander comments on the show's build-up in *Trips:* "A good portion of the audience still couldn't see and they were furious. Crowds stormed the front of the stage and were turned back by the police. Some were trying to scale the stage and others cheered them on. Morrison spun around and ground the songs out half-heartedly, ad libbing, improvising, doing an ominous dance. Hysteria was building. Morrison shrieked, moaned, gyrated, and minced to the edge of the stage, hovering. Hands reached out and grabbed him and the cops had to pry them away. The camera crew ducked a piece of broken chair which came flying onto the stage.

Morrison caught it and heaved it back into the crowd. The Doors were hardly visible from any angle because there were about twenty cops onstage." (Ellen Sander, *Trips*, New York: Charles Scribner's Sons, 1973)

By the time the Doors begin to perform "The End," the crowd is in an incredible uproar. Morrison vainly attempts to "sssshhhh" the audience, but there is no response and he begins appealing to them. "Hey, this is serious, everyone! Get quiet, man! You're going to ruin the whole thing."

Following the opening stanzas of the song, Morrison drifts into an expansive passage of poetry, beginning with "Fall down now; strange Gods are coming." With decidedly steady pacing, he advances through a series of poems until he unexpectedly screams, "Don't come here! Don't come in!" Proceeding from this flare-up into "Ensenada," Morrison is continually assailed with clamorous screams of "Morrison is King!" from the crowd. He calmly begins to recite the Oedipal section of the song, but when he pauses at one significant part, the audience impatiently roars the delayed lyrics "he walked on down the hallway, baby!" The crowd momentarily becomes quiet again, until Jim reaches the conclusion of the Oedipal section with "Mother, I want to . . ." and the Singer Bowl bursts into pandemonium with the audience finishing the lyrics. The band accelerates into the musical passage and Morrison hits the stage, writhing in agony like the death knell of a hideous serpent while the crowd goes wild. The instrumental passage climaxes with a horrendous blood-curdling scream from Morrison, followed by Krieger's guitar set on some wildly unrestrained echo. By now no one remains seated in the crowd and the police are forming a barricade in front of the stage. The audience is defiantly screaming "Sit down, cop!" as Krieger finishes the song with a long trail of feedback.

Just before midnight, as the Doors conclude their performance, a horde of people begin demolishing the wooden seating section in front and hurling portions of the splintered benches at the stage. The debacle turns into a complete riot when the crowd charges the police barricade, forcing the Doors to abandon the stage amid a torrent of plummeting debris. As the police struggle to regain control of the crowd, Vince Treanor and the equipment crew desperately try to defend their gear.

Pete Townshend, lead guitar player for the Who, observes the entire disturbance from the side of the stage and is both fascinated and appalled by Morrison's apparent indifference to the situation. According to Who biographer Dave Marsh, it is Morrison's aloof and mystifying demeanor in the face of intensifying chaos that prompts Townshend to write the Who's composition "Sally Simpson."

- Also performing: The Who; the Kangaroo
- Filmed for *Feast of Friends*
- Promotion: Gary Kurfist and Shelley Finkel
- Capacity: 17,500

> Jim reaches "Mother, I want to ..." and the Singer Bowl bursts into pandemonium with the audience finishing the lyrics.... Morrison hits the stage, writhing in agony like the death knell of a hideous serpent while the crowd goes wild.

SAT. AUG. 3 1968 CLEVELAND PUBLIC AUDITORIUM
Cleveland, OH

[introductions]
Break on Through (instrumental) »
  [introductory jam without Morrison]
Break on Through »
Back Door Man »
Five to One (extended version)
When the Music's Over »

"Vast Radiant Beach" »
[Krieger's guitar instrumental] »
"The Royal Sperm" »
When the Music's Over »
Soul Kitchen (extended version) »
Light My Fire

After a prolonged delay, announcements are made for upcoming shows featuring Janis Joplin, Jimi Hendrix, and Country Joe and the Fish. As the introduction

finishes, the Doors begin a driving instrumental jam on "Break on Through," but there is still no sign of Jim Morrison. As the instrumental comes to a close, an extremely intoxicated Morrison saunters onstage grasping a bottle of whiskey in one hand, while he flips off the audience with the other. At points during the show he is clearly incoherent and seems compelled to converse endlessly with the audience. The formidable influence of the previous night's performance at the Singer Bowl carries over into Cleveland, where the Doors put on such an outrageous show it comes close to the Miami fiasco that will take place in March 1969.

The band starts the standard "Break on Through" and Morrison shouts and grunts throughout the song while Krieger seems to be enthralled at the increasingly bizarre feedback squealing out of his guitar amp. Toward the end of "Back Door Man," Jim appears to be perplexed and the band is rapidly becoming louder and so discordant that it is almost impossible to discern which song is being performed. As the medley goes into "Five to One," it becomes apparent that Morrison can't hear his own monitor as he angrily barks "I can't hear myself! I'm gonna give you a good time . . . I want it real soft. If I can't hear myself I'm going to get a gun and kill some people! I want to hear my little voice!"

Jim then begins to direct the band to "Play real soft. Softer. Softer!" until the music comes to a complete standstill. For a full five minutes he mischievously engages in a dialogue with the audience, eliciting frequent laughter and applause. Responding to an audience member, "You've got a real dirty mind don't you! FAWK! [applause] Listen! I'm not kidding. I want you to feel it! I want you to FEEL IT!" Then the band quietly begins playing "Five to One" again, while Jim continues his observations. "That little cowgirl is lookin' reeeaal good! Later, later!" He demands, "Listen here! You've got to feel it right NOW!" and then returns to the lyrics from "Five to One," but he sings the song so sluggishly that the band is forced to stop and wait for him to catch up. By the end of the piece, the music has deteriorated into chaos, with the musicians all playing out of tempo with each other, and Morrison growling out in the chaos: "Get together one more time."

The medley ends and Morrison repeatedly states, "We're gonna have a real good time, right?" "When the Music's Over" starts, and Jim is still asking, "Well, what are we gonna do now?" He's singing the song in a flat southern accent, entirely missing his cue for "Until the end!" Krieger then tears into an absolutely bizarre lead that collapses into chaotic feedback at the end. At that point, Morrison grabs the mike again: "Fine! You old fellows are gonna get it now! Yeah! Softer, you're getting softer. Softer. I want to tell you people a few things I don't think you know about! We're getting real soft now, come on! Softer, baby. Softer, baby. Softer, baby. Gotta feel it inside. Take it deep inside!" The audience begins laughing and Krieger applies massive echo to his guitar. "Hey Listen! I want to give you a history of me!" Jim continues, "All right! I have a few things to say if you don't mind. . . . I don't know how I got here! But I did!" He then recites "Vast Radiant Beach," and Krieger follows him with some wild echo set on such long delay that it is impossible to tell what he is playing. Almost incoherently, Jim recites "The Royal Sperm" and continues with "You know we want it and we're gonna get it. Speak up, I can't hear you! What are we gonna get? We're gonna get everything! We want it! We want it! We want it! We want more! We want more! Hey, everybody take a real deep breath. We. We want. We want all. We want all. We want all! You ready? You ready? You ready! We want the world and we WANT IT NOW!" At this, the entire band bursts into an incredibly loud and dissonant musical passage where each musician is playing completely out of sync with the others. At the end of the song Morrison laughingly says "Yeah! Lookin' *real* good!"

By now the concert is beyond any saving grace and the audience is getting precariously unruly. "Hey, what do you want to hear?" asks Jim, "One at a time, I can't hear you! Can anyone pass a Marlboro to me? They're the best! Come on out to California and have some fun!" The band then plays a rapid introduction to "Soul Kitchen." By this time, Morrison is incoherent and Krieger covers him with an extended guitar solo. Toward the conclusion of the song, Jim leaves his microphone and does something at which the audience bursts into applause, while Manzarek unceasingly repeats the final stanzas of the piece. When it seems as if the song will never reach a conclusion, they finally break into "Light My Fire." By now Morrison is in far worse shape than he will be at the infamous Miami show,

I want it real soft. If I cant hear myself Im going to get a gun and kill some people! I want to hear my little voice! ... You've got a real dirty mind dont you! FAWK! ... That little cowgirl is lookin' reeeaal good! Later... Hey Listen! I want to give you a history of me! ... I dont know how I got here! But I did!

endlessly repeating "Come on! Come on!" throughout Ray's solo. As Krieger begins his solo, Morrison screams at the top of his lungs: "You know I can't take it! I CAN'T TAKE IT! Come on, yeah, COME ON!" and then maniacally leaps into the crowd with his microphone. Pandemonium erupts—the screaming is so loud it effectively drowns out the band. Several fights break out as Jim is carried along across the hands of the audience, all the while diabolically repeating "All right! Come on! DO IT!" He somehow arrives back onstage and can barely finish the song, his voice is breaking up so badly. Afterward, the Doors flee the stage as the crowd explodes with chants of "Jim! Jim! Jim!" When it appears that no one is going to leave, the announcer gets onstage and implores them with "Thanks very much for coming! Have a safe trip home! The Doors are on their way to Philadelphia!"

There is extensive damage to the venue's seating and adjacent property. Following the performance, the clean-up crew notes that the destruction is worse than when Jimi Hendrix's performance sparked a near riot there on March 26. The enormous hanging curtains in the auditorium have sustained numerous lacerations and even huge wooden doors have been torn off their hinges.

- Also performing: The Blues Establishment
- Promotion: Belkin Productions
- Filmed for *Feast of Friends*
- Capacity: At least 9,200

SUN. AUG. 4 1968 Philadelphia Arena
Philadelphia, PA

When the Music's Over »
  (Leave the poor kid alone!) »
  "The Royal Sperm" »
When the Music's Over
Alabama Song »
Back Door Man »

Five to One
Spanish Caravan
Texas Radio and the Big Beat (WASP)»
Hello, I Love You »
Wake Up! »
Light My Fire

After a brief introduction, the Doors lead off with "When the Music's Over." The show that follows is very fast paced, almost rushed. Police are scattered around the front of the stage, facing the audience as if in anticipation of difficulties. Their imposing presence seems to provoke the crowd. Midway through the first song, someone in the audience begins to taunt one of the officers. Morrison, observing the situation, speaks to the person in the audience saying, "Oh, leave the poor kid (referring to the policeman) alone! He's just doing his job. Just think what would happen! All those criminals and assassins!" Then after a brief pause, Morrison leads into his poetry, "The Royal Sperm."

Robby Krieger's guitar playing is phenomenal tonight. As "Back Door Man" moves into "Five to One," he takes a commanding solo that screeches with wild distortion, while John Densmore attacks his drums with equal fury. After this medley, they pause long enough for Jim to make a request for a cigarette and a beer from the audience. Then Krieger vaults into what must be one of the most dramatic versions of "Spanish Caravan" he's ever performed, complete with piercing loops of feedback that reverberate throughout the arena.

Before their finale, Morrison asks the crowd, "What do you guys want to hear?" and everyone began shouting at once. Jim barks in response, "One at a time, I can't hear you!" but to no avail. He settles the matter by beginning to recite "Texas Radio and the Big Beat." This leads directly into "Hello, I Love You," and without missing a beat they jump into "Wake Up!" and then "Light My Fire." By the time this final medley arrives at "Light My Fire," Morrison is going wild. He shouts and grunts throughout the song, while the police, visibly disturbed, begin to form a dense semicircular barricade in front of the stage. At the end of Ray's solo, Jim maniacally calls out to no one in particular, "Yeah! Have you got anything to say?" Before there is a chance for any response, Krieger bursts into an incredibly loud and wildly distorted solo. The Doors finish "Light My Fire" and swiftly exit the stage, determined to avoid any suggestion of an encore.

One reader of Philadelphia's *Distant Drummer* writes these comments on the show in a letter to the editor: "The Doors' concert Sunday night at the Arena was one time which the long hot wait really paid off. When the Doors' performance finally did get underway (around 10:30), the result was one of the finest, if not the greatest, shows I've ever seen. Between the tremendous vocal talent of Jim Morrison, and the musical competence of the entire accompanying group, the night was well worth the sweat and discomfort." (G. Dangel, "Readers' Feedback," *Distant Drummer*, Aug. 1968)

🐝 Also appearing: Mandrake Memorial; All That the Name Implies; emcee Bob Borden

FRI. AUG. 30 1968 Merriweather Post Pavilion
Columbia, MD

Back Door Man
Five to One
Break on Through
When the Music's Over
Crystal Ship
Soul Kitchen »

Celebration of the Lizard »
Rock Me »
Celebration of the Lizard
Light My Fire
The End

The Doors' performance goes remarkably well tonight, and they do an elaborate version of "Celebration of the Lizard," plus an extended rendition of "The End." Opening under a deluge of flash-bulbs, the band is in fine form, especially Manzarek whose flowing organ passages fuels the improvisational tone of the evening. The *Washington Star* applauds his work: "There is a considerable amount of rhythmic skill, particularly in the playing of the organist, Ray Manzarek, who can produce syncopations that are only slightly off the beat in a manner so precise as to suggest overdubbing more than live performance." (Donald Mintz, "The Doors Bang Out Hint of Inventiveness," *Washington Star*, Aug. 31, 1968)

🐝 Also performing: Earth Opera; All That the Name Implies; emcee: Jim Stewart
🖐 Set-list incomplete
🎥 Filmed for *Feast of Friends*
🎭 Capacity: 14,000

SAT. AUG. 31 1968 Asbury Park Convention Hall
Asbury Park, NJ

Late Show
Break on Through
Love Me Two Times
When the Music's Over
Soul Kitchen

Spanish Caravan
Light My Fire
The End (encore)

The Doors perform two shows this evening, and the second is reportedly the more powerful. As the late show opens, Morrison slowly saunters up to his microphone, closes his eyes, throws his head back, and stands motionless for a long time with the exception of one hand that almost imperceptibly caresses the mike during the silence. The tension continues to build throughout the hushed auditorium until, as if on some transcendental cue, Densmore kicks off the introductory beat to "Break on Through," and the band is off to a phenomenal show.

After the Doors' finale of "Light My Fire," the audience is well on their way to the exits when Morrison unexpectedly reappears onstage. Somewhat shyly he announces, "Hey! The show was supposed to end with that number, but [pause] I don't see why we can't go on!" All at once, the entire crowd reverses in a huge surge, cheering, shouting, scaling chairs, and prompting the hall's security forces to encircle the stage. The mesmerizing opening chords of "The End" serve to induce a calm trance throughout the scores of people crushed against the stage, and the Doors conclude the show with a terrific version of the song.

- Set-list may be incomplete
- Filmed for *Feast of Friends*
- Early (7:00 p.m.) and late (9:45 p.m.) shows

SUN. SEPT. 1 1968 (1) Saratoga Performing Arts Center
Saratoga Springs, NY

Back Door Man
When The Music's Over
Hello, I Love You
Light My Fire
The End

This Saratoga Springs show is the Doors final performance before their European tour, as well as the last concert filmed for *Feast Of Friends*. The following day, the Doors are scheduled to depart for London. While backstage before the show, Ray Manzarek warms up for the show by playing John Coltrane's "Dahomey Dance" at the grand piano situated in the center of their dressing room. Then Jim Morrison spontaneously takes Ray's seat and devises the clever and astute "Ode to Friedrich Nietzsche." This impromptu innovation is captured on film by the documentary crew and is featured in both "The Soft Parade" video and *Feast of Friends*.

The Doors' performance opens with a very indifferent Morrison leisurely strolling toward his mike as the band begins "Back Door Man." His initial mannerisms seem entirely detached from the proceedings going on around him, until he erupts into some particularly fierce vocals that set the tone for the entire evening. Toward the conclusion of the show, as the intensity escalates, he finally explodes into offhand shrieks of "Touch me, baby!" and "If you want to move around when I sing, do it. DO IT!" Perhaps the tensest moment of the night comes when the Doors came back on stage after a tumultuous standing ovation. Morrison saunters out, takes a perfunctory bow, and then vaults into the audience as a startled squadron of police fly into the crowd to steer Morrison back on stage. At the conclusion of the show, the impassioned audience remains for more than a half-an-hour, standing on their chairs, screaming and chanting, until a frantic local deejay pleads with them to leave and behave like "ladies and gentlemen!" It is a ludicrous plea considering the emotional state of this crowd, but people do finally begin making their way reluctantly toward the exits. (Quotes from "The Doors' Concert an Unforgettable Experience," Jake Sherman, Albany *Times Union*, Sept. 3, 1968)

> Morrison spontaneously takes his seat and devises the clever and astute "Ode to Friedrich Nietzsche."

- Also performing: Earth Opera
- Set-list incomplete
- Attendance: 12,500
- *Feast of Friends* filming concludes

SUN. SEPT. 1 1968 (2) The Aerodrome
Schenectady, NY

After the Saratoga show, Jim Morrison appears at this popular stopover while en route to New York. After strolling through the audience for a while, he gets onstage and sits in with an undetermined blues band for a few numbers.

EUROPEAN TOUR: SEPTEMBER 1968

The Doors had a tentative date to perform at the Saville Theater in London in late 1967 as their first European show. Due to complicated logistics, that particular show never occurred. They were later scheduled for a joint appearance with the Jefferson Airplane at the Royal Albert Hall on April 13, 1968, which was cancelled as well. Preparations were made for this European tour in the fall.

Note: Jefferson Airplane [RCA Records] and Canned Heat [Liberty Records] were touring Europe as well in September and arrangements were made, according to feasibility, for these bands to alternate double billings with the Doors on their tour. The Airplane had just made their British debut at the Isle of Wight festival on August 31, and were continuing with their European tour.

Kennedy International Airport, Queens, NY

SEPTEMBER
2
MONDAY

The Doors, their associates, and their equipment crew depart for London on Air India on a 6:00 p.m. flight, which is delayed until 11:00 p.m. They arrive at London's Heathrow Airport on Tuesday, where the Granada Television film crew meets them at the gate.

THU. SEPT. 5 1968 Top Of The Pops
BBC-1 TV, London, England

Hello, I Love You (live)

I didnt realize they turned out everyone like sausages.... I doubt if we will do it again

Top of the Pops is the BBC's response to the success of ITV's several television rock programs, especially the acclaimed *Ready, Steady, Go!*

London's *Melody Maker* reports Morrison's reaction to the show: "He was not so enamored with the group's appearance on 'Top of the Pops.' 'I didn't realize they turned out everyone like sausages on that show,' he said. 'I doubt if we will do it again.'" ("Super Jim, the angel faced Rasputin," *Melody Maker*, May 2, 1970)

Also appearing on the show: Canned Heat

FRI. SEPT. 6 1968 The Roundhouse
London, England

(soundcheck: Hello, I Love You)

Early Show (7:00 p.m.)

Back Door Man	Wild Child
Break on Through	Money
When the Music's Over	Light My Fire
Alabama Song	The Unknown Soldier*
Hello, I Love You	The End

Late Show (10:00 p.m.)

Five to One	Celebration of the Lizard (abridged version)
Break on Through	"A Little Game" »
When the Music's Over	"The Hill Dwellers" »
Alabama Song »	"Wait! There's Been a Slaughter Here!" »
Back Door Man »	"Not to Touch the Earth" »
Crawlin' King Snake »	"I Am the Lizard King!"
Back Door Man	Hello, I Love You
Spanish Caravan	Moonlight Drive »
Love Me Two Times	Horse Latitudes »
Light My Fire	Moonlight Drive »
The Unknown Soldier	Money
Soul Kitchen	

Both of these performances at the Roundhouse go exceptionally well. The band is in terrific form and Morrison, although a tad reserved in comparison to the summer performances, is in fine voice.

The late show opens with irrepressible energy from the band, with Morrison adding his graveliest snarl to the lyrics. The usually staid British audience breaks into applause at the introductory notes of "When the Music's Over" and Krieger rips into some fascinating Indian mantra–style leads during the piece. Morrison is quite animated during the gutsy "Back Door Man" and integrates "Crawlin' King Snake" into the midpoint of it while the band maintains the "Back Door" beat. Of note is their inclusion of a moderately abridged rare version of "Celebration of the Lizard." They conclude with a medley of "Moonlight Drive" intersecting with "Horse Latitudes" and wrapping up with the classic "Money."

London's *Melody Maker* comments on the early show: "He walked majestically on stage clad in a tight black leather suit, white shirt and brown shoes. The crowd applauded him and Morrison, taking a stance at the mike, smiled briefly and belted into his first song. His singing is every bit as powerful as the Doors albums suggest, while the backing trio of organist Manzarek, drummer Densmore, and Krieger, guitar, are really together and play with precision and timing that are quite remarkable. The Doors are undoubtedly one of the most professional groups on the scene anywhere. Everything hangs together well and there is an underlying feel of calculation and presentation which projects the music to its full [sic]." (*Melody Maker*, Sept. 14, 1968)

Both of these performances were filmed by Granada Television for the *Doors Are Open* special telecast on October 4, although the program used only footage from the second show.

On their first night, the Doors open for Jefferson Airplane, and on the following night the Airplane open for the Doors. The first night's performances are delayed while negotiations as to which band will appear first continue past 10:30 p.m. Initially, it had been determined that the Airplane would be first on the stage, but Granada Television pleads for the Doors, and the ensuing discussions continue for several hours while the audience remains remarkably patient. Advertisements for the shows announced the performance time as from 7:30 till dawn, so the audience was already anticipating a long night.

These shows are attended by many London music scene luminaries, including members of the Rolling Stones, Traffic, and the Crazy World of Arthur Brown.

✳ At the early show, "The Unknown Soldier" may actually have been performed before "Light My Fire."

⚖ Note: "Money" was written by Berry Gordy Jr. and Janie Bradford, and was originally performed by Barret Strong in 1960.

☡ Also performing: Jefferson Airplane; Terry Reid [probably on the bill as well]; Blossom Toes

♛ Lighting by San Francisco's Glenn McKay's Head Lights Co.

☡ Capacity: 2,500

SEPTEMBER
7
SATURDAY

ICA Gallery, The Mall, London, England

The Doors hold a press conference at the Institute for Contemporary Arts Cybernetics, which is also filmed by Granada Television and incorporated into their broadcast special.

Early Show*

Five to One	Light My Fire
Break on Through	The End »
When the Music's Over	"Ensenada" »
Wake Up! »	The End

The early show opens with some strong vocals and blistering guitar work on "Five to One." It sets the stage for the evening, which continues in the same vein. During "When the Music's Over," Krieger erupts into a grinding, twisting, note-bending guitar solo and Morrison's voice is coarse and sharp with precise inflections. This is a well-executed show right through to "The End," where Krieger again bursts into dramatic, crashing guitar chords with a twisting and churning that evokes a free-falling plunge. Near the conclusion of the song the difference between the British and American audience becomes evident. The British remain politely still during the quiet passage following the instrumental climax, while American audiences usually erupt into cheers.

Jim Morrison later stated that he thought the late show on their second night at the Roundhouse was probably one of the band's best performances: "The audience was one of the best we've ever had. Everyone seemed to take it so easy. It was different because in the States they are there as much to enjoy themselves as to hear you. Whereas at the Roundhouse, everyone was there to listen. It was like going back to the roots again and it stimulated us to do a good performance. They really took me by surprise. I expected them to be a little resistant, a little reserved, but they were fantastic. That's all I can say. I enjoyed playing at the Roundhouse more than any other date for years." (Nick Logan, "Elvis influenced Doors Jim," *New Musical Express*, Sept. 21, 1968)

In 1969, Jim reflected on the Doors' European tour: "Well, a lot of people had cautioned us that there'd be a lot of hostilities towards an American group, but it didn't happen that way. The Germans were really boorish, but, other than that, the audiences were really great. Especially London, they were fantastic. It's probably the most informed, receptive audience I've ever seen in my life, the one at the Roundhouse. An old converted railway roundhouse now used for theatrical performances." (Hank Zevallos, "Jim Morrison," *Poppin* magazine, 1969)

- Also performing: Jefferson Airplane; Terry Reid; the Crazy World of Arthur Brown; Blonde On Blonde
- Early (7:00 p.m.) and late (10:00 p.m.) shows
- Lighting by San Francisco's Glenn McKay's Head Lights
- Capacity: 2,500
- Set-list may actually be from late show

FRI. SEPT. **13** 1968 (1) Frankfurt Romer Square "4-3-2-1 Hot & Sweet" TV Show

Hello, I Love You
Light My Fire

At one o'clock in the afternoon, the Doors tape a segment for the West German ZDF-TV *4-3-2-1 Hot & Sweet* television show. They lip-synch an outdoor presentation to their two most popular European hits. (Host: Suzanne Doucet)

FRI. SEPT. 13 1968 (2) The Drugstore
Frankfurt, West Germany

This is a press conference at Frankfurt city hall.

SAT. SEPT. 14 1968 Kongresshalle
Frankfurt, West Germany

Early Show (6:00 p.m.)

Break on Through	Texas Radio and the Big Beat (WASP) »
Alabama Song »	Hello, I Love You
Back Door Man	Light My Fire
When the Music's Over	The Unknown Soldier

Late Show (9:00 p.m.)*

Five to One	Light My Fire
Alabama Song »	Little Red Rooster
Back Door Man	I'm a Man
When the Music's Over	The End (encore: an extended version)

The early show goes well, although the audience seems somewhat restrained. While Manzarek's playing is powerful, Morrison is a bit subdued, even tired. Nevertheless, his grotesque laughter during "Back Door Man" elicits cheers from the crowd. The finale of "The Unknown Soldier" is particularly powerful, with loud, distorted, raging guitar from Krieger, and Jim pushing some real fury into the lyrics. That song elicits the greatest applause of the evening. It is particularly significant for the numerous G.I.s in the audience.

The late show opens with a particularly gritty rendition of "Five to One," which concludes with Morrison delivering a nasty, clenched-teeth snarl of "Get the whole fucking thing together just one more TIME!" His voice is particularly melodic tonight, making his unpredictable outbursts even more startling. After a substantial portion of the audience has already left at the conclusion of the late show, the Doors reappear to do an extended encore with an approximately thirty-minute version of "The End."

Portions of this show are filmed by German television (possibly by a station in Frankfurt, which also recorded a number of the Jimi Hendrix Experience shows). The songs televised include portions of "Light My Fire" and "Five to One."

🎤 Also performing: Canned Heat

📋 Promotion: Lippman and Rav and SBA

❋ Late show set-list possibly incomplete

SUN. SEPT. 15 1968 Concertgebouw
Amsterdam, Holland, Netherlands

Late Show (9:00 p.m.)*

Break on Through »	Back Door Man
"There You Sit!" »	Hello, I Love You
Break on Through	Light My Fire
Soul Kitchen	The Unknown Soldier
Alabama Song »	

In Amsterdam, the Doors are obliged to perform without Jim Morrison. During the afternoon, Morrison has graciously consumed an abundant amount of hashish, which admirers have presented him while he is sightseeing around the city. Whenever he is given any hashish, he just pitches it in his mouth and swallows it whole.

The delayed reaction from ingesting the gratuities this way eventually catches up with him just as the Jefferson Airplane are opening the show. Morrison strolls onstage during their performance of "Plastic Fantastic Lover" and begins dancing outlandishly, twirling and wrapping himself in and out of guitar cables. After one spirited spin, Morrison collapses briefly, and then staggers backstage, where he crumples to the floor and is briskly transported to a local hospital. The physicians there diagnose the problem, but cannot prescribe any remedy to counteract Jim's exhaustion and get him back to the show. Instead, it is recommended that he remain overnight and sleep it off.

Meanwhile, when it is confirmed that Jim will be unable to perform, road manager Vince Treanor is elected to make an announcement that, although Jim cannot perform, the band wishes to go on with the show, and that people can request a refund and leave if they chose to do so. It is soon evident that scarcely anyone wishes to leave, and the three Doors perform to a capacity house.

The Doors' performance is exceptional this night. Fueled by their frustration with the extenuating circumstances, notably Jim, they catapult into an aggressive and vibrant set with the majority of the vocals taken on by Ray Manzarek, whose inflection is uncannily reminiscent of Morrison's.

🎤 Also performing: Jefferson Airplane; Terry Reid [probably on the bill as well]

♀ Early and late shows

✳ Set-list may actually be from early show

TUE. SEPT. 17 1968 Falkoner Centret (Concerthall)
Copenhagen, Denmark

Early Show (6:00 P.M.)
When the Music's Over　　　　　Hello, I Love You
Back Door Man »　　　　　　　　Light My Fire
Five to One　　　　　　　　　　Alabama Song
Break on Through　　　　　　　Unknown Soldier

Late Show
Back Door Man »　　　　　　　　Texas Radio and the Big Beat (The WASP)* »
Five to One　　　　　　　　　　Hello, I Love You
Soul Kitchen　　　　　　　　　Light My Fire
Love Me Two Times　　　　　　　The Unknown Soldier
When the Music's Over »　　　　The End

Reportedly, the Doors appearance in Copenhagen was a bit unsettling to Danish audiences. According to *down beat*, the audience's overall reaction was one of disappointment due to their perception of Morrison as being overly aggressive.

✳ Note: In all probability the Doors perform "Texas Radio" as their intro to "Hello, I Love You," as was the case in numerous concerts in the last months. However, this is not confirmed as all that is written for the set-list is "poetry."

🎤 Also performing: Cy Nicklin and the Day Of Phoenix; and probably Savoy Brown

🕴 Capacity: 2,000

WED. SEPT. 18 1968 Television-Byen
Gladsaxe, Copenhagen, Denmark

Alabama Song »　　　　　　　　Love Me Two Times
Back Door Man　　　　　　　　　When the Music's Over
Texas Radio and the Big Beat (The WASP)　The Unknown Soldier

The Doors reportedly appear at the Gladsaxe Television-Byen studio at ten in the morning, not exactly an ideal time to capture them in performance. With no audience other than the camera crew to interact with, they make a valiant effort to reproduce a live performance on film. Although they appear to suffer from want of sleep, they are determined to provide a show for an invisible audience of television viewers who will see them across parts of Europe. The show is introduced by Edmondt Jensen.

⚐ Note: These recordings of "Love Me Two Times" and "Texas Radio and the Big Beat" were included in the album *Alive She Cried* and the video "Dance on Fire."

FRI. SEPT. 20 1968 Konserthuset
Stockholm, Sweden

Early Show

Five to One	"A Little Game" »
Love Street	"The Hill Dwellers" »
Love Me Two Times	Light My Fire
When the Music's Over	The Unknown Soldier (encore)

Late Show

Five to One	"Confusion" »
(Ballad Of) Mack The Knife* »	When the Music's Over
Alabama Song »	Wild Child
Back Door Man	Money »
You're Lost Little Girl	Wake Up! »
Love Me Two Times	Light My Fire
When the Music's Over »	The End (encore)

Both of these performances go exceptionally well. The first show includes a rare live rendition of "Love Street," and the second an infrequent take of the Brecht/Weill composition "(Ballad of) Mack the Knife." The entire late show is outstanding— a fine representation of the Doors' live performances at the time.

Both the early and late shows are recorded in their entirety for broadcast on Stockholm's Radiohuset radio station.

⚐ Note: "Prologue: Ballad of Mack the Knife" follows the introductory overture from the Brecht/Weill *Threepenny Opera*.

⚐ Note: This show had been originally scheduled on September 21 with Canned Heat as the opening act.

✦ Also performing: Jefferson Airplane; Terry Reid [was probably on the bill]; Savoy Brown [were probably scheduled to perform as well]

Return To Los Angeles

The Doors and their accompanying road crew return to London and then fly on to Los Angeles, with the exception of Jim Morrison and Pamela Courson, who remain in London at the Belgravia Hotel through October 20.

MON. SEPT. 23 1968 Studio Two
Abbey Road Studios, London

In the evening, Jim Morrison visits one of the Beatles' recording sessions at Abbey Road Studios. At the time, the Beatles are recording multiple takes of John Lennon's "Happiness Is a Warm Gun" for their *White Album*. The rumors that Morrison sat in on the chorus for one of these takes are unsubstantiated and highly improbable.

OCT. 1968 The Doors Workshop
Hollywood, CA

While Jim Morrison is in London, the other band members are approached by Buick with a lucrative offer for the use of "Light My Fire" as an underscore to a commercial. Although the idea is appealing, Manzarek, Densmore and Krieger are apprehensive about accepting the offer. After efforts to contact Jim fail, they agree to the proposal.

Upon Jim's return, it is clear that he is enormously upset by their acceptance of the offer. Jim firmly maintains that allowing the use of their music for any such enterprise is antithetical to everything the Doors stand for. He is distressed by what he perceives to be a violation of trust, and the result of the dispute is an agreement that all future decisions will be unanimous. To the relief of all concerned, Buick rescinds their offer and the song is never used commercially.

> Note: At the time that the Doors were considering "Light My Fire" as a commercial soundtrack, Jefferson Airplane had done a scarcely known advertisement for Levi's and Cream had made a plug for Falstaff Beer.

> Note: The use of the "Come on Buick, Light My Fire" commercial in Oliver Stone's movie *The Doors* is a fictitious portrayal of this incident.

FRI. OCT. 4 1968 The Doors Are Open
Broadcast On BBC/Granada TV

Introduction
When the Music's Over
Five to One
Spanish Caravan
Interview selections from the ICA Gallery Press conference
Hello, I Love You (from the soundcheck, with Ray Manzarek on vocals)
Interviews
Back Door Man »
Crawlin' King Snake »
Back Door Man
Interview with Jim Morrison
Wake Up! »
Light My Fire
The Unknown Soldier
Conclusion

This special is an earnestly designed semidocumentary that seeks to equate the Doors with the emotional political climate of the time. Although the inclusion of provocative newsreel footage from various demonstrations adds an excitement to the visual components of the show, it frequently creates a distraction from the band's music. As an historic document, however, it does well, placing the band in the context of the times. At the height of their only European tour, *The Doors Are Open* is a fitting portrait of the band from a British perspective.

🖳 Note: The original working title of this BBC Special was *When the Mode Of the Music Changes, The Walls Of the City Will Shake,* which is a quotation from Plato.

🖳 Note: The performance used for this broadcast was recorded at the late show on September 6 at the London Roundhouse.

🖳 Note: This show may have been rebroadcast on October 6, but the 4th was the scheduled date for its first presentation in London. It was broadcast nationally by Granada on Saturday, November 16 at 10:00 p.m. and again on December 17. Granada was part of the ITV [Independent Television] network of stations that operated throughout the United Kingdom independently of the BBC.

🎬 Produced by Jo Durden-Smith

OCTOBER 13 SUNDAY

Belgravia

While in London, Jim Morrison meets with San Francisco Beat poet Michael McClure, and they establish a personal working relationship that endures until Jim's death. (McClure's relationship with the Doors continues to this day; he and Ray Manzarek periodically join forces for a recital of McClure's poetry with Ray on piano.)

OCTOBER 1968

The Doors Fan Club

Leon Bernard is officially employed as the administrator and public relations representative for the rapidly expanding Doors Fan Club.

The Soft Parade
Rehearsals Begin for the Fourth Album

FALL 1968: MIDWEST TOUR

THU. OCT. 31 1968 Freedom Hall
Louisville, KY
Halloween '68

Soul Kitchen
Back Door Man
Rock Me

Wake Up! »
Light My Fire

The Freedom Hall performance goes very well despite the fact that Manzarek's piano bass breaks down just prior to the show. Morrison saunters onstage in baggy white jeans, a cigarette clenched between his teeth, while rolling up the sleeves on a crumpled blue shirt. The show is relatively calm, and despite the periodic obscenity, there isn't much interaction with the audience.

A local paper comments on the show: "A more subdued Morrison enables one to put the rest of the group in perspective. The 'other three'—drummer John Densmore, guitarist Robby Krieger, and organist Ray Manzarek—are very, very good.

They improvise in tight, together flourishes, creating great musical tensions and then releasing them with those cold steel pauses that have distinguished the group. The Doors' jam on 'Light My Fire' was the best of the night, particularly the work of Manzarek and Krieger, the latter running long, whining notes into one another." (Jack Lyne, "Doors opened in Louisville," *The Kentucky Kernal,* Nov. 4, 1968)

- Also performing: Tom Dooley and the Lovelights; the Waters
- Set-list incomplete
- 8:00 p.m. show
- Promotion: Belkin Productions presents

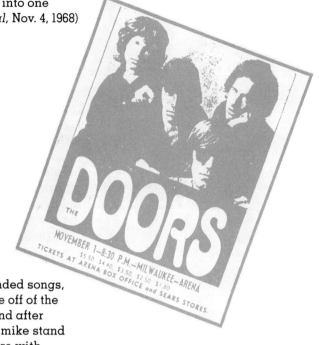

FRI. NOV. 1 1968 Milwaukee Arena
Milwaukee, WI

When the Music's Over
Light My Fire
The End
Gloria (encore)

The Doors play a good solid show, performing both of their extended songs, which utilize improvisational poetry. Morrison takes a suitable plunge off of the stage at the conclusion of "The End." The crowd is roaring for more, and after about five minutes the band returns to the stage. Morrison knocks his mike stand over, which elicits more cheers, and then slowly introduces their encore with "Okay, baby, this song is gonna bring the house down!" Krieger rips into the opening notes of "Gloria," and the band takes off into a wild version of the song. Morrison leaps about the stage with abandon, periodically letting loose emotional screams and random comments like "Gotta little girl. Hey! Gotta little girl!" It is a fitting climax to a solid show.

The *Milwaukee Journal* remarks: "The Doors, to the uninitiated, are no wooden set of guitar pickers and brassy vocalists. They are perhaps the leading popular exponents of acid rock—acid in terms of drug oriented, perhaps; acid in terms of social commentary, certainly. They plug in to Morrison as 1,300 watts of amplified sound blast into their minds, a sound so loud it drives thought out, a sound so loud it pins the value judgments of the adult world to the far wall of the Arena and leaves them squirming helplessly. From 'Light My Fire' to 'The End' . . . the sinister lyrics socked their satanically sensual message to the crowd." (Pierre-Rene Noth, "Acid rock singers etch their message," *Milwaukee Journal,* Nov. 2, 1968)

They plug in to Morrison as 1300 watts of amplified sound blast into their minds, a sound so loud it drives thought out.

- Also performing: Midwest Hydraulic Company
- Set-list incomplete
- Note: There is a remote chance "Gloria" may have actually been the encore at Madison on November 8th.

SAT. NOV. 2 1968 Veterans Memorial Hall
Columbus, OH

Early Show (7:00 p.m.)
Five to One
Not to Touch the Earth
Light My Fire

- Set-list incomplete
- There is no information on the late (10:00 p.m.) show
- Capacity: 3,944

SUN. NOV. 3 1968 Chicago Coliseum
Chicago, IL

Back Door Man
When the Music's Over
Break on Through
Tell All the People

Love Me Two Times
Celebration of the Lizard (complete version) »
Light My Fire

Unlike the Door's rowdy appearance here in May, this performance is restrained to the point of being hypnotic. From the outset, it is clear that the band is in a solemn and pensive mood, and the audience responds accordingly. Although Morrison is unusually subdued and experiences some obvious difficulty remaining on key, his vocals are remarkably graphic and the rendition of "Celebration of the Lizard" lends a sense of foreboding to the concert. The band is in superb form, dramatically emphasizing Jim's poetry, and concludes the show with a rather airy version of "Light My Fire," which is in sharp contrast to the hysteria at the end of their preceding appearance at the Coliseum.

🦎 Note: The exact sequence of "Break on Through" and "Tell All the People" in the set is uncertain.

🕺 Also performing: Holocaust

👤 One show at 3:30 p.m.

🎭 Promotion: Triangle Theatrical Productions & Franklin Fried Presents

THU. NOV. 7 1968 Arizona State Fair
Veterans Memorial Coliseum
Phoenix, AZ

Tell All the People (opening song)
When the Music's Over
Light My Fire
The Unknown Soldier (finale)

This one-hour performance is disrupted from the start by multiple equipment failures. Jim Morrison fills in the intervals by expressing his fundamental distrust of the evolving political climate in the country. Richard Nixon has just been elected to his first term in office and Morrison bitterly declares that, "We have a new president and he has not made any mistakes . . . yet. If he does, we will get him! [loud cheering] We are not going to stand for four more years of this bullshit!"

The interruptions created by the technical glitches, combined with Jim's political slurs and his invitations for people to get up out of their seats, inspire an estimated five hundred fans to rush the stage toward the end of the concert. Morrison urges the crowd to stand up and to clap their hands near the end of "Light My Fire," then someone launches a handful of sparklers onto the stage as the balconies empty onto the already congested floor. One of the stagehands rushes onto the platform and douses the sparklers with a fire extinguisher. As the Doors conclude their performance with the "The Unknown Soldier," the crowd pelts the stage with clothing, and Jim mischievously hurls most of it back at them. Before the song is over, the power has been briefly turned off and the coliseum lights brought up. The Doors finish "The Unknown Soldier" and depart the stage, leaving a large milling crowd of young people who, despite a few shoving matches, peacefully make their way toward the exits.

While some reports state that the crowd is generally orderly and composed, others describe the audience as unruly and difficult to disperse. There are a few arrests for disorderly conduct (most for loud and vulgar language), and seven people are admitted to the local hospital with minor injuries (mostly from altercations with police when they tried to rush the stage). Afterward, the captain of the Arizona Highway Patrol says Morrison was "right on the brink" of being arrested several

> "We have a new president and he has not made any mistakes ... yet. If he does, we will get him! [loud cheering] We are not going to stand for four more years of this bullshit!"

times for obscene language and instigated the evening's major difficulties when he encouraged people to leave their seats, thereby disregarding police orders.

The Doors are repeatedly accused of inciting near-riot situations, and the local media exaggerate the incident considerably. The actual scenario seems to have been that the crowd is fairly compliant. However, the Doors are condemned by coliseum executives as being vulgar and obscene and the band is permanently barred from future appearances there. The executive director of the fairgrounds, Wes Statton, promises that "the Doors will never be booked into this Coliseum again. Their conduct before those kids was unprofessional, common and embarrassing." In addition, the Doors face several indictments stemming from their alleged unlawful misconduct, all of which are ultimately dismissed. Nevertheless, they never perform in Arizona again.

A few weeks later, this declaration of "persona non grata" is also bestowed upon the Fraternity of Man, after their appearance (opening for the Crazy World of Arthur Brown and Genesis) is deemed obscene.

The Arizona State Fair runs from November 1 through 8, and opening night features comedian Pat Paulsen and the First Edition. Other performers during the eight-day event include Diana Ross and the Supremes, Jim Nabors, Bobby Goldsboro and the King Sisters.

- Also performing: Albert King; Sweetwater; possibly Sunshine Company and Hamilton Street Car
- Promotion: Scenic Sounds/Richard Linnell
- Set-list incomplete
- Capacity: 17,000; attendance: 9,600

FRI. NOV. 8 1968 Dane County Memorial Coliseum
Madison, WI

Back Door Man (opening song)
When the Music's Over
Crystal Ship
Light My Fire
Celebration of the Lizard (finale)

The Doors put on a captivating show in Madison despite the fact that the coliseum is only half sold out. They open the show just before 10:00 p.m. with an extended version of "Back Door Man," into which Morrison inserts some spontaneous prose. The band's emphasis on intense dynamics is not lost on the crowd, many of whom spend the evening getting chased out of the aisles and back to their seats in the more distant sections of the venue. Morrison is in an irritable mood tonight, and reportedly demolishes his microphone during the finale of "Light My Fire." However, the mike (or its replacement) seems to be working fine when the band reappears after a cigarette break for an encore presentation of "Celebration of the Lizard." That piece always seems to bring about an unanticipated response from the audience, and tonight's crowd is no different. After its conclusion, they sit entranced, mutely staring at a vacant stage.

- Set-list incomplete
- Also performing: Midwest Hydraulic Company
- Capacity: circa 10,000

SAT. NOV. 9 1968 Kiel Auditorium
St. Louis, MO

The Doors' performance in St. Louis is a moderately good one, despite the sense that neither Morrison nor Krieger have their hearts in it. An uncharacteristically shy Morrison avoids any unnecessary dialogue, dedicating himself rather more to consuming a prodigious quantity of beer while onstage.

A curious preconcert promo of the show in the *St. Louis Post* says: "The Doors, who are guaranteed to do something outrageous, will be at Kiel Nov. 9. After the performance, lead singer Jim Morrison is expected to beat up Snow White and the Seven Dwarfs (*sic*)." (Harper Barnes, "New album by Bill Cosby," *St. Louis Post*, Nov. 1, 1968)

SUN. NOV. 10 1968 Minneapolis Concert Hall
Minneapolis, MN

Soul Kitchen
Break on Through
When the Music's Over
  [introduction for Tony Glover]
Back Door Man* »
  (Tony Glover's Blues Jam #1)* »
  "Next One Comin' Down the Line"* »
Back Door Man* »
Little Red Rooster*
Wild Child* »
Money*

Love Me Two Times* »
  (Tony Glover's Blues Jam #2)* »
  "Love My Girl, All Night Long"* »
  "I Hate to End My Song"* »
Mystery Train* »
Love Me Two Times
Light My Fire »
  Summertime (instrumental) »
  Eleanor Rigby (instrumental) »
Light My Fire

Local author and harmonica player extraordinaire Tony Glover is invited to perform onstage with the Doors for a significant portion of the show. Glover was one of the founding members of the Koerner, Glover and Ray blues group (also produced by Paul Rothchild for Elektra Records), which was held in high regard by other musicians such as Janis Joplin.

The show opens with a lengthy overture to "Soul Kitchen" until Jim eventually strolls onstage and says, "Well, let me get a good look at you!" The prolonged opening song expands even further to include an intriguing jam in the middle.

During "Break on Through," Manzarek provides an instrumental passage that gives the song a decidedly different texture. Morrison intentionally garbles his vocals at the beginning of "When the Music's Over," and then unexpectedly shifts into a gruff articulation where he clearly enunciates every syllable. Immediately following his lyrics "Ear down to the ground," he begins laughing uncontrollably. His comedic spirit takes hold of the situation and he begins a long improvised succession of grunts and laughter that keeps the audience in stitches. Shifting gears again, he breaks the humor when he thunders out "We want it now!" in an anguished scream.

After a short delay, Morrison introduces Tony Glover and the band performs a lengthy version of "Back Door Man." During the song, Glover delivers an expansive solo, which is followed by some off-the-cuff lyrics by Jim centered around the stanza "Little girl, you're lookin' fine. Next one comin' down the line. . . ." After reciting some explicitly obscene lyrics, Morrison begins laughing again before returning the improvisation into "Back Door Man."

Introducing the next tune, Jim announces, "This is an old blues song! Howlin' Wolf wrote it, I think. Oh! Muddy Waters wrote it, I think!" Robby Krieger then leads off "Little Red Rooster" with some scorching slide guitar. Again Morrison brings peals of laughter from the audience when, after the lines "Dogs begin to bark, hounds begin to howl," he begins to bark and howl with an uncanny imitation of a lonesome hound wandering the back hills.

During the interval before the next song, one member of the audience takes the opportunity to shout "Fuck you!" Ever quick on his feet, Jim retorts, "This is a democracy, you first! Ha! Democratic sex . . . you did it to each other!"

Tony Glover continues onstage with the Doors through the next number where they merge "Wild Child" into "Money," and finishes his appearance with an expansive rendition of "Love Me Two Times." Glover again vaults into an outstanding harmonica instrumental, followed by Jim's tightly paced lyrical improvisations, which conclude with "Mystery Train" set to the beat of "Love Me Two Times."

The Doors' finale of "Light My Fire" includes distinct instrumental variations on "Summertime" during Manzarek's solo and "Eleanor Rigby" during Krieger's. Overall, it is a night of sparse and succinct emphasis on the blues interspersed with good-natured humor from Jim Morrison.

Elektra Sound Studios
Hollywood, CA

After rehearsing their new material, the Doors enter the studio with producer Paul Rothchild and begin recording *The Soft Parade*. For this album, they want to combine their hard rock sound with an orchestral ambience. During these sessions, Beatle George Harrison visits them and remarks that the session bears a remarkable resemblance to the complexity required for the *Sergeant Pepper* recordings.

WED. DEC. 4 1968 Smothers Brothers Comedy Hour
CBS Television City, Los Angeles, CA

Wild Child
Touch Me (with Curtis Amy and the Smothers Bothers Orchestra)

This is the probable recording date for the Doors' only appearance on the Smothers Brothers' television show. They perform two of their recently completed songs. During "Touch Me," they are accompanied by saxophonist Curtis Amy and the Smothers Brothers Orchestra.

Robby Krieger is sporting an unmistakable black eye during the performance. When asked about it afterward, Krieger jokes that Morrison punched him out, then later states that he walked into a door. Most recently (in the Doors laser disc), he reveals that he and Morrison had been accosted by some rednecks, and while Jim got away relatively unscathed, Robby took a rather severe blow to the face.

The *Smothers Brothers Comedy Hour* (CBS) is a phenomenally successful show designed as an alternative to the standard variety shows of the time. It is fueled by Tom and Dick Smotherses' irreverent style of social and political satire, which brazenly assaulted every contemporary "establishment" taboo through a very cleverly designed maze of hip double-talk and metaphor. Their charming, seemingly innocuous delivery keeps the "Program Practices" censorship department on red alert from their first broadcast in February 1967 until their cancellation. One of the highlights of each show is comedian Pat Paulsen's brilliant deadpan sardonic commentary, which targets relevant topics of the day and delights the more precocious audiences while going right over the heads of the more conservative viewers.

On March 9, 1969, CBS cancels the evening's broadcast over a dispute on the inclusion of Joan Baez's introduction to "Green, Green Grass of Home," featuring a dedication to husband David Harris, who has been sentenced to three years in prison for draft resistance. That program is ultimately broadcast on March 30, but the uneasy animosity between the network and the hosts continue despite the show's success. CBS finally cancels the show on June 8.

- Note: The broadcast date of this performance is December 15.
- Note: The delay between recording and broadcast for performances on the *Smothers Brothers* was typically about ten days.

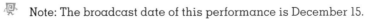

SAT. DEC. 14 1968 L.A. Forum
Inglewood, CA

Tell All the People
Love Me Two Times
Who Scared You
Spanish Caravan
Crystal Ship

Wild Child
Touch Me
Light My Fire
("What are you all doing here!?" exchange)
Celebration of the Lizard (complete version)

To perform selections from *The Soft Parade,* the Doors incorporate a string sextet and brass ensemble into their stage show.

After Sweetwater's half-hour set, Jerry Lee Lewis performs a set of straight-ahead country music and the impatient audience treats him quite crudely. (Although he does include "Great Balls of Fire" as his second number, and concludes with "Whole Lotta Shakin'," the crowd's booing prompts him to ferociously counter with, "I don't care if you all get heart attacks!")

The Doors open quietly with their new "Tell All the People" and move smoothly into "Love Me Two Times." The show seems pretty sedate until Morrison lets go with a series of grunts, pops, and groans in the midsection of that song. Next, their version of "Who Scared You" is long and rather disjointed, receiving minimal applause. This leads into a fairly routine "Spanish Caravan," and then a fine "Crystal Ship," where Manzarek takes a memorable, beautiful lead. While "Touch Me" is augmented with strings, it is a surprisingly lackluster performance.

It is at this point that the impatient crowd begins intensifying their cries of "Light My Fire" and even "Do something!" This is not a bad night for the Doors, but a significant portion of the music is so new it will not appear on an album for six months, and much of it is rather quiet compared to previous Doors' shows.

The incessant clamoring for "Light My Fire" makes the audience seem harshly unsympathetic to anything else the band want to introduce. The attitude of these ever-increasing "top 40" fanatics who demand nothing but the hits will contribute significantly to the band's disgust with the way rock 'n' roll is—or isn't—developing. The Doors have observed a change in the audience as their music became more popular. Their apprehensions will peak within a few months when they record the spontaneous "Rock Is Dead" session and Jim Morrison accosts the audience at Miami's Dinner Key Auditorium.

Next comes the piece everyone has been calling for, and it is a showstopper. This version of "Light My Fire" is terrific, as evidenced by the audience breaking into spontaneous applause no less than four times during its performance. Sometime during the song, someone launches a large handful of sparklers onto the main floor, igniting great commotion as many others follow by raising lit matches over their heads. The police became visibly distressed at these events.

After the conclusion of "Light My Fire," there is a long pause before Morrison sits down cross-legged on the stage and begins to ask the audience what they *really* want. Although he seems relaxed, there is a mocking and confrontational tone in his voice as he suggests that the band could play music all night long, but that what the audience really wants is "something different, something more." He then leads the band into their "Celebration of the Lizard," incorporating lyrics that are quite different from the version finally released on the live album. The audience reaction is mixed. Some seem interested in the piece, others bored. A few aggravated patrons even bark out some obscenities during the first portion of the song.

As tonight's rendition of "Celebration of the Lizard" draws to a conclusion, each of the band members leaves the stage individually. First John Densmore inconspicuously strolls off, then Robby Krieger unplugs his guitar and follows. Finally Ray Manzarek leaves, with Morrison alone onstage as he quietly recites the final poetic verses of the composition and then solemnly walks off the stage. The effect is transcendent. As opposed to the usual thunderous applause exhibited at the end of the show, the somewhat stunned audience of over 18,000 send out a brief ripple of quiet acknowledgment, and then stare mutely before leaving the venue in near silence.

Cash Box describes the concluding song of the night: "A feeling of indescribable tension filled the Forum as the music stopped and the poetry began. 'Is everybody in? The ceremony is about to begin,' said Morrison, crouching with microphone in hand in front of the audience. The crowd squirmed, fidgeted, and started shouting obscenities. They wanted Morrison to sing, not to recite. He realized what they were waiting for, and in a mocking voice still wallowing in his own glow, proceeded to recite more poetry." ("Talent On Stage," *Cash Box,* Dec. 28, 1968)

Also performing: Jerry Lee Lewis; Sweetwater; Tzon Yen Luie [who plays the Chinese stringed instruments the Pi pa and the chin]

Promotion: Scenic Sounds/Richard Linnell

Art: Bob Masse

Capacity: 18,679

SAT. DEC. 15 1968 Smothers Brothers Comedy Hour
Los Angeles, CA

This is the broadcast date of the December 4 recording.

The Doors
on the road
1969

FRI. JAN. 24 1969 Madison Square Garden
New York, NY

Touch Me

The Soft Parade

Tell All the People

Love Me Two Times

Who Scared You

Spanish Caravan

Wild Child

Light My Fire

Back Door Man

The Devil Is a Woman

Five to One

When the Music's Over

ONE PERF. ONLY
FRI. JAN. 24
at 8:30 P.M.

THE doors

Also THE STAPLE SINGERS
PRICES: $6.50, 6.00, 5.00, 4.00 MAIL ORDERS ACCEPTED
Tickets now on sale at Madison Square Garden Box Office
MADISON SQUARE GARDEN
PENNSYLVANIA PLAZA, 31st to 33rd STS., 7th to 8th AVES.

The Doors give one performance at 8:30 p.m. to a sell-out crowd. The esteemed bass player Harvey Brooks and a small orchestra appear with the band.

The colossal Madison Square Garden, with a seating capacity of twenty thousand, was at that time an exceptionally difficult venue to perform in. It featured a revolving stage, which aggravated the Garden's already horrendous acoustics.* The Doors performance suffers despite Vince Treanor and the equipment crew's efforts to dampen the hall's massive reverberations.

Regardless of these problems, this show is a resounding success. The Doors put on a fabulous performance, and Morrison's presence is electric. The stage is awash in a constant deluge of instamatic flashes that give the whole show a bizarre strobelike effect. The Doors exit the stage in a deafening roar of appreciation from their hard-core New York following.

Describing the event, *Cash Box* elaborates: "As matters turned out, none were disappointed at the show. It may well have been the rapport which uplifted the quality of this show, or the electricity that is created between a worshiping, yet contained, audience and its object of affection. In any case, the crowd was Morrison's—to an extreme that called for special police protection; and, in return, he was theirs." ("Talent On Stage," *Cash Box*, Feb. 8, 1969)

New York Times critic Mike Jahn comments: "It was hard to hear the lyrics, and a large measure of the Doors' value is based on those lyrics. To many in the audience, the performers were a speck in the distance, and this was unfortunate since much of the group's popularity is based on the onstage theatrics of Jim Morrison. Few groups match their ability to make rock music sound eerie and magical. Few lyricists can match Morrison's ability to create effective, often terrifying, images. As it turned out, the Doors were good despite the shortcomings of the arena." (Mike Jahn, *New York Times*, Jan. 25, 1969)

According to *Variety*: "The Doors made a triumphant return to New York Friday night after many months in absentia. The Doors, performing with an orchestra and led by Jim Morrison, one of the major personalities in rockdom, remain one of the more bizarre and theatrical turns in the idiom. Some of the material was familiar, but crisply executed." (Bent, "The Doors," *Variety*, Jan. 29, 1969)

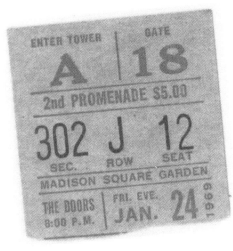

A few months after this show, the Felt Forum, which was a smaller venue with a seating capacity of four thousand located in the Madison Square Garden complex, underwent extensive restorations by multimedia designer Pablo. When the Doors appeared in New York in January 1970, they decided to perform at the more acoustically sound Felt Forum.

Note: Harvey Brooks, one of the rare people to have performed with the Doors for an entire show, had worked with Bob Dylan on the "Like a Rolling Stone" sessions and was briefly a member of Dylan's first official touring band along with Robbie Robertson, Levon Helm and Al Kooper. He went on to become one of the founding members of the Fabulous Rhinestones, was a major player in the legendary 1970s Shaboo scene in southern New England, and toured extensively with the "Rock 'N' Soul Revue," which also featured John Sebastian and members of the Rascals.

Note: When the legendary Blind Faith performed there six months later, the acoustics were so abominable that large portions of the audience could barley discern what was being played. Frustrated and disappointed fans finally stormed the stage at the conclusion of the show.

Also performing: The Staple Singers

Lighting: Chip Monck

Capacity: 20,000

FRI. FEB. 14 1969 San Diego International Sports Arena
San Diego, CA

The Doors are tentatively scheduled to perform here with the Iron Butterfly, but the show never takes place.

TUE. FEB. 25 1969 Sunset Sound Recorders
Hollywood, CA
"Rock Is Dead" Session

When I Was Back in Seminary School #1
When I Was Back in Seminary School #2 »
Whiskey, Mystics & Men (with musical accompaniment)
Love Me Tender
Rock Is Dead (Pt. 1)
Me and the Devil (The Devil Is a Woman)
Rock Is Dead (Pt. 2) ("Are You Ready?!") »
  "Listen, I don't want to hear no talk about revolution . . ." »
  "We're Gonna Have a Good Time! Let's Roll!"
  "I'm Talkin' about the Death of Rock 'n' Roll" »
  "Rock and Roll Woman" »
  "Baby, Love Me" ("The Queen of the Magazine") (slow blues)
Pipeline
Rock Me (improvisation) »
Mystery Train »
When I Got Home
Rock Is Dead »
My Eyes Have Seen You (jam) »
Rock Is Dead! (conclusion)

It is during the recording sessions for *The Soft Parade* that the Doors spontaneously record this commemoration to the history of rock 'n' roll. After taking a break for dinner at a local Mexican restaurant, the band returns to the studio and whimsically begins to improvise on a succession of blues numbers. Within half an hour, the impromptu parody begins to develop into a showcase of rock classics. At this point, the master recording is interrupted by the necessity to change reels, and a significant portion of the unanticipated session is lost before a new reel is prepared. The engineers succeed in capturing more than half of the session, and what is captured on tape is a fascinating montage of musical styles underscored by Jim Morrison's increasing disenchantment.

While the Doors maintain that "Rock Is Dead" will not be released because an integral section has not been recorded, subsequent reexamination of the reels' contents have again opened up the possibility that choice segments of the acclaimed jam session might be made available in the future.

It is during these *Soft Parade* sessions at Sunset Sound that the Doors also record a rendition of "Albinoni's Adagio in G minor" with an entire orchestra.

⚑ The Albinoni's "Adagio in G Minor" is not from this date, but is from the sessions around this time period. The Doors recorded "Adagio" with a full orchestra in the studio.

⚑ The "Roadhouse Blues Interlude" often appears at the start of recordings of this session but is actually from sessions for *Morrison Hotel*. The harmonica in the background certainly sounds like John Sebastian.

> After taking a break for dinner at a local Mexican restaurant, the band returns to the studio and whimsically begins to improvise on a succession of blues numbers.

FRI. FEB. 28 1969 Bovard Auditorium
UCLA, Los Angeles, CA

Throughout the week prior to the Doors' Miami show, Jim Morrison religiously attends performances by the Living Theater at the University of Southern California. At this time, the theater ensemble, led by Julian Beck, concentrates on four different productions, of which the tour de force is *Paradise Now*. *Paradise Now* is conceived as a confrontational, street-wise variation on guerrilla theater. The performance frequently runs in excess of three hours, systematically and dynamically challenging all boundaries, restrictions, moral codes, laws and regulations. The similarities in perspective between Morrison and the theater group encourage Jim to step up his own intransigent performances.

The Living Theater, established in New York's East Village, was conceived by Julian Beck and Judith Malina and began its succession of dramatic live performances in 1951. It possesses the distinction of being the oldest "avant-garde repertory acting company" in New York. Their main theater was located at 530 Sixth Avenue until an audit by the IRS in October of 1963 seized the theater and the group of performance artists relocated in Europe as a nomadic tribe. They remained there until their triumphant return at the end of the decade when they present the performances that Jim Morrison finds so exhilarating just prior to the Doors' Miami fiasco. In an early manifesto from the Living Theater quoted in the *Greenwich Village Guide*, the Becks stated that "The theater is love, drama, ritual, poetry, prose, reality. It is a place of intense experience, a thing in itself; it is a place where the spectator must participate by feeling and comprehending. It must be more than an entertainment. It is as terrifying and as amusing, as painful and as pleasurable as life is. It is a place in which one's senses are keenest. Everything that occurs is deeply aimed. The theater is not an imitation of life. It is life itself. . . ." This might well be a description of a Doors' concert.

The Living Theaters performances this week are as follows:

Monday	Feb. 24	*Mysteries and Smaller Pieces*
Tuesday	Feb. 25	*Frankenstein*
Thursday	Feb. 27	*Antigone*
Friday	Feb. 28	*Paradise Now*

> The theater is love, drama, ritual, poetry, prose, reality ... as terrifying and as amusing, as painful and as pleasurable as life is.

Break on Through Jam »
  "I ain't talkin' about no revolution #1" »
Back Door Man »
  "Hey listen, I'm lonely" »
Five to One »
  "You're all a bunch of f-kin' idiots" »
Five to One
  "I'm not talkin' about no revolution #2"
Touch Me (abrupt halt)
Love Me Two Times (crooned in a humorous blues style)
When the Music's Over »
  "I used to think the whole thing was a big joke" »
Away in India »
  (dialogue with woman in audience) »
  "There are no rules, no laws" »
  "I was born here in this state" »
When the Music's Over
Wake Up! »
Light My Fire »
  (Jim is given a lamb to hold while still onstage)* »
  "I want to see some action out there" »
  "No Limits, no laws!"
  (Promoter: "I don't want you to get hurt!")
  "We're not going to leave until we all get our rocks off!"
  (Jim Morrison is thrown into the audience and the performance ends in commotion)

This is the infamous Miami performance, which results in a warrant for Jim Morrison's arrest and subsequent indictments for multiple offenses. The progression of events begins when the *Miami Herald* published two articles (by staff writer Larry Mahoney) entitled "Rock group fails to stir a riot" and "Public reacts to rock show." The articles indignantly maintains that Morrison had exposed himself and feigned masturbation. The controversy also fuels some fierce debate on Miami's talk radio station WKAT. Legal proceedings begin on March 5, with twenty-year-old Robert Jennings as legal complainant against Morrison. The accusations are as follows:

1) lewd and lascivious behavior (felony)
2) indecent exposure (misdemeanor)
3) open profanity (misdemeanor)
4) drunkenness (misdemeanor)

The immediate result of these accusations is that the Doors lose their entire spring tour and are temporarily banned from performing in nearly every venue across the country. In addition, Jim Morrison is now confronted with the likelihood of an arduous trial in which a conviction could conceivably entail a prison term at Rainford Prison, one of the most brutal penitentiaries in the country.

Over the years, there have been innumerable accounts of this performance and the subsequent trial. Jim Morrison was faced with the felony arraignment of "lewd and lascivious behavior," in addition to several misdemeanors, all of which kindled the unsubstantiated accusation that he had exposed himself during the performance. Sexual misconduct, alleged or otherwise, has always been a convenient method of defaming and discrediting prominent personalities. Political

The articles indignantly maintains that Morrison had exposed himself and feigned masturbation

figures and media celebrities are especially vulnerable to the perceived scandals that feed the voracious appetite of the nation's tabloid industry. Needless to say, Morrison found such sleazy exploitations particularly loathsome.

Several factors contribute to the Miami debacle. The Doors' formerly sophisticated audiences have been replaced by teenyboppers who want only to hear their hit songs and who become noticeably irritated at Jim's poetic aspirations. In addition, Morrison has begun actively exploring the potential of confrontational theater, such as he had recently witnessed in the Living Theater's productions. The Doors' mystique has always centered around their quest into cryptic enigmas of existence, and Morrison urgently feels that the larger venues in which they now work demand an improved dramatic method through which to convey their ideas.

By the time Morrison hits the stage in Miami, he is exasperated. He has left LA following a bitter argument with girlfriend Pamela Courson and has consumed considerable amounts of alcohol while on the flight. In addition to grimly anticipating the incessant demands for "Light My Fire," Jim is infuriated to learn upon his arrival that the promoters have deceived the band by drastically overselling the venue after removing the seating and have then tried to defraud them by insisting that such is not the case. Jim strides out onstage and begins mercilessly assaulting the audience with the accusation that they are nothing but "a bunch of slaves!" He then challenges them to throw off their chains and reject all the mindless regulations forced upon them. He declares that "There are no limits, no laws!" When Morrison later reflects in *Rolling Stone* on the concert he says, "I think that was the culmination, in a way, of our mass performing career. Subconsciously, I think I was trying to get across in that concert—I was trying to reduce it to absurdity, and it worked too well." (Ben Fong-Torres, "Jim Morrison's got the blues," *Rolling Stone*, Mar. 4, 1971; used with permission: © Straight Arrow Publishers, Inc. 1996)

During the resulting trial, no hard evidence ever substantiates the criminal accusations, and most charges are eventually dropped. Even the promoter, Ken Collier, who is understandably upset with the whole situation, exclaims to Miami's *Daily Planet:* "I was right there and I didn't see anything like that happen!" The dilemma urgently calls for a drastic self-reappraisal for everyone concerned. The Doors themselves begin to venture back into their musical heritage of blues and jazz.

The Doors find themselves at the forefront of fierce controversy, with Jim Morrison held up as a primary example of the alarming deterioration of values sweeping the country. Although Miami aspires to be a cosmopolitan city, the Doors' performance that night would probably not have generated such repercussions in New York or Los Angeles. Miami was unquestionably the wrong place at the wrong time.

The climate of this trial closely parallels comedian Lenny Bruce's predicament a few years earlier, invoking a déjà vu experience for anyone acquainted with Bruce's New York arrests in March and April of 1964. During the testimony of police officers who had been in attendance, Bruce is repeatedly accused of having made masturbatory gestures during his act at the Cafe Au Go Go, while no one else at the performances claimed to have seen anything of the kind. Despite the numerous witnesses who denied having seen any of the obscene gestures referred to, the court leaned heavily on the police's testimony and ultimately found Bruce guilty.

Although Jim Morrison's arrest in Florida receives the most publicity, Janis Joplin is also arrested onstage in Tampa on November 15 for using "vulgar and indecent language," Allen Ginsberg's poetry reading at Miami's Marine Stadium on December 22 is abruptly terminated when a city manager decides it includes too many profanities, and Arthur Brown (The Crazy World of Arthur Brown—"Fire") is arrested in Fort Lauderdale in April for "disturbing the peace and inciting a riot" when he practices his performance in a motel room prior to a show and attracts a large gathering of vacationers.

Meanwhile in Massachusetts, Country Joe (of Country Joe and the Fish) has a warrant issued for his arrest in March as well, citing him as a "lewd, lascivious and wanton person in speech and behavior" after he leads the audience in the "Fish" cheer in Worcester. Even John Lennon has over 22,000 copies of his *Two Virgins* album seized in Elizabeth, New Jersey, on January 24, with an ultimatum issued to dealers: "Don't sell or else!" And finally, Lou Reed has the privilege of joining the "obscenity" ranks several years later when he is arrested after a perfor-

I was trying to reduce it to absurdity, and it worked too well.

mance at the Miami Beach Convention Hall on June 1, 1973. Apparently the local police were still being directed to act on any offensive lyrics in songs.

The ensuing controversies engulf Florida in tumultuous debates and create considerable embarrassment as Miami tries to salvage its reputation as a city that is not antagonistic to the arts.

🎵 Promotion: Thee Image—Ken and Jim Collier

MAR. 1 1969 Transcript, Miami Dinner Key Auditorium

The following is an unedited transcript of this performance as recorded by a member of the audience. The reference recording opens with a brief series of harmonica notes from Jim Morrison. Morrison then engages in a dialogue with the audience that apparently was already in progress.

Yeah! Now looky here!

I ain't talking about no revolution.

And I'm not talking about no demonstration.

I'm talkin' about having a good time.

I'm talkin' about having a good time this summer.

Now, you all come out to LA.

You all get out there.

We're gonna lie down there in the sand and rub our toes in the ocean and we're gonna have a good time.

Are you ready [eight times]?!

Are, ahh, ahh, ahh, whew, whew, whew, whew. . . .

[Music selection begins: "Back Door Man"]

Fuck! Louder! Come on band, get it louder, come on! Yeah baby! Louder! Yeah! Yeah!

[Morrison proceeds with the first two stanzas of "Back Door Man" and Krieger takes his lead.]

Yeah, hey! Yeah, hey! Suck me, baby. You gotta. . . . [Morrison howls] Hey softer, baby. Get it way down. Softer, sweetheart. Get it way down low. Soft [five times]. Sock it to me. Come on softer.

Hey listen, I'm lonely! I need some love, you all. Come on. I need some good time lovin' sweetheart. Love me! Come on!

I can't . . . I can't take it without no good love. Love, I want some lova, lova, lova, lova love me sweet. Come on.

Ain't nobody gonna love my ass! Come on! [audience laughter]

I need you. There's so many of you out there. Nobody's gonna love me sweetheart, come on. I need it [three times]. I need ya, need ya [six times]! Huh! All right!

Hey! There's a bunch of people way back there that I didn't even notice!

Hey, how about 50 or 60 of you people come up here and love my ass? Come on! [audience laughter, cheers and whistles] Yeah! I love ya! Come on!

Yeah, la la la la [five times].

[Audience member: "Let it all hang out!"]

Nobody gonna come up here and love me huh? Come on!

[Music selection begins: "Five to One"]

All right for you baby. That's too bad. I'll get somebody else, yeah!

[Morrison recites the first two stanzas from "Five to One" with a noticeable slur and Krieger takes his lead. Morrison begins screaming and berating the audience.]

You're all a bunch of fuckin' idiots!!! [loud audience applause and laughter]

Lettin' people tell you what you're gonna do! Lettin' people push you around!

How long do you think it's gonna last?!

How long are you gonna let it go on?!

How long are you gonna let them push you around?

How long??

Maybe you like it.

Maybe you like being pushed around!

Maybe you love it!

Maybe you love getting your face stuck in the shit! Come on!

[Morrison pauses briefly and the commotion in audience becomes increasingly noticeable.]

Maybe you love getting pushed around.

You love it, don't ya! You love it!

You're all a bunch of slaves. Bunch of slaves.

You're all a bunch of slaves! Letting everybody push you around.

What you you gonna do about it [five times] ?!!!

What are you gonna do [three times]???

[Morrison returns to the lyrics of the song, "Your ballroom days . . ." and at the conclusion of the song, Jim leaps in with:]

Hey, I'm not talkin' about no revolution.

I'm not talkin' about no demonstration.

I'm not talkin' about getting out in the streets.

I'm talkin' about having some fun.

I'm talkin' about dancing.

I'm talking about love your neighbor . . . 'til it hurts

I'm talkin' about grab your friend.

I'm talkin' about love

I'm talkin' about some love [three times]. Love [seven times].

Grab your [pause] fucking friend and love him! Come On! Yeah!

[The band begins with the opening notes to "Touch Me" and Morrison sings the first two lines, then abruptly brings it to a halt because the tempo is too fast.]

Hey, wait a minute! Wait a minute! Wait a minute! Hey, wait a minute, this is all fucked up! Now, wait a minute, wait a minute. Wait a minute. You blew it [three times]! Now, come on! Wait a minute. I'm not gonna go on.

[The band attempts to continue the song to no avail.]

Now wait a minute! I'm not gonna take this shit! I'm copping out. Now, wait a minute. Bullshit! [nervous laughter from the audience]

[The rest of the band stops playing as Manzarek fades the song out on the organ. After a brief pause, they try to begin the song again and that effort doesn't work either. They scrap "Touch Me" and decide to play "Love Me Two Times." Morrison humorously recites the song in a flat, lifeless, monotone vocal style, screwing up the final verse.]

[The Doors next perform "When the Music's Over" and Morrison quite intentionally slurs some of the words almost beyond recognition. Instead of the poetic midsection of the song, Jim begins another dialogue with the audience.]

Now listen, I used to think the whole thing was a big joke.

I used to think it was something to laugh about.

And then the last couple of nights I met some people who were doing something.

They're trying to change the world, and I want to get on the trip.

I wanna change the world.

Wanna change it. Yeah! Yeah! Change it!

The first thing we're gonna do is take over all the schools! [moderate audience applause]

After we take over all the schools, we're gonna take over all the . . . the . . . [sentence not completed]

[Morrison then begins singing "Away in India," which is followed by a brief instrumental passage. Following that, Morrison continues with the lyrics from "When the Music's Over" ("Before I sink . . .") until he starts to whisper to some people in the audience just before the climactic "We want the world" verse.]

Huh? What's that? What you say, baby? Say huh?

Say what? Say what [three times]? What's that? [audience yelling]

What's that, honey? Come on, tell me again. Aw, come on, I can't hear you. Now tell me what you say. [audience yelling]

"Do what to your what? [Portions of the audience begin booing.] Huh? I can't hear you.

Yeah, right!

[The band unsuccessfully attempts to initiate an uptempo rhythm to persuade Jim out of his diversions, but Morrison at this point just seems lost in his own orbit.]

I used to think the whole thing was a big joke. I used to think it was something to laugh about. And then the last couple of nights I met some people who were doing something. They're trying to change the world, and I want to get on the trip.

Guy says he's no animal. What are you? What's your name, man? I used to know someone who had that name. Has anybody out there, anybody out there got a cigarette?

Hey, I'm getting lonely up here, I need some love. [moderate laughter and applause]

Hey, I can't believe all those people sitting way over there, man. Why don't you all come down and get with us, man. Come on!

What are you, in the fifty-cent section or what? Come on! [loud audience laughter]

Come on down here, come on! Get closer man. We need some love! [pause] You're gonna stay way away. [pause]

You know, I was born here in this state, you know that? [audience applause]

Yeah, I was born right here in Melbourne, Florida, in 1943.

I think they call it Cape something or other now. I don't know what they call it.

Yeah, then I left for a little while and I came back and I went to a little junior college in St. Petersburg. You know where that is? And I left there and I went up to a little college in Tallahassee called F.S.U.

Then I got smart and I went out to a beautiful state called California. [audience cheering]

Went out to a little city named Los Angeles.

Now Listen! I'm not talkin' about no revolution!

And I'm not talkin' about no demonstration!

I'm talking about having fun!

I'm talking about dancing.

I want to see you people get up and dance.

I want to see you people dancing in the street this summer.

I want to see you have some fun.

I want to see you roam around.

I want to see you paint the town.

I want to see you wring it out.

I want to see you shout.

I want to see some fun. I want to see some fun from everyone.

We are together. We're together. We're together, baby. We're together.

[Morrison sings the words as hecklers curse from the audience.]

We want the same thing, don't we. We want the same thing.

We want the whole hog, don't we, baby?

We want the world and we want it . . . Now!

[The band returns to the song and proceeds with the instrumental passage following this section of the song. They then conclude the song without further digressions, although Morrison again intentionally slurs the words beyond recognition.]

[Jim Morrison then recites the "Wake Up!" section from "Celebration of the Lizard," which leads into "Light My Fire." During Manzarek's instrumental passage, Morrison encourages him with "Don't Stop!"]

[After Krieger's solo, Morrison begins talking to the audience again.]

I want to see some dancing. Yeah, I want to see some fun. I want to see some dancing.

There are no rules!

There are no laws!

Do whatever you want to do! Do it! All right!

[By this point, Jim has been handed a lamb onstage and he cradles the animal in his arms for a few minutes. Lewis Marvin, a member of Moonfire, has been travelling with the lamb as a icon reflecting his philosophies of vegetarianism and nonviolence.]

I'd fuck her but she's too young. [loud audience laughter]

Yeah! Now listen! Anybody that wants to come up here and join us and do some dancing and have some fun, just get on up here. Come on! Come on!

[The band proceeds into the final stanza of "Light My Fire" and they finish the song. During the applause, Morrison begins yelling at the audience.]

All right! All right! I want to see some action out there [five times].

I want to see you people come on up here and have some fun! Now come on, let's get on up here!

There are no rules! There are no laws! Do whatever you want to do! Do it! All right! ... I'd fuck her but she's too young.

No limits! No laws! Come on! Come on!

This is your show. Anything you want goes! Now, come on! Anything you want and let's do it! Let's do it! Let's do it!

[At this point, another person's voice (most likely promoter Ken Collier) announces to the audience "Someone's going to get hurt!" Morrison continues with:]

All right! We're not going to leave 'til we all gets our rocks off!"

[At this point, the reference recording runs out, but it is not far from the conclusion of the show, and probably just moments before Morrison is flipped off the stage by a karate expert. Jim then initiates a snake dance through the crowd, which is quickly joined by an extended line of participants, as the band winds down and leaves the stage. Morrison shortly thereafter breaks from the procession, only to swiftly reappear in the balcony quietly surveying the bedlam, and then departing for the dressing room.]

MARCH 5 WEDNESDAY — The Dade County Sheriff's Office, Dade County, FL

The case for "The State of Florida vs. James Douglas Morrison" is filed when Robert Jennings, a twenty-year-old clerk in the State Attorney's Office, acts as the complainant against Morrison with regard to the Miami performance.

The multitude of cancellations of Doors performances has a profound effect on the entire music industry. Auditorium directors, fearful of any repeat of the Miami situation, now insist on stricter regulations for all rock performances. Promoters are threatened with liabilities that had previously been considered unsuitable. Nevertheless, in the spring of 1969 the general consensus is that the repercussions of the Miami show will gradually fade into the background.

SUN. MAR. 9 1969 — Veterans Memorial Sports Coliseum — Jacksonville, FL — CANCELLED

Immediately following the Miami incident, Mayor Hans Tansler cancels the show. Though the Doors are not even scheduled to play Tampa, the city's mayor announces on WFLA-TV that he will not allow the band to play there. He also declares that his position reflects the consensus of the mayors of five of Florida's largest cities, who are presently discussing how to prevent questionable rock performers from ever appearing in Florida.

SUN. MAR. 16 1969 — The Los Angeles Image Publishes Dry Water

The Los Angeles Image magazine includes an excerpted edition of a poem by Jim Morrison's entitled "Dry Water."

MON. MAR. 17 1969 — The Electric Theatre — Pittsburgh, PA — CANCELLED

New proprietor Pat DiCesare is inundated with objections to the upcoming performance after having spent a considerable sum promoting it. As a new promoter, his reputation is at considerable risk, and the Doors' booking agency, Ashley Famous, releases him from the contract on March 12.

TUE. MAR. 18 1969 Philadelphia Spectrum
Philadelphia, PA

CANCELLED

Music Fair Enterprises unsuccessfully attempts to reschedule the March 19 cancellation at the Convention Center to this night at the Spectrum.

✻ Also scheduled to perform: Pacific Gas & Electric

WED. MAR. 19 1969 (1) Convention Center (Hall) Auditorium
Philadelphia, PA

CANCELLED

On advice of the city solicitor, executive director Harry Ferleger declines confirmation of either of the two Philadelphia contracts. The public relations director for promoters Music Fair Enterprises is led to believe that any application they present would be an "exercise in futility."

✻ Also scheduled to perform: Pacific Gas & Electric

WED. MAR. 19 1969 (2) Philadelphia Spectrum
Philadelphia, PA

CANCELLED

Promoter John Wanamaker's efforts to schedule the Doors for tonight at the Spectrum fail as well.

THU. MAR. 20 1969 Rhode Island Auditorium
Providence, RI

CANCELLED

FRI. MAR. 21 1969 Maple Leaf Gardens
Toronto, Ontario, Canada

CANCELLED

✻ Also scheduled to perform: Pacific Gas & Electric, who are rescheduled for a week at Toronto's Electric Circus instead

SAT. MAR. 22 1969 Pittsburgh Arena
Pittsburgh, PA

CANCELLED

SUN. MAR. 23 1969 Kent State University
Kent, OH (DU)

CANCELLED

Rally For Decency, Miami, FL

The outrage at the Doors' Miami show culminates in an immense "Rally for Decency," at the Orange Bowl. The rally is designed to elicit the endorsement of a predominately right-wing audience disturbed by what they perceive as an affront to their devout convictions regarding decency. Spearheaded by nineteen-year-old Mike Levisque, it also features Jackie Gleason, the Lettermen, Anita Bryant, Roslyn Kind, Kate Smith, and the Miami Drum and Bugle Corps. Radio station WIOD's Ken

Collier serves as an adviser to the undertaking, and Catholic Archbishop Coleman F. Carroll also lends his support. The rally runs into difficulties when their announcements herald that "longhairs and weird dressers" will be refused admittance, and the promoters are accused of unlawfully obstructing civil rights. President Richard M. Nixon dispatches a letter of congratulation and appreciation to the organizers four days after the rally.

On May 26, Mike Levisque helps organize another decency rally in Baltimore that erupts into a race riot when the living god James Brown fails to appear. It is described as the worst violence since the previous year's riots, with multiple knifings requiring hospitalization. Police fire shotguns into the air in an effort to quell the disturbance. Levisque continues to promote additional rallies in Columbus, Ohio, and a particularly controversial one in Enterprise, Alabama, featuring Governor George Wallace.

THE DOORS CONCERT CANCELLED
REFUNDS AVAILABLE AT
OLYMPIA BOX OFFICE
HUDSON'S AND GRINNELL'S
M. BELKIN

FRI. MAR. 28 1969 Olympia Stadium
Detroit, MI
CANCELLED

- Also scheduled to perform: Sky
- Promotion: Belkin/Gibbs Presents

SAT. MAR. 29 1969 Cleveland Public Auditorium
Cleveland, OH
CANCELLED

SUN. MAR. 30 1969 Cincinnati Music Hall
Cincinnati, OH
CANCELLED

On March 10, the Music Hall Association requests that Mayor Ruehlman announce that the necessary permits have been denied for the Doors' appearance at the Music Hall. Promoters Roger Abramson and Frank Wood III (aka WEBN-FM's Michael Xanadu) find themselves caught in the typical scenario of "falling dominoes" as Doors concerts are cancelled across the country.

MAR. 1969

Elektra Sound Recorders
Hollywood, CA

In That Year
When Radio Dark Night Existed . . .
Vast Radiant Beach
Moonshine Night
Frozen Moment by a Lake »
Bird of Prey (song)
Indians Scattered on Dawn's Highway
Under Waterfall (song)
Tell Them You Came (The Hitchhiker)
Why Does My Mind Circle Around You?
Winter Photography (song)
Whiskey, Mystics and Men (song)
Orange County Suite (song)
All Hail the American Night
And So I Say to You (aka Far Arden)
The Truth Is on His Chest »
Texas Radio and the Big Beat (#1)
He Was No General »

The Dark Los Angeles Evening »
In Conclusion Darling
The American Night (with piano)
My Name Is the Holy Shay
Adolf Hitler Is Still Alive
Hey Man, You Want Girls?
   A) To Come of Age
   B) Black Polished Chrome
   C) Latino (Chrome)
There's a Belief by the Children of Man
(Indian, Indian) What Did You Die For?
(I Am the) Woman in the Window (song)
She's Selling News in the Market »
They Haven't Invented Music Yet (aka Book Of Days) »
I Have a Vision of America
A One Armed Man »
Motel, Money, Murder, Madness
Earth, Air, Fire, Water
Discovery
Now Listen to This (Texas Radio and the Big Beat #2) »
Stoned Immaculate
And the Carnival Immediately Begins (Babylon Fading)
Thank You, Oh Lord (for the White Blind Light)

In March, Jim Morrison records an hour's worth of poetry at Elektra Sound Recorders with engineer John Haeny.* Jim combines a mixture of prose and melody throughout the session, recording such notable pieces as "Orange County Suite." Portions of this session are included on *An American Prayer*, which also consists of selections from a recording on December 8, 1970.

🀄   These titles were created by recognizing the first lines of the poems (unless they have been otherwise interpreted), an accepted literary means for defining the works of a deceased author. They are by no means intended to be the final titles to these pieces; that will be determined by the estate of Jim Morrison.

🀄   Note: Some sources suggest this session was actually at Sunset Sound Recorders.

✳   John Haeny had been appointed chief engineer for Elektra in February, and previously had been on the mixing staff at Hollywood's RCA Victor Studios.

MAR. 1969 Feast Of Friends Completed

Soundtrack:
Strange Days
Albinoni's "Adagio in G minor" (with voiceovers)
Wild Child
Albinoni's "Adagio in G Minor"
Moonlight Drive
   (Dialogue)
Five to One
Not to Touch the Earth
   (Dialogue)
Poetry
"Dahomey Dance" (Manzarek performs the John Coltrane piece on piano)
Robby Krieger on Guitar
"Ode to Friedrich Nietzsche" (Morrison performs this impromptu poetry piece on piano)
The End (from the Hollywood Bowl performance on July 5, 1968)
Credits (featuring concluding music: "Neptune, The Mystic" from Gustav Holst's "The Planets."

Feast of Friends is an interesting, almost avant garde, succession of events captured on film. It is an unusual and fascinating portrayal of the Doors on tour, featuring a strong emphasis on the personal side of the band in situations as diverse as a discussion of the war in Vietnam while riding on a subway, to Jim Morrison tending an injured audience member while backstage after the Singer Bowl riot in New York. Despite the positive reviews, the film is never officially released, although portions of it have subsequently been released in other videos. It is presented at several film festivals in 1969, as well as at numerous benefit screenings.

Selections from the stockpile of outtakes from the documentary have been utilized in later productions as well. Some of the most spectacular footage is featured in the "Roadhouse Blues" video from the "Dance on Fire" collection.

CREDITS:

1) Paul Ferrara: Director of Cinematography (Film and Design) Paul began with 16 mm black-and-white, then switched to color.
2) Babe Hill: Location Live Sound Recording (utilizing a portable Nagra reel-to-reel tape recorder).
3) Frank Lisciandro: Editor.

Author Jerry Hopkins describes the movie in a review in *Rolling Stone:* "Many filmed dramas and documentaries about rock have shown the clutching hands and ecstatic faces that confront the musician or singer, but no film before *Feast* has captured in so exciting a manner what actually takes place during a near-riot. Police and college-age guards ringed the edge of one concert stage shown and Morrison tried futilely to squeeze through them so he and the audience could see each other. Then the audience rebelled. They hurled themselves at Morrison, pulling the microphone chord, scrambling between cops' legs. The guards picked the kids up and bodily hurled them back. Finally the concert is stopped and Morrison is led away. Morrison has often said the film is an attempt to capture some of what they see in their travels. In an impressionistic and carefully paced filmic collage, this goal was achieved. *Feast of Friends* is a familiar statement nicely made, a pleasing way to spend 40 minutes." (Jerry Hopkins, "Doors' Movie is a Feast for Friends," *Rolling Stone,* July 12, 1969; used with permission: © Straight Arrow Publishers, Inc. 1996)

Jim Morrison commented on the production of the film later in the year, after interviewer Hank Zevallos asked him about the sailing scene's conclusion of the film: "The way that film was made was just a small crew following us around for about four months, through a lot of different concerts. They gathered all this footage together, and then the photographer and the editor got a rough cut while we were in Europe, and that was their idea. Yeah . . . because if it had ended on "The End," it would have been a little bit . . . left everybody a little bit too down, and that has a nice refreshing quality at the end." (Hank Zevallos, "Jim Morrison," *Poppin* magazine, 1969)

MARCH

Hwy (aka Hiway) Productions
Clear Thoughts Building, Los Angeles, CA

Jim Morrison establishes a company called HWY Productions with the intention of realizing several of his cinematic ambitions. He employs the technical crew from *Feast of Friends,* which includes Frank Lisciandro, Paul Ferrara, and Babe Hill. Their first project begins with the shooting of Jim's screenplay, *HWY,* outside Palm Springs, California, during Easter week. *HWY* is a condensed avant-garde film intended to be a predecessor to a full-length production that would expand on this original premise.

Morrison comments on the film's progress toward the end of the year: "Well, it's about a hitchhiker who—essentially it's just a movement from a state of nature gradually to city. I don't want to say too much about it now because I don't want to ruin the trip. But, it's a pretty good film. I had the idea for it, and I play the hitchhiker. I won't say that I directed the film, but I'm producing it and overseeing the whole production. The film created itself. We finished a version of it and I think what's going to happen is instead of ending up with a short film like 40 or 50 minutes, we're going to add to it, and make it longer. It's really interesting in its present form but we would like to get it seen by people and unless it's feature length, it's not going to be taken very seriously. We're going to have to shoot a lot more, and then edit all that." (Hank Zevallos, "Jim Morrison," *Poppin* magazine, 1969)

Jim Morrison later comments on the movie in an interview with Bob Chorush: "There's no story really. No real narrative. Except there's a hitchhiker who . . . We don't see it, but we later assume that he stole a car and he drives into the city and it just ends there. He checks into a motel and he goes out to a nightclub or something. It just kind of ends like that." (Bob Chorush interview, "The Lizard King reforms," *Los Angeles Free Press*, Jan. 15, 1971)

The FBI Investigates

APRIL
3
THURSDAY

Jim Morrison, accompanied by his lawyer Max Fink, turns himself in to the FBI in downtown Los Angeles to face charges stemming from the Miami Dinner Key Auditorium show on March 1. The FBI becomes involved with the case when a federal warrant is issued citing interstate flight to avoid prosecution.

FRI. APR. 4 1969 Dallas Memorial Auditorium
Dallas, TX

~~CANCELLED~~

The tentative contract with Concerts West is declined by the auditorium manager.

SAT. APR. 5 1969 Sam Houston Coliseum
Houston, TX

~~CANCELLED~~

Jim Morrison Released On $5,000 Bail

APRIL
4
FRIDAY

FRI. APR. 25 1969 Boston Garden
Boston, MA

~~CANCELLED~~

SAT. APR. 26 1969 Buffalo Memorial Auditorium
Buffalo, NY   ~~CANCELLED~~

SUN. APR. 27 1969 Onondaga Memorial Auditorium
Syracuse, NY

~~CANCELLED~~

MON. APR. 28 1969 PBS Studios
Critique Recording Sessions
New York, NY

Tell All the People
Alabama Song »
Back Door Man

Wishful, Sinful
Build Me a Woman
The Soft Parade
Light My Fire*

Over the course of two days, the bulk of the material for the *Critique* show is recorded at the PBS Studios. The first day is devoted to performing their music, and the second to interviewing.

※ "Light My Fire" was reportedly recorded as well but was not included in the broadcast

TUE. APR. 29 1969 PBS Studios
Critique Recording Sessions
New York, NY

The interview segment with Richard Goldstein for *Critique* is recorded. The panel discussion is recorded later, around May 13.

For additional details, see the broadcast information on June 25.

MAY 1 THURSDAY
Sacramento State College Gallery, Sacramento, CA

Jim Morrison, Michael McClure, and Dr. Wagner hold a poetry reading/performance at the gallery for one night beginning at 8:30 p.m.

SAT. MAY. 3 1969 Whisky A Go Go
West Hollywood, CA (DU)

Jim Morrison joins Eric Burdon and the Blues Image onstage for several songs. Eric Burdon was the renowned lead singer for the Animals who joined forces with Robbie Krieger in the early 1990s for some notable shows featuring several Doors songs.

Regarding Eric Burdon's relationship with Jim, a *Melody Maker* interviewer reports, "I had spent the previous day with Eric Burdon who is alive and unhappy and living in exile in L.A., but seems to have found a 'spiritual' companion in Jim. Eric has become a much loved 'local' as he would anywhere and I related to Jim how the owners of the Whisky, apparently afeared of Morrison in his more boisterous moods, would get Eric to sooth the savage beast. Eric described himself as feeling like 'the cow sent in to pacify the bull' on these occasions. But Morrison liked Burdon. 'I like anyone who will get drunk with me for the right reasons in the right way.'" ("Jim, the angel faced Rasputin," *Melody Maker*, May 2, 1970)

DU Note: Eric Burdon and the Blues Image performed at the Whisky from May 1 through 4. Morrison may have joined them on stage on May 4. (A review of the show on May 2 makes no mention of Morrison.)

Also performing: Tarantula

MON. MAY 19–THU. 22 1969 Whisky A Go Go
Hollywood, CA

Cancelled. The Doors originally intended to record a live album during these special shows at the Whisky. The dates were cancelled when they confirmed their appearance at the Aquarius Theater later in July. Albert Collins had been selected as the opening act.

🎤 Also scheduled to perform: Albert Collins

FRI. MAY. 30 1969 Cinematheque 16
Hollywood, CA

This is the first of two poetry readings and midnight film screening benefits for Norman Mailer's New York mayoralty campaign. Films included the Doors' *Feast of Friends* and Andy Warhol's *I, a Man*.

Presenting their poetry were Jim Morrison, Michael McClure, Tom Baker, Seymour Cassel, Michael C. Ford, Mary Waronov and Jamie Sanchez.

Jim Morrison reads the long version of "An American Prayer," and he is visibly nervous. Afterward, he is joined by Robby Krieger on guitar and they run through a repertoire of rhythm and blues songs including Elvis Presley's "I Will Never Be Untrue."

SAT. MAY. 31 1969 Cinematheque 16
Hollywood, CA

This is the second night of the poetry and film benefit for Norman Mailer's campaign. The films and poetry readings are again presented, this time with Jack Hirshman replacing Michael McClure.

Morrison once more contributes his long version of "An American Prayer" and is accompanied by Robby Krieger for some rhythm and blues standards.

Tonight's presentation is recorded, and the portion featuring Jim and Robby performing "I Will Never Be Untrue" is included in the 1978 album release of "An American Prayer."

FRI. JUN. 6–SUN. 8 1969 Cinematheque 16
Hollywood, CA

The Cinematheque presents the world premiere of *Feast of Friends*.

Other films include Ron Houge's *The Door*, *The Red Umbrella*, and Newsreel's *Chicago* (about the 1968 Democratic National Convention) and *Yippie* (about the Youth International Party).

Elektra Sound Recorders
Hollywood, CA

In early June, the Doors and Producer Paul Rothchild complete their fourth album, *The Soft Parade*, after nearly a year of preparation, recording, and mixing.

SUN. JUN. 8 1969 (2) Queen Elizabeth Theater
Vancouver, Canada
Eleventh Vancouver International Film Festival

Feast of Friends is presented at 9:30 p.m. along with *Jusqu'au Coeur* by Jean-Pierre Lefebvre.

FRI. JUN. 13 1969 Kiel Auditorium
St. Louis, MO ~~CANCELLED~~

Performances continue to be cancelled due to Miami.

☩ Also scheduled to perform: The Staple Singers

🐞 Promotion: Belkin Productions

SAT. JUN. 14 1969 Chicago Auditorium Theater
Chicago, IL

Early Show (7:30 P.M.)

When the Music's Over	Touch Me
My Eyes Have Seen You	The Soft Parade
Back Door Man	Light My Fire (1st encore)
Tell All the People	Maggie M'Gill (2nd encore)

Late Show (10:30 p.m.)

Roadhouse Blues	When the Music's Over
Ship of Fools	Light My Fire (encore)

These are the Doors' first scheduled performances after the cancellations following the Miami debacle. Promoters across the country are paying close attention, not only to watch for any disruptions but also to see if the shows will be a financial success after all of the negative publicity.

The Doors open their first set since Miami with a spellbinding version of "When the Music's Over," where Morrison allows the introduction to build and build, until he finally erupts in a dash from the drum riser to his mike and bursts into a spectacular, deafening scream. After this formidable version of the song, they go on to present an exceptional show. Concluding their set with a rare live version of "The Soft Parade," they encore with "Light My Fire" to a rapturous standing ovation, and then return again for a bluesy "Maggie M'Gill."

The second show begins shortly after midnight and continues with the same tremendous energy of the first one. Morrison becomes even more animated as he repeatedly leaps into the air and tumbles across the stage. He also peppers the two-hour set with his contagious sense of humor, which brings everyone into high spirits, and the band finally concludes the set with an encore of "Light My Fire."

☩ Also performing: The Staple Singers

🎭 Capacity: 4,100 per show

🎶 Set-list incomplete

🐞 Promotion: Belkin Productions

Back Door Man	Maggie M'Gill* »
Break on Through	(Tony Glover harmonica solo) »
When the Music's Over	Maggie M'Gill*
Wild Child*	Celebration of the Lizard
Gloria*	Light My Fire (encore)

The Doors' performance tonight is not as exciting as those from the previous evening in Chicago, but it definitely has its moments. The band opens with rather a restrained version of "Back Door Man" during which Morrison coasts into some disjointed dialogue. After signaling the band to settle into a groove by saying, "Quiet down now; give the singer a chance," Morrison becomes slightly tongue-tied. Some audience members begin goading him with Miami references like "Take it off!" and "Jack it off!" and Jim counters with "No, you ain't gonna get *that* one again." He then proceeds with some ludicrous but witty dialogue that includes a comment on how the president called him a few nights previously, but he refused to take the call because he was playing with his cat and just didn't feel like being interrupted by a telephone conversation. The show picks up with "Break on Through," and is in high gear by "When the Music's Over," featuring some stunning guitar work by Krieger. Then Tony Glover, the harmonica virtuoso who joined them on their last appearance in Minneapolis, joins them for several songs beginning with "Wild Child." They then jam on "Gloria," which features some scorching bottleneck work by Krieger in unison with Glover's resourceful harp playing. On their final song together, the evolving "Maggie M'Gill," the Doors push Glover into the forefront for a bluesy harp solo that enhances the song perfectly.

After Glover leaves the stage, the band takes a pause and asks for song requests, which the audience proceeds to call out diligently for almost ten minutes. Finally, the band settles on their "Celebration of the Lizard" as the finale. That choice is a surprising detour from the evening's previous material, and the audience apparently doesn't quite know what to make of it. At its conclusion, the applause is warm but hardly the response a more familiar composition would have elicited. The Doors return for an excellent "Light My Fire," propelled by some fiery organ work from Manzarek.

Belkin Productions sends out a press release following these shows in Chicago and Minneapolis stating, among other things, that "the Doors . . . receiving national publicity due to an alleged incident in Miami . . . have returned to the concert trails this past weekend. The audiences were well behaved with the age group between 14 and 23. There was absolutely no incident in either city which would cause any disfavor among public officials or concerned parents. Jim Morrison . . . seemed very concerned that the entire group put forth a good show."

❇ Featuring Tony Glover on harmonica

⛩ Promotion: Belkin Productions

🐾 Capacity: 8,000

THU. JUN. 19 1969 P.N.E. Garden Auditorium
Vancouver, Canada

Feast of Friends is presented as part of a "Free Press Benefit for the Georgia Straight Defense Fund." Performances at the benefit include Country Joe McDonald and Barry Melton (from Country Joe and the Fish), the Collectors, and Dr. Eugene (HIP-Pocrates) Schoenfeld.

FRI. JUN. 20 1969 Memorial Arts Center
Atlanta, GA
The Second Atlanta International Film Festival
(June 16 to 21, 1969)

This is the Atlanta Film Festival's premiere of *Feast of Friends*. It is shown during the Friday afternoon session of this six-day event, and Jim Morrison attends the screening with Frank Lisciandro.

SAT. JUN. 21 1969 Awards Ceremony
Regency Hyatt House Hotel
Atlanta, GA

Jim Morrison and photographer/film editor Frank Lisciandro are presented with a Gold Medal Award for *Feast of Friends*. The following day, Jim and Frank drive to New Orleans and spent four days there.

TUE. JUN. 24 1969 The Reach
New Orleans, LA (DU) (LU)

Jim Morrison makes an impromptu guest appearance with a local New Orleans band, probably White Clover or Deacon John and the Electric Soul Band, singing four songs including "Crawlin' King Snake" and a cleverly improvised version of "Little Red Rooster."

Note: Date and location uncertain but probable. There is a possibility this performance may have been on Wednesday the 25th.

WED. JUN. 25 1969 CRITIQUE
PBS Studios, (WNET/Channel 13)
New York, NY
A profile of Jim Morrison and the Doors - On and Off Stage

Five to One
    (introduction by Richard Goldstein)
Tell All the People
Alabama Song »
Back Door Man
Wishful, Sinful
Build Me a Woman
    (additional introductions by Richard Goldstein)
    (interview with the Doors, including a discussion on shamanism)
The Soft Parade

This is the original New York broadcast date for the *Critique* show.

The three different segments that comprise the show are recorded on separate days. The Doors' music is recorded on April 28, the interview with Richard Goldstein on April 29, and the panel discussion a couple of weeks before the broadcast.

Critique was an educational television series that provided critical analysis of contemporary works in the arts and humanities. It premiered on November 19, 1968.

The Doors were reportedly thrilled to be doing a show for the Public Broadcasting Service, which at that time was still a relatively new phenomenon on television. All of the restrictions of commercial broadcasting were suspended in this format, and the band could perform their magic within a serious context without fear of censorship or being cut off by a commercial.

The band seems relaxed, eager to talk, and they perform an excellent set of new and vintage material. Morrison appears in loose clothes sporting a newly grown beard that gives him a Che Guevara look. In addition to the music, he even attempts to read from his book *The Lords and the New Creatures,* but discontinues it after a few lines, somewhat shyly saying that he just isn't very good at reciting this material. The Doors reportedly record a rendition of "Light My Fire" for this show.

The show is a production of WNDT in New Jersey. It is directed by Jack Ofield, and produced by Stephen Rabin, with audio by Frank Hanley. The discussion segments feature *Village Voice* music critic Richard Goldstein, WNEW-FM's William "Rosko" Mercer, Patricia Kennealy, and Alfred G. Aronowitz. It is broadcast in New York on June 25 and rerun on June 29, and in Los Angeles on July 19.

❋ Note: There is a doubtful possibility that this show was first shown on May 23, the Sunday night spot for *Critique,* as an unadvertised broadcast. *Critique* usually was broadcast twice a week, first on Wednesday, then a rerun on Sunday. The June 25 broadcast was advertised as the debut of the Doors episode, to be rebroadcast on June 29. The previous rock group on *Critique* had been the New York Rock & Roll Ensemble.

FRI. JUN. 27 - MON. 30 1969 The Forum
Mexico City, Mexico

The Doors were originally scheduled to appear on May 31 in Mexico City at the enormous Plaza Monumental, the largest bullfighting ring in the world (boasting a seating capacity of 48,000). The performance is then tentatively rescheduled for June 27, but promoter Mario Olmos is unable to secure the required authorizations from city officials. As a result of the disruptive student revolts the previous year, President Gustavo Diaz and Mayor Corona Del Rosal are extremely wary of authorizing such an event at the Plaza, especially since it is so close to the anniversary of the student unrest. This was the third time that they retracted permission for the performance. Their apprehensions were magnified following a stadium riot in March, during which newspapers burned and chairs flew through the air while the Mexican band Tijuana played "Light My Fire." Apparently all hell had broken loose when it was announced that the Union Gap would not perform for such an unruly crowd.

In addition to these Plaza Monumental negotiations, preparations are being considered for a benefit designated for either the United Nations or the Red Cross, to be held at the Camino Real Hotel and/or an expensive dinner club. Such a benefit would contribute to the citizens of Mexico as well as further the political agendas of Mexican officials. Attempts are even made to schedule the Doors into the 18,000-seat National Auditorium. A television special is also discussed.

Finally, Mario Olmos approaches Javier Castro, who was the owner of the 1,000-seat diner club the Forum, and offers him the Doors for four consecutive nights at approximately $5,000 each evening. Javier and his brother Arturo had almost given up on the entertainment business after their involvement with the Union Gap fiasco, and Sammy Davis Jr. had cancelled his Forum appearance on May 12. When this offer arrives, Castro immediately seizes the chance and schedules the Doors over a four-day weekend with a cover charge equivalent to a steep $16. Surprisingly, the Doors are never consulted about this situation, and upon arriving they are quite upset when they realize that the exorbitant cover charge will prevent many fans from attending. Despite the awkwardness of the situation, all four of the Doors' shows are reportedly outstanding.

Mexico City's major newspaper runs two half-page advertisements for the broadcast association to air the first show on June 27. However there is no confirmation that this broadcast ever transpired. Similarly, arrangements to film one of the concerts for later use by both American and Mexican networks never materialize.

Their apprehensions were magnified following a stadium riot in March, during which newspapers burned and chairs flew through the air while the Mexican band Tijuana played "Light My Fire."

On opening night, Jim Morrison greets the audience in their native language to considerable applause. "*Buenos noches, señores y señoritas,*" he rings out and then introduces the band members as "Ramon Manzarek, Juan Densmore, and Roberto Krieger."

The Doors are besieged with requests for "The End" throughout the evening. When they finally oblige, an uncomfortable silence pervadeds the room until Jim begins the Oedipal section and the entire audience roars out the lyrics in unison with him. It is not until later that the astonished Doors are informed that in Mexico such lyrics are especially revered for their daring and courage.

🔲 Promotion: The Castro Brothers

🔲 On Saturday June 28, the Doors visit the Indian Pyramids.

🔲 On the afternoon of June 30, the band and constituents visit the Anthropological Museum.

Jim begins the Oedipal section and the entire audience roars out the lyrics in unison with him. It is not until later that the astonished Doors are informed that in Mexico such lyrics are especially revered for their daring and courage.

THU., FRI. JUL. 3, 4 1969 H.I.C. Arena
Honolulu, HI
CANCELLED

The Director of Auditoriums again rejects a proposal for the Doors, maintaining that he does not think "the show is in the best interest of the people of Hawaii."

FRI. JUL. 4 1969 Willingdon Juvenile Detention Home For Girls
Vancouver, Canada

Announcements that the Doors *Feast of Friends* film will be shown are met with uninhibited applause and cheers of anticipation. However, at the conclusion of the film, the girls sit motionless before leaving the screening room without uttering a word.

SAT. JUL. 5 1969 Sicks Stadium
Seattle, WA
CANCELLED

In addition to the cancellation of their entire spring tour, the Doors continue to be plagued with additional losses such as these shows.

🐸 Also scheduled to performed: Taj Mahal; the Impressions; Ballin' Jack; Annie

The Soft Parade
Fourth Album Released (Elektra Us 75005) (DU*)

The Doors.

Side One (A)
Tell All the People
Touch Me
Shaman's Blues
Do It
Easy Ride

Singles
Touch Me / Wild Child (E-45646)
Running Blue / Do It (E-45675)
Wishful, Sinful / Who Scared You (E-45656)
Tell All the People / Easy Ride (E-45663)

Side Two (B)
Wild Child
Runnin' Blue
Wishful Sinful
The Soft Parade

Their new album is here. The Soft Parade. It is Jim Morrison. And John Densmore and Ray Manzarek and Robby Krieger. The Soft Parade. It is Touch Me. It is Wishful Sinful. It is Tell All The People. It is much more. It is today and tomorrow. It is emotion. It is perception and poetry. It is the Doors and their search for things known and unknown. For things real and unreal. The Doors. The Soft Parade.

FRI. JULY 18 1969

❧ Additional musicians include Harvey Brooks (bass), Douglas Lubahn (bass), Curtis Amy (sax), George Bohanan (trombone), Champ Webb (English and additional horns), Jesse McReynolds (mandolin), Jimmy Buchanan (fiddle), and Reinol Andino (conga/percussion)

❀ Note: This album was released the week of July 18, possibly earlier than Friday.

SAT. JUL. 19 1969 KCET Los Angeles Broadcasts CRITIQUE

MON. JUL. 21 1969 Aquarius Theater
Hollywood, CA
Elektra Records Showcase Concert Series*

Elektra Records showcases a number of its artists during an inexpensive series of concerts at the Aquarius Theater on consecutive Mondays throughout the summer.

Soundcheck:
Gloria
Back Door Man
Crawlin' King Snake

Early Show (8:00 p.m.)

Back Door Man
Break on Through
Soul Kitchen
You Make Me Real
I Will Never Be Untrue
When the Music's Over
Universal Mind
People Get Ready* »

Mystery Train* »
Away in India* »
Crossroads*
Build Me a Woman
Who Do You Love (false start)
Who Do You Love
Light My Fire
Celebration of the Lizard (complete version)

Late Show (10:30 p.m.)

Back Door Man
Break on Through
When the Music's Over
You Make Me Real
Universal Mind
People Get Ready* »
Mystery Train* »
Away in India* »
Crossroads*
Little Red Rooster
Gloria »
    "Coda Queen" »
Crossroads »

Gloria
Touch Me
Crystal Ship
Light My Fire
Celebration of the Lizard (complete version)
    [break for crowd control]
Soul Kitchen
Close to You
Peace Frog (instrumental) »
Blue Sunday
Five to One
Rock Me

These highly acclaimed Aquarius shows are uniformly regarded as the Doors' definitive "comeback" performances. The music is fluid, yet exceptionally tight and dynamic, and the entire band radiates an unprecedented musical maturity and revitalized atmosphere of assurance and conviction. Jim Morrison dispenses with his rock star persona, sports an outlandish full beard, and delivers a vocal performance that is nothing short of outstanding. He skillfully interacts with the audience in an unusually casual and easygoing manner, sometimes amiably seated on a stool at center stage. His introduction to the audience goes something like, "For a long time we've wanted to record a live album. Tonight's the night . . . but, we're going to keep it loose and almost casual. Ready? Let's go!"

The shows are being recorded for a forthcoming double live album and the sound is acoustically superb throughout the theater. Morrison's only attempt at theatrics comes during the second show at the opening of "Celebration of the Lizard" when he appears in the right balcony illuminated solely by a deep blue light and then grasps a rope and swings down onto the stage. Artistically, these Aquarius shows are a real stepping stone for the band. Aside from being much more congenial onstage, they have reembraced their roots in authentic American blues music.

These are first of a series of shows recorded for the upcoming *Absolutely Live* album. The cover of that record features a photograph from these performances with another photograph of Morrison superimposed on it.

It is later determined that additional shows will be recorded because, as is periodically the case with live recordings, an extraordinary performance does not necessarily translate successfully to tape.

After the second show, the Doors present *Feast of Friends* for the remaining audience.

Jim Morrison's recent poetic remembrance, "Ode to L.A. While Thinking of Brian Jones—Deceased" is distributed at each of the Aquarius shows at his own expense. Brian Jones, a pivotal member of the Rolling Stones, drowned in the swimming pool at his home in England on July 3.

The Aquarius Theater shows replace the scheduled appearances at the Whisky A Go Go on May 19 through 22, where the Doors originally planned to record a live album. Despite this cancellation, the Doors are still quite interested in doing some minimally advertised appearances at the Whisky at a later date.

The following comments are selected from reviews of the show:

Cash Box: "The Doors, fully cleansed from the unfortunate after-affects of their highly-publicized Miami exhibition, emerged from many months of self exile to give to a native Los Angeles crowd one of the best and most powerful exhibitions of music performance ever witnessed locally. Morrison came back . . . and then some. His new visual appearance and new ease-of-stage-presence combined to create a new image . . . sort of a 'thinking man's singer.' Morrison can no longer be stereotyped as a 'rock singer.' Of the ample new material the Doors displayed, it ran the gamut from hard rock to uptempo blues to ballads . . . all led by the new, more confident Jim Morrison. They ended their set, an encore, with a rare performance of their chilling (literally) theatrical piece, "The Celebration of the Lizard," which combined poetry and song in a truly sardonic (but artistically successful) mixture." (P.S., "The Doors," *Cash Box*, Aug. 2, 1969)

Los Angeles Herald-Examiner: "The Doors are an assertive, demanding group. They preach revolution. They reach out for love. They play beautiful rock 'n' roll. Robby Krieger is a brilliant eclectic and often volcanic guitarist. The Krieger-Manzarek-Densmore instrumental passages are among the most intelligently conceived in contemporary popular music. As an encore—or perhaps an afterthought—Morrison performed one of his tortured paranoid poems set to music. He slowly left the stage, telling the audience to 'retire not to your dreams.' And what dreams the Doors inspire. They are controlled, compressed nightmares." (Michael Ross, "The exciting Doors record a 'live' album," *Los Angeles Herald-Examiner*, July, 1969)

Los Angeles Free Press: "This album, I'm sure, will convince everyone that the Doors have gotten it together, because the electricity in the air, the magic that was created that evening, was a testament to the fact that whatever it was the Doors had once upon a time, when they and their world were younger, they not only had again in spades but had the added virtue of being as sublime and self-assured as they were once brash and vulgar. There was Jim Morrison, more the rabbinical student than the Sex God and looking more comfortable in the new guise. Seeming less self-conscious, but singing, if anything, better than even his greatest fans thought he could sing. How can Morrison be accused of singing less well just because the hostility and the sensuality has given way to something richer textured, fuller, more aggressively grim? They have approached Art, no matter how much they have offended, amused, or even thrilled the rock critics. The standards by which their art must be measured are older and deeper." (Harvey Perr, "Stage Doors," *Los Angeles Free Press*, Aug. 8, 1969)

... sublime and self-assured as they were once brash and vulgar. There was Jim Morrison, more the rabbinical student than the Sex God.

* Note: This medley is often referred to as the "People Get Ready" jam, an impromptu composite of several songs that reappears in several of the Doors' later performances. "Away in India" evolved from the "Latin BS #2" instrumental that the Doors performed on the slower nights at the Whisky A Go Go.

🚗 Poster artist for concert: Leon Bernard

🎵 Both shows recorded for *Absolutely Live*

🎬 *Feast of Friends* is shown after the performance

TUE. JUL. 22 1969 Aquarius Theater
Hollywood, CA

I Will Never Be Untrue
Peace Frog (instrumental) »
Blue Sunday
Maggie M'Gill
You Need Meat (Don't Go No Further) »
You Gotta Love Somebody »
Close to You [Ray and Jim on vocals]
Gloria
People Get Ready »
Mystery Train »
Crossroads »
Double Dose of Love (I'm Your Doctor) [Ray Manzarek on vocal]
Build Me a Woman
Cars Hiss by My Window »
   "Blues Jam" »
The Devil Is a Woman »
   "Extended Blues Jam" »
The Assassination

For a surprise encore performance, Elektra Records and the Doors negotiate for an additional evening at the Aquarius Theater. The unscheduled event is a single performance, which is also recorded for the live album, "Absolutely Live."

FRI. JUL. 25 1969 Cow Palace
(San Francisco), Daly City, CA

Instead of playing the Fillmore West or Winterland, the Doors are scheduled for this significantly larger venue just south of San Francisco.

🎸 Also performing: Elvin Bishop; Lonnie Mack

📋 Promotion: Bill Graham Presents

🎯 Capacity: 14,700

SAT. JUL. 26 1969 Hayward Field
University Of Oregon, Eugene, OR
The Eugene Pop Festival (2:00 to 11:00 pm)

This is the final day for the four-day F.A.M.E. Expo '69. The main headliners for the day were to have been the Byrds, with the Youngbloods and the Doors as the featured attractions. However, the Youngbloods never arrive, and the Byrds arrive too late to set up their equipment and play. The potential disaster is offset by the Doors, who help out by extending their scheduled 45-minute set to 70 minutes. The Doors arrive just minutes before their set in a car that drives directly

through the festival audience with Eugene police officers stationed on the fenders. Morrison emerges onstage dressed not in leather but in jeans, a sheepskin jacket, and a flat-brimmed hat sporting a feather in its band. They perform a very good set before a genuinely enthusiastic audience, with no hint of the controversy that surrounded them since Miami.

- Also performing: Them; Alice Cooper; Rockin' Foo; Peter; River; Truth; the Bumps; ZU; emcee: KEED's Gordon Scott. Scheduled but not performing: The Byrds; the Youngbloods; Tyme; and Grant's Blue Boys
- Promotion: Tom Lasley's Northwest Sounds and F.A.M.E. Foundation Expo '69 Presents
- Attendance: 5,000

SUN. JUL. 27 1969 — GOLD CREEK PARK
Woodinville, Seattle, WA
Seattle Pop Festival

When the Music's Over* (opening song)
Light My Fire
   (Morrison's frustrated dialogue with the audience) »
Five to One
The End »
   "Maggie M'Gill" »
The End

This three-day festival is the largest event of its kind in the Northwest to date and attracts a crowd of more than 50,000 from all over the West. Alcohol consumption plays a very prominent role, with one truckload of wine selling out within minutes, and this had an undeniable influence on the interaction between audience and performers.

The Doors are already developing an intense aversion to outdoor performances, maintaining that the open-air venues greatly diminish the energy and intimacy that an interior environment can provide. Thus, their performance this evening at the Seattle Pop Festival proves something of a challenge. The dramatic differences between it and the previous week's superb Aquarius Theater shows lend credence to the band's convictions about appropriate venues for their style of performance.

Jim Morrison arrives by helicopter in the afternoon and immediately retreats into a Cadillac provided by Gram Parsons of the Flying Burrito Brothers, where he remains until show time.

During the Doors' performance, Morrison continuously ridicules the audience, prompting them to shout obscenities back at the stage. The Doors open with a strong introduction to "When the Music's Over," but it isn't long into the song before Morrison begins his diatribe. At its conclusion, an irate fan heaves a cup at him, and Morrison gives him the finger to audience cheers. As the show progresses, the band runs through a spiritless version of "Light My Fire", and then the antagonistic interchange with the audience resumes. After someone hurls a particularly abusive insult toward the stage, Morrison ferociously responds, calling him a "big-mouthed bastard," and demanding that he say it again. "Get it all out," Morrison continues, "all the little hatreds, everything that's boiled up inside you. Let me have it." As the predictable "Fuck you" retaliations arise from the crowd, Morrison sarcastically belittles their response, "That's the word I wanted to hear. That's the very little word." The band continues with "Five to One,' but the audience has become icily unreceptive. The Doors conclude with a erratic version of "The End," and during it

Morrison drifts into some of the developing lyrics from "Maggie M'Gill." At the conclusion, Morrison silently strikes a crucifixion pose under the red spotlight, and maintains it long after the applause from the bewildered audience has died down. He finally exits the stage to an awaiting helicopter as the next act prepares to go on. (Quotes from Edd Jeffords, "Doors At Seattle," *Poppin* magazine, 1969)

Later, Led Zeppelin's Robert Plant comments on Morrison's performance: "We only played with the Doors once, in Seattle, and it seemed like he was screwed up. Morrison went on stage and said 'Fuck you all' which didn't really do anything except make a few girls scream. Then he hung on the side of the stage and nearly toppled into the audience, and did all those things that I suppose were originally sexual things but as he got dirtier and more screwed up, they just became bizarre. He was just miles above everyone's head. It seemed that he realized the Doors were on the way down. He went on stage with that opinion and immediately started saying all those strange things which nobody could get into." ("Robert Plant," *New Musical Express*, Apr. 11, 1970)

The Doors were promptly followed by Led Zeppelin at about 11:30 p.m.

🎆 Also performing: Bo Diddley; Chuck Berry; the Flying Burrito Brothers; Led Zeppelin; Vanilla Fudge; Ten Years After; Guess Who; Albert Collins; Santana; the Youngbloods; Tim Buckley; It's a Beautiful Day; the Byrds; Santana; the Flock; Charles Lloyd; Lee Michaels; Spirit; Blacksnake; Chicago Transit Authority; Lonnie Mack; and more

🖐 Set-list incomplete

🎆 Promotion: Boyd Grafmyre, the promoter who ran the acclaimed Eagles Ballroom in Seattle, presented this festival with the assistance of John Chambless and the staff of the New American Community.

FRI. AUG. 8 1969 Electric Circus
New York, NY

Performance never occurred. Although many flyers/posters were distributed, the Doors never performed at the Electric Circus. "The Jam Factory" was scheduled to perform there from August 5 through 10.

MON. AUG. 18 1969 Solomon Little Theatre
United States International
University, San Diego

The "Creative Arts Conference" at the California Western Campus of the United States International University is held from August 18 through 29.

"The Film Maker" series includes a personal appearance by Jim Morrison of the Doors representing his film *Feast of Friends*.

The following night features Michael McClure, author of *The Beard*, at the University of California Matthews Campus Art Gallery. The conference features ten appearances by authors and filmmakers.

SUN. AUG. 24 1969 KQED San Francisco
Broadcasts CRITIQUE

SUN. AUG. 31 1969 Edinburgh Film Festival
Edinburgh, Scotland

Feast of Friends, Easy Rider, and the Rolling Stones' *One Plus One* (which had been recently retitled *Sympathy for the Devil*) are presented at this film festival, which runs from August 24 through September 6.

Morrison ferociously responds, calling him a "big-mouthed bastard," and demanding that he say it again. "Get it all out," Morrison continues, "all the little hatreds, everything that's boiled up inside you. Let me have it." As the predictable "Fuck you" retaliations arise from the crowd, Morrison sarcastically belittles their response, "That's the word I wanted to hear. That's the very little word."

SAT. SEPT. 6 1969 Varsity Arena
Toronto, Canada
The Toronto Rock & Roll Revival Rally:
Featuring a Festival of Doors Films

This promotional rally includes presentations of *Feast of Friends, Break on Through,* and *The Unknown Soldier.* It is scheduled to begin at 9:00 p.m., and is sponsored by CKFH with "Your Freak Out Host—Kim Fowley."

SAT. SEPT. 13 1969 Varsity Stadium
Toronto, Ontario, Canada
Toronto Rock & Roll Revival

When the Music's Over	Crystal Ship
Break on Through	Wake Up! »
Back Door Man »	Light My Fire
"Maggie M'Gill" »	"Illustrious Musical Geniuses" (introduction) »
"Roadhouse Blues" »	The End
Back Door Man »	

This one-day 13½-hour festival is originally promoted as a tribute to the influential rock 'n' roll musicians of the 1950s. It is the second festival of its kind that summer, the first being the Toronto Pop Festival in June. When ticket sales prove to be insufficient, the promoters work to secure the Doors, and also invite John Lennon to emcee the proceedings. In an amazing sequence of events, Lennon, long an enthusiastic fan of '50s rock, offers to perform at the event and hastily assembles the Plastic Ono Band with Eric Clapton on lead guitar. They had recently released "Give Peace a Chance" (July 4), and this performance is released by Apple Records on December 15, entitled "Live Peace in Toronto."

The entire revival is a well-staged event, proceeding smoothly through the various bands with minimal set-up time between acts. There are numerous memorable performances at this legendary Varsity Stadium show, in addition to Lennon and the Doors. Chuck Berry's set burns with enthusiasm from the minute he hits the stage, and Alice Cooper pulls out all the stops for his theatrical nightmarish exposition. This is the performance where groundless rumors start that he has orally decapitated a live chicken. Actually he unceremoniously launches the hapless bird into the audience, as well as freeing live pigeons, showering the audience with feathers propelled by a large fan, and firing off a flare gun at the conclusion. (Cooper began his illustrious career by provoking a mass audience exodus at the Los Angeles Cheetah, arousing such a negative and indignant response that Frank Zappa's new Straight Records promptly signs them to the label.)

The Doors' entourage is escorted the ten miles from the airport to Varsity Stadium by 150 members of the Vagabond motorcycle club, some of whom shoulder Pennebaker's film equipment. The entire festival is being filmed by D. A. Pennebaker, Inc., whose previous films include *Don't Look Back* and *Monterey Pop.** At the show, the Doors are placed in the unenviable position of following John Lennon and Eric Clapton. The audience is clearly becoming fatigued toward the conclusion of the all-day event, not to mention the conclusion of the Plastic Ono Band set, which features Yoko Ono screeching through two extended numbers. However, the Doors put on a solid, musically proficient performance, and Morrison pauses before their finale of "The End" to express his reverence for the exceptional line-up of talent that has preceded them.

Morrison's reverence for the early rock 'n' roll artists was clear. When asked once about what influence early rockers like Elvis had had on him, he responds, "Along with many of the early rock singers, Little Richard, Fats Domino, Jerry Lee Lewis, Gene Vincent, [Elvis] had an influence on me because of the music and the fact that I heard them at an early age when I was kinda ready for an influence. It was a strong influence and they just seemed to open up a whole new world to me. They were very exciting and presented a strong intense landscape that I had only vaguely glimpsed before." (Nick Logan, "Elvis influenced Doors' Jim," *New Musical Express,* Sept. 21, 1968)

Toronto's *Globe and Mail* reports: "The appearance of the Doors was almost anti-climatic. People were getting tired. But the Doors were a beautiful anti-climax. Jim Morrison, his hair cut off shorter, in faded denim, looked less beautiful than he was expected to. The sound for the Doors was clear, and Morrison's dramatic voice came across pure and clean. The Doors seemed rather down. Their songs are full of morbid images and their vibes were depressed and dramatic. Morrison's greatness as a performer still is evident, in his bursts of movement, and the exciting climax at the end. He seemed to alternate between a controlled emotional tension and letting it all hang out. His singing of 'The End' might not have been what it once was, but it was great. (Melinda McCracken, "Rock joy fully revived," *Globe and Mail,* Sept. 15, 1969)

🕷 Also performing: John Lennon's Plastic Ono Band; Bo Diddley; Chicago; Tony Joe White; Alice Cooper; Chuck Berry; Cat Mother and the All Night Newsboys; Jerry Lee Lewis; Gene Vincent; Little Richard; Doug Kershaw; Whisky Howl

✳ Note: Reportedly, the darkened stage during the Doors' set interfered with the quality of the filming.

🦂 Promotion: John Brower & Ken Walker Enterprises

🦋 Capacity: 22,000

🦑 This was not the Toronto Pop Festival, an entirely different event held in June.

SUN. SEPT. 14 1969 Montreal Forum
Montreal, Canada

Back Door Man (opening song)
Heartbreak Hotel
Light My Fire (finale)

The Montreal show opens with a message sent from John Lennon expressing his appreciation for the reception he received there this summer. The audience responds with enthusiastic cheers and their ignited matches illuminate the auditorium. The announcement sets the general mood of the evening, and the Doors put on a good show to an appreciative crowd.

The *Montreal Star* reviewer is clearly no admirer of the Doors, but makes this memorable remark in his contemptuous verdict of the show: "The Doors were easily the most boring of the groups last night because they were the most pretentious. *Morrison doesn't sing; he roars and screeches like both ends of an automobile accident.*" (Juan Rodriguez, "The Doors bore but the boppers loved it all," *Montreal Star,* Sept. 15, 1969)

🕷 Also performing: Trevor Payne Group; La Revolution Francaise

♀ 8:00 p.m.

🦂 Promotion: Donald K. Donald presents

🖐 Set-list incomplete

FRI. SEPT. 19 1969 United Kingdom Tour CANCELLED
Royal Albert Hall, London

In June 1969, a brief minitour through the United Kingdom comes close to materializing but never reaches fruition. Although the tour appears almost definite in June, continued difficulties stemming from the Miami incident prevent the dates from being confirmed. It was to have opened at London's Royal Albert Hall on September 19 and was tentatively scheduled to include Manchester, Glasgow, and Dublin.

🦂 Organizational efforts for the tour were being directed by Roy Guest of Nems.

Morrison doesn't sing; he roars and screeches like both ends of an automobile accident.

"We want the DOORS ... and we want them NOW! DONALD K. DONALD presents ...

the doors

LA REVOLUTION FRANCAISE

with guest star TREVOR PAYNE WITH THE CFOX GOOD GUYS AND ROBERT ARCAND OF CJMS
SUN. SEPT. 14 - 8 P.M.
TICKETS $3 4 5, AVAILABLE AT THE FORUM AND CFOX STUDIOS
MONTREAL FORUM

FRI. SEPT. 19 1969 Philadelphia Arena
Philadelphia, PA

Early Show

Back Door Man

Break on Through

When The Music's Over

The Soft Parade

Light My Fire (finale)

The City of Philadelphia attempts to cancel the September 19 appearance by revoking the "amusement permit" as they had done the previous March and on the same grounds—the infamous show in Miami. On September 11, promoter Fred Samango challenges the revocation through an appeal by his attorney Herbert L. Olivieri, which states that the action has "a chilling effect on the Constitutional rights of free speech and free expression." Samango continues to advertise the show while he takes legal recourse against the Department of Licenses and Inspections. On the morning of the performance, a last-minute court decision over-turns the earlier revocation, and the show goes on as scheduled without incident.

Originally, they are scheduled for one appearance at 8:00 p.m., but all of the attendant publicity prompts the addition of a second show. The majority of Doors' enthusiasts seem to gravitate toward the late show, while the somewhat sparsely attended early show (estimated between 2 and 3.5 thousand) appears to attract a crowd of curiosity seekers lured by the possibility of a lewd and obscene presenta-tion. Morrison stations himself firmly at the mike with one foot planted on the stand's base, and sings quite well even though he restricts his characteristic screams, concluding "When the Music's Over" in a faint, whispery voice. It is at the opening of "The Soft Parade" that the show begins to really take off. After tearing off the blue windbreaker he's been wearing, Morrison bounds into the introductory "Seminary School" passage and continues with what is probably the highlight of the evening show. Despite an impressive performance, the Doors fail to connect with the dispassionate audience, and promptly exit the stage at the conclusion of "Light My Fire." Fortunately, the second show fares better.

The *Philadelphia Inquirer* appraises the first show: "In rock concerts, there has to be a thing between the musicians and the audience. Call it chemistry or rapport or anything else. . . . This is especially so with a group such as the Doors, where there has to be emotion . . . fire . . . because that's the way the group per-forms. He [Morrison] is a powerful entertainer just standing on a stage, cupping the microphone in his hands and wailing his brand of music. And on Friday night, that's all he did. That was enough—that and the strong backing he received from Ray Manzarek on the organ and the others in the group. (Jack Lloyd, "Ban lifted, Doors perform," *Philadelphia Inquirer*, Sept. 20, 1969)

And Philadelphia's *Distant Drummer* remarks on the shows: "The Doors turned in a good show powerful enough to put them back in the first rank of rock acts. . . . While the Doors will always be remembered as the world's best Oedipal blues band, Friday night they were at a near peak of their performing powers. Stripped of the garbage they're one of the tightest groups in the idiom, and it showed. They started to get together on 'Back Door Man' and, since the crowd couldn't make enough noise to drown them out, every note came over clear and perfect. Krieger was off on the subtle runs that make him one of the most under-rated guitar players in rock; Manzarek on organ was superb, pounding out the beat with his left hand and showing some great improvisation with his right, perfectly complementing Densmore, quiet and tasty on drums. And if Manzarek's organ is the backbone of the Doors, there was always Morrison as the guts, singing, raving, whispering and chanting. They still generate more energy than nearly everybody else in rock combined. . . ." ("Pop" column, *Distant Drummer*, Sept. 1969)

- Also performing: Jim & Dale
- Early (7:00 p.m.) and late (10:00 p.m.) shows
- Promotion: Fred Samango Presents
- Capacity: 7,000

SAT. SEPT. 20 1969 Pittsburgh Civic Arena
Pittsburgh, PA

Break on Through (opening song)	The Soft Parade
Back Door Man	Light My Fire
When the Music's Over	Soul Kitchen (encore)

Overall, tonight's performance goes very well except that, at one point, the standing-room-only audience becomes so rambunctious that the show has to be temporarily stopped. The Doors open with a blistering take of "Break on Through," and the show progresses into a noteworthy version of "When the Music's Over" that has the audience erupting into loud screams and exhilarated cheers. Following that, Morrison leads off "The Soft Parade" with its "Seminary School" prelude and the audience goes wild. Their fervor escalates from there, and by the time the band introduces "Light My Fire," the crowd's response ascends into sheer mayhem. People start scaling the sides of the stage, only to be vigorously shoved and clubbed back by a rapidly assembling barrier of policemen. The subsequent collisions between retreating fans with those advancing toward the stage result in several injuries. The security forces form a steadfast barrier at the front of the stage as the Doors do "Light My Fire." When the song is concluded, the police bring the concert to a halt. Rather than terminating the performance, they simply insist that everyone returns to their seats before it continues. When some semblance of order has been restored, the Doors reappear for an impressive encore of "Soul Kitchen." At its conclusion, the band members quickly exit the stage and their manager (Siddons) comes on and thanks everyone for coming and vows that they'll return soon.

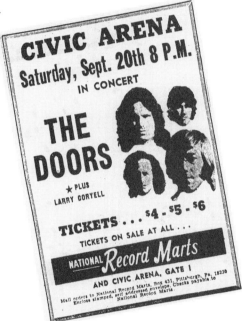

🕺 Also performing: Larry Coryell; Lonnie Mack [possibly cancelled]

👤 One show at 8:00 p.m.

🕺 Capacity: 17,500

SUN. SEPT. 21 1969 University Of Toledo
Field House
CANCELLED
Toledo, OH

The cancellation occurs after the student board is unable to secure a rider to the contract from Bill Siddons providing that the payment of $15,000 will be withheld if the show features the "public indecency" that occurred in Miami. Meanwhile, university officials claim that they have been besieged with "abnormal pressures from the public, city councilmen and state legislators" to cancel the performance. The "Move to Restore Decency" assemblage launches a telephone campaign against the show and proclaims they will organize a demonstration if the Doors appear.

🕺 Also scheduled to perform: The James Gang featuring Joe Walsh

TUE. SEPT. 23 1969 Philadelphia Civic Center
CANCELLED
Philadelphia, PA

After the spring cancellation, the city attempts to cancel this performance as well. This time the Department of Licenses and Inspection insists that it had been unaware of granting any license for a Doors performance and immediately revokes it, declaring that it had been "in error." However, when the efforts to terminate the performance are challenged as illegal and unconstitutional, the show is allowed to proceed on the originally scheduled date of September 19.

MON. SEPT. 29 1969 Lincoln Center's 7th New York Film Festival

Feast of Friends is one of the special events presented by the Film Society of Lincoln Center. It is screened at 5:00 p.m. along with *Charles Lloyd—Journey Within* by Eric Sherman and *Cycles* by Bill Tannem.

Jim Morrison attends the festival.

FRI. OCT. 17 1969 U.C. Santa Cruz Film Festival
Santa Cruz, CA (DU)

Presentation of *Feast of Friends*.

SUN. OCT. 26 1969 Balboa Stadium
San Diego, CA

This was to have been an afternoon performance. On June 23, this stadium is the site for a "Youth for Decency" rally.

- Also scheduled to perform: Ike and Tina Turner Revue
- Promotion: West Coast Productions/Richard Linnell

FRI. OCT. 31 1969 Masonic Hall
San Francisco, CA

13th Annual San Francisco Film Festival midnight presentation of *Feast of Friends*. Jim Morrison personally attends the festival and is there to see what is probably the most unreceptive audience the film will ever have. *Feast of Friends* is presented along with *Popcorn* (featuring appearances by many bands including the Rolling Stones doing "Jumping Jack Flash") and *Thank You Masked Man* (an animated cartoon featuring Lenny Bruce doing all of the voices). Other films featured during the festival include *Easy Rider* and *Sympathy for the Devil*, Jean Luc Goddard's fascinating portrayal of the Rolling Stones. The San Francisco Film Festival opens on October 22 and runs for twelve days.

SAT. NOV. 1 1969 Las Vegas Ice Palace
Las Vegas, NV

Out on Bail

NOVEMBER 9 SUNDAY

Jim Morrison turns himself in to the Dade County Public Safety Department and is arrested at 9:50 p.m. He makes the $5,000 bail pre-set by Judge Murray Goodman at 10:10 p.m. and is released. A formal "not guilty" plea is entered. Ironically, the Living Theater had put on an unhampered presentation a week earlier (November 2) at Bayfront Park in Coconut Grove.

Drunk and Disorderly

NOVEMBER
11
TUESDAY

Jim Morrison and Thomas Baker (an actor who appeared in Andy Warhol's film "I, A Man") are arrested at the Sky Harbor International Airport in Phoenix, Arizona, on charges of "drunk and disorderly conduct" and "interference with a flight crew" upon landing in Phoenix on a Continental Airlines flight. They are en route to see the Rolling Stones at the Phoenix Veterans Coliseum that night. The Captain of Flight 172, Craig A. B. Chapman, is required to abandon his post three times to go back to the cabin and attempt to maintain the peace with the intoxicated passengers. He requests police assistance upon arrival at the airport. Complaints are filed, and Morrison and Baker are hauled off to jail. The intoxicated duo is initially quite unaware of the gravity of the charges: Public intoxication is a relatively minor offense, but "interference with a flight crew" is a federal matter.

Assault and Intimidation

NOVEMBER
12
WEDNESDAY

Morrison and Baker appear in court in the morning and plead "not guilty" to the charges of "drunk and disorderly conduct." The arraignment is set for December 2 and they are responsible for $66 bail each. Rather than being released, they are immediately surrendered to a U.S. marshal. A hastily convened federal grand jury indicts them on the felony counts of "assault, intimidation and threatening a flight attendant on an interstate flight." Bail is set at $2,500 each and an arraignment is scheduled for November 24.

The Unauthorized Doors

NOVEMBER
15

"Jim Morrison and The Doors: An Unauthorized Biography," by Mike Jahn, the first of many on the Doors, is published. It is not so much a biography as an imaginative description of the Doors' performance at the Fillmore East on March 22, 1968. Author Mike Jahn was also a frequent contributor of music reviews to the *New York Times*, including reviews of Doors performances in the New York vicinity. The book is released in softcover by Grosset & Dunlap Books, and is reviewed in *Rolling Stone* on this date.

Elektra Sound Recorders
Hollywood, CA

The Doors begin recording *Morrison Hotel* with producer Paul Rothchild. Additional musicians sitting in on the session include Lonnie Mack and Ray Neapolitan on bass guitars, and John Sebastian on harmonica under the pseudonym of G. Puglese.

Some of the material, notably "Waiting for the Sun" and "Roadhouse Blues," is also mixed down at Sunset Sound Studios.

The original working title of this album is *Hard Rock Cafe*.

FRI., SAT. NOV. 21, 22 1969 Felt Forum, Madison Square Garden
New York, NY

Cancelled. These two shows are rescheduled for January 17 and 18. The cancellation has nothing to do with Miami; rather, it is a schedule mixup. Sam and Dave and Ike and Tina Turner play on the dates instead.

Federal Court, Phoenix, AZ

James D. Morrison and Thomas F. Baker appear before U.S. District Court Judge William P. Copple, under representation of attorney Craig Mehrens, and enter a plea of "not guilty." Copple informs them that they could face prison terms of up to twenty years and a $10,000 fine for each of the three charges. The judge also explains to Morrison that, due to his age, the court could adjudge him under the Youth Corrections Act, and thereby limit his maximum sentence to four years. The trial is set for February 17, 1970 at the federal court in Phoenix.

The Doors
on the road
1970

THE "ROADHOUSE BLUES" TOUR

SAT. JAN. 17 1970 Felt Forum
Madison Square Garden, New York, NY

This very successful series of concerts at the Felt Forum, a smaller venue inside the Madison Square Garden Complex, allows the band to perform in a more intimate setting than the Garden would allow, similar to the ambience of the Aquarius Theater shows the previous summer.

Early Show

Roadhouse Blues	Five to One
Ship of Fools	Who Do You Love
Break on Through	Little Red Rooster
Peace Frog »	Money
Blue Sunday	Light My Fire
Alabama Song »	Soul Kitchen (encore)
Back Door Man »	

The Doors are in fine form. The early show begins somewhat awkwardly, with the band requiring several numbers to get warmed up. After "Peace Frog," the energy begins intensifying and the show shifts into higher gear, expanding with each number and climaxing with a well-received encore of "Soul Kitchen."

Late Show

Roadhouse Blues	Wild Child [after two false starts,
Break on Through	they forego the song and move on]
Ship of Fools	When the Music's Over
Crawlin' King Snake	Light My Fire
Alabama Song »	Soul Kitchen
Back Door Man »	"Bring Out Your Dead!" »
Five to One	The End »
Build Me A Woman	"Across the Sea" »
Who Do You Love	The End

MADISON SQUARE GARDEN PRODUCTIONS and ANDAR FIVE present THE doors

JAN. 17th · 8 & 11 P.M. PERFORMANCES
SOLD OUT
JAN. 18th · 7:30 P.M. PERFORMANCE
$3.50 Tickets Available
JAN. 18th · 10 P.M. PERFORMANCE
$4.50 & 3.50 Tickets Available

the felt forum
MADISON SQUARE GARDEN CENTER
8th AVE. BETWEEN 31st & 33rd Sts.
FOR FURTHER INFORMATION CALL 564-4400

Jim Morrison opens the show with the exclamation that "Everything is fucked up as usual!"

The momentum of the second show picks up where the first one left off. Although Morrison restrains his characteristic screams, he and the band are on solid footing. Of particular note is their finale of "The End," which Jim introduces with the macabre wailing of "Bring out your dead!" The mournful cries evoke the corpse gatherers during the Black Plague (Death) in fourteenth-century Europe.

Hofstra University's *Chronicle* comments on the late show: "The Doors have gone back to their earth, their roots, way back to those 1967 Whisky moments in L.A., where singer and musicians come together in a tightly interwoven package of melodic delight. They have given up the orchestrated stuff and didn't do one song from the *Soft Parade* album. The closest they came to that material was when they started 'Wild Child' and couldn't get it together; the guitar wasn't harmonizing with Morrison's voice and they stopped dead, he held his nose, shook his head and groaned 'uunnh-uuhh,' meaning 'no good.' They did a haunting chant in the 'Horse Latitudes' vein where Manzarek tinkled bells, Krieger emitted eerie squeaks by playing his guitar strings below the bridge and Densmore rubbed the cymbals in scraping rasp all the while James is screaming 'Bring out your Dead . . . Bring out your Dead' like some twelfth-century flagellant. They ended their first night with 'The End,' and when they left you could see they had drained all their passions out and were completely spent, like the boy who has just finished his first taste of love-making. The audience clapped and clapped, as they had been doing all night." (Douglas Sizer, "Morrison, Doors at the Felt Forum: Pre-Parade Style Scores Heavily," Hofstra *Chronicle*, Jan. 1970)

New York Times critic Mike Jahn commented: "Saturday, at least two dozen teen-age girls and quite a few boys had to be dragged away from the Doors' singer, Jim Morrison, by stagehands. The other three Doors played on unperturbed. Mr. Morrison has had trouble before when the police of other cities found his performances variously lewd, lascivious, indecent and profane. But by the standards of the Off-Broadway stage, Mr. Morrison's performance is fairly tame. The Doors played their familiar songs quite well, much better than in last year's concert in the Garden." (Mike Jahn, *New York Times*, Jan. 19, 1970)

🔯 Note: Lonnie Mack, who was also featured on *Morrison Hotel,* had released an album several years earlier entitled *The Wham of That Memphis Man* with a single of "Memphis," and although they received superb reviews, they were essentially buried under the avalanche of British Invasion releases. In 1969, Elektra bought the rights to the album and released "Glad I'm with the Band" and "Whatever's Right." He was now making a reappearance in the music business fronting a powerful blues trio featuring himself on guitar and vocals, backed by a driving rhythm section of David Byrd on organ and Mike Mahoney on drums. Despite the lavish praise extended to the trio, Lonnie Mack decided to quit the music business in late 1971.

🔯 Note: These shows were originally scheduled for November 21 and 22, 1969, but were moved to these January dates after a scheduling mixup.

🎭 Also performing: The Lonnie Mack Trio

🌀 Both shows are recorded for *Absolutely Live*

🎯 Capacity: 4,000 to 5,000

SUN. JAN. 18 1970   **FELT FORUM**
Madison Square Garden, New York, NY

Early Show
Roadhouse Blues
Ship of Fools
Break on Through
Universal Mind
Alabama Song (the band leads off out of tune, abruptly ends, and starts again)
Alabama Song »
Back Door Man »
Five to One
Moonlight Drive »
   "Horse Latitudes" »
Moonlight Drive*
Who Do You Love
Money
Light My Fire
When the Music's Over

After opening with "Roadhouse Blues," the Doors spring into a particularly sarcastic "Ship of Fools" that features some brusque vocals from Morrison. Later, the band introduces their rarely performed (only five other known times) "Universal Mind." Toward the end of the medley concluding with "Five to One," Morrison begins toying with the audience. After repeatedly saying "One more," he hesitates as if he were going to erupt into "Time!" but then drifts off on a tangent that circles back again to "One more." The audience's laughter lets him know they are with him, and he wistfully follows "One more" with a bashful, questioning "Time," and the crowd bursts into laughter and applause as the band finally finishes the song. Later, after doing two cover songs back-to-back ("Who Do You Love" and "Money"), Morrison acknowledges the crowd with "Hey, thank you all for being so patient with us tonight. It usually takes an hour or so to get warmed up, you know. So I hope nobody has to go anywhere for a while [applause]." Then he concludes with "Why don't we do a famous radio song," and the band breaks into "Light My Fire." After that, they bring the show to a close with a very good "When the Music's Over."

Commenting on the early show, *Billboard* reports: "The Elektra Records artists actually were more businesslike than often has been their wont, but Morrison conveyed none of his famed eroticism. His voice, however, was distinctive whether singing or screaming. The concentration was on blues and simple rock. 'Light My Fire,' which gave organist Ray Manzarek and guitarist Robby Krieger good instrumental bits, was a fitting climax." (Fred Kirby, *Billboard*, Jan. 31, 1970)

Late Show

Roadhouse Blues	Light My Fire
Peace Frog	Rock Me* »
Alabama Song »	Close to You*
Back Door Man »	Ship of Fools
Five to One	Goin' To New York**
Celebration of the Lizard	Maggie M'Gill**
Build Me a Woman	Gloria »
When the Music's Over	"Coda Queen" »
Soul Kitchen	My Eyes Have Seen You
"When I Was Back in Seminary School!" »	

Jim Morrison opens their final Felt Forum show with a display of his wry sense of humor, saying: "How you doing, man?! All right, everybody [pause]. Everybody sit down—come on, listen! [pause] Hey! Get those people to sit down, man! There's too much activity around here! You people spend much too much time in those restrooms, I'll tell you that! Yeah, we know what you're doing in there! All right! Is everybody ready? . . ."

The standout performance of these four shows is this final set, which includes exemplary renditions of their songs and a generous finale featuring John Sebastian and Dallas Taylor. Jim is in high spirits, leading off with a strong "Roadhouse Blues," from which they hardly pause before launching into "Peace Frog." This flows into "Alabama Song" during which a mischievous Morrison follows the lyrics "we must die" with a jocular "hope not!" Then, as they connect into "Back Door Man," Jim brings out his grating screams and caustic yelps, while appreciative audience members collectively yelp back.

One of the highlights of the evening is a rare performance of the entire "Celebration of the Lizard," which is met with hearty enthusiasm by the New York audience. Introducing the song, a cunning Morrison announces, "Alright listen, man, we've gotta special treat for you right now. This is a little tour de force that we've only done a couple of times in front of strangers. And it starts off kind of quiet, so if everybody would just kind of relax, take a few deep breaths, think about your eventual end, and what's gonna happen tonight. *[laughter]* And we'll try and do something good to your head . . . right man?!" When the audience refuses to settle down, Jim resourcefully proceeds: "Now listen, listen. I want to remind you of something very important. I don't know if you're aware of it, but this evening is being taped for eternity, and beyond that too. *[applause]* And so listen, man, if you want to be represented in eternity with some uncouth language *[laughter]*, then I hope you'll stand up on the top of your seat and shout it out very clearly or we're not gonna get it on tape, right?! *[enthusiastic cheers and applause]*."

This evening is being taped for eternity, and beyond that too. [applause] And so listen, man, if you want to be represented in eternity with some uncouth language [laughter], then I hope you'll stand up on the top of your seat and shout it out very clearly or we're not gonna get it on tape, right?!

After "Celebration," the show continues with an excellent succession of songs, including an impressive "Soul Kitchen" in which Ray and Jim blend dramatically on the chorus. As an introduction to "Seminary School," Morrison wittily announces "All right, now listen! For fear of getting too patriotic, we're going to attempt a rendition of the National Anthem. *[applause]* So everyone will respectively, respectfully, get up on their feet, at full attention, right?! Shhhh, all right, have some respect now, have some respect please. Shhhh. Pretend you're at a football game!" *[laughter]* Everyone respectfully gets very quiet. And then as the audience settles down, Jim unexpectedly launches into "When I Was Back in Seminary School!" and the entire audience breaks into loud cheers and applause. New York audiences revere this kind of humor.

Later, the Doors bring out Gotham City's own John Sebastian, who Jim simply introduces as "a very talented guy" to tumultuous applause, and they jam with him on a succession of numbers, some of which also include Crosby, Stills, Nash and Young's drummer Dallas Taylor.

A memorable night that evokes the whole gamut of human emotions, it will not to be forgotten for a long time to come.

🥁 Also performing: The Lonnie Mack Trio

✳ With John Sebastian

✳✳ With John Sebastian and Dallas Taylor

📻 Note: "*Goin' To New York*" by Jimmy & Mary Reed, © 1958, 1968 Conrad Music

🎶 John B. Sebastian originally hailed from Greenwich Village in New York City, and was just about to begin a series of shows at the Bitter End. Before forming the Lovin' Spoonful, he had studied directly under such blues masters as Lightnin' Hopkins. The Spoonful formed in 1965, and during 1966 was topping the charts with such songs as "Summer In the City," "Daydream", and "Do You Believe in Magic." When the Lovin' Spoonful folded, he branched out on a solo career, performing at Woodstock and the Isle of Wight festivals. At this time, he was completing his first solo album, with Paul Rothchild producing. Sebastian also contributed his harp playing to Crosby, Stills, Nash and Young's *Deja Vu* album.

🎶 Dallas Taylor was the drummer with Crosby, Stills, Nash and Young.

MON. JAN. 19 1970 Hilton Hotel Penthouse Suite
New York, NY

The Doors host a press party at the New York Hilton the day after the Felt Forum shows.

SUN. JAN. 25 1970 Honolulu International Center (H.I.C.) Arena
CANCELLED
Honolulu, HI

Honolulu's Director of Auditoriums, Guido Salmaggi, apparently rescinds his decision to prohibit the Doors from performing there, but he insists on a special contract clearly designed to dissuade the Doors from wishing to do so. The contract stipulates that the "Leasor (Guido Salmaggi) shall have the absolute right in its sole discretion to terminate the performance in progress and, regardless of whether the performance is terminated, to delay and withhold payment and settlement of all accounts and funds related to monies collected or received by coliseum under this agreement until completion of an investigation relating to any incident thought to be a violation." Further, should Salmaggi decide there had been any violation, he can automatically refund all money collected from the gate receipts to the patrons. The promoters bring up the very sensible proposal that, in all fairness, a small panel, consisting of at least one clergyman, could be assigned to more objectively determine the status of any possible violations, but Salmaggi steadfastly refuses to relinquish absolute jurisdiction. Rather than allow themselves to be subject to the questionable intentions of one inflexible and clearly biased individual, the Doors immediately cancel the date. The cancellation results in the loss of thousands of dollars in probable revenue for the city.

Morrison Hotel
(aka Hard Rock Cafe)
Fifth Album Released (E-75007)

FEB. 1 1970

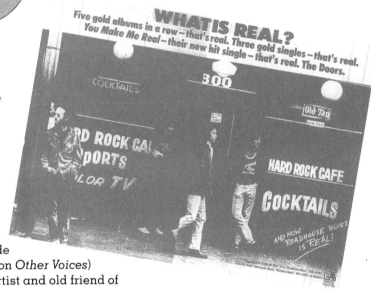

WHAT IS REAL?

Five gold albums in a row – that's real. Three gold singles – that's real. You Make Me Real – their new hit single – that's real. The Doors.

Side One (A)
Roadhouse Blues
Waiting For The Sun
You Make Me Real
Peace Frog
Blue Sunday
Ship of Fools

 Single
You Make Me Real / Roadhouse Blues (E-45685)

Side Two (B)
Land Ho!
The Spy
Queen of the Highway
Indian Summer
Maggie M'Gill

Initially, the proposed title for this album was to be *Hard Rock Cafe* on one side and *Morrison Hotel* on the other. Additional musicians performing on the album include Lonnie Mack and Ray Neapolitan (who would also perform on *Other Voices*) on bass guitars. John Sebastian, who was also an Elektra artist and old friend of Paul Rothchild from his days in New York, contributes the harmonica portions to "Roadhouse Blues" under the pseudonym of G. Puglese, and later performs live with the Doors on several occasions during the tour.

- Producer: Paul Rothchild.
- Engineer: Bruce Botnick.
- Note: The album was released during the first week in February and had achieved "gold" status by February 23.

THU. FEB. 5 1970 Winterland Arena
San Francisco, CA

When the Music's Over
Five to One
Roadhouse Blues

The Doors' final performances in San Francisco go exceptionally well, and Morrison unleashes his full ability to navigate the aural spectrum from deafening screams to gentle whispers.

- Also performing: Doug Kershaw; Cold Blood; Commander Cody and the Lost Planet Airmen
- Lighting by Holy See
- Promotion: Bill Graham Presents

FRI. FEB. 6 1970 Winterland Arena
San Francisco, CA

Carol!
Rock Me

The Doors put on an excellent show, as is clearly evidenced through these two songs. Krieger's guitar work is gutsy and primitive, while Morrison continuously pushes his vocals to the breaking point.

- Also performing: Doug Kershaw; Cold Blood; Commander Cody and the Lost Planet Airmen; [Bigfoot])
- Promotion:Bill Graham Presents
- Tickets did include Commander Cody and the Lost Planet Airmen on the same bill, however it is possible that they didn't perform on these two nights.

SAT. FEB. 7 1970 Long Beach Sports Arena
Long Beach, CA

Roadhouse Blues
Alabama Song »
Back Door Man »
Five to One
Ship of Fools
When the Music's Over
    "I'm Calling You!" »
When the Music's Over »
    "You Know I Had a Friend . . ." »
When the Music's Over
The Spy in the House of Love
Break On Through
    [Jim engages in humorous dialogue with the crowd]
Peace Frog
Universal Mind
Gloria
Blue Sunday
    "When I Was Back In Seminary School!" »
Light My Fire »
Summertime »
Fever »
Light My Fire

1st Encore:
Soul Kitchen »
    [Morrison harmonica solo] »
Soul Kitchen
    [Jim: "Listen! Does anyone have to go home early tonight?"]

Additional Encores:
Love Me Two Times
Maggie M'Gill
Crystal Ship
Touch Me
The End

The Flying Burrito Brothers open the show with a surprisingly lackluster set, and are followed by an impassioned one-hour show by Albert King. The Doors follow with a leisurely paced two-hour concert, which continuously alternates between accelerated and slow tempos. They open with a superb version of "Roadhouse Blues," with Krieger brilliantly punctuating Morrison's lyrics. "Ship of Fools"

introduces part of an instrumental jam that will later be incorporated into their "People Get Ready" jam.

The two previous nights of intense singing at Winterland have left Jim's voice quite hoarse and on the edge of cracking. Songs that require full vocal stamina, such as "Break on Through," suffer as a result. But Morrison is in good spirits, stretching out where he can, but cautiously restraining himself during strenuous passages such as the "Jesus, save us!" portion of "When the Music's Over." "Light My Fire" is extended into a long medley incorporating other songs and works so well that the Doors continue to use this medley throughout the rest of the year. During the encore of "Soul Kitchen," Jim breaks out his harmonica and inserts a brief solo before the final stanza. Every time the chorus comes around to "I guess we have to go now," the audience replies with a resounding "No!" and following one of the concluding verses of "We'd really like to stay here all night!" the auditorium roars with an affirmative "Yeah!"

When the crowd is leaving after the show, Jim unexpectedly reappears onstage under the blinding houselights and grabs his gold microphone. "Hey listen! Does anyone have to go home early tonight?" echoes throughout the startled arena, eliciting a thunderous "No!" as the crowd stops at the exits. Morrison continues with "You'd like to listen to some more, right?" which provokes a deafening "Yes!" as the crowd hastens back into the arena. In response to the audience's enthusiasm, the Doors launch into a passionate version of "Love Me Two Times," followed by "Maggie M'Gill." Jim then lightheartedly asks for a vote on either "Crystal Ship" or "Touch Me," and "Crystal Ship" garners the loudest applause. At the conclusion of "Crystal Ship," the band surprises the crowd by immediately springing right into "Touch Me." Then, after a brief interval on the darkened stage, the opening chords for "The End" echo through the arena, and the Doors conclude the night with a full rendition of the song. This is one of the longest performances the Doors ever play, with the encores themselves practically comprising an entire show. The band finally leaves the stage well after one in the morning.

☀ Also performing: Albert King; the Flying Burrito Brothers

♛ Capacity: 12,000 to 14,000

▥ Promotion: West Coast Promotions–Linnell/Branker

▥ Note: The precise sequence of songs remains uncertain.

FRI. FEB. 13 1970 Allen Theatre
Cleveland, OH

Early Show (7:30 p.m.)

Roadhouse Blues (opening song)	Light My Fire »
Ship of Fools	Fever »
When the Music's Over	Light My Fire

Late Show (10:00 p.m.)

Roadhouse Blues	Light My Fire »
Ship of Fools	Fever »
Five to One	Light My Fire
When the Music's Over	Encores: Who Do You Love »
Maggie M'Gill (an extended version)	Money »
Peace Frog	Little Red Rooster
The Spy in the House of Love	Break On Through

At the start of the first show, Morrison confidently sprints on stage, picks up some maracas, and announces "We're gonna have a real good time." Then the band launches into "Roadhouse Blues," and the Doors are off into a very solid show. Morrison is quite animated and spontaneous. The band closes with their extended version of "Light My Fire'" but does not return for an encore.

As it turns out, the first show is a warm-up for an exciting second show, which concludes with three encores. At the late show, Morrison seems to really come alive with frequent and often humorous communications with the audience. There is some initial trepidation when a large group of Hell's Angels lines up in front (since this is shortly after Altamont), but it is quickly determined that they are just there to dig the show. High spirits pervade the set, and Morrison playfully does things like disconnecting his microphone stand's neck from the base, parading it around like a cheerleader's baton, and then humorously threatening to spear members of the audience with the chrome javelin. After "Light My Fire," the audience is already heading for the exits when Morrison reappears and announces that they aren't ready to call it a night, and the band breaks into a blues medley as the elated audience races back to their seats. The band wraps up with a grand finale of "Break on Through."

Both performances are superb, with the band putting their heart and soul into the texture of rustic blues that dominate their recently released "Morrison Hotel." Their fabricated media persona has been shattered by recent events, and without that pressure the Doors are able to focus on their musical heritage, which is rooted deeply in rhythm and blues. This recent focus comes through solidly, and the audience is treated to a rekindled sense of freedom that the band hasn't experienced in a long time. The transformation enables the Doors to relax into a groove that recalls the innovative humor of the days preceding Miami.

- Set-list incomplete.
- Also performing: Eli Radish
- Promotion: Belkin Productions/Cleveland After Dark
- Capacity: 2,800 to 3,000

SAT. FEB. 14 1970 Allen Theatre
Cleveland, OH

Roadhouse Blues
Ship of Fools
Maggie M'Gill

The Doors are invited back for an encore performance that is only advertised on the day of the show. They do one show at 8:00 that is every bit as exciting as the previous night's.

- Also performing: Eli Radish [probably opened tonight's show as well]
- Set-list incomplete.
- Promotion: Belkin Productions/Cleveland After Dark
- Capacity: 2,800 to 3,000

SUN. FEB. 15 1970 Chicago Auditorium Theatre
Chicago, IL

Early Show (8:00 p.m.)
[A brief tune-up while Manzarek plays "Spy in the House of Love" on acoustic piano]

Roadhouse Blues
Ship of Fools
Alabama Song »
Back Door Man »
Five to One
Peace Frog »
Blue Sunday
Crawlin' King Snake
When the Music's Over
Will the Circle Be Unbroken »
Spy in the House of Love

Break on Through »
 "There You Sit!" »
Break on Through
The Soft Parade
Light My Fire »
 [Manzarek's instrumental] »
Fever »
 [Krieger's instrumental]»
Summertime »
 "Please Don't Cry" ("Summertime") »
Light My Fire

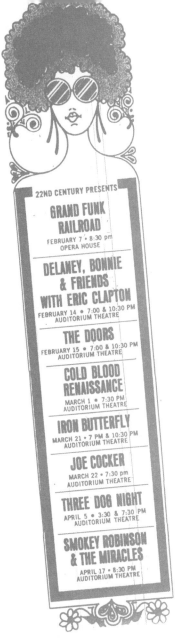

The Doors nonchalantly take the stage and proceed with a very relaxed but unusually tight performance. Ray Manzarek comes to the musical forefront with dynamically clear and distinct keyboard playing, which is beautifully augmented by Densmore's steady and concise percussion.

On a special note, "Spy in the House of Love" is preceded by Morrison initiating an impromptu rendition of "Will The Circle Be Unbroken" during which Ray quickly jumps in on acoustic piano. This may well have been the only time the band played this song. The show concludes with a lengthy "Light My Fire" jam during which Manzarek takes an extended solo and Morrison concludes "Summertime" with numerous repetitions of the song's plaintive stanza, "Please don't cry."

Late Show
The End (finale)

Throughout the second performance, Jim frequently inserts selected poetry into the songs, eliciting mixed reactions from the audience. Ray Manzarek fondly remembers the late show, likening it to the nights at the Whisky when Jim would drift into a stream of spontaneous prose. Many appreciate the variations, but others seem to be frustrated by these detours. Overall, the performances go remarkably well, with much of the audience delighted by the Doors' immersion into the blues.

Billboard gives a somewhat negative evaluation of the shows that seems to miss the point of the second one entirely: "The Doors just couldn't put it together despite playing for nearly two hours in both shows. The first show was clearly superior to the second, which was drowned in the ocean of free verse by singer Jim Morrison. The second show found Morrison and the rest of the group to be in separate worlds. Although fine instrumentally, especially Densmore, Morrison frequently got caught up in his own lyrics, mixing lines from different songs, and generally confusing everyone. The concert closed, appropriately, with 'The End,' featuring a strong solo by Manzarek." (George Knemeyer, "Talent In Action," *Billboard*, Feb. 28, 1970)

Note: There was an initial scheduling error in advertisements for the show, placing it on March 14 when Delaney & Bonnie and Friends featuring Eric Clapton performed.

Also performing: The Staple Singers

Late show set-list incomplete.

Promotion: Belkin Productions

Capacity: 4,000

Reindicted

The grand jury in Phoenix reindicts Jim Morrison and Tom Baker on charges stemming from the incident on a Continental Airlines flight the previous November. The indictment is designed to correct a previous faulty indictment.

MARCH
3
TUESDAY

MAR. 13 1970 Aardvark Cinematheque
Chicago, IL

This is the midwest premiere of *Feast of Friends*.

MAR 15 TO APR 4 1970 Proposed Tour of Japan

Although tentative plans were still being arranged as recently as January, this anticipated tour never materializes.

Stewardess Testifies: "Intoxicated, obnoxious..."

Jim Morrison and Tom Baker appear in federal court, Phoenix, Arizona, for the trial stemming from the charges of two counts of "assaulting, threatening, intimidating, and interfering with the performance of a flight crew" in November. Defense attorney Craig Mehrens contests the charges, maintaining that the laws under which his clients are being prosecuted were established for the purpose of curtailing hijacking incidents. U.S. District Court Judge William P. Copple finds Morrison guilty of the reduced charge of simple assault, which carries a maximum three-month imprisonment and $300 fine. Tom Baker is acquitted when the prosecution fails to produce any verification that he had continued to harass the stewardess after being warned to refrain. Morrison's sentencing is set for April 6.

The stewardesses testify that Morrison and Baker were intoxicated, obnoxious, and began shouting obscenities when refused additional liquor on the flight. One of the women further testifies that Morrison had repeatedly clasped her arm and shoulder until she finally had to summon Captain Craig Chapman, who radioed ahead to the airport requesting that authorities meet the plane. Her confusion over who had done what, and which of the men was Morrison, eventually leads to Jim's being acquitted.

> Shouting obscenities when refused additional liquor on the flight, Morrison had repeatedly clasped her arm and shoulder until she finally had to summon Captain Craig Chapman.

FRI. MAR. 27 1970 Queen Elizabeth And Orpheum Theaters
Vancouver, Canada

This is the "Jim Morrison Film Festival" as presented by Ihor Todoruk as a benefit for Canada's *Poppin* magazine. The highlight of the festival is the world premiere of *HWY*. Other presentations include Granada Television's *Doors Are Open*, Elektra Records' promotional *Break on Through*, and the Doors' own *Unknown Soldier*.

Jim Morrison has intended to make a personal appearance at the festival (along with Frank Lisciandro) and is en route to Vancouver from his trial in Phoenix when a friend in San Francisco recommends that he reconsider leaving the country, because of his legal difficulties. He sends the producers of the festival a telegram explaining his predicament and wishing them the best of luck.

The festival is presented at the Queen Elizabeth Theater, with the exception of *HWY*, which debuts at midnight at the Orpheum Theater.

Mistaken Identity

The judge for the Continental Airlines trial defers sentencing until later in April after defense attorney Max Fink insists that there had been a case of mistaken identity on the part of the stewardess.

APR. 7 1970 The Lords and the New Creatures
Released by Simon and Schuster

The first printing of the hard-bound copies of *The Lords and the New Creatures* is released in April under the author's full name, James Douglas Morrison. With the support and encouragement of poet Michael McClure, Jim is successful in securing a publisher that will present his work as that of a serious young poet, and not use his rock-star status.

Jim Morrison
his first book of poems
The Lords AND The New Creatures
$3.95 • Simon and Schuster

This volume combines Morrison's *The Lords: Notes on Vision* with *The New Creatures*, which he had privately published the previous year in a limited edition of 100 copies.

When Jim receives his advance copies of the book, he is reportedly thrilled that Simon and Schuster have handled it with genuine respect and honored his request that it be presented without reference to his being the lead singer of the Doors.

FRI. APR. 10 1970 Boston Arena
Boston, MA

Early Show (7:00 p.m.)

"Rock Me" (vocal introduction) »
Roadhouse Blues
Ship of Fools
Alabama Song »
Back Door Man »
Five to One »
  "I Want to Love You, Baby" »
Five to One
When the Music's Over

Rock Me
People Get Ready »
Mystery Train »
Away in India »
Crossroads
Wake Up! »
Light My Fire »
  "Let's Roll, All Night Long!" »
Light My Fire

The Doors' Boston shows go well, although the first show is not nearly as impressive as the second. Morrison precedes their raw, gutsy version of "Roadhouse Blues" with a brief a cappella introduction based on lyrics from "Rock Me." With hardly a pause, the band then leaps into an energetic version of "Ship of Fools" featuring some atmospheric organ work from Manzarek. Later, Morrison's legendary, guttural screams erupt during the transition from "Alabama Song" into "Back Door Man." Following that medley, they do an excellent version of "When the Music's Over." Before the "We want the world" portion, the arena is silent and Jim asks "What do you want?" After the wild response, Morrison queries in a singing voice "What would you do with it?" to boisterous laughter and applause. And then quite unexpectedly, Morrison flatly states "I think I'll pass" to a knowing applause that indicates they understand what he is driving at. After that song, the band does a sparse, bluesy rendition of "Rock Me" that showcases Krieger's guitar prowess, and then quietly initiate their "People Get Ready" jam. As the tempo begins to accelerate into "Mystery Train," the audience breaks into spontaneous applause and the band is off to a respectable version of the medley, despite the fact that Morrison's vocals are becoming increasingly slurred. Next, after his opening shriek of "Wake Up!" Morrison interjects his poetic "Vast Radiant Beach" before bursting into "Wake Up" a second time, as their now customary prelude to "Light My Fire." Robby Krieger digresses into a waltz melody during his lead in "Light My Fire" that bears similarities to John Coltrane's "My Favorite Things" and the Doors' instrumental "Summertime."

Late Show (10:00 p.m.)

Break on Through
When the Music's Over
Roadhouse Blues*
The Spy in the House of Love
Alabama Song »
Back Door Man »
Five to One
Build Me a Woman
You Make Me Real
People Get Ready »
Mystery Train »

Away in India »
Crossroads
  (band introductions)
Light My Fire »
Fever »
Summertime »
St. James Infirmary Blues »
  "Graveyard Poem" »
Light My Fire
Been Down So Long
  (stage power cut)

The second performance tonight is outstanding despite the stage power being cut off when the show goes overtime. Morrison hits the stage in a fury of energy that never seems to subside as he spins and reels about the stage throughout the show. During "Alabama Song," he slips while climbing a speaker stack, landing flat on his back in front of the speakers and proceeds with the song that way without missing a beat.

The late show opens with a vigorous "Break on Through" with Morrison bulleting out onto the stage right after the introductory notes and erupting into the song. The show starts at 12:18 a.m. and is running excessively late when the frustrated hall manager loses all patience and disconnects the band's stage power around two a.m. The electric instruments all go down, but the house PA system, including Jim Morrison's microphone, is still live. As the crowd screams for more, Jim is furious that their power had been cut and clearly growls "Cocksuckers!" into the live mike. He continues with "We should all get together and have some fun, because they're going to win if you let them!," Manzarek leaps from his keyboards, cups Jim's mouth, and emphatically reminds him that any controversial incidents could further damage the already excessively scrutinized tour. Morrison then angrily smashes his microphone stand into the floor and follows Ray off the stage.

The following day Morrison tells a reporter from *Melody Maker:* "When I freak out on stage it's usually for one reason, I can't stand them stopping the show. It happened again last night in Boston. Just as we got the audience going some—comes up and pulls the plugs. I got mad not just for us but for the audience who had been cheated as well. The result was that they cancelled the next booking in Salt Lake City." ("Super Jim, the angel faced Rasputin," *Melody Maker,* May 2, 1970)

The *Boston Globe* comments: "The Doors performed non-stop for almost two hours—until the Arena management turned the power off, and it would be [an] understatement to say the show was a complete success. Morrison is a showman. He prances and reels about the stage, miraculously staying on his feet. The end of the show was tense. After Morrison's insistence to sing, the power was shut off. The crowd chanted for more; Manzarek implied that if they didn't quit, they would be blackballed from halls across the country." (Barry Gilbert, *Boston Globe,* April, 1970)

At this point in the music business, there was still no generally agreed upon concluding time for live concerts and there were enormous variations from venue to venue. Some halls staged their legendary "Dance Marathons" with groups such as the Grateful Dead and Allman Brothers, which continued into the daylight hours, while others tended to emphasize contractual deadlines. The Doors were just one of a multitude of bands that enjoyed performing into the late hours, but its reputation for late-night concerts was no doubt exaggerated because of the band's other reputation—for pushing the limits of the law. This tendency to spotlight the Doors in an extreme fashion lent credence to Jim Morrison's conclusion that "We're the band people love to hate."

- Also performing: Gordon Lowe; Axis
- Promotion: Fred Samango
- The band may have decided against performing "Roadhouse Blues" in this set
- Note: This show was originally scheduled for April 17.
- Both performances recorded for *Absolutely Live*

This tendency to spotlight the Doors in an extreme fashion lent credence to Jim Morrison's conclusion that "We're the band people love to hate."

SAT. APR. 11 1970 The Salt Palace CANCELLED
Salt Lake City, UT

The manager of the Salt Palace, Earl Durea, is flown to Boston in order to give a firsthand account of the Doors' performance to his board of directors. He is present during the second show when the power is disconnected, and based on his observations, the board decides to cancel this evening's performance.

- Promotion: West Coast Promotions–Linnell/Branker

SUN. APR. 12 1970 University Of Denver Arena
Denver, CO

Back Door Man   When the Music's Over
Break on Through   Light My Fire

The Doors and the promoters for this show are greeted by the notorious
Denver vice squad known as "McKevitt's Marauders." The "Marauders" proceed to
scrutinize every aspect of this production, hauling in cameras and tape recorders
to capture any indiscretion that might offend the moral sensibilities of the community and, incidentally, bring them some welcome political leverage.

At one point during the show, for example, Jim Morrison is spotted consuming
a beer, which he puts down in huge gulps frequently followed by an uninhibited
belch, and the squad moves in to arrest him for consuming alcoholic beverages in
public. However, the promoter is quick on his feet and challenges the squad to consider the consequences if he has to go on stage and explain why the show is being
shut down. McKevitt reexamines the situation and backs down, satisfied that at
least Morrison's backstage beer supply has been cut off. When Morrison discovers
this, he approaches the audience with the request for a beer and is deluged with
about two dozen cans.

Overall, it is a flamboyant and theatrical two-hour concert that grips the
audience's attention from beginning to end, largely owing to Morrison's genius for
"formulated spontaneity." As the opening notes to "Back Door Man" resound, Morrison leaps onto the stage bathed in red and purple lights, reeling and spinning
until he latches onto the microphone to spit out a frightful, high-pitched laugh and
the introductory verse without missing a beat. Throughout the show, he alternately
paces the stage and rhythmically straddles the microphone stand, periodically
collapsing onto the stage in wrenched contortions. Ultimately, the only dissatisfied
members of the audience are the vice squad, who leave empty-handed.

🐝 Promotion: Continental Artists; DU Special Events Committee

✍ Set-list incomplete

✗ Capacity: 6,000

SAT. APR. 18 1970 Honolulu Convention Center
Honolulu, HI

Back Door Man »   Love Me Two Times
   "Love Hides" »   Rock Me »
Five to One »   Wake Up! »
Roadhouse Blues   Light My Fire »
   (Morrison demands lighting changes) Fever »
Break on Through   "Love Hides" (reprise) »
When the Music's Over   Light My Fire
Peace Frog »   Encore: The End »
The Crystal Ship   "Across the Sea" »
People Get Ready »   The End »
Mystery Train »   "Accident" »
Away in India »   "Ensenada" »
Crossroads »   The End (Oedipal section) »
People Get Ready   "Coda Queen" »
Love Me Two Times »   The End (finale)
Baby, Please Don't Go »

The Doors' final performance in Hawaii soars like a wild two-hour amuse-
ment-park ride. Prior to the show, the Doors partake of the Hawaiian Islands' legendary Paka Lolo, a particularly potent variety of marijuana. As the band starts its
introductory medley, Morrison pleads for the brilliant stage lights to be turned
down. By the conclusion of "Roadhouse Blues," he is furious that the lights are still

so bright, and accuses the lighting personnel of being "incompetent, immaterial, irrelevant and unnecessary" and insists the lights be readjusted to "something dark with gloom, and just leave it at that!" The stage goes dark to audience applause and the Doors burst into a jazzy, incendiary version of "Break on Through." Manzarek takes an extended solo before the climax and then draws it to a fiery conclusion in a vocal duet with Morrison that elicits thunderous applause. However, by the conclusion of "When the Music's Over," Morrison is becoming noticeably intoxicated and continues to become more so as the evening wears on. He begins eliciting requests from the audience, an activity that always seems to create pandemonium. The band brings the fast-tempoed "Peace Frog" to an abrupt ending and deftly shifts down into a beautiful version of "Crystal Ship." The "People Get Ready" jam is particularly vital tonight, as Densmore drives the band with a furious locomotive percussion into "Mystery Train," and then Manzarek graciously leads them out of it with a melodic solo that melts into a relaxed instrumental version of "Across the Sea." Instead of concluding the jam at the end of "Crossroads," they drift back into "People Get Ready" to bring the jam full circle.

Another unusual twist this night is the insertion of "Baby, Please Don't Go" during "Love Me Two Times." Toward the end of "Rock Me," Morrison begins a hypnotic repetition of "All right! All right! All right!." until exploding into a raucous "Wake Up!" which introduces the concluding "Light My Fire" jam.

The encore of "The End" presents a fitting conclusion to the show. Morrison seems to effortlessly insert select portions of poetry throughout the piece, bringing the evening's performance to a dramatic finale that provides something special for everyone in attendance.

Promotion: West Coast Promotions–Linnell/Branker

Note: The Doors did not play Honolulu on Friday, April 17.

Testimony Reversed

APRIL

20

MONDAY

In Federal Court, Phoenix, Arizona, Jim Morrison is acquitted in the Continental Airlines case when the complainant reverses her testimony, stating that she had mistaken James Morrison for the other defendant.

FRI. MAY 1 1970 THE SPECTRUM
Philadelphia, PA

Who Do You Love
Roadhouse Blues
Break on Through »
  "Feel It!" »
Break on Through
Back Door Man »
  "Love Hides" »
Back Door Man
Ship of Fools
Universal Mind
When the Music's Over
People Get Ready »

Mystery Train »
Away in India »
Crossroads »
Wake Up! »
Light My Fire
Maggie M'Gill
Roadhouse Blues (reprise) »
Been Down So Long »
Rock Me
Carol »
Soul Kitchen

This is a terrific show from start to finish. The band comes on full of compelling energy, which propels the show to innumerable heights and elicits consid-

Their listeners are exhausted from an experience which is the best musical version of an LSD trip given by any contemporary rock group.

erable applause from the audience. The "Roadhouse Blues" from this show is included in the 1978 release of Jim Morrison's poetry called *An American Prayer.*

Philadelphia's *Evening Bulletin* lauds the show: "Their music paints a spiraling turbulence which increases in thrust and power as they progress through each number. By concert's end, they and their listeners are exhausted from an experience which is the best musical version of an LSD trip given by any contemporary rock group. Morrison's gut blasts and drawn out moans from his powerful voice combine with Manzarek's organ arrangements to lull the Doors' audiences into a turbulent, hypnotic trance . . . the trance never wore off last night." (S. Robert Jacobs, "Morrison Steals Show From the Other 3 Doors," *Evening Bulletin,* May 2, 1970)

Commenting on an interview done with Jim earlier in the day for *Downbeat,* Michael Cuscuna says: "In Jim Morrison, I found to my surprise a beautiful human being who, not unlike Charles Mingus, has been a victim of sensational publicity and harassment by silly journalists. This same Jim Morrison seems trapped in the routine of success, with a public image to live up to, while his best musical and cinematic talents and ambitions remain stifled and/or untapped. Whatever part of their musical history appeals to you—if any—the Doors are one of the most important forces in rock." (Michael Cuscuna, *Downbeat,* May 28, 1970)

- This performance is recorded for *Absolutely Live*
- Also performing: The Staple Singers; the Blues Image
- Attendance: 14,027

SAT. MAY 2 1970 Pittsburgh Civic Arena
Pittsburgh, PA

Back Door Man »	Crossroads »
"Love Hides" »	Blues Jam
Five to One	Universal Mind
Roadhouse Blues	Someday Soon
People Get Ready »	When the Music's Over
Mystery Train »	Close To You (Manzarek on vocal)
Away in India »	Light My Fire

The Doors are a little slow getting started tonight, but by the time they arrive at their "People Get Ready" jam they are in high gear. That unreleased jam goes over exceptionally well with the crowd, who are subsequently introduced to two additional new songs—"Universal Mind" and (the still unreleased) "Someday Soon." The only other known time that "Someday Soon" is performed will be one month later in Seattle, and that version is pitiful in comparison to this one. After superb versions of both of songs, the audience is busy shouting for favorites when Manzarek suddenly bursts into the opening lines of "When the Music's Over" and the crowd goes wild. Morrison turns toward Krieger and breaks into a wide smile and Robby reciprocates in kind. Tonight's version of the song rises to new heights when Morrison begins inserting rare snippets of his poetry in between his legendary howls and groans. When the song is over, the band takes a pause and Morrison requests a cigarette from the audience. He is bombarded with single butts and full packs. Morrison gratefully scoops up a handful, strolls over to Manzarek, and the two of them take a brief smoke break. During it, one heckler successfully provokes Morrison into flipping him off, and then, after a few moments, Jim returns to his mike and makes some brief comments about his experiences in Miami. Then the band continues with another unreleased song—a rendition of "Close to You" featuring Manzarek on lead vocals, during which Morrison moves to the side of the stage. As Manzarek cries out his invitation of "Wanna get close to you, Pittsburgh," a portion of the audience responds by spilling out of their seats and advancing toward the stage. The arena management reacts by bringing up the house lights, but by now nothing can interfere with the high spirits that pervade the auditorium.

At one point, he gathers up all of the bras that have been hurled at him and playfully holds them up like some sort of a preposterous trophy.

After the song, the band members joke around, Robby dances a jig, and Manzarek is beaming with a radiant smile as he breaks into the introductory organ passages to "Light My Fire." During the instrumental excursion, Morrison spins about the stage, stopping frequently to lean over and kiss or be kissed by impassioned women in the audience. At one point, he gathers up all of the bras that have been hurled at him and playfully holds them up like some sort of a preposterous trophy.

🌀 This performance is recorded for *Absolutely Live*

🦋 Also performing: The Blues Image

🐵 Capacity: 17,500

FRI. MAY 8 1970 COBO ARENA
Detroit, MI

Roadhouse Blues (abrupt halt)
  (greeting and introduction)
Break on Through
Alabama Song »
Back Door Man »
Five to One
Roadhouse Blues
You Make Me Real
Ship of Fools
When the Music's Over
People Get Ready »
Mystery Train »
Away in India »
Crossroads »
Carol
Light My Fire
Been Down So Long* »
  "Love Hides"* »
  "Ray's Blues"* »
Close to You*
King Bee** »
Rock Me** »
Heartbreak Hotel**
Little Red Rooster**
The End »
  "Across the Sea" »
  "Come on, Baby, Take a Chance with Us!" »
  "Vast Radiant Beach" »
  "Come, They Crooned, the Ancient Ones" »
  "Everything Is Broken Up and Dances" »
  "Wake Up!" »
The End

The Cobo Arena show is reportedly one of the most powerful and outstanding performances of 1970. During the overtime portion of the show, John Sebastian joins the Doors on stage with his harmonica and guitar for an extended blues jam. It is his second time sitting in with the group, and proves to be even more engaging than the memorable occasion in New York in January.

The conclusion of "The End" is a very unusual collage of poetry, which makes it unique even among the previous variations on the song. Jim's singing on the piece is precise, intentional, and emphasized by his clearly pronounced vocals, which make the unusual progression of lyrics even more remarkable. He sings concluding verses of the song at the beginning of the piece, then drifts into a very calm version of "Come with me, across the sea," and then unexpectedly moves into the climactic lyrics "Come on, baby, take a chance with us!" However, instead of building this into its usual crescendo, Jim tones it down and gracefully coasts the verses into "Vast Radiant Beach." There follows a mixture of poetic imagery, beginning with "Come, they crooned, the ancient ones; Beneath the moon beside the lake . . ." and concluding with "Everything is broken up and dances," which abruptly crashes into "Wake Up!" From there, the band sprints into the rapidly accelerating instrumental climax of "The End," and Morrison explodes into a fury of motion, culminating with his collapse on the stage as innumerable arms stretch out to connect with him. This spectacle is followed by a brief harmonica contribution by Morrison and the concluding verses, bringing this fine but highly unusual version of the song to a close.

Tonight's contract with the arena specifies that the concert is to conclude no later than midnight; however, with Morrison's prompting to "Don't let them push us out!" the Doors continue to play for an hour overtime. As a consequence, the manager of the Cobo Arena permanently bars them from ever appearing there again.

✹ With John Sebastian on harmonica
✹✹ With John Sebastian on guitar
🐚 Recorded for *Absolutely Live*
🕺 8:30 p.m. show

SAT. MAY. 9 1970 Fairfield University
Fairfield, CT   CANCELLED

This performance is purportedly cancelled due to a management dispute over the limitations on audience capacity. However, the campus newspaper's front-page headlines announces that the concert has been cancelled after an emergency meeting of the board of trustees on April 30 was organized in order to prevent the Doors from appearing at the upcoming "Dogwood Weekend." Following that session, the board issues a statement insisting that, "It is not in the best interests of the Fairfield community to have as its star attraction at spring weekend a person such as Mr. James Douglas Morrison." The statement goes on to warn that "undesirable and immoral elements might infiltrate the campus under the guise of watching the concert." The cancellation creates enough of an uproar to warrant coverage by the *New York Times* when approximately half of the student body protests with a boycott and calls for the resignation of the university's president. The university paper ceases publication at this point, and how discussions progress between the student body and the heads of the university is somewhat vague. There appears to have been some sort of compromise, because the next band to appear after this dispute is the Grateful Dead on May 17! (Quote from *The Stag*, May 1970)

SAT. MAY 9 1970 Veterans Memorial Auditorium
Columbus, OH

🐾 Capacity: 4,000

Back Door Man	I Will Never Be Untrue
Five to One	Light My Fire
Roadhouse Blues	The Crystal Ship
Heart Break Hotel	Encore: Summertime jam »
Carol	People Get Ready »
When the Music's Over	Mystery Train »
Peace Frog	Away in India »
Ship of Fools	Crossroads »
Land Ho!	People Get Ready

During the Doors' opening "Back Door Man," people flood the orchestra pit in front of the stage prompting security to have all the house lights brought up. This not only destroys the atmosphere of the show, but disorients the band, which is accustomed to performing in darkened halls. At the conclusion of the song, Morrison immediately begins requesting that the lights be turned back down, stating, "Hey man, we need some atmosphere! We've got to have some atmosphere! Could the man who controls the house lights turn them off?" He further stipulates that "We're not going to play anymore unless you do!" It quickly becomes apparent that the lights will not be turned down unless people clear the aisles, and even Morrison pleads with them to do so, punctuating his requests with some caustic remarks. Eventually the situation seems to resolve itself: The lights are dimmed and the show goes on.

Although their performance is far from their most exciting of the tour, the Doors play flawlessly and interject some unusual songs into their repertoire. During "Light My Fire," Morrison "inadvertently" falls into the orchestra pit, but maintains a firm grip on his microphone. For a few eerie moments, hundreds of curious audience members rush to catch a glimpse of him, as the disembodied vocals continue without missing a beat. Finally, the stage security, which has inundated the area, succeed in hauling Morrison out of the pit, just in time for him to recite the concluding verse to the song.

- Also performing: Insect Trust; the Rigg
- Note: Exact sequence on concluding songs may be out of order
- Promotion: Premier Attractions and Fred Samango Present
- Poster art: Dale Beegly/Creative Posters, Inc.
- Capacity: 13,641

MON. MAY 11 1970 Village Gate
New York, NY
"Holding Together" benefit for Tim Leary

Jim Morrison reportedly attends (and may have read some poetry at) this benefit designed to help finance Tim Leary's appeals in the U.S. Supreme Court against an inequitable and apparently vindictive sentencing for possession of a small quantity of marijuana. A similar benefit had just taken place at the Family Dog in San Francisco on April 16 and featured Michael McClure (who read "Poem for Olson & Kerouac"), Allen Ginsberg and Philip Lamantia. Holding Together is a nonprofit organization that defends the rights of individuals who are threatened because of their religious, political, or scientific beliefs.

- Also announced for tonight: Jimi Hendrix, Noel Redding, Johnny Winter, the Grateful Dead, Allen Ginsberg, Alan Watts, Wavy Gravy, and others

Jim in North Beach

In late May, Jim Morrison and Babe Hill (sound technician for Jim's HWY Productions Company) go to San Francisco where Jim sits in with some bands in North Beach.

FRI. JUN. 5 1970

SEATTLE CENTER COLISEUM
Seattle, WA

Back Door Man
   "Love Hides" »
Back Door Man
   "Adolf Hitler Is Still Alive"
Roadhouse Blues
When the Music's Over
   [Morrison's feedback escapade] »
When the Music's Over
People Get Ready »
Mystery Train (instrumental) »

Baby, Please Don't Go
Mystery Train* »
Away in India (instrumental) »
Crossroads
Break on Through
Someday Soon
Five to One
   "When I Was Back in Seminary School" »
Light My Fire
The End [power cut before conclusion]

❊   With Jim Morrison on harmonica

This Seattle performance is undoubtedly one of the most difficult and regrettable shows of the 1970 tour. For unknown reasons, there are obvious hostilities between the audience and the Doors from the moment the band takes the stage. After the icy reception, Morrison seems withdrawn and remote throughout the show. The Doors' last appearance in Seattle (at the Pop Festival) had not gone well and may have contributed to the fact that only one-third of the available seats in the 15,000-seat Coliseum have been sold. There are long pauses between songs that last up to nine minutes, and the catcalls from the audience grow more intense after each song. During the lull after a weary opening version of "Back Door Man," Jim observes there's "Lot's of trouble [equipment] here tonight," then recites the poem "Adolf Hitler Is Still Alive" as if he were filling the time. He follows rhythmically with "Lots of trouble, lots of blues. Whole lot of nothing and nothing to lose. All right!" People in the audience continually shout "Remember Miami!" and call out requests for Jim to take his clothes off, until the band breaks into "Roadhouse Blues." The song gets off to a good start and sounds like it might resuscitate the show, but Morrison just doesn't seem to have his heart in it.

Tonight's version of "When the Music's Over" is particularly dreadful. Morrison appears to be lost in another world, preoccupied and depressed. During the central passage he keeps making ludicrous noises into the mike and then begins passing his microphone in front of his monitors, effecting a long series of howling, ear-piercing feedback that essentially butchers the song. Afterward he apologizes, saying, "Thank you for your patience. It takes a few songs to get warmed up; you know what I'm talking about?"

As the band prepares for the "People Get Ready" jam, Jim continues to converse with the audience. At one point he claims, "You know, I haven't been to Seattle in about two years; And good riddance they say [referring to this crowd]." The audience corrects him, recalling last year's Seattle Pop Festival, and he asks, "Was it a year ago?" As he remembers that other unfortunate performance, he quotes the Latin phrase, "Tempus fugit [Time flies], right?" with a distinctly obscene mispronunciation on "fugit." Jim then seeks to infuse some humor into the situation with, "Well you know, driving into Seattle from the airport . . . Seattle

> You know, driving into Seattle from the airport ... Seattle reminds you of a late 1930s version of twenty years in the future. You know what I mean?!

reminds you of a late 1930s version of twenty years in the future. You know what I mean?!" Some do and break into laughter, but the wry reflection seems to go over many people's heads.

The "People Get Ready" jam falls apart when Jim, for whatever reason, doesn't sing "Mystery Train," leaving the band to carry on with the instrumental until Morrison unexpectedly comes in with a passionless version of "Baby, Please Don't Go." The jam temporarily comes to a standstill until "Mystery Train" is started again, but the songs are decidedly unenthusiastic.

The show begins to improve with "Someday Soon," an unreleased song about the inevitability of death that is in retrospect ominously appropriate.

During their finale of "The End," the power is abruptly cut off and the house lights turned on. The Doors began at 10:20 and were to have been done by midnight. At 12:05, the concert is abruptly terminated and one of the stagehands leads Morrison offstage.

The *Seattle Times* reports: "When Jim Morrison sauntered on stage he got the coldest reception this town has ever accorded a rock star. Audience unrest flared as Morrison, in simple blue tee shirt and black pants, dawdled inexcusably between selections. There were periods of no music, no talk, no action for up to 9 minutes each. Obscene expletives bounced from many parts of the stadium. As cat calls increased, Morrison grew more remote. Morrison was piqued enough at one point to simulate an act, which back in the 1950s even a Seattle audience would have called self abuse. Equipment failures complicated matters. During one selection Manzarek's electric organ was dismantled and replaced. The disappointed promoters said afterward it was not a typical concert." (Victor Stredicke, "The Doors stumble through a concert," *Seattle Times*, June 6, 1970)

And the *Seattle Post-Intelligencer* gives this scathing review: "Morrison, once thought to be a sex symbol on the order of Brando or Presley, is now a parody of his former self. His voice, which once produced soul-chilling screams and sweet, soft, almost boyish emotion, is now without any real expression. His screams are perfunctory, his gentle tones raspy. His movements are now forced and not natural. Where once his performance was a rock communion with his audience, it is now without life. He seems to be quite bored with what he is doing. Morrison and the Doors, meanwhile, are well on their way to becoming an anachronism." (Patrick MacDonald, "Doors a parody of past power, *Seattle Post-Intelligencer*, June 6, 1970)

Albert King's performance goes quite well, featuring powerful versions of "Born Under a Bad Sign" and "Oh, Pretty Woman." The contrast between the two bands make the Doors appear to be well past their prime to Seattle audiences.

Also performing: Albert King

Promotion: West Coast Promotions–Linnell/Branker

Capacity: 15,000

SAT. JUN. 6 1970 P.N.E. Coliseum
Vancouver, Canada

Roadhouse Blues »
Alabama Song »
Back Door Man »
Five to One
When the Music's Over
Love Me Two Times
Little Red Rooster*
Money*
Rock Me*
Who Do You Love*
    "When I Was Back in Seminary School!" »
Light My Fire »

"My Favorite Things" (instrumental) »
Fever »
Summertime »
St. James Infirmary Blues »
Fever »
    "There You Sit! (All By Yourself)" »
Light My Fire
The End »
    "Across the Sea" »
The End »
    "Ensenada" »
The End

Although this performance is not one of the highlights of the 1970 tour, it is significantly better than the previous night's show. The Doors get off to a good start with "Roadhouse Blues" and the whole show goes quite well, sustained by the solid foundation provided by Ray Manzarek. Unfortunately, his keyboard patch into the house PA is plagued with an intermittent connection during "When the Music's Over," but the situation is quickly remedied. Morrison's voice seems a little hoarse, which he astutely compensates for by sometimes dropping an octave or avoiding higher pitches.

During this tour, Albert King frequently appears as the opening act for the Doors. At this show he joins them on stage, along with his Gibson Flying V, "Lucy," for several songs.

Albert King had been cutting his mean Mississippi Delta slide guitar for a long time before he came into prominence in the mid-1960s. By this time, he was renowned for his formidable and fierce style of bottleneck guitar that seemed to explode with all the powerful emotion held within his massive six-foot-four frame. King was a featured act in the major rock venues and festivals of the era, and it was indeed a fortunate occurrence that he was scheduled to appear on the bill with the Doors at several of their 1970 performances. One of his better-known songs, "Born Under a Bad Sign," was reverentially covered by Cream on *Wheels of Fire*. When scheduled as an opening act, Albert King's group was one band that would have been impossible for the audience to overlook. Albert King died from a heart attack on December 21, 1992, in Memphis at the age of sixty-nine.

Also performing: Albert King

Note: These songs feature Albert King on second lead guitar

Promotion:West Coast Promotions–Linnell/Branker

Poster art: Random Hazard. Design by John Van Hammersveld

Outside Police Jurisdiction

JUNE
9
TUESDAY

James Morrison's attorney, Max Fink, files a motion at the Metropolitan Dade County Justice Building, Miami, Florida, to end the trial on the grounds that Morrison's conduct is outside police jurisdiction. The motion is denied.

Exile at the Georges V Hotel

JUNE
27
SATURDAY

Jim Morrison and the Doors' public relations representative Leon Bernard arrive in Paris. Jim expresses a strong desire to spend time there working and absorbing the culture. He returns to Paris in April 1971.

Absolutely Live
Sixth Album Released (E-9002)

JULY
1970

Side One (A):
Who Do You Love
Medley: Alabama Song »
Back Door Man »
 "Love Hides" »
Five to One

Side Two (B):
Build Me A Woman
When the Music's Over

Side Three (C):
Close to You
Universal Mind
Break on Through #2

Side Four (D):
Celebration of the Lizard (breakdown):
 1) Lions in the Street and Roaming »
 2) Wake Up! »
 3) A) (Once I Had) A Little Game »
    B) And the Rain Falls Gently on the Town »
 4) The Hill Dwellers »
 5) A) Names of the Kingdom »
    B) Let the Carnival Bells Ring »
    C) Wait! There's Been a Slaughter Here! »
 6) Not to Touch the Earth »
 7) I Am the Lizard King »
 8) The Palace of Exile
Soul Kitchen

Absolutely Live is released at a time when there is a plethora of live albums on the market. In 1970, repeated attempts are made to capture the raw, vital energy of a live performance on vinyl, and the spirit of the times is very apparent in the multitude of rock festivals taking place. Virtually every band feels an obligation to rerelease their material in the live format to meet the demands of fans and record companies alike. Some translate well to vinyl, while others do not. Attempting to capture the Doors live presents difficulties. The band's interaction with the audience does not translate through sound alone, and the timing appropriate to a live performance may later seem entirely inappropriate on a sound recording.

Nevertheless, the Doors' double live album stands as a fair representation of their live concert appearances. Although the album gets decidedly mixed reviews, it is well received by fans in a market flooded with live releases, and to this day continues to be in demand (in its new CD format).

After the concerts for the live album have been recorded, producer Paul Rothchild takes on the task of constructing a cohesive double album from the master tapes. He laboriously listens to all the multiple takes of different songs until choosing the ones that hold up as the most consistent versions. Then, applying his mastery of sound production and editing, he selects the strongest segments from different takes of the same song, and meticulously pieces them together, producing the finest possible rendition of every piece chosen for the album. His craftsmanship is superb, and it is virtually impossible to detect the many edits he made in putting together the album.

The sound quality of the album also proves to be exceptional for the time, especially considering that all of the performances were recorded on an eight-track machine. Two of those eight tracks were designated as ambient audience microphones, leaving only six tracks available for recording the band. Aided by engineer Bruce Botnick's painstaking recording techniques, Rothchild is able to construct a live album that is not only equivalent to, but often surpasses, the sound quality of many albums of the time, which had the advantage of being recorded on the then state-of-the-art, sixteen-track machines.

Despite its drawbacks, *Absolutely Live* stands as a testament to Paul Rothchild's brilliance. Years later, his sound production on *The Doors* movie will serve to further establish his reputation as one of the true production geniuses in the industry.

🌀 Recorded live at the Felt Forum, Aquarius Theater, Cobo Arena, Boston Arena, Philadelphia Spectrum, Pittsburgh Civic

SAT. JUL. 18 1970 Hyde Park National Amphitheater
London, England

While in London during his European travels, Jim Morrison attends this famous free concert by Pink Floyd at Hyde Park, which draws an estimated crowd of 20,000.

SAT. AUG. 1 1970 The Now Explosion
WPIX-TV (Channel 11), New York, NY

Wake Up! »
The End (with Oedipal section omitted)

This is the American debut of the Doors' performance from the CBC's *The Rock Scene*, which was originally recorded on September 14, 1967, and broadcast in Canada on October 16 that same year.

♀ This episode of the *Now Explosion* was broadcast twice, at 4:30 p.m. and again at 11:00 p.m.

☀ Also performing on this show: Bobby Sherman; Frankie Avalon; Kenny Rogers; the Flaming Embers

Miami Trial

AUGUST 6: Jim Morrison and the Doors arrive at the Carillon Hotel, Miami, Florida, to begin the trial.

AUGUST 10: *The State of Florida vs. James Douglas Morrison*, Metropolitan Dade County Justice Building, Miami, Florida. Case #69-2355. The trial stemming from charges filed after the Doors' Dinner Key Auditorium performance officially begin on this date. Morrison is slated to appear in Division D of the County Justice Center, and is represented by attorney Max Fink as well as Robert Josefsberg, an attorney from Miami. However, due to an over-capacity docket, the start of the trial is delayed until Wednesday.

AUGUST 12: This is the first day of jury selection for the trial.

AUGUST 14: The jury selection is completed and the members are sworn in. The jury consists of four men and two women.

AUGUST 6 THURSDAY THROUGH AUGUST 14 FRIDAY

FRI. AUG. 14 1970 (2) The Hump, Marco Polo Resort Hotel
Miami, FL

Back Door Man
Rock Me
Fever
I'm a Man

Jim Morrison, with friends Babe and Tony, begin their evening by going to the Miami Beach Convention Center to see Credence Clearwater Revival perform. Afterward, they proceed to the nightclub known as the Hump (the reference is to the camel's humps featured throughout the room) to see Canned Heat, who are just beginning a weeklong engagement at the club. After being spotted by the Bear (Canned Heat's Bob Hite), Morrison is coaxed into joining the band onstage as the lead vocalist for a 45-minute set. Although the management is extremely apprehensive, considering the situation in Miami, the set goes remarkably well and the audience is enthralled.

Canned Heat had long been one of the Doors' favorite Los Angeles blues bands. At this time the band featured founding members Bob "The Bear" Hite and Al "Blind Owl" Wilson. Acclaimed Detroit guitar player Harvey Mandell and Larry Taylor (bass) had just left the group to join John Mayall. Jim Morrison's guest appearance with them occurs shortly before Al Wilson's death on September 3. Both Hite and Wilson were avid blues enthusiasts and were regarded as two of the foremost authorities of the genre. Among other things, the band is remembered for its legendary appearances at Monterey and Woodstock, and for their tour with John Lee Hooker, which produced the LP *Hooker 'n' Heat*.

Later that week, Canned Heat is joined by members of the Jefferson Airplane, Jorma Kaukonen and Jack Cassady (who comprised Hot Tuna) for a momentous two-plus-hour jam.

🏋 Capacity: 800

AUGUST 17 MONDAY THROUGH AUGUST 20 THURSDAY

The State of Florida vs. James Douglas Morrison

Metropolitan Dade County Justice Building, Miami, Florida.

AUGUST 17: The trial begins at 10:30 a.m. with opening statements from prosecution and defense lawyers. The state brings forth two witnesses who testify that they saw Morrison expose himself. Then, the Doors' attorney intensely cross-examines them and points out blatant inconsistencies between their sworn statements of two months previous and today's testimony. Fink also presents a request that the defense be allowed to introduce contemporary works such as Woodstock in order that Morrison might be judged according to "community standards." He also asserts that despite the presence of twenty-six police at the concert, there was no arrest made because there was no crime.

AUGUST 19: Over 100 photographs taken by Jeffrey Simon are presented and none indicates that Morrison has committed the offense he is charged with. Simon also testifies that he did not observe Morrison expose himself even though he was within three to five feet of the stage.

AUGUST 20: Judge Murray Goodman refuses the defense's request for admission of evidence pertaining to "community standards."

FRI. AUG. 21 1970 Bakersfield Civic Auditorium
Bakersfield, CA

When the Music's Over
Wake Up »
Light My Fire
The End

This performance lasts for three hours and features three encores.

🗺 Note: The tentative free concert in Miami scheduled for this weekend never took place.

🎸 Also performing: Genetic Drift

📋 Promotion: West Coast Promotions–Linnell/Branker

🏋 Capacity: 3,041

Break on Through
Money
Little Red Rooster
Back Door Man
Medley: "Poetic Improvisation" »
Carol! »
Louie, Louie »
Lions in the Street and Roaming »
Wake Up! »
Once I Had A Little Game »
The Hill Dwellers »
Wait! There's Been a Slaughter Here »

Not to Touch the Earth »
The Names Of The Kingdom »
Heartbreak Hotel »
Light My Fire »
Fever »
Summertime »
St. James Infirmary Blues »
Eleanor Rigby (instrumental) »
Easy Ride »
St. James Infirmary Blues »
Fever »
Light My Fire

Jim Morrison strides purposefully on stage to introduce the show, rhythmically announcing that "This whole thing started with rock 'n' roll, and now it's out of control!" Five years later, Ray Manzarek chooses this introductory phrase as the title for his second solo album.

The Doors again play an exceptionally long show and conclude with what is perhaps the longest improvisational medley they have ever performed. Morrison remains composed throughout the show, pacing across the stage, requesting cigarettes and every so often playfully generating feedback from the speaker stacks, all the while sipping from a continually replenished container of beer.

In front of the stage, the crowd is packed like sardines, and everyone seems to be vying for a closer position. The band is tight, even in this improvisational format, with Manzarek sustaining the pulse and Morrison grinding out an earthy, gutsy, blues-engrossed vocal.

🎵 Also performing: Crabby Appleton
🎵 Promotion: West Coast Productions Linnell/Branker
🎵 Capacity: 15,000
🎵 Set-list may be incomplete

AUGUST 25 TUESDAY THROUGH AUGUST 27 THURSDAY

The State of Florida vs. James Douglas Morrison (continued)

AUGUST 25: A policewoman testifies that no effort was made to arrest Morrison because of their fear of retaliation from the audience. Max Fink later counters the testimony by pointing out that an arrest could have been made later in the dressing room, but wasn't. He asserts once again that there was no arrest made because there had been no crime until the "news media fueled a hysteria" that essentially coerced police into filing charges.

AUGUST 26: Jim Morrison, Ray Manzarek, and Babe Hill use this day off from the trial to take a trip to the Everglades.

AUGUST 27: The prosecution plays a recording of the Doors' March 1, 1969, Dinner Key Auditorium performance. Conspicuously missing is any remark about exposing himself, which prosecution witnesses testified Morrison had made prior to doing so. Ironically, *Hair* is premiered tonight at the Coconut Grove Playhouse in Miami.

Isle of Wight

After the rest of the Doors have departed, Morrison takes a late flight to London and then to the East Afton Farm site for the 1970 Isle of Wight Festival.

SAT. AUG. 29 1970 East Afton Farm
Isle of Wight, England
1970 Isle Of Wight Festival

Back Door Man »
Break on Through
When the Music's Over
Ship of Fools
Light My Fire
The End »

"Across the Sea" »
"Away in India" »
Crossroads »
Wake Up! »
  [instrumental climax] »
The End
(Roadhouse Blues)*

Until now, the Doors have avoided all of the major rock festivals, only reluctantly agreeing to appear at some of the smaller ones in Toronto and on the West Coast. Ever since the Seattle Pop Festival, they have been wary of all outdoor appearances. Now they are scheduled to appear at what is often referred to as the last of the great festivals.

Prior to their appearance, the Doors, without Morrison, meet the press at a tiny riverside pub in Hammersmith. John Densmore comments on the rock festivals: "We don't usually play many festivals in the States because they are so disorganized. Promoters who aren't really promoters put them on to make money and they are terrible. There are so many kids there and they can't see you at all. We would prefer to play a nice hall where the fans can sit down and watch in comfort." ("Enter the Doors minus Jim," *Melody Maker*, Sept. 5, 1970)

Saturday's show opens with a superb two-plus-hour set by John Sebastian, which also features an unexpected appearance by ex-Lovin' Spoonful colleague Zal Yanovsky. After Shawn Phillips and Lighthouse, Joni Mitchell takes the stage solo and has to confront the deteriorating attitude of the audience. After only a few songs, she is almost reduced to tears by the continuing disruptions, but she regains her composure and comments that some audience members are behaving like obnoxious "tourists." Her spirited confrontation works, and she is able to continue her set uninterrupted. Tiny Tim and Miles Davis follow, and then the evening shifts into adrenaline overdrive as Ten Years After takes the stage with the tumultuous energy that made them so memorable in Woodstock. The Doors had originally been scheduled to appear directly following Ten Years After, but are delayed until after Emerson, Lake and Palmer.

The Doors are exhausted from their traveling and the previous weeks' court dates in Miami. Arriving at the festival, the weary band finds themselves sandwiched between Ten Years After and Emerson, Lake and Palmer on one side, and the Who and Sly and the Family Stone on the other. Their intense reflective music is out of synch with acts renowned for their fast and furious pacing. Sometime between one and two in the morning, the Doors take the stage at the chilly outdoor festival and are immediately troubled by the somewhat meager sound reinforcement and lighting systems. They focus primarily on material from their first two albums (with the exception of "Ship of Fools") and keep their set much shorter than the expansive shows they had been giving in the States that summer. Morrison bypasses the improvised inclusion of other songs they had been incorporating into "Light My Fire," but then steps in with some unreleased poetry during "The End." Their show proves to be quite restrained. Rumors circulate that perhaps John Sebastian, who had played harmonica on "Roadhouse Blues," will join them for an encore of that song, but it doesn't come to pass. The Doors are followed by the Who, who, true to their reputation, put on a dynamic and highly acclaimed marathon.

Afterward, Jim Morrison is so troubled by their exhausted appearance that he hints to the rest of the band that he hopes it will be their final live performance. Ultimately, the Doors agree to play two more shows in December, in Dallas and New Orleans, and those prove to be their final performances with Jim Morrison.

The following night (Sunday) at the Isle of Wight, Jimi Hendrix also plays one of his final live performances, just a few weeks prior to his untimely death on September 18.

Billboard comments: "The Doors, one of the Saturday night headliners, turned in a solid performance. Lead singer Jim Morrison's visit to England was very brief, coming as it did in the middle of his Florida trial for alleged self-exposure at a festival there last year." ("Wight makes right but may be last festival," *Billboard*, Sept. 1970)

Meanwhile, the Isle of Wight Festival is experiencing such severe gate-crashing difficulties that by Sunday it is declared a free event. Earlier predictions had insisted that the large pop festivals were a dying phenomenon and that this would be the last major event of its kind. The complete unmanageability of this year's festival quickly turns this prediction into a reality, and before the end of the festival the promoters declare that they have abandoned all hopes of any similar venture next year. The majority of festivalgoers are able to maintain a somewhat relaxed and enjoyable mood despite surging attendance estimates that approximate anywhere from 250,000 to 400,000. Perhaps the most discouraging aspect of all this is that the music festivals are becoming less and less concerned with music. The *London Times's* Karl Dallas reflects after the festival: "It is difficult to write about a pop festival like Isle of Wight in purely musical terms. Indeed, there are some—like the fierce young musical radicals whose attempts to force the organizers into declaring it a free event were a constant peripheral obligato to what went on in the main enclosure—for whom the music is obviously not necessarily the main thing." (Karl Dallas, "Soundtrack for a lifestyle," *London Times*, Aug. 31, 1970)

This portion of the festival was also to have featured the very first satellite broadcast of a rock concert, with capacity to cover the event in forty cities throughout the U.S. and Canada. A company called Video Rangers made arrangements for the broadcast to be reflected off of the Atlantic satellite in color with high-fidelity sound as a special "Metavision" show to be broadcast in New York at 9:00 p.m. and California at 6:00 p.m. Video Rangers were to have worked alongside Joshua Television (both utilizing the equipment of Management Television Systems, Inc.), which had recently brought screen magnification to a Who performance in Tanglewood, Massachusetts. Joshua White was designated to direct the "telecast." Scheduled for the monumental broadcast were the Doors, Jimi Hendrix, Chicago, and Joan Baez. However by early August, it became apparent that there were an insufficient number of venues still available to broadcast the show, and reluctantly Video Rangers had to cancel the event.

The Pye Records Mobile Studio is hired by Columbia to record the entire Isle of Wight Festival, employing the services of producer Ted Macero and four recording engineers. The Doors' set is also filmed; however, the shadowy lighting results in rather dark film footage.

- Note: The Doors performance took place at 2 a.m. on the morning of August 30.
- Also performing on Saturday: John Sebastian; Shawn Phillips; Lighthouse; Joni Mitchell; Tiny Tim; Miles Davis; Ten Years After; Emerson, Lake & Palmer; the Who; Sly and the Family Stone; [and possibly] Cat Mother and the All Night Newsboys; Mungo Jerry; Spirit
- Also performing on Sunday: Kris Kristofferson; Heaven; Ralph McTell; Free; Donovan; Pentangle; Moody Blues; Jethro Tull; Jimi Hendrix; Joan Baez; Richie Havens; Leonard Cohen
- Promotion: Fiery Creations Presents
- According to some sources, there may have been an encore performance of "Roadhouse Blues"

SUN. AUG. 30 1970 Second European Tour CANCELLED

      Tentative arrangements had been made for a second European tour starting with the Doors' appearance at the Isle of Wight Festival. However, Judge Goodman insists that the original court schedule of Morrison's Miami trial be maintained. This results in many European fans never being able to see the band live.

      The following night's performance had been scheduled for Montreux, Switzerland, with Black Sabbath opening. The Doors are replaced by Cactus and Taste.

      The European tour was to have included the following scheduled dates:

AUG. 31 1970 Montreux Festival, Switzerland CANCELLED

SEPT. 2 1970 K.B. Hallen, Copenhagen, Denmark CANCELLED

SEPT. 10 1970 Bremen, Germany CANCELLED

SEPT. 11 1970 Rome, Italy CANCELLED

SEPT. 12 1970 Milan, Italy CANCELLED

SEPT. 14 1970 Olympia, Paris, France CANCELLED

      In addition, a brief tour set for March 1971 was being tentatively scheduled by Barry Dickins of the Harold Davison offices and was supposed to include three live performances and one television appearance.

Miami, Hendrix, and Joplin

SEPTEMBER 2 THROUGH OCTOBER 30
WEDNESDAY — FRIDAY

      SEPTEMBER 2: The prosecution rests its case and the defense begins presenting its witnesses. Although they have sixty witnesses ready to contradict the prosecution's testimony, Judge Goodman orders them to restrict the number to seventeen.

      SEPTEMBER 3: An eleven-day recess is called. During the recess, Jim Morrison spends much of his time with Frank Lisciandro and Babe Hill. They attend an Elvis Presley concert in Miami and take a combination fishing and skin diving trip to the Bahamas accompanied by attorney Max Fink.

      SEPTEMBER 14: The defense resumes.

      SEPTEMBER 16: Jim Morrison and other members of the band are called to testify.

      SEPTEMBER 17: Jim Morrison and the Doors testify.

      SEPTEMBER 18: The defense rests. Jimi Hendrix dies in London, England.

SEPTEMBER 19: The prosecution and defense give their closing arguments.

SEPTEMBER 20: The jury returns with verdicts of not guilty on the felony charges of "lewd and lascivious behavior" and "public drunkenness." However, they do find Morrison guilty of the misdemeanors of "open profanity" and "indecent exposure." The jury is unaware that, while they were in recess, Judge Goodman has expressed his opinion that it is "already proven beyond a shadow of a doubt that Mr. Morrison didn't expose himself." Morrison is instructed to return for sentencing on October 30. Following the trial, Rolling Stone's "Random Notes" reports: "Jim Morrison drove back to L.A. from Miami following his trial and stopped off in New Orleans. After visiting the St. Louis Cathedral there, he sent off a picture postcard to the rest of the Doors with the message: "Don't worry; the end is near, Ha Ha!" The picture he sent was the Sacrifice of the Divine Lamb." (*Rolling Stone*, Nov. 26, 1970; used with permission: © Straight Arrow Publishers, Inc. 1996)

OCTOBER 4: After the deaths of Janis Joplin and Jimi Hendrix, Jim Morrison tells his friends that they're "looking at number three."

OCTOBER 30: Jim Morrison returns to Miami and is given the maximum sentences of two months for "profanity" and six months for "indecent exposure," to be served in the Dade County jail. Attorney Max Fink immediately files an appeal with the United States District Court. The basic consensus of the legal community is that the sentencing will be overruled in the higher courts.

13
First compilation album released

Side One (A):
Light My Fire
People Are Strange
Back Door Man
Girl
Moonlight Drive
Crystal Ship
Roadhouse Blues

Side Two (B):
Touch Me
Love Me Two Times
You're Lost Little

Hello, I Love You
Land Ho!
Wild Child
The Unknown Soldier

TUE. DEC. 8 1970 Village Recorders
West Los Angeles, CA

On Jim Morrison's twenty-seventh birthday, he goes to Village Recorders with engineer Jon Haeny to record a three-hour session of his poetry. This renowned session is commonly referred to as the "An American Prayer" poetry reading. Portions of this session appear in Frank Lisciandro's compilations of Jim Morrison's poetry *Wilderness* and *The American Night*. The 1978 *An American Prayer* album includes a mixture of recordings from this and Jim's other studio poetry reading in March 1969. Depending on future decisions concerning Jim Morrison's estate, there is always the possibility of an official release of his poetry.

Note: The unofficially released recordings of poetry are an edited version of the 1969 studio session.

FRI. DEC. 11 1970 State Fair Music Hall
Dallas, TX

Early Show

Love Her Madly »
  [instrumental jam] »
Back Door Man

Ship of Fools
The Changeling »
L.A. Woman »
When the Music's Over

Late Show

Riders on the Storm
Light My Fire (finale)

The Doors' performances tonight are quite unusual and include the debut of much of their new material from the forthcoming *L.A. Woman*. They haven't performed in many months, having endured the ordeals of the Miami trial, and they are bound to be somewhat rusty. The first show opens with "Love Her Madly," which surges into a spontaneous instrumental that emerges into "Back Door Man." Later in the set, the group doesn't even pause between songs, fusing "The Changeling" into "L.A. Woman," and then coming out of that song straight into "When the Music's Over."

Morrison seems a bit weary from the start, and becomes progressively more withdrawn as the show continues, perhaps due to the prodigious amount of beer he is consuming. "L.A. Woman" seems relatively tame compared to the album version, though its debut should have been a showstopper.

Not a bad night for the group, although it is uncustomarily sedate. Apparently there is some real concern about Morrison's condition prior to the second show. He is exhausted, and the alcohol is further sapping his energy. Onstage, he is reportedly having difficulty maintaining his equilibrium, as if he might keel over at any moment. He also keeps his back to the audience throughout much of the set. During the late show, the band runs through a series of their new songs, concluding the relatively short set with "Light My Fire." However, there is a definite tension building on stage and the volcano finally erupts toward the show's conclusion. Morrison and Krieger apparently collide into one another during the apex of one song, and both topple to the floor, narrowly missing a plunge off the stage.

The *Dallas News* reports: "Morrison has vocal style similar to John Kay's (Steppenwolf). Subtly aggressive, insinuating, it drones on, weaving itself around the band's rock/blues progression. Their performance was casual, informal. No encore was played, but the set was a satisfying one that rounded out their music, giving it an electronic blues dimension that doesn't come through as strongly on record." (Pat Pope, *Dallas News*, Dec. 23, 1970)

🜚 Also performing: Courtship

🜚 Late show set-list incomplete

🜚 Promotion: Richard Linnell

SAT. DEC. 12 1970 The Warehouse
New Orleans, LA
The Doors' Final Performance with Jim Morrison

Soul Kitchen
  [Jim Morrison narrates some vapid jokes to the audience]
Break on Through
Light My Fire (finale)

The Doors' performance begins in customary fashion, but there is a dramatic turn of events halfway through the abbreviated show. Jim Morrison begins to omit key lyrics and then abruptly slumps against the microphone stand as if a puppeteer had suddenly let go of his strings. Ray Manzarek later describes the incident as watching Jim's strength drain out of him and dissipate into the air as if some mysterious force had wrenched his life energy right out of him. He begins to halfheartedly mutter a few jokes to the audience, which are basically unintelligible, and the house becomes very quiet. It is obvious to everyone in attendance that something indefinable, and extremely troublesome and disorienting, has happened to Jim.

The Doors cautiously continue with their set after Morrison seems to regain enough stamina to do so. Jim appears to grasp onto the microphone stand for support, and passively mouths the lyrics to songs. The band brings the show to a quick conclusion by limiting additional songs, and jumps into the "Light My Fire" finale. It is during this song's instrumental passage that Morrison seems to disintegrate totally. He slumps down on the drum riser and, when it comes time for him to return to his microphone, he doesn't budge. The band compensates by cycling back through their instrumental passages. When it becomes apparent that Jim is not going to get up off the platform again, Densmore takes his hi-hat foot and firmly shoves Morrison toward the front of the stage. Morrison grimly rises up, returns to his microphone, mutters something, and tries to complete the song. Accounts vary as to whether he completes the song first, but what follows is an explosion. In tormented frustration, he repeatedly smashes his microphone stand into the stage with such force that the boards splinter. He then throws the mike stand onto the floor in front of the audience, and storms off the stage.

Although the Doors complete their performance, Morrison's equilibrium and vitality never return, and the entire band experiences a disturbing premonition that this may very well be their last appearance together. They later agree to discontinue live performances, at least for the time being, and fly back to Los Angeles.

The proprietors of the Warehouse choose not to repair the damage to the stage floor for years after this show because of its historical significance.

🖐 Set-list incomplete
🐾 Promoter: Beaver Productions

MID DEC. 1970 The Doors Break from Touring

After their excruciating night in New Orleans, the Doors unanimously resolve to stay off the road for a while, and focus primarily on their studio work. The years have taken their toll, and the band members feel a sense of relief at the prospect of a break. They hope that when they return to touring they can do so with renewed strength and optimism.

John Densmore: "The reason we were so negative about the road was because toward the end we just didn't think it was worth it. We were getting hassled so much by various establishment people—police, narcotics, vice squad, etc.—and the audience expected some kind of a spectacle rather than music, you know, because of Jim's image. So he grew his beard, gained a little weight and went off to Paris, and we all just said, well, the road, ugh, for a while." (Bob Nirkind interview "The Doors' Aftermath," *Phonograph Record Magazine*, April, 1972)

Jim Morrison comments to *Rolling Stone:* "We're kind of off playing concerts; somehow no one enjoys the big places anymore, and to go into clubs more than just a night every now and then is kind of meaningless." (Ben Fong-Torres, "Jim Morrison's got the blues," *Rolling Stone,* March 3, 1971; used with permission: © Straight Arrow Publishers, Inc. 1996)

Finally, Jim Morrison tells an interviewer from the *Daily Planet* in Miami that they will not be doing any more live concerts. When asked further about it, he says, "It just won't happen." He does not say that the band is breaking up, but does indicate that they will be branching out and exploring different avenues. (*Daily Planet*, Miami, April 10, 1971)

Sunset Sound Recorders
Hollywood, CA

Before the Doors decide to produce their next album at the Doors Workshop, they record some rudimentary versions of "L.A. Woman" and "Riders on the Storm" at Sunset Recorders.

DEC. 1970 The Doors Workshop
Hollywood, CA

At Elektra Sound Studios, the Doors preview some of their new material, including "Riders on the Storm," for their producer, Paul Rothchild. The band is experiencing an off day, and the performance is lackluster. Paul had recently suffered through the death of friend Janis Joplin while recording her final studio album, *Pearl,* and is probably quite sensitive to Jim's excessive alcohol consumption. He listens intently to the new material and afterward approaches the band with genuine reluctance and explains that he feels that there is nothing he can do with what they have given him. Paul goes on to suggest that with their extensive experience in the recording studio, they should consider producing the album themselves.

During the ensuing discussions, Jim suggests that they could record the album themselves at their Workshop and their recording engineer Bruce Botnick offers to help co-produce it.

After considering their options, they unanimously agree to work with Bruce at their "home away from home," the Doors Workshop. Botnick arranges to borrow the old-eight track mixing console from Sunset Sound Recorders and the Doors set out to transform their Workshop into a recording studio. The situation turns out to be ideal, with the band able to organize their own schedule to optimal recording times and free to experiment with ideas without the usual pressures of blocked studio time. This atmosphere creates a favorable mood that permeates the entire record, revealing a band that is both relaxed and inspired by their recording environment.

The Doors also hire Jerry Scheff on bass guitar and Marc Benno on rhythm guitar for the sessions.

In the Bob Nirkind interview for *Phonograph Record Magazine,* Robby and Ray reflect on the decision. Robby: "Paul Rothchild is an absolute ruler when it comes to producing. Once a group does five or six albums, they don't really need that kind of producer because an act who has been into it that long will instinctively know how to produce their own albums. He felt like he wasn't being useful, so together we decided it would be better to go it alone." Ray: "He's a great producer though. Boy, that guy knows his stuff. Yeah, he's really good. It was just time, you know, it was one of those things where you had a relationship and it's like . . . like being in school. Some guys that I went to school with I was best friends with, I've never seen again. You drift apart. I don't know why, it just happens." (Bob Nirkind interview,"The Doors Aftermath," *Phonograph Record Magazine,* April 1972)

FEB. 1971

The Doors' Workshop
Hollywood, CA

Toward the middle of February, the Doors successfully finish recording their new material for *L.A. Woman*. The majority of the material is recorded during an energetic two-week stretch in January. Their "live" recording method—with the entire band playing as a unit—helps to accelerate the process. Additional time is required for some polishing and the addition of sound effects.

FEBRUARY 15

Safe Haven

Pamela Courson, Jim Morrison's girlfriend, checks in to the Georges V Hotel in Paris, where Jim had stayed during his previous stay there. Jim is to join her a short while later. The luxurious hotel, one of the most expensive in Europe, is considered a "safe haven" for celebrities.

LATE FEB. 1971

Poppy Studios
Los Angeles, CA

The Doors and Bruce Botnick complete the mixing for *L.A. Woman*.

EARLY 1971 Whisky A Go Go
West Hollywood, CA

The Doors almost make one last appearance together. The idea of performing at the Whisky A Go Go comes up often during the last days before Jim's departure. The band members have fond memories of the exciting nights of experimentation that preceded their rise to prominence. Live performances in an intimate environment have become a distant recollection after years of riots, warrants, New Haven, Miami, great press, terrible press, TV shows, arenas, vice squads, accusations, arrests, court dates and cancelled dates.

The Whisky would have been a terrific place to have premiered *L.A. Woman* in its entirety—their own version of "bringing it all back home." Unfortunately, it is not to be. The days fly by and before long Jim is en route to Paris.

The following is a compilation of quotations regarding the Whisky:

Elmer Valentine from the Whisky reflects in *Rolling Stone:* "When they started getting big and doing concerts, he [Morrison] was unhappy that he couldn't come back to the club. He missed working out their material, the way "Light My Fire" was done, with the audience like a barometer. Well, they were going to do it, just before he went to Europe. Jim tried to get the fellas to do it, and for one reason or another, it couldn't happen. Then the night they were going to, Jim didn't show up. Of all people. . . ." (Ben Fong-Torres, "James Douglas Morrison, Poet: Dead at 27," *Rolling Stone,* Aug. 5, 1971; used with permission: © Straight Arrow Publishers, Inc. 1996)

During the spring 1970 tour Morrison tells interviewer Michael Cuscuna: "When we were working clubs, we had a lot of fun and could play a lot of songs. A lot of things were going on. Now we just play concert after concert, and we have to play the things the audience wants to hear. Then we record and go out into the concert halls again. The people are very demanding, and we don't get to do a lot of new or different things." (Michael Cuscuna, *down beat,* May 28, 1970)

Jim Morrison later tells interviewer Bob Chorush of the *Los Angeles Free Press:* "A few years ago I wanted to do live performances. I was trying to get everyone to do free surprise spots at the Whisky, but no one wanted to. Now everyone wants to, and I totally lost interest. Although I know it's lot of fun, I just don't have the desire to get up and sing right now." (Bob Chorush, "The Lizard King reforms," *Los Angeles Free Press,* Jan. 15, 1971)

MAR. 1971 United Kingdom Tour Plans Never Materialize

Immediately following their Isle of Wight appearance, tentative plans are made (by Barry Dickins of the Harold Davison offices) for a tour in England that would feature three live performances and one television appearance. By October, the proposed itinerary is expanded to include additional destinations such as Amsterdam, Copenhagen, Paris, Switzerland, and Germany (and possibly even Australia). This tour never gets off the ground, and their final appearance at the Warehouse in New Orleans basically nixes any proposals for further engagements.

Jim Morrison Leaves for Paris

**APRIL
15
THURSDAY (DJ)**

Upon his arrival, Jim and Pamela Courson check into the Le Maris, located on the Right Bank. The exact date is uncertain.

L.A. Woman

Seventh Album Released (E-75021)

LATE APR. 1971

Side One (A)
The Changeling
Love Her Madly
Been Down So Long
Cars Hiss by My Window
L.A. Woman

Side Two (B)
L'America
Hyacinth House
Crawlin' King Snake
The WASP (Texas Radio and the Big Beat)
Riders on the Storm

 Singles
Love Her Madly / (You Need Meat) Don't Go No Further
Riders on the Storm / The Changeling

Despite the recent advent of sixteen-track recording technology, the Doors choose to record this album entirely on an eight-track machine at their own workshop. The album still serves as a testimonial to the quality and integrity that can be maintained in "live studio" recording, where the band members record in unison. The vitality and synergistic elements of a group can be lost in multitrack when an exaggerated emphasis is placed on the production.

- 🖳 Notes: "L'America" was originally recorded as part of the soundtrack for Antonioni's movie *Zabriskie Point*, but was never used for that purpose.

- 🖳 Among the unreleased outtakes from these sessions is a song entitled "The Paris Blues," which is a blues-oriented cut featuring Morrison singing about his upcoming journey to Paris.

- 🖳 Note: "The WASP," also known as "Texas Border Radio," was a pirate radio station that favored the dynamic rhythm and blues virtually ignored on commercial radio. Every midnight, the airwaves shook as the underground station's remarkably powerful signal broadcast as far north as Chicago and east as Florida. In their younger years, both Manzarek and Morrison tuned into the station to keep abreast of the rapidly evolving rock 'n' roll music. When their paths crossed years later, this tribute to WASP developed out of their mutual admiration for the legendary underground station from Texas with the "big beat."

- 🖳 *L.A. Woman* achieves gold status on July 22

APRIL
Morocco

Jim Morrison and Pamela Courson leave Paris in mid-April and spend about three weeks traveling through France, Spain and Morocco.

"Love Her Madly"

Single released in the United Kingdom

EARLY MAY 1971 **Astroquet**
Paris, France (DU)

Crawlin' King Snake

Jim Morrison sits in with an American band called the Clinic.

MAY
7
FRIDAY
Oscar Wilde, Herve Muller, and Yvonne Fuka

Jim meets Herve Muller and Yvonne Fuka, who both work for *Best*, one of France's leading rock magazines. After staying the night, Jim takes them to lunch at the Alexander Restaurant.

Early in the month, Jim and Pamela Courson stay for a few weeks at L'Hotel de Nice on the Left Bank, where Oscar Wilde lived at the end of his life.

The Lost Paris Tape

Jim Morrison reportedly jams with two street musicians at a studio where he had been listening to his poetry earlier in the day. The result is a brief moment of historical value, but a terribly inept attempt at recording "Orange County Suite."

The Doors Workshop
Hollywood, CA

The Doors begin working on new material while Jim is in Paris. Exactly what direction the band is going to pursue is in question. Jim has even suggested that they work on some instrumental material, personally hoping it will include some heavy blues compositions.

Jim Morrison Dies in Paris

17 Rue De Beautreillis (Marais District), Paris, France. Jim's death was originally believed to be a heart attack brought about by a respiratory ailment. However, some associates of his from Paris came forward in 1990 and indicated that he may have actually died from a heroin overdose, primarily due to his unfamiliarity with the powerful narcotic. Ultimately, it is impossible to determine exactly what happened without a comprehensive autopsy report, which was not required in this circumstance because the attending physician had discerned that the death was due to natural causes. Any number of undiagnosed physical maladies may have contributed to Jim's death, even at such a young age.

Previous to this, Morrison had a strong aversion to hard drugs, choosing instead the legal, but equally addictive and potentially deadly drug alcohol. However, he may well have begun experimenting with heroin. If this was the case, he unfortunately underestimated the potency of this deadly substance.

Morrison was awakend by Pamela in the early morning hours because he apparently was having great difficulty breathing. He drew a bath to relax, and at some point in the next few hours, drifted into unconsciousness. Pamela awoke later to discover him unconscious in the bath, summoned help, but was too late. The final outcome was the signing of a death certificate at their place of residence at 17 rue Beautreillis, Paris.

A Call from London

After repeated inquiries from European journalists concerning Jim Morrison's death, Clive Selwood, the director of Elektra's London offices, calls Doors' manager Bill Siddons in Los Angeles concerning the influx of rumors. Bill calls Pamela Courson in Paris and she reluctantly admits that the rumors are true. He decides he had better arrange for the first available flight to Paris, and calls Ray Manzarek, who agrees. Bill Siddons arrives in Paris the next day.

Buried at Père Lachaise Cemetery

The funeral is held on Wednesday afternoon. Attending are Pamela Courson, Bill Siddons, Alan Ronay, Agnes Varda and Robin Wertle.

DEPARTMENT OF STATE
FOREIGN SERVICE OF THE UNITED STATES OF AMERICA

REPORT OF THE DEATH OF AN AMERICAN CITIZEN

FINAL   American Embassy, Paris, France, August 11, 1971
                              (Place and date)

Name in full __James Douglas MORRISON__   Occupation __Singer__

Native or naturalized __BORN ON December 8, 1943 AT Clearwater,__ Florida   Last known address

in the United States __8216 Norton Avenue, Los Angeles, California__

Date of death __July__ __3__ __5:00 a.m.__ __1971__   Age __27 years__
              (Month) (Day) (Hour) (Minute) (Year)   (As nearly as can be ascertained)

Place of death __17, rue Beautreillis, Paris 4, France__
              (Number and street) or (Hospital or hotel)   (City)   (Country)

Cause of death __Heart Failure__
                              (Include authority for statement)

__As certified by Dr. Max Vassille, 31, rue du Renard, Paris, France__

Disposition of the remains __Interred in Pere Lachaise Cemetery, 16th Division, Paris,__
__France on July 7, 1971.__

Local law as to disinterring remains __May be disinterred at any time upon the request of__
__nearest relative or legal representative of the estate. See Decree Law of December__
__31, 1941, Journal Officiel, January 26-27, 1942, Page 378.__

Disposition of the effects __In the custody of Pamela Courson, friend.__

Person or official responsible for custody of effects and accounting therefor __Rear Admiral George S.__
Informed by telegram: __Morrison, father.__

NAME	ADDRESS	RELATIONSHIP	DATE SENT
N/A			

Copy of this report sent to:

NAME	ADDRESS	RELATIONSHIP	DATE SENT
ear Admiral George S. Morrison	Chief Naval Operations	Father	August 11, 1971
	OPO 3B - Room 4E 552		
	Pentagon, Washington, D.C. 20350		

Traveling or residing abroad with relatives or friends as follows:

NAME	ADDRESS	RELATIONSHIP
Miss Pamela Courson	17, rue Beautreillis	Friend
	75 - Paris 4, France	

Other known relatives (not given above):

NAME	ADDRESS	RELATIONSHIP
Unknown		

This information and data concerning an inventory of the effects, accounts, etc., have been placed under File 234 in the correspondence of this office.

Remarks: __U.S. passport number J 900083, issued at Los Angeles, California,__
__on August 7, 1968 cancelled and returned to father.__

Filing date and place of French Death Certificate: __July 3, 1971 at the Town Hall__
__of Paris 4, France.__

_____ (Continue on reverse if necessary.)

                         Mary Ann Meysenburg
                              (Signature on all copies)

[SEAL]   Vice Consul _____ of the United States of America
No fee prescribed.

Statement Regarding the Death of Jim Morrison

After returning from Paris with Pamela Courson, Bill Siddons releases a prepared statement to the press (via a public relations firm) regarding Jim Morrison's death.

"I have just returned from Paris, where I attended the funeral of Jim Morrison. Jim was buried in a simple ceremony, with only a few friends present.

"The initial news of his death and funeral was kept quiet because those of us who knew him intimately and loved him as a person wanted to avoid all the notoriety and circuslike atmosphere that surrounded the deaths of such other rock personalities as Janis Joplin and Jimi Hendrix.

"I can say that Jim died peacefully of natural causes—he had been in Paris since March with his wife, Pam. He had seen a doctor in Paris about a respiratory problem and had complained of this problem on Saturday—the day of his death.

"I hope that Jim is remembered not only as a rock singer and poet, but as a warm human being. He was the most warm, most human, most understanding person I've known."

Jac Holzman, president of Elektra Records, makes his public announcement.

"Jim was able to sustain a bemused and detached perspective on his aura, his art and his stardom. His exciting qualities as a performer and writer are universally known to a fascinated public for whom Jim was always news.

"Jim admired those people who stretched their lives to the fullest, who lived out on the edge of experience. He possessed special insight into people, their lives and into the dark corners of human existence.

"But beyond his public image, he was a friend to many and those of us at Elektra who worked with him and the Doors so closely over the past five years will remember him as one of the kindest and most thoughtful people we have known. He is already missed."

("Morrison, of Doors, Dies of Heart Attack in Paris," *Billboard*, July 17, 1971)

The previous year had been a devastating one for the rock 'n' roll world with the loss of Jimi Hendrix and Janis Joplin. Unfortunately, fate was to continue to deal a black hand through 1971 with the additional losses of the extraordinary Duane Allman, King Curtis, and Canned Heat's Al Wilson.

L.A. Woman Released in the United Kingdom

JUL. 9 1971

THE DOORS – OTHER VOICES

AUG. 1971 The Doors Workshop
Hollywood, CA

After they begin to adjust to the shock of Morrison's death, the Doors discuss their next course of action. They debate whether they should audition a new vocalist, whether they should retain the name the Doors, and even whether they should disband. They decide to keep their name, but hire no new vocalist. Another vocalist would be inevitably compared to Jim Morrison and found wanting. Moreover, the psychic communication that had developed among the band members just couldn't be duplicated, no matter how competent the new singer was.

Manzarek elaborates further for the *Los Angeles Free Press:* "We'd thought about it; we'd thought about maybe finding another guy. But it kind of seemed impossible to bring in another singer, to bring in another psyche, another personality. We'd been together so long, and the four of us had worked together so long that the psychic communication is so strong that to bring in an outside personality and try to adapt it to our vibrational wavelength and harmonize with another person's vibrations—it takes a long time to really build that up, and maybe you do build up, and what if he's not the right guy?" (Chris Van Ness, "The Doors after Morrison," *Los Angeles Free Press,* Nov. 26, 1971)

John Densmore tells *Los Angeles Times* reporter Robert Hilburn: "After the shock of Jim's death wore off a little, we got together and talked about the future. Actually, we had been thinking about the future for some time. Our contract with Elektra had run out and Jim wasn't sure what he wanted to do. He went to Paris to do some writing and some thinking. It was one of those awkward periods. We didn't know what was going to happen. After Jim's death, we decided that we did want to stay together. We felt we had a lot of music left inside us. Besides, we were friends and we knew each other's moves musically. When Ray does something on organ, for instance, Robby and I just know where he's going. You don't give up something like that. We decided against bringing in a new vocalist. No matter how good he was, people would say he wasn't as good as Jim. We really didn't know what to do about a vocalist. Then, fortunately, Ray stepped forward and began singing." (Robert Hilburn, "Doors out to prove themselves as trio," *Los Angeles Times*, Oct. 26, 1971)

Ultimately, Ray Manzarek takes on the demanding and unenviable task of handling the lead vocals. Ray comments on this in an interview shortly into their first tour: "We sort of had reservations at first. It had been a long time since any of us sang and we were a little shaky. Then we figured Oh boy, here we go!' The first time in front of the mike there were a lot of frogs in the throat. But then it started to get easier." (Jack Lloyd, "Three Doors and the Ghost of Jim Morrison," *Philadelphia Inquirer*, November 21, 1971)

The Doors negotiate a new contract with Elektra Records, and Jack Conrad joins them on bass guitar. They also prepare for recording their first album without Jim Morrison. Some of these rehearsals are held at the Wilshire Ebell Theater (at Wilshire and Lucerne).

SEPT. 1971 The Doors Workshop
Hollywood, CA

The Doors begin recording their eighth album, selecting as a title *Other Voices*. In a later interview, the Doors discuss their methods for composing music.

Ray: "Everything gets shared pretty equally. Somebody will bring a song in with some lyrics, or without lyrics, or we'll jam and get an idea. You know it's really the way it's always been—we've always done the same thing. Everybody gets to contribute what they feel like."

Robby: "Because we're the same three musicians and we play our instruments the same way. It's the same style. But it's just the three of us now, doing all of the lyrics, so it's a little different in its philosophical base."

(Quotes from an interview with John Keating, "Doors Discuss Style," *The Flat Hat*, Feb. 25, 1972)

SEPT. 1971 The Lords and the New Creatures is Released in Paperback

Other Voices

Eighth Album Released (U.S. 75017)

LATE OCT. 1971

Side One (A)
In the Eye of the Sun
Variety Is the Spice of Life
Ships with Sails
Tightrope Ride

Side Two (B)
Down on the Farm
I'm Horny, I'm Stoned
Wandering Musician
Hang onto Your Life

Singles
Tightrope Ride / Variety Is the Spice of Life (E-75757) (released 11/71)
Ships with Sails / In the Eye of the Sun (E-45768) (released 12/71)

Additional musicians include: Jerry Scheff (bass) from the L.A. Woman sessions, Jack Conrad (bass), Ray Neapolitan (bass player who worked on *Morrison Hotel*), Willie Ruff (bass), Wolfgang Meltz (bass), Francisco Aguabella (percussion) and Emil Richards (also playing a variety of percussion instruments)

OCT. 1971 UCLA
Los Angeles, CA

The "Jim Morrison Film Fund" is established by the UCLA Foundation. The idea originated during a conversation between Jim Morrison and Elektra's President Jac Holzman when Jim was distressed over the lack of finances for his film ideas.

OCT. 1971 An Artist in Hell
FM Special Broadcast

This engaging special includes interviews with the Doors, producer Paul Rothchild, etc., and incorporates readings of Jim Morrison's poetry.

NOV. 1971 KPFK-FM
Pacifica, CA

After months of silence, Ray Manzarek and Robby Krieger give an interview in which they state that they will continue as the Doors. They also begin their Northern Tour on November 12, accompanied by Bobby Ray on rhythm guitar and background vocals, and Jack Conrad on bass guitar.

OTHER VOICES
MIDWEST & NORTHEAST TOUR - FALL 1971

The Doors book smaller venues for their first tour without Jim since it is impossible to predict the public's reaction to such a tour. In addition, they are outright opposed to playing the big halls that had become such a scene while Jim was in the band. The superior acoustics and more intimate settings of the smaller venues also appeal to them.

The performances during this tour always seem to start with an anticipatory edginess from the audience, who don't know what to expect from the band without

Morrison. Their concerns are quickly alleviated as the band progresses through their first few songs. It is obvious that the musicians are proficient players who have adjusted to their loss and generated a cornucopia of new material that unmistakably defines them.

Manzarek later comments on that first tour: "As you can well imagine, it was a little strange, but the audience was warm and receptive. Thankfully, most of them came with an open mind to see us and not for any seance during which we would try to raise a ghost. I've got to say that we're most happy and grateful with the way in which the audiences have accepted us." (Roy Carr, "People must realize it: Jim is dead," *New Musical Express*, Feb. 19, 1972)

FRI. NOV. 12 1971 Pershing Municipal Auditorium
Lincoln, NB

Opening night of this first Doors tour without Jim Morrison shows great promise for the trio, which is accompanied by Bobby Ray and Jack Conrad. Ray Manzarek plays exceptionally well. The *Lincoln Journal* comments: "Keyboard man Ray Manzarek receives the star on his dressing room for his Friday evening performance at Pershing Auditorium. He is super talented on both the organ and piano. When he tears into the blues, he really is a superstar." (Holly Spence, *Lincoln Journal*, Nov. 13, 1971) They open with a solid version of "Tightrope Ride," and other highlights of the show include "Variety Is the Spice of Life," "Ships with Sails," and "Hang onto Your Life."

🕴 Also performing: The Spencer Davis Group; Ballin' Jack
🎫 Promotion: Richard Linnell

SAT. NOV. 13 1971 Augsburg College Melby Hall
Minneapolis, MN

🕴 Also performing: The Spencer Davis Group
🎫 Promotion: Schon Productions
🕗 8:00 p.m. show
🎫 Note: The concert was originally scheduled for the Auditorium Concert Bowl.

SUN. NOV. 14 1971 St. Lawrence Market
Toronto, Canada

The Doors' performance in Canada goes exceptionally well despite the somewhat sparse attendance. The band is in fine shape and delivers the distinct impression that, even without Jim, they are still a band to be reckoned with.

🎫 Note: This performance was originally scheduled for October 6.

WED. NOV. 17 1971 Ottawa Civic Center
Ottawa, Canada

This performance was originally scheduled for October 5.

THU. NOV. 18 1971 Peace Bridge Center
Buffalo, NY

FRI. NOV. 19 1971 The Carousel CANCELLED
Schenectady, NY

SAT. NOV. 20 1971 East Town Theatre
Detroit, MI

MON. NOV. 22 1971 Boston Music Hall
Boston, MA

TUE. NOV. 23 1971 Carnegie Hall
New York, NY

Tightrope Ride	Down on the Farm
Variety Is the Spice of Life	Close to You
In the Eye of the Sun	Ships with Sails
I'm Horny, I'm Stoned	Good Rockin'*
Hang on to Your Life	Light My Fire
Love Me Two Times	Hoochie Coochie Man*

The Doors highly touted appearance at New York's prestigious Carnegie Hall is not only one of the highlights of the hall's season, but probably one of the best shows the Doors ever perform without Jim Morrison. After opening with an explosive "Tightrope Ride," they proceed directly into a bustling version of "Variety Is the Spice of Life." Later, "In the Eye of the Sun" features some mesmerizing keyboard work from Ray Manzarek, particularly during the instrumental passage, which delivers numerous eerie overtones reminiscent of "Riders of the Storm." They conclude "Sun" with frequent high-spirited references to New York City, which are embraced with the appropriate cheers from this stronghold of Doors fans. Tonight, even the peculiar "I'm Horny, I'm Stoned" is highlighted with some feverish guitar sequences from Krieger. Although "Hang on to Your Life" commences as a fairly routine version of the song, toward its conclusion the entire band suddenly vaults into an exceptional jam that so vividly invokes the spirit of Jim Morrison that one can readily imagine Jim's high-pitched howls, fueled by the intensity of the instrumental, rising in the air.

The Doors then step back into their previous repertoire with a lively "Love Me Two Times" and a very rock 'n' roll-flavored "Close to You." Following that, Ray introduces Tony Glover, who had sat in with the Doors on some memorable nights in Minneapolis, and the band breaks into a very blues-influenced version of "Good Rockin'." Glover's steady, locomotive harmonica style adds some exquisite flavor to this rock classic. The band closes with the highly anticipated "Light My Fire," which builds into an remarkably energetic instrumental passage followed by a vigorous final chorus that concludes to tumultuous cheers and applause from the enthusiastic audience. The Doors then return with Tony Glover to bring the superb evening to a close with a salty version of "Hoochie Coochie Man."

Variety reports: "One of the most eagerly awaited concerts of the N.Y. fall season was a knockout at Carnegie Hall. The Doors, appearing in Gotham for the first time without the late Jim Morrison, were exciting all the way. . . . Their second encore was "Light My Fire," a Krieger composition that had been the group's biggest hit." (Krib, *Variety*, Dec. 1, 1971; reprinted with permission of © Variety, Inc. 1996)

Hofstra University's *Chronicle* also praises the show: "The group emphasized its instrumental performance over the vocals and lyrics by playing lengthy numbers from 'Other Voices' at extremely high volumes. . . . Were it not for the uncommonly refined instrumental talents of John Densmore, Robby Krieger and Ray Manzarek, the Doors' decision to retain their name and continue as a trio could have proven fatal. As it stands, the group fronts an impressive attack that could be strengthened and improved by turning down the volume a bit and incorporating more familiar material into its current repertoire." (John Koegel, "Doors' 'Other Voices' Weaken Carnegie Show," *The Chronicle*, Dec. 2, 1971)

Cash Box delivers a reflective and insightful overview of the performance, with some prophetic comments about the Doors having come "full circle" long before that album was released: "No audience would let them get away [with] a complete about face on their musical backgrounds; Jim's image is still very much with them, musically and spiritually. Ray Manzarek, who looks too calm for it all, is the new leader. And he wears his role with enough reluctance so that it is readily acceptable. His keyboards are mightier than ever and the sum total of the group's 'other voices' convey much of the richness that made Jim so unique. The new music bears Jim's mark, but this is both expected and welcomed. Morrison was and forever will be a Door. That's the way the crowd wants it. That's the way fate planned it. Manzarek-Krieger-Densmore: they are one and they are three. They are the audience and the audience is them. Full circle, round circle, beautiful circle. Death is not an end when life is strong." (R.A., "The Doors, The Wackers," *Cash Box*, Dec. 4, 1971)

- Also performing: The Whackers
- Capacity: 2,804
- With Tony Glover on harmonica

WED. NOV. 24 1971 Irvine Auditorium
University Of Pennsylvania, Philadelphia, PA

The Doors' performances go well this evening, demonstrating their musical abilities aptly. The mood of the evening is light and open.

- Also performing: The Wackers
- Early (8:00 p.m.) and late (10:30 p.m.) shows.
- Promotion: Electric Factory Concerts & Univ. Penn Union Council

FRI. NOV. 26 1971 Hollywood Palladium
Hollywood, CA

Tightrope Ride	Love Me Two Times
Variety Is the Spice of Life	Down on the Farm
In the Eye of the Sun	Close to You
[introductions]	Ships with Sails
I'm Horny, I'm Stoned	Hoochie Coochie Man
Hang on to Your Life	Light My Fire (encore)
[farewell to road manager Vince Treanor]	

The Doors' first performance in Los Angeles without Jim Morrison is met with universal praise for their craftsmanship, inspiration, and capacity to persevere despite the loss of their lead singer.

Billboard comments: "The music of the Doors still deals with apocalypse, but now the group tends to be doing a rueful little dance along the edge of the abyss. The death of lead singer Jim Morrison seemed to make survivors Ray Manzarek, Robby Krieger and John Densmore a lot freer in their musicianship and more consistently able to express their heavy metaphysical outlook with touches of cosmic humor. Onstage minus Morrison they have obviously lost something in fiery charisma at this early phase of their new career. But their return L.A. set showed craftsmanship of a high order and a touching eagerness to communicate all-out. The Doors trio is sure to remain a major force in rock for many more years." (*Billboard*, Dec. 1971)

The *Los Angeles Free Press* comments: "As far as almost all of the audience was concerned, the group could do no wrong; and to be honest, they were good—damn good. The five men, together with engineer-producer Bruce Botnick who mixed the show, delivered one of the tightest sounds you'd want to hear. They don't have to rely on old material; the set was well-paced and the excitement level was consistently high. *Other Voices* is like a rough sketch of the kind of finished masterpiece they can create on stage. It's a new group, and it is an exciting group. And it is a group that I would even go out of my way to see again. And coming from a reviewer who, more often than not, has to force himself to go to a concert that is quite a compliment." (Chris Van Ness, *Los Angeles Free Press*, Dec. 3, 1971)

This is the Doors' road manager Vince Treanor's final gig with the Doors, and the band expresses their high regard for him onstage.

After the show, Electra gives an immense Welcome Home party at Theda Bara's Los Angeles mansion.

🛬 Also performing: Dr. John the Night Tripper; Curved Air

🎭 Capacity, 4,400

THU. DEC. 2 1971 Berkeley Community Theatre
Berkeley, CA

Light My Fire (finale)

This concert is unfortunately marred by sound difficulties that affect all three bands. The Doors seem to be slightly uncomfortable with this sole performance in the Bay Area, sounding much more like they did with Jim than they have in recent performances. They even pull back on their instrumentals during songs like "Light My Fire," as if half expecting to see Morrison suddenly appear offstage engaging in some of the craziness he loved to enact during the instrumental passages.

🛬 Also performing: Albert King; Dan Hicks and his Hot Licks

🎦 Promotion: West Coast Promotions–Linnell/Branker

📯 Note: This show was originally scheduled for December 7.

🎭 Capacity: 3,700

The Doors on the road
1972

FRI. JAN. 7 1972 Aerial Tramway Lodge
Riviera Hotel, Palm Springs, CA
Elektra On Parade

Elektra's first national sales convention is held at the Riviera Hotel and Country Club from January 6 through 9. In addition to the Doors, highlights of the convention include the debut of the brilliant Harry Chapin, and an appearance by Carly Simon.

The Doors perform for the convention in a lodge above the aerial tramway in Palm Springs. *Cash Box* appreciate their set: "The Doors were another treat. They're a powerful rock group with great sounds, including some amazing work by guitarist Robby Krieger. And you seem to appreciate their musical ability more now that your attention is not riveted to one individual like of the giant, handsome idol Jim Morrison. Fascinating entertainment at the Elektra Meeting." (M.O.,"Talent On Stage." *Cash Box*, Jan. 22, 1972)

Note: This actually turns out to be Vince Treanor's final show with the Doors.

Weird Scenes Inside The Gold Mine
Second Compilation LP Released (8E-6001)

SIDE ONE (A)	SIDE TWO (B)
Break on Through	The End
Strange Days	Take It As It Comes
Shaman's Blues	Running Blue
Love Street	L.A. Woman
Peace Frog	Five to One
Blue Sunday	Who Scared You*
The WASP	(You Need Meat) Don't Go No Further*
End of the Night	Riders on the Storm
Love Her Madly	Maggie M'Gill
Spanish Caravan	Horse Latitudes
Ship of Fools	When the Music's Over
The Spy in the House of Love	

✳ These two songs were previously unreleased "B" sides

"Tightrope Ride"
Single Released in Great Britain

A&M Recording Studios
Hollywood, CA

The Doors begin recording their second album as a trio. This time they opt to produce themselves, and work on it for several months in between tour schedules.

EAST COAST TOUR - 1972

The Doors are pleased to embark on this brief predominantly college tour of the East Coast because ticket prices can be kept affordable and, as Ray puts it: "College audiences are good because they're not going to scream and run up on stage. They're really there for the music." (Quote from "Doors Aim for Inexpensive College Dates," *Cash Box*, Dec. 25, 1971)

THU. MAR. 2 1972 C.W. Post College Dome Auditorium
Greenvale, NY

The Doors perform a moderately good set tonight, complete with all the rough edges anticipated on the opening night of a tour, and are hailed back for at least two encores.

🐸 Also performing: Badfinger

FRI. MAR. 3 1972 Painters Mill Music Theatre
Owings Mill, MD

Tightrope Ride
Variety Is the Spice of Life
Mosquito (instrumental jam)
Eye of the Sun
I'm Horny, I'm Stoned
Love Me Two Times

Ships with Sails »
   Percussion »
Ships with Sails
Good Rockin'
Light My Fire (encore)

The Doors perform a tight set before a capacity audience, opening with a raucous version of "Tightrope Ride" with some strong lead vocals by Manzarek. Later, as he introduces "In the Eye of the Sun," Ray drifts into a dreamy preamble: "Now it's time for outer space. Time for that long trip back where we all came from." As the music begins, he continues: "Getting back, back, back. Flying out. Flying out to the sun. Go to the sun. Out to the eye of the sun. . . ."

"Ships with Sails" is the highlight of the evening. The band is obviously enthusiastic about the song and Krieger takes an inspired and melodious lead on guitar toward its conclusion. The *Baltimore Sun* praises the show: "In performance, the Doors' music shows an admirable tightness, made possible by their long years of playing together, and a simultaneous spontaneity of ideas that is very enjoyable." (James D. Dilts, "The Doors appear at Painters Mill," *Baltimore Sun*, Mar. 6, 1972)

🐸 Also performing: Badfinger; David Pomeranz

SAT. MAR. 4 1972 College of William and Mary Hall
Williamsburg, VA

Ships with Sails
Light My Fire (encore)

Despite an audience comprised of a quantity of Badfinger fans, some of whom shouted affronts like "Don't let the Doors on!," tonight's performance goes very well. The band is solid and grabs the audience's attention with a riveting "Ships with Sails."

Also performing: Badfinger; David Pomeranz

Capacity: 11,200

SUN. MAR. 5 1972 County Auditorium
Charleston, SC

Also performing: Badfinger

WED. MAR. 8 1972 Carolina Coliseum Arena
University Of South Carolina, Columbia, SC

Also performing: Badfinger

THU. MAR. 9 1972 Atlanta Municipal Auditorium
CANCELLED
Atlanta, GA

This appearance in Atlanta is cancelled by the manager of the auditorium who cites the Doors as a "riot-causing act" based on a communiqué from the International Auditorium and Arena Managers asserting that the Doors provoke trouble.

Also scheduled to perform: Badfinger

FRI. MAR. 10 1972 Pirates World
Dania, Miami, Miami, FL

Tightrope Ride
Love Me Two Times
Light My Fire

This performance marks the return of the Doors to Miami, an event that probably never would have occurred had Jim still been alive. Even with Jim gone, there is still some apprehension, but none of the media blitz that surrounded their last appearance in Miami.

The crowd is unusually quiet before the band appears. As the Doors take the stage, there is appreciative applause and the group goes right into their first number. Circumstances demand that something be said about the return engagement of a band that created such a furor in this city exactly three years and ten days ago. With more than a sprinkle of their sly humor, the band members at one point launch a quantity of hot dog balloons into the audience, suggesting their shape be interpreted as phallic symbols. Then during "Light My Fire," Manzarek brazenly thunders out an obscenity as if to declare: "Get a load of this Jim! Here we are, back in Miami!"

- 7:30 p.m. show
- Set-list incomplete
- Attendance: 6,000
- Note: This Doors' performance is featured as the first live FM broadcast in Florida, presented by WBUS and H.B.S. Productions.
- This performance was almost scheduled at the Sportatorium, which would have accommodated a larger audience, but the band had expressed a desire for smaller venues and the promoters agreed.
- Also performing: Badfinger; David Pomeranz

SAT. MAR. 11 1972 Tallahassee Sports Stadium
Florida State University, Tallahassee, Miami, FL

- Also performing: Badfinger; David Pomeranz
- 8:00 p.m. show

SUN. MAR. 12 1972 Fort Homer Hesterly Armory
Tampa, Miami, FL

Tightrope Ride
In the Eye of the Sun
I'm Horny, I'm Stoned
Mosquito (instrumental)
 [introductions]
Love Me Two Times
Ships with Sails »
 [percussion] »
Ships with Sails

The final show of the Doors brief East Coast tour is a lively one. They kick their set off with an enthusiastic "Tightrope Ride." An instrumental rendition of "Mosquito" is one of the highlights of the performance, and features some exemplary leads from Manzarek and Krieger, anchored solidly by Densmore's frenetic drumming. "Ships With Sails" concludes the show and also features some melodic keyboard work by Manzarek, breakneck percussion, and a fine vocal chorus.

- Also performing: Badfinger

APR. 1972 Phonograph Record Magazine Quotes Ray Manzarek

During this interview, Ray makes a memorable statement regarding the future of the Doors, and portions of this are subsequently cited in countless other publications: "I think we'll get into some explorations of light as opposed to darkness. We've spent a lot of time exploring the dark side of the soul . . . a lot of time in the unconscious mind, the subconscious mind, finding all the strange, weird things down there. Now we're going to come up for a breath of air. Come up for some light, for some sunshine, and get some light into those dark corners."

EUROPEAN TOUR - 1972

THU. APR. 27 1972 Tivoli Koncertsal
Copenhagen, Denmark

Also performing: Atomic Rooster
Note: This show was originally scheduled for May 8.

FRI. APR. 28 1972 Circus Krone
Munich, West Germany

Note: The Beatles performed at this venue on their final European tour.

SAT. APR. 29 1972 Jahrhundert Halle
Frankfurt, West Germany

SUN. APR. 30 1972 Montreux Jazz Festival
Montreux, Switzerland

The Doors perform afternoon and evening shows, which are both well received. The respectful applause that greeted them at the beginning of the tour quickly evolves into increasingly enthusiastic cheers as it quickly became apparent that the new band excels beyond everyone's expectations.

MON. MAY 1 1972 Olympia Theater
Paris, France

In the Eye of the Sun	Ships with Sails
I'm Horny, I'm Stoned	Good Rockin'
Love Me Two Times	Light My Fire
Verdillac	Hoochie Coochie Man
Close to You	(including lyrics from "Close to You")

The Doors' sole appearance in Paris occurs less than a year after Jim Morrison's death there, and they present a pleasing show to a warmly appreciative audience. Early in the set, they do a relaxed version of "In the Eye of the Sun" that sets the mood for the rest of the evening. There is an overall light feeling to the song, and Krieger slips in with some uncharacteristic sharp, angular slide guitar work. "Verdillac" is especially good tonight and they appear to enjoy introducing one of the newest additions in their repertoire to this Paris audience. After a very melodic "Ships with Sails," they close with a traditional "Good Rockin'." Later, after encoring with "Light My Fire," the band concludes the show with an interesting blend of "Close to You" and "Hoochie Coochie Man," where the lyrical content of both songs keeps intersecting until they are united as one piece.

✳ There may have been some songs prior to "In the Eye of the Sun."
Note: This show was originally scheduled for April 27.

WED. MAY 3 1972 Beat Club
Radio Bremen TV, Bremen, West Germany

Good Rockin'
Tightrope Ride
In the Eye of the Sun
I'm Horny, I'm Stoned
Love Me Two Times

Verdillac
Ship with Sails (false start)
Ships with Sails »
  [percussion] »
Ships with Sails

The *Beat Club* was the name of a television show that featured prominent musicians. It was recorded live at the Radio Bremen Television studios. The Doors do a good set, although it may have lacked the immediate vitality that a live audience could have provided. The band is in high spirits and has a good-natured laugh at themselves when they blow the introduction to "Ships with Sails" and have to start over again.

This show is broadcast on May 27.

"Ships with Sails"
Single Released in Great Britain

FRI. MAY 6 1972 Rotterdamse De Doelen
Rotterdam, Holland

Ships with Sails
I'm Horny, I'm Stoned
Light My Fire

Eleanor Rigby (instrumental) »
  My Favorite Things (instrumental) »
Light My Fire

Set-list incomplete

SUN. MAY 7 1972 Amsterdamse Carre Theater
Amsterdam, Holland

Tightrope Ride
Ships with Sails
Variety Is the Spice of Life
In the Eye of the Sun
I'm Horny, I'm Stoned

Close to You
Light My Fire
Love Me Two Times
Verdillac

The Doors' performance tonight is a rather flamboyant affair, with Robby Krieger playing guitar on his back and striding across the stage like a psychedelic Chuck Berry, while Manzarek periodically assails the piano with his feet.

Also performing: Max Marritt and M

Note: Exact sequence of songs is uncertain (one of them was performed a second time as an encore).

TUE. MAY 9 1972 Old Grey Whistle Test
BBC 2 TV Centre, London, England

Old Grey Whistle Test is a magazine-format program devoted to covering music beyond the top 20 and presenting it in a documentary framework. It was first broadcast on September 21, 1971, as a successor to *Disco 2*. The program includes the finest of British and American music with a special emphasis on presenting American groups on tour in the United Kingdom. In addition to the Doors, other bands featured this spring include the Beach Boys, Don McLean, Buddy Miles and Carlos Santana, Kris Kristofferson, and more.

☙ Also performing: Tom Paxton

☙ Producer: Mike Appleton; Director: Colin Strong; Compere: Bob Harris

WED. MAY 10 1972 City Hall
Newcastle-Upon-Tyne
Newcastle, England

THU. MAY 11 1972 Kinetic Circus
Birmingham, England

FRI. MAY 12 1972 Imperial College Great Hall
London, England

Tightrope Ride	Ships with Sails
In the Eye of the Sun	Good Rockin'
I'm Horny, I'm Stoned	Light My Fire
Love Me Two Times	Mosquito
Verdillac	Hoochie Coochie Man »
Close to You	Close to You

This performance receives praise from the critics despite an initial apprehension at seeing the band without Jim Morrison. Review after review praises the show as a triumph for the band, applauding their exuberant energy.

The band is in good spirits and their elevated mood comes through in the music. The encore "Hoochie Coochie Man," which incorporates lyrics from "Close to You," is a solid version reminiscent of the days when Jim Morrison would ad lib verses from different songs.

SAT. MAY 13 1972 Reading University
White Knights Park
Reading, England

SUN. MAY 14 1972 Guildford City Civic Hall
Guildford, England

Tightrope Ride	Verdillac
In the Eye of the Sun	Ships with Sails
I'm Horny, I'm Stoned	Good Rockin'
Love Me Two Times	Light My Fire
Close to You	Hoochie Coochie Man

Before the Doors' tour itinerary was changed, they were also scheduled to appear on May 20 in Mannheim, West Germany, and on May 22 at Geelan, Holland.

MAY 1972 Midnight Hour
Swedish Radio Special

This special includes the Doors performing songs from *Other Voices* as well as interviews with Ray Manzarek and John Densmore.

Full Circle
Ninth Album Released (Eks-75038)

Side One (A)
Get Up and Dance
Four Billion Souls
Verdillac
Hardwood Floor
Good Rockin'

Side Two (B)
The Mosquito
Piano Bird
It Slipped My Mind
The Peking King and the New York Queen

 Singles
Get Up and Dance / Tree Trunk
The Mosquito / It Slipped My Mind
Piano Bird / Good Rockin'

- Additional musicians include: Jack Conrad, Chris Ethridge, Charles Larkey, Leland Sklar (all play bass on different songs), Bobbi Hall and Chico Batera on percussion, Charles Lloyd on sax and flute, and backing vocals by Clyde King, Melissa Mackay, and Venetta Fields

- Recorded at A & M Recording Studios, Hollywood, CA

- Produced by the Doors

- Engineered & coordinated by Henry Lewy

- Note: The album was released with a zoetrope of the cover designed to display a moving image of a fetus that progresses to an old man and returns to a fetus when placed on a turntable. It was designed by Pacific Eye and Ear, which also designed Cheech and Chong's *Big Bamboo* and Alice Cooper's *School's Out* panty/desk package.

FINAL AMERICAN TOUR

Featuring Ron Starr on sax, Jack Conrad on bass, and Bobby Ray on guitar/timbales

Many performances were opened by Dr. John the Night Tripper, and by Phlorescent Leech and Eddie.

- Note: Phlorescent Leech and Eddie [aka Mark Volman (Flo) and Howard Kaylan (Eddie)] had played with the Doors before, first as founding members of the Turtles (for whom the Doors had opened at the Whisky in 1966), and then as a prominent feature with Frank Zappa and the Mothers of Invention as "Flo and Eddie." In 1972 they formed Phlorescent Leech and Eddie with other members of the Mothers, Gary Rowles from Love (on guitar), and British drummer Aynsley Dunbar. During their brief career, they worked with David Bowie and toured with Alice Cooper.

FRI. JUL. 21 1972 Aragon Ballroom
Chicago, IL

In the Eye of the Sun
I'm Horny, I'm Stoned
Verdillac
Love Me Two Times

Mosquito
Ships with Sails
Good Rockin'
Light My Fire

The opening night of what is to be the Doors' final tour is a lively show, delivered with some praiseworthy musicianship from the entire band. Manzarek frequently makes comments about how good it is to be home in Chicago and his high spirits are contagious. They open with a bustling version of "In the Eye of the Sun," and conclude with an uptempo encore of "Light My Fire," which features a rocksteady beat and swells with some fine jazz-flavored instrumentation.

🜊 Also performing: Dr. John the Night Tripper; Phlorescent Leech and Eddie

🜨 Note: This show was broadcast on WGLD-FM in Oak Park, Chicago.

SUN. JUL. 23 1972 Summerfest Amphitheater
Main Stage
Milwaukee, WI

Mosquito
Love Me Two Times
Verdillac

This almost ten-hour concert is the spectacular conclusion to the Milwaukee Summerfest series. The Doors headline an impressive lineup of talent that takes the stage at 3:20 in the afternoon and doesn't let up until the Doors conclude their set at 12:40 a.m. It is an eventful day in the history of Wisconsin's musical performances, featuring the still relatively unknown Mahavishnu Orchestra with John McLaughlin, and a nearly two-hour show by Quicksilver Messenger Service just prior to the Doors.

🜋 Set-list incomplete

🜨 Note: This show was originally scheduled for the Milwaukee Auditorium Arena.

🜊 Attendance: Almost 60,000

SUN. AUG. 13 1972 Balboa Stadium
San Diego, CA
Rock Liberation Festival

Tightrope Ride
In the Eye of the Sun
I'm Horny, I'm Stoned
Love Me Two Times
Verdillac

Close to You
Mosquito
Ships with Sails
Good Rockin'
Light My Fire (encore)

Tonight's performance includes a high-energy version of "Light My Fire" into which Krieger incorporates instrumental segments from "Eleanor Rigby" and "My Favorite Things," as he had during the 1970 tour.

🜊 Also performing: Canned Heat; Kris Kristofferson; Rita Coolidge; Cold Blood; Elvin Bishop Group; Stoneground; Bones; Boones Farm

MON. AUG. 14 1972 Cobo Arena
Detroit, MI

This concert most likely replaced the September 3 appearance at the Michigan Palace. It was originally scheduled for July 22.

TUE. AUG. 15 1972 Ritz Theatre
Staten Island, NY

- Also performing: Phlorescent Leech and Eddie
- Promotion: The Ungano's Present
- Note: The Doors returned for an encore performance on August 23.
- Capacity: 2,100

WED. AUG. 16 1972 Boston Common
Boston, MA
Sunset Series on the Common
[for the benefit of Summerthing]

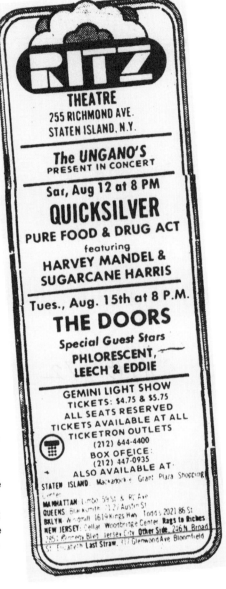

Tightrope Ride	Good Rockin'
In the Eye of the Sun	Light My Fire
Love Me Two Times	Close to You
Verdillac	

The Doors perform a tight, well-paced show to an audience of almost 12,000, who enthusiastically cheer throughout the show and refuse to allow the band to leave after only one encore. The band is off to a good start with "Tightrope Ride." Each member of the band displays superb musicianship, including Ron Starr, who performs a tremendous flute solo during "Verdillac."

The *Boston Globe* reports: "The Doors put together a fine rocking set last night at the Sunset Series on the Common. The group has modified its sound in the past year or so. Most of last night's numbers were from their new book which ventures a little more boldly into a jazz sound. They are still, however, basically a rock band, and a good one. The Doors have always had an appeal to a variety of people because of their hard-edge rock and because it is a performing group that communicates directly to the audience in a way that goes beyond music. The group got stronger as the set went on last night. Their last three numbers left both them and the crowd in tatters." (Ray Murphy, *Boston Globe*, Aug. 17, 1972)

- Also performing: Dr. John the Night Tripper
- Set-list incomplete
- Promotion: Falstaff Presents

FRI. AUG. 18 1972 Dillon Stadium
Hartford, CT

Love Me Two Times
Mosquito
Light My Fire

The Doors headline this event in Hartford, which features several major acts. "Phlo and Eddie" open the show and are followed by the Kinks, who are promptly followed by an intermittent rainstorm that shuts down the concert for an hour. After the delay, the Beach Boys come on stage for a superb set, and are followed by the Doors, who keep the momentum going until 1:30 a.m.

🦗 Also performing: the Beach Boys; the Kinks; Phlorescent Leech and Eddie

🐛 Set-list incomplete

🕷 Attendance estimates: 14,000 to 20,000

SAT. AUG. 19 1972 Loews Theater
Providence, RI

SUN. AUG. 20 1972 DAR Constitution Hall
Washington, DC

For whatever reasons, neither the Doors nor Dr. John have good shows tonight. The Doors' opening songs are apparently so rough that a number of people actually head for the exits. The opening act Phlorescent Leech and Eddie practically steal the show.

🦗 Also performing: Dr. John the Night Tripper; Phlorescent Leech and Eddie

🕴 8:00 p.m. show

MON. AUG. 21 1972 Wollman Memorial Rink
Central Park, New York, NY
The Schaefer Music Festival

Tightrope Ride	I'm Horny, I'm Stoned
In the Eye of the Sun	Good Rockin'
Mosquito	Ships with Sails
Love Me Two Times	Light My Fire
Verdillac (with Charles Lloyd)	Close to You (with Charles Lloyd)

The Doors' final appearance in New York, the city that had so passionately embraced them from the start, is met by an exceptionally enthusiastic audience. It is a polished show that clearly evidences the strong influence that jazz is having on the direction of the band. After opening with a smooth "Tightrope Ride," the band continues with an effective version of "In the Eye of the Sun," which prominently features the increasing subtlety of Krieger's slide guitar. During "Verdillac," they are joined by Charles Lloyd, and they do a lengthy version of the song. Toward the conclusion of the performance, the Doors do an expansive "Ships with Sails," which has evolved into a jazz-flavored piece featuring extended percussion and flute segments. The feeling of the song is appreciably different from previous versions, even though the structure is essentially the same. Even the succeeding "Light My Fire" now features a sax instrumental following Manzarek's traditional one on keyboard. After the instrumental, Manzarek comes in a little late on the verses, and the crowd, which had actually been clapping in time during the passage jumps right in with the lyrics and continues to sing along with the band through the conclusion. There is an unmistakable fondness for the band in the air tonight. To wrap up the show, Charles Lloyd joins the band again for their grand finale of "Close to You."

Variety reports: "[The] original members of the Doors led the revised combo through a stirring set at the Schaefer Music Festival in Central Park last Monday, one of the summer season's best Gotham concerts. Charles Lloyd, a top jazz musician, joined on tenor on 'Verdillac,' as he does on disk, and flute on 'Ships with Sails.' The rousing encore was their oldie 'Light My Fire.' Manzarek's strong organ playing and vocals did justice to his composition, which had been associated with Jim Morrison, the Doors' late vocal star. Krieger was solid on lead guitar, as was Densmore on drums." (Krib, *Variety*, Aug. 30, 1972; reprinted with permission of Variety, Inc. ©1996)

🕴 Also performing: Phlorescent Leech and Eddie

🕺 This performance was originally scheduled for July 17.

THU. AUG. 24 1972 Norfolk City Hall
Norfolk, VA

FRI. AUG. 25 1972 Dick Cavett Show
ABC 58th St. Theater, New York, NY

The Mosquito
Good Rockin'

The *Dick Cavett Show* was one of the best discussion programs of the time, and catered to an intelligent perspective on contemporary topics. Among the memorable rock music appearances were Jimi Hendrix and the Jefferson Airplane the night after Woodstock, and George Harrison's appearance to discuss Bangladesh.

The shows were taped at 6:00 p.m. and then broadcast later at 11:30 p.m. New York time.

FRI. AUG. 25 1972 (2) Atlanta Municipal
Auditorium
Atlanta, GA

CANCELLED

The Atlanta city officials again insist on canceling this performance, despite the fact that Jim Morrison is deceased. When it is explained to them that drastic changes have occurred within the band, they repeatedly refer back to articles detailing Morrison's legal difficulties. All attempts to provide them with factual information prove fruitless.

"Get Up And Dance"
Single Released in Great Britain

SUN. AUG. 27 1972 County Music Hall
Memphis, TN

FRI. SEPT. 1 1972 Majestic Theater
Dallas, TX

🕴 Also performing: Phlorescent Leech and Eddie

🕺 8:00 p.m. show

SAT. SEPT. 2 1972 New Orleans City Auditorium
New Orleans, LA

🏛 Note: This show was originally scheduled for Aug. 26

SUN. SEPT. 3 1972 Michigan Palace
Detroit, MI

🎭 Also performing: Phlorescent Leech and Eddie; Ursa Major
🎤 8:00 p.m. show

MON. SEPT. 4 1972 Erie Canal Soda Pop Festival

CANCELLED

Bull Island in the Wabash River, Carmi, IL

Although this festival does occur, it is reportedly a fiasco due to the difficulties the overwhelmed promoters have to endure when threats of injunctions disrupt their plans at Chandler Raceway Park, and a final festival site could not be secured until Friday. By Monday, three days of chilling rain and a lack of food convince most of the audience that they have had enough and they begin pouring out of the festival encampment. The promoters had expected 75,000 people, but the crowd is estimated at 275,000. On the final day, aggrieved audience members burn the stage, topple the lighting towers, and participate in other acts of destruction.

Apparently, the Doors never appeared at the Monday evening concert. Nor did the Faces, Fleetwood Mac, and Nazareth, all of whom were also to have performed.

🎭 Also performing: the Allman Brothers, John Mayall and many others for September 2 to 4.

SUN. SEPT. 10 1972 Hollywood Bowl
Los Angeles, CA

Final Performance as The Doors (without Jim Morrison)

Tightrope Ride
In the Eye of the Sun
Mosquito
Love Me Two Times
Piano Bird*

Verdillac
I'm Horny, I'm Stoned
Ships with Sails
Light My Fire

Appropriately, this is a bizarre final night for the Doors. First, Frank Zappa premieres the Grand Wazoo, a twenty-piece orchestra performing contemporary jazz and classical pieces, to a somewhat stunned audience.

The Doors performance tonight is tight and well paced, with a driving gutsy blues sound that fuels the entire evening. Manzarek is in high spirits, mischievously introducing Krieger's "Mosquito" with "Okay, Robby, brilliant . . . the divine . . . the sexy Robby Krieger is going to deliver the high school Spanish course for the evening. Everybody had two years of Spanish, but Robby's a four-year man! He's had enough! We're going to do the Mosquito."' Appropriately, Krieger responded with some tasteful guitar work.

While introducing "Light My Fire," Ray Manzarek delivers what in retrospect could be considered a eulogy for the band: "When we first started out there were four of us, and one of the guys is missing now, I don't know whether you know that or not. But he met with a little unfortunate accident and he's not here right now. But he'll be back! He'll be back next time we play the Bowl! And we're going to try and do this whether or not he's not just hanging around somewhere digging it. We're going to do this one for our own Jimbo. Okay, Jim, get ready! I know you're out there somewhere man, so get ready for it 'cause here it comes!" The Doors proceed through their finale with gusto and at the conclusion, Ray loudly exclaims their farewells with "Thank you very much. Thank you Jim! We'll see you!"

✥ Also performing: Frank Zappa and the Grand Wazoo Orchestra; Tim Buckley

✥ Promotion: KRLA/Concert Associates

✥ Following the show, there is a posh party at Theda Bara's vintage Hollywood Hills mansion that lasts until dawn.

✥ Note: This show has been inaccurately reported as having occurred at the Hollywood Palladium. That confusion probably stems form their appearance at the Palladium a year before.

✥ Charles Lloyd joins the Doors for "Piano Bird" and stays with them for the remainder of the set.

THE END # #

Aftermath

AUG. 1 1973
Best of the Doors
(Quadraphonic) Third compilation released (EO-5035)

Side One (A)
Who Do You Love
Soul Kitchen
Hello, I Love You
People Are Strange
Riders on the Storm
Touch Me

Side Two (B)
Love Her Madly
Love Me Two Times
Take It As It Comes
Moonlight Drive
Light My Fire

Jac Holzman and Elektra Records were in the forefront of quadraphonic technology when it was being introduced in 1973 as the logical extension to stereophonic sound systems. When the Doors' first LP was released in 1967, it was in both monophonic and stereophonic editions, which was common industry practice at the time. Since then, mono had become essentially obsolete and stereo dominate the market. The proposed quadraphonic market was not heralded as the technology that would make stereo obsolete, but rather focused on the growing audience of serious audiophiles seeking to expand their enjoyment of the music. Despite the release of many popular albums in quadraphonic, the idea never really caught on, and by 1975 had been largely abandoned.

Note: The slightly different sound mix on the mono edition has made it a highly sought-after collector's item.

MID-APRIL 1974

THE OBSCENE DOORS LIVE

During a visit to New York to promote his *Golden Scarab* album, Manzarek mentions that he wants to begin a collaboration with Elektra Records for a new album consisting of previously unreleased Doors material. He reflects on their one live album and aspirations to release another one: "When we released the live album, there was a lot of so called dirty language on some songs which we were afraid to put out because the censors would have jumped all over it. I think we could get away with releasing it now because there was a lot of good stuff that Morrison was on top of at the time—a lot of it, obscene. I'd like to see a live, unexpurgated album of it, *The Obscene Doors–Live*. There's also an obscene version of "The End." Jim didn't hold anything back on that, so maybe we can get that on it too." ("From Morrison's Shadow." Barry Taylor, *Observation Post*, May 1, 1974)

THU. APR. 25 1974
Pamela Courson Morrison dies in Hollywood, California

During the settlement of Jim Morrison's estate, it is determined that Pamela Courson will be legally recognized as the wife of the deceased, and therefore one of the beneficiaries of the estate. Still considerably distraught over Jim's death, she dies almost three years later.

MON. APR. 29 1974
Memorial service for Pamela Courson Morrison

The memorial service is held at Forest Lawn's Old North Church, and includes services for both Jim Morrison and Pamela Courson Morrison. Pamela's ashes were buried alongside Jim in Paris. During the proceedings, Ray Manzarek paid tribute to them with the performance of "When the Music's Over," "Love Street," and "Crystal Ship" on the organ.

NOV. 1978
An American Prayer
Tenth album released (5E-502)

Side One (A)	Side Two (B)
Awake	American Night
Ghost Song	Roadhouse Blues
Dawn's Highway	Lament
Black Polished Chrome	The Hitchhiker
Angels & Sailors	An American Prayer
The Movie Curses	The End
Invocation	

Regarding this project, Ray Manzarek comments to the *Los Angeles Times*: "It's a different Jim Morrison from the one the AM radio public knows. It's the Jim Morrison we always knew. He was a very warm person. The guy on stage was another person. We did this album to show the side of Jim which has been under-rated all these years. As far as we were concerned, Jim was a poet. But being the Lizard King has overshadowed the fact that he did some incredible poetry. That was always a sore point for him, that people never appreciated him as a poet. Now that he's been gone for seven years and you can forget what a good performer he was, you can begin to realize that he was probably one of the major poets of his time." (Richard Cromelin, *Los Angeles Times*, Nov. 19, 1978)

In addition to the LP, the Doors release an edited version for airplay that deletes material considered inappropriate for radio. The original length of 38 minutes 40 seconds is edited down to 24 minutes 36 seconds.

SUN. DEC. 8 1978
Palais Club
Paris, France

Love Me Two Times
Light My Fire
Close to You
Ghost Song

This is an impromptu "live" reunion during their promotional tour for *An American Prayer*.

JAN. 1979
Roadhouse Blues (live) / Albinoni's Adagio (The Severe Garden)
Fourteenth single released (Elektra E-46005)

1980
Apocalypse Now
Soundtrack released (Elektra K-12400)

The End
Delta

This maxi-single features the Doors portion of the movie soundtrack.

1980
The Doors Greatest Hits
Fourth compilation released (SE-515)

Side One (A)	Side Two (B)
Hello, I Love You	Break on Through
Light My Fire	Roadhouse Blues
People Are Strange	Not to Touch the Earth
Love Me Two Times	Touch Me
Riders on the Storm	L.A. Woman

JUL. 3 1981
Père La Chaise Cemetery, Paris, France

The Doors visit the gravesite of Jim Morrison on the tenth anniversary of his death.

WED. JUN. 2 1982
The Museum of Rock Art, Hollywood, CA

The museum begins a six-week exhibit of Frank Lisciandro's *Jim Morrison & The Doors* photograph collection.

1983

Alive She Cried
Eleventh album released (60269-1)

Side One (A)
Gloria
Light My Fire »
   "Graveyard Poem" »
Light My Fire
You Make Me Real

Side Two (B)
Texas Radio and the Big Beat »
Love Me Two Times
Little Red Rooster
Moonlight Drive »
Horse Latitudes »
Moonlight Drive

APR. 11 1985

Dance On Fire video released

Break on Through (original Elektra promotional clip)
People Are Strange (from Ed Sullivan and Murray the K special)
Light My Fire (from Ed Sullivan)
Wild Child (from an Elektra recording session)
L.A. Woman (a new film directed by Ray Manzarek)
The Unknown Soldier (original Elektra promotional clip: banned in 1968)
Roadhouse Blues (from 1968 film footage)
Texas Radio and the Big Beat »
Love Me Two Times (from the Danish television special)
Touch Me (from the Smothers Brothers Comedy Hour)
Horse Latitudes »
Moonlight Drive (from the Jonathan Winters debut show)
The End (from the Hollywood Bowl, July 5, 1968)
Crystal Ship (from American Bandstand)
Adagio (by Tommasso Albinoni; arranged by Paul Harris and the Doors)
Riders on the Storm (conclusion/credits)

Directed by Ray Manzarek, the film premieres at the Roxy in Los Angeles on this evening.

1985

Classics
Fifth compilation released (60417-1)

Side One (A)
Strange Days
Love Her Madly
Waiting for the Sun
My Eyes Have Seen You
Wild Child
The Crystal Ship
Five to One

Side Two (B)
Roadhouse Blues (live)
Land Ho!
I Can't See Your Face in My Mind
Peace Frog
The WASP: Texas Radio and the Big Beat
The Unknown Soldier

JUL. 16 1987

The Doors: Live at the Hollywood Bowl video released

When the Music's Over
Alabama Song »
Back Door Man
Five to One
Moonlight Drive »
Horse Latitudes »
   "A Little Game" »
   "The Hill Dwellers" »

Spanish Caravan
The Unknown Soldier
Light My Fire
The End »
   "Accident" »
   "Grasshopper" »
   "Ensenada" »
The End

Directed by Ray Manzarek and released by MCA Home Video.
Filmed and recorded at the Hollywood Bowl on July 5, 1968.

FRI. MAR. 1 1991

The Doors—movie directed by Oliver Stone—released

The Oliver Stone presentation of *The Doors* incites a great deal of controversy as to its authenticity and its portrayal of the band's meteoric rise to stardom and abrupt decline. Keyboardist Ray Manzarek likens it to a movie of a hedonistic, self-destructive punk band from the late 1970s with likenesses of the Doors substituting for the band members. Friends and acquaintances of the Doors frequently comment that they find it difficult to recognize their own colleagues onscreen. Events are exaggerated or fictionalized for dramatic effect, and unsubstantiated rumors from questionable sources are presented as fact. Aside from this, Oliver Stone has made an attempt to convey the shamanistic influences on the Doors, as well as their reputation as being one of the most intelligent and well-read rock groups to have ever appeared on the scene. The live performance sequences are quite good (the sound production is outstanding), but the simulated Hollywood embellishments destroy authenticity, especially in the portrayals of the Doors' audiences.

In viewing the movie, one has to remember that this is an expensive Hollywood entertainment production based on the Doors, and *not* a documentary designed to present solid facts in a historically accurate way, or provide genuine insight into the driving forces behind the band.

In conclusion, I must agree with what innumerable others have expressed—that the actual story is considerably more interesting.

MAR. 7 1991

The Doors (movie soundtrack)
Sixth compilation released

The Movie
Riders on the Storm
Love Street
Break on Through
The End
Light My Fire
Ghost Song
Roadhouse Blues

Heroin (Velvet Underground & Nico)
Carmina Burana: Introduction–
   (Atlanta Symphony Orchestra & Chorus)
Stoned Immaculate
When the Music's Over
The Severed Garden (Adagio)
L.A. Woman

MAY 1991

The Doors in Concert
Seventh Compilation Released

CD Disk #1

[house announcer]
Who Do You Love
Medley: Alabama Song »
Back Door Man »
   "Love Hides" »
Five to One
Build Me a Woman
When the Music's Over
Universal Mind
Petition the Lord with Prayer
Medley: "Dead Cats, Dead Rats" »
Break on Through (#2)
Medley: Celebration of the Lizard
Lions in the Street »
Wake Up! »
A Little Game »
The Hill Dwellers »
Not to Touch the Earth »
Names of the Kingdom »
The Palace of Exile
Soul Kitchen

CD Disk #2

Roadhouse Blues
Gloria
Light My Fire »
   "Graveyard Poem" »
Light My Fire
You Make Me Real
Texas Radio and the Big Beat »
Love Me Two Times
Little Red Rooster (with John Sebastian on harp)
Moonlight Drive »
Horse Latitudes »
Moonlight Drive
Close to You
The Unknown Soldier
The End

This CD release includes "Absolutely Live" and "Alive She Cried" in their entirety, as well as "Roadhouse Blues" from *An American Prayer*, and two selections from the Hollywood Bowl, July 5, 1968 concert.

SEPT. 1991

The Soft Parade video released
Directed by Ray Manzarek

This video, based on the PBS *Critique* show, includes terrific previously unseen footage of the band, including some remarkable sections with Jim Morrison that should furnish new insights into the warmth and spiritual nature of the man.

The Changeling (Doors Archives 1967, 1968)
Wishful, Sinful (PBS archives and private archives)
Wild Child (newly discovered Cinema Verité of the recording sessions)
Build Me A Woman (PBS archives)
Unknown Soldier (Dazzling new edit from all existing performances)
Soft Parade (PBS archives and private archives)
Hello, I Love You (Doors archives from Europe)

TUE. JAN. 12 1993

Rock 'n' Roll Hall of Fame induction ceremonies
Century Plaza Hotel, Los Angeles, CA

The Doors perform three numbers in celebration of the event, with Eddie Vedder admirably handling the lead vocals:

Roadhouse Blues
Break on Through
Light My Fire

The other Hall of Fame inductees include: Cream, Creedence Clearwater Revival, Van Morrison, Sly and the Family Stone, Ruth Brown, and Etta James.

MAR. 30 1995

Paul Rothchild dies

Legendary producer Paul Rothchild dies at the age of fifty-nine after a five-year battle with lung cancer. Prior to the Doors, Paul had worked with various Elektra artists including Love and the Paul Butterfield Blues Band.

MAY 23 1995

An American Prayer released on CD

This long-awaited release of *An American Prayer* on CD features two new selections with Jim Morrison's vocals—"Bird of Prey" and "Babylon Fading"—as well as a reworking of the instrumental track on "The Ghost Song," which is supported by a music video featuring rare clips from the unreleased HWY film. A promo CD single features "The Ghost Song," plus a rare interview with Morrison by Lennart Wretlind for Stockholm radio.

AUG. 1995

No One Here Gets Out Alive
CD/cassette released

This auditory adaptation of the bestselling book by Jerry Hopkins and Danny Sugerman is read by Sugerman himself.

DEC. 19 1995

The Doors Collection (laser disk)

This remarkable laser-disk compilation of Doors material is released following both private and public receptions at the Virgin Mega Store in Los Angeles.

Post-Doors Albums & Projects

MID MAR. 1973

The Doors officially disband in London

London newspapers (particularly the *New Musical Express*) announce that Jess Roden has joined the Doors, replacing Jim Morrison, and that Ray Manzarek has left the band. Krieger and Densmore book some time at Trident Studios at the end of the month under their old moniker the Doors, but end up cancelling the session.

Immediately thereafter, it is clarified that Krieger and Densmore are not reconstructing the Doors; rather they are forming an entirely new group to be called the Butts Band, with Roden as lead vocalist.

Meanwhile, Ray Manzarek directs his attention toward the concepts that will evolve into his first LP, *The Golden Scarab*. Later he describes the break: "Everybody started writing songs and each of us had enough material for an entire album. When it got around to doing our third LP without Jim, I had had enough. I thought, hell, I want to do my songs, my way. What I hear in my ear is what I want to put down on a disc." (Quote from Ellot Sekular, "Insight & Sound," *Cash Box*, March 16, 1974)

During the summer of 1974, Manzarek poignantly reflects: "The only thing to do after Jim died was to keep making music, but it wasn't right without Jim. Quite honestly, the new Doors was some other band that I didn't care to be in. But that whole period was the beginning of me as a composer. I'd never written much before but when Jim died the rest of us had to start writing." (Barbara Charone, "Manzarek? Alive & Well," *New Musical Express*, July 13, 1974)

In another interview, Ray goes right to the point: "I have to date the death of the Doors with the death of Jim Morrison, even though we did two more albums after that. I've been away from the whole Doors thing for three years now, and I'm still in the process of exploring all kinds of musical facets and styles, but on the other hand, I know I'll never get completely away from the Doors. Everything I'll probably ever do, you'll be able to trace back to the Doors. I could be making music 50 years from now, and people will be able to say, "Oh, that guy was with the Doors; that's terrific.'" (David Seay, "George Segal came by to play a little banjo," *The Gig*, Nov. 15, 1974)

MID AUG. 1973

Ray Manzarek forms new group

Announcements are made that Manzarek has formed a new group featuring some of the "heavy" musicians in the industry. Of primary note is that the legendary Tony Williams has joined Manzarek's new band. (Williams is a highly respected musician whose fusion group, the Tony Williams Lifetime, had attracted Jack Bruce after the dissolution of Cream.) Also featured are Larry Carlton, who played guitar on the Crusaders' albums, and Jerry Scheff, who had played bass behind Elvis Presley. The new group begins rehearsals in Los Angeles for the *Golden Scarab* album and tour.

LATE AUG. 1973
Butts Band formation

After considerable speculation, announcements for the newly christened Butts Band confirm that the group will not continue under the name of the Doors, especially after the departure of Ray Manzarek.

OCT. 1973
Sunset Sound Studios, Hollywood, CA

Ray Manzarek begins recording his first post-Doors album, *The Golden Scarab*, with Tony Williams (drums), Jerry Scheff (bass) and Larry Carlton (guitar).

JAN. 1974
The Butts Band
First LP by group featuring Robby Krieger and John Densmore

Side One (A)	Side Two (B)
Won't Be Alone Anymore	Be with Me
Baja Bus	New Ways
Sweet Danger	Love Your Brother
Pop-a-Top	Kansas City

Krieger and Densmore consider a number of vocalists, including Kevin Coyne and Howard Werth, before settling on Jess Roden. Roden had worked as the vocalist with the Alan Brown Band in the mid-1960s and had officially resigned as lead vocalist for Bronco on March 11, 1972. After some speculation about him joining Deep Purple as the replacement for Ian Gillan, and work on a solo album, Roden is offered the position of lead vocalist in a tentative group with Krieger and Densmore. Roden introduces them to Chen and Davies, and the band was formed.

Roden later reflected on his invitation into the band: "I wasn't too sure about it at the time because I know I'm no Jim Morrison. That's just not my cup of tea at all. And I'm really not the kind of guy who could hold the position of being an outrageous singer fronting a group. But I realized the band probably wouldn't carry on as the Doors anyway, once other musicians were introduced. And that's the way it worked out." ("Roden faces 10,000 mile split," *New Musical Express*, June 22, 1974)

The *Rolling Stone* review noted: "The debut LP of the Butts Band provides many pleasurable moments with its economical medium-tempo rock. Roy Davies' jazzy electric piano, coupled with Krieger's tenuously blended lead guitar, recalls the Doors' "Riders of the Storm." Jess Roden sings wildly, in a style reminiscent of Burton Cummings, and some will find his harshness repelling. There's plenty of variety. They go from conga-addled soul rhythms to floating synthesized reveries, but the album coheres well. The band shows further promise in elevating mediocre songs into listenable cuts through creative arranging." (Harold Bronson, *Rolling Stone*, May 9, 1974; used with permission: © Straight Arrow Publishers, Inc. 1996)

With Jess Roden (vocals), Philip Chen (bass), and Roy Davies (keyboards), replacing Mick "Frog" Weaver.

Note: Side One was recorded at Olympic Studios, London (engineer, Keith Harwood) and Side Two at Dynamic Sound Studios, Kingston, Jamaica (engineer, Bruce Botnick). Both were mixed at Hollywood Sound.

The Roxy, Sunset Strip, Hollywood, CA

Blue Thumb Records plays host to an introductory party for the Butts Band featuring Robby Krieger, John Densmore, Jess Roden, Roy Davies and Philip Chen.

The Butts Band do a brief tour in March/April, which includes the following performances:

March 13–18	Max's Kansas City, New York, NY
March 20–23	The Bijou, Philadelphia, PA
March 25–30	Performance Center, Cambridge, MA
April 3–7	Quiet Knight, Chicago, IL
Early April	Dallas, TX

The Butts Band returns to England in June and does a brief tour, which is highlighted by their appearance with the Kinks at the London Palladium:

June 15,	Links Pavilion, Cromer
June 16 (1)	London Palladium (opened for the Kinks)
June 16 (2)	Greyhound, Croydon
June 18	Barbarella's, Birmingham
June 19	The Penthouse, Scarborough
June 21	University of Hull, Hull (opened for Sparks)
June 22	University of Reading, Reading

MAR. 1974

The Golden Scarab (A Rhythm Myth)
First LP by Ray Manzarek released

Side One (A)	**Side Two (B)**
He Can't Come Today	The Purpose of Existence Is?
Solar Boat	The Moorish Idol
Down Bound Train	Choose Up and Choose Off
Golden Scarab	Oh, Thou Precious Nectar Filled Form
	(Or, A Little Fart)

In an interview with *Cash Box*, Manzarek reflects on his first album apart from the Doors: "After the [Doors] split, it was as if I had opened the valves somewhere—songs started pouring out. I had seven years' worth of material back there, seven years' of bottled up experience that I had never expressed. I would sit down to write lyrics and it was as if someone else was writing them. It was sheer inspiration." Ray goes on to describe the perception of the album as a "psychic journey" of a man's search for meaning. "The guy goes through a journey through the cosmos, a trip through hell. He explores ancient Egypt and at one point worships idols he knows to be false. Finally, at the end of the story, he comes to the realization that its not left or right, not north or south. There's a level of consciousness above and beyond all choices. In the last song, he comes back into contact with a reality that he already understood, but one that he's seeing through new eyes, eyes that have been through heaven and hell." (Quote from Ellot Sekuler, "Insight & Sound," *Cash Box*, March 16, 1974)

The *Rolling Stone* review comments: "This record should dispel the notion that Jim Morrison alone was the Doors. Manzarek accelerates the jazz pace woven into the Doors' later albums through the use of several name jazz sidemen, among them guitarist Larry Carlton and drummer extraordinaire Tony Williams. Though on its face an unworkable collaboration, the interplay of this bunch gives *The Golden Scarab* a halo of tight professionalism that accentuates Manzarek's mastery of song form. Although not without disappointments (Manzarek's singing often sounds too affected), *The Golden Scarab* is an intelligent album, showing that one of rock's best minds is back on the track." (Gordon Fletcher, *Rolling Stone*, May 23, 1974; used with permission: © Straight Arrow Publishers, Inc. 1996)

Musicians included Larry Carlton (guitar), Jerry Scheff (bass), Tony Williams (drums), and three additional percussionists: Mluto, Steve Forman, and Milt Holland. Recorded primarily in late August 1973.

MAY 2 – AUG. 1974
Golden Scarab Tour featuring Ray Manzarek

Ray Manzarek begins touring the U.S. on May 2 with his "Golden Scarab" lineup, primarily performing music from the new album. Performances include:

May 28–June 10	Max's Kansas City, New York, NY
July 3–7	Whisky A Go Go, Los Angeles
July 29, 30	Cape Camus, Montreal, Canada
August 1–4	My Father's Place, 19 Bryant Ave., Roslyn, NY
August 7–10	Max's Kansas City, New York, NY

TUE. JUN. 4 1974
The Midnight Special, ABC Television Studios, CA

The Butts Band record two songs for this program:

Be with Me
Love Your Brother

TUE. JUN. 11 1974
Old Grey Whistle Test
BBC 2 TV Centre, London, England

The Butts Band appears on this BBC television show. Their set was most likely recorded on Monday afternoon, just before the broadcast. (Also appearing on the program: Bridget St. John.)

WED. JUL. 3 – SUN. 7 1974
Whisky A Go Go, Los Angeles, CA

Notable Show: The "Jim Morrison Memorial Disappearance Party."
On the opening night of this memorial, which marks the third anniversary of Morrison's death, Ray Manzarek teams up with Iggy Pop and Iggy sings "Back Door Man," "L.A. Woman," and "Maggie M'Gill."

AUG. 1974
First Butts Band breaks up

This first configuration of the Krieger/Densmore British Butts Band disbands because of difficulties caused by band members living so far apart. Krieger and Densmore are based in Los Angeles and the remainder of the band is based in London.

After the dissolution of the first Butts Band, Roden works on a solo project with the (New Orleans) Meters and producer Allen Toussaint. Philip Chen goes on to work with Jeff Beck (on the *Blow by Blow* album) and Rod Stewart, among others.

NOV. 1974
Second Butts Band formed
Featuring Robby Krieger and John Densmore

This second configuration of the Butts Band is assembled in Los Angeles featuring Mike Zorkowitz (drums), Carl "Slick" Rucker (rhythm guitar), Alexandra Richman (vocals and keyboard). They are the first American group playing reggae music.

JAN. 1975
The Butts Band–Here & Now
Second LP by Krieger and Densmore released

Side One (A)
Get Up! Stand Up!
Corner of My Mind
Caught in the Middle
Everybody's a Fool
Living and Dying

Side Two (B)
Don't Wake Up
If You've Got to Make a Fool of Somebody
Feelin' So Bad
White House
Act of Love

With Michael Stull on vocals, guitar and piano (Blue Thumb Records).

JAN. 1975
The Whole Thing Started with Rock & Roll, Now It's out of Control
Ray Manzarek's second LP released (Mercury SRM-1-1014)

Side One (A)
Whole Thing Started with Rock & Roll
The Gambler
Whirling Dervish
Begin the World Again

Side Two (B)
I Wake up Screaming
Art Deco Fandango
Bicentennial Blues
Perfumed Garden

Ray Manzarek completes the recording sessions for his second album in December, and the LP is promptly released in January. The recording band includes Joe Walsh (guitar), Flo and Eddie, Gary Mallaber (drums), Nigel Harrison (bass), and Patti Smith. After Smith's appearance at the Whisky, Ray invites her to Amigo Studios in mid-November to recite Morrison's "Ensenada" and her "Screamin'." Some other musicians make guest appearances on the album including George Segal, who contributes banjo on "Art Deco Fandango."

FEB. 1977
Nite City
Ray Manzarek's third LP released (20th Century Fox)

Side One (A)
Summer Eyes
Nite City
Love Will Make You Mellow
Angel with No Freedom
Midnight Queen

Side Two (B)
Bitter Sky Blue
Caught in a Panic
In the Pyramid (instrumental)
Game of Skill

Nite City tours following the release of the album, including some excellent high-energy shows at New York's legendary Bottom Line on March 28 and 29. The band included Paul Warren on guitar, Jimmy "Mad Dog" Hunter on percussion, Nigel Harrison on bass, and Noah James on vocals. The album was coproduced by Manzarek and Jay Senter.

SEPT. 1977
Robby Krieger and Friends
First solo LP by Robby Krieger released (Blue Note Records)

Side One (A)
Gunpopper
Uptown
Everyday
Marilyn Monroe

Side Two (B)
The Ally
Low-Bottomy
Spare Changes
Big Oak Basin

1977
Versions
Second solo LP by Robby Krieger released (Passport Records)
(rereleased in 1982)

Side One (A)
Tattooed Love Boys
Her Majesty
East End, West End
The Crystal Ship
Street Fighting Man

Side Two (B)
Reach Out, I'll Be There
Gavin Leggit
Under Waterfall
I'm Gonna Tell on You
Harlem Nocturne

1978
Golden Days & Diamond Nights
Fourth LP by Ray Manzarek released (second with Nite City)

Side One (A)
Riding on the Wings of Love
The Dreamer
Holy Music
Ain't Got the Time

Side Two (B)
Die Hard
Blinded by Love
Barcelona (instrumental)
America

This album is released in West Germany only (20th Century Fox).

1979
Red Shift group featuring Robby Krieger

Red Shift is primarily a punk rock and new wave-oriented band that features Arthur Barrow, Mack McKenzie, and Vinnie Caliutta. They perform around the Los Angeles vicinity but never release an album.

1980
Ray Manzarek becomes the producer for "X"

After seeing the renowned L.A. band X live, Manzarek is terrifically impressed and subsequently signs on as their producer. He does four albums with them.

1982
The KGB Band featuring Robby Krieger

Toward the end of the year, Robby Krieger performs around Los Angeles in the KGB Band, which includes Arthur Barrow, Bruce Gary, Burton Avarre (from the Knack), and Marty Gibarro. Arthur Barrow had contributed some synthesizer work on *An American Prayer*. Robby Krieger had been playing with Barrow and Bruce Gary since 1977.

THU. NOV. 18 1982
The Roxy, Los Angeles, CA

Notable Show: John Densmore appears on stage with the KGB Band for a rendition of "Love Me Two Times."

1983

Carmina Burana

Fifth LP by Ray Manzarek (A&M Records)

This album is based on the work of German composer Carl Orff, who in 1935 had adapted the writings of mystically oriented thirteenth-century monks (which had been lost for centuries) into this this cantata.

1983

Reggae Bonanza

Third LP (Maxi) by Krieger and Densmore released (Rhino Records)

Side One (A)	Side Two (B)
Kinki Reggae (1983)	Get Up! Stand Up! (1975)

"Get Up, Stand Up" was recorded in December 1975. Produced by Jerry Fuller.

1985

Krieger

Third Solo LP by Robby Krieger released (Cafe Records) Mobile Fidelity

Side One (A)	Side Two (B)
Bag Lady	Costa Brava
Reggae Funk	Noisuf
Bass Line Street	

FEB. 24 1986

Los Angeles Forum, Inglewood, CA

Notable Show: This memorable evening is the "Welcome Home" Vietnam Veterans benefit where Robby Krieger & Friends perform and are joined by John Sebastian and actor-singer Steven Bauer. They perform:

Love Me Two Times
My Sharona (instrumental)
The Unknown Soldier
Roadhouse Blues (with John Sebastian on harp)

Also performing: Neil Young and Graham Nash; John Sebastian; Richie Havens; Herbie Hancock and Wynton Marsalis; Stevie Wonder; Buddy Miles Express; Nils Lofgren; Chris Hillman; Buffalo Springfield Revisited

1986
Robby Krieger Dance Single
(12" Single) (Macola Records)

Side One (A)
Nasti Kinki (Radio Mix)

Side Two (B)
Nasti Kinki (Dance Version)

1989
Guitar Speak Vol. 1
Compilation album featuring Robby Krieger (IRS Records)

Robby Krieger contributes "Strut-a-various" to this album.

1989
Night of the Live Guitars-Live
Compilation featuring Robby Krieger (IRS Records)

A double multiartist LP featuring Robby Krieger on "Love Me Two Times" with Steve Hunter.

1989
No Habla
Fourth Solo LP by Robby Krieger (IRS Records)

Side One (A)
Wild Child
Eagles Song
It's Gonna Work Out Fine
Lonely Tear Drops
Love It or Leave It

Side Two (B)
The Big Hurt (Doleres)
Piggy's Song
I Want You, I Need You, I Love You
You're Lost Little Girl

This is an all-instrumental album.

1989
Door Jams
The Best of No Habla and Krieger & Friends

This compilation features selections from Krieger's first (1977) and fourth (1989) solo LPs.

1990
Robby Krieger and Eric Burdon

Robby Krieger joins forces with Eric Burdon (the legendary lead vocalist with the Animals) on a U.S. tour. They are occasionally joined by Brian Auger. They perform such classics as the Doors' "Back Door Man" and "Roadhouse Blues," and the Animals' "Don't Let Me Down," "House of the Rising Sun," and "Don't Let Me Be Misunderstood."

SEPT. 1990
Riders on the Storm
(book by John Densmore)

Subtitled "My Life with Jim Morrison and The Doors," this publication is John Densmore's autobiographical account of his years with, and following, the Doors.

1991
The Robby Krieger Band

This band is more oriented toward rock music than were Krieger's previously jazz-flavored efforts. It even includes songs from his days with the Doors, a welcome addition to his repertoire—especially to old fans. Featured in the lineup are Wah Wah Watson ("King" of the funk guitar), Robby's son Waylon (on rhythm guitar and vocals), Berry Oakley Jr. on bass (his father had played bass with the original Allman Brothers Band), and Dale Alexander on drums.

OCT. 1991
Love Lion
First video by Ray Manzarek released (Mystic Fire Video)

Ray Manzarek and Michael McClure. This video documents a poetry reading by renowned San Francisco beat poet Michael McClure, fortified by Ray Manzarek's improvisational brilliance on piano.

SPRING 1995
RKO Live
Fifth LP by Robby Krieger (with Robby Krieger Organization) released

This CD, recorded live, is released along with a video of the "Spanish Caravan/Spain" medley from the CD.

And Now . . .

ROBBY KRIEGER continues periodically to perform live, and works on various soundtracks for film and television.

JOHN DENSMORE continues to work as an actor. The response to his book has been very favorable.

RAY MANZAREK is focused on a number of personal projects. He occasionally joins Michael McClure (and additional poets such as Allen Ginsberg) for poetry/music performances.

Bibliography

NOV. 1969

Jim Morrison & the Doors: An Unauthorized Biography

Author Mike Jahn's book on the Doors' March 22, 1968 shows at the Fillmore East (Grosset & Dunlap).

APR. 1970

The Lords and the New Creatures by James Douglas Morrison

Hardcover version released by Simon & Schuster.

SEPT. 1971

The Lords and the New Creatures by James Douglas Morrison

Softcover version released by Simon & Schuster.

MAR. 1974

Jim Morrison An Dela Des Doors by Hervé Miller

Journalist Hervé Miller periodically associated with Jim Morrison during his final days in Paris.

1980

No One Here Gets Out Alive by Jerry Hopkins and Danny Sugerman

The bestselling biography of Jim Morrison and the Doors by journalist Jerry Hopkins and Doors associate Danny Sugerman (Warner Books).

MAY 1982

An Hour for Magic by Frank Lisciandro

A "photo journal" on the Doors containing text and photos by Frank Lisciandro (Delilah Books). Now a collector's item.

1983

The Doors: The Illustrated History by Danny Sugerman

This is an excellent compilation of reviews, interviews, and photographs assembled by Danny Sugerman. It includes an outstanding, previously unreleased, interview with Jim Morrison by Lizzie James (William Morrow and Company).

1988

Wilderness—First Compilation of James Morrison's Poetry

The first book in a series of releases of Jim Morrison's poetry by Villard Books in New York. Compiled by Frank and Katherine Lisciandro, and the Coursons.

1988

The Doors: In Their Own Words by Andrew Doe and John Taylor

A selection of quotations compiled by Andrew Doe and John Taylor (Omnibus & Pedigree).

FEB. 1989

Wonderland Avenue: Tales of Glamour and Excess by Danny Sugerman

This autobiographical retrospective recounts his associations with members of the Doors before and after Jim's untimely death. Although the book is not specifically about the Doors, Sugerman graphically describes his association with the band, especially in the years following their dissolution.

SEPT. 1990
The American Night—Second Compilation of James Morrison's Poetry

The second book in a series of James Douglas Morrison's poetry released by Villard Books. It includes, for the first time ever, the complete version of "An American Prayer." Compiled by Frank and Katherine Lisciandro and the Coursons.

SEPT. 1990
Riders on the Storm: My Life with Jim Morrison and The Doors by John Densmore

Doors' percussionist John Densmore's autobiographical account of his life with the Doors and the effect that it had on his life (Delacorte Books).

1990
The End by Bob Seymour

(Omnibus Press)

FEB. 1991
Dark Star by Dylan Jones

This book was originally released by Britain's Bloomsbury Press and is authored by Dylan Jones, the editor of Britain's men's magazine *Arena* (Viking Star Books).

APR. 1991
Morrison: A Feast of Friends by Frank Lisciandro

This is Doors' associate Frank Lisciandro's second book concerning Jim Morrison. This superb book includes interviews with fifteen people who spent intimate time with Jim Morrison, providing genuine insight into the man during different stages of his life.

APR. 1991
Mr. Mojo Risin' by David Dalton

Says Oliver Stone of *Mr. Mojo Risin'*: "Dalton writes like a mad, inflamed poet. . . . Morrison and the Doors as I've never seen described." David Dalton is the author of numerous biographies including *El Sid* (St. Martin's, fall 1997), and the coauthor of *Faithfull* with Marianne Faithfull, and *Living with the Dead* with Rock Scully.

MAY 1991
Break on Through by James Riordan and Jerry Prochinicky

A comprehensive biography and analysis of Jim Morrison, focusing on his influences and cultural impact (William Morrow and Co.).

JUN. 1991
Images of Jim Morrison by Edward Wincentsen

This nicely designed tribute book includes a satisfying assortment of photographs, poetry and memorabilia from the Andrew Hawley collection (Vergin Press).

JUL. 1991
The Essential Jim Morrison by Jerry Hopkins

This book includes information not included in *No One Here Gets Out Alive*, as well as a compilation of select interviews with Jim Morrison (Plexus Books).

OCT. 1991
The Doors' Complete Book of Lyrics by Danny Sugerman

Features all of the lyrics to the Doors' compositions as well as numerous rare photographs (Hyperion Books).

MAY 1992
Strange Days by Patricia Kennealy

This book is not specifically about the Doors; rather, it is an autobiographical account of the author's time spent with Jim Morrison.

1993
Rimbaud And Jim Morrison: The Rebel As Poet by Wallace Fowlie

(Duke University Press)

JUN. 1993
The Doors Collectors Magazine

This exceptionally well produced and increasingly popular magazine began publishing in 1993 as a tribute to the band and to furnish information on their current activities. It regularly features memorable interviews, concert reviews, recent and upcoming events related to the band, as well as being an astonishing outlet for memorabilia of every variety. Proprietor Kerry Humpherys diligently searches the globe for all aspects of rare and valuable Doors memorabilia, and a segment devoted to his archives was recently included on *The Doors Collection* laser disk. The magazine has been a welcome arrival to Doors enthusiasts everywhere.

Subscriptions for the magazine ($20.00 annually, 4 issues) or inquires may be addressed to TDM Inc., PO Box 1441, Orem, UT 84059-1441. Their internet address is: http://www.doors.com

U.S. & Canada Order Line: (800) 891-1736. All other calls: (801) 224-7390. Fax: (801) 224-5723

1994
The Complete Guide To The Music Of The Doors by Peter Hogan

(Omnibus Press)

1995
Moonlight Drive by Chuck Crisifulli

(Carlton Books Ltd)

1996
The Doors Artistic Vision by Doug Sundling

(Castle Communications)

JUN. 1996
Jim Morrison: My Eyes Have Seen You by Jerry Prochnicky and Joe Russo

This self-published volume is an extraordinary photo-documentary of the Doors ranging from Jim Morrison's high school yearbook photo to the band's induction into the Rock 'n' Roll Hall of Fame. The chronologically fashioned feast of rare and exquisite photographs was compiled by *Break on Through* author Jerry Prochnicky and lead singer for the Soft Parade tribute band, Joe Russo. (Copies may be ordered from Prochnicky for $23.00 at 1611-A South Melrose Dr., #121, Vista, CA 92083.)

Unreleased Recordings

The following is a comprehensive listing of all the underground recordings circulating among collectors. These are not bootleg LPs or CDs—bootlegs are commercial products manufactured by a bootlegger who obtains copies of these source tapes.

The exchange of tapes among collectors is almost always an equilateral exchange that excludes monetary remuneration.

The list shows date of show, location of show, source (e.g., Rec), length (e.g., 0:17), quality (e.g., 9–), and whether it is available in video (V).

5/65	Rick and the Ravens: Aura Records Singles (DU) Soul Train, Geraldine, Henrietta, Just for You, Big Bucket "T," Rampage.	Rec	0:17	9–
9/2/65	The Doors Original Acetate Demos: Aura Records Moonlight Drive, Hello I Love You, Summer's Almost Gone, My Eyes Have Seen You, End of the Night, A Little Game (Go Insane). Recorded at World Pacific Studios for Aura Records.	Rec	0:16	7–
3/4/67	Avalon Ballroom, San Francisco, CA (DU) Moonlight Drive, Back Door Man.	Sbd	0:15	8
3/7/67	The Matrix, San Francisco, CA Set 1: Back Door Man, My Eyes Have Seen You, Soul Kitchen, Get Out of My Life, Music's Over. Set 2: Close to You, King Snake, Can't See Your Face, People Are Strange, Alabama Song, Crystal Ship, 20th Century Fox, Moonlight Drive, Summer's Almost Gone, Unhappy Girl. Set 3: The Devil Is a Woman » Rock Me, Break on Through, Light My Fire, The End.	Sbd	1:50	8
3/10/67	The Matrix, San Francisco, CA Set 2: My Eyes Have Seen You, Soul Kitchen, I Can't See Your Face, People Are Strange, Music's Over. Set 3: Money, Who Do You Love » Moonlight Drive, Summer's Almost Gone, King Bee, Gloria, Break on Through, Summertime (instrumental), Back Door Man, Alabama Song, The End.	Sbd	1:30	8
7/9/67	Continental Ballroom, Santa Clara, CA (DU) Soul Kitchen, Break On Through, Alabama Song » Back Door Man . . . The End.	Aud	0:27	7+
8/67	Love Me Two Times (acetate)	Rec	0:04	8+
9/14/67	CBC Television Studios, Toronto, Canada Wake Up! » The End (aka "Now Explosion" broadcast in New York on August 1,1970). Circulates in video as well.	Sbd	0:10	8 V
9/17/67	*Ed Sullivan Show,* Ed Sullivan Theater, New York, NY People Are Strange, Light My Fire.	TV	0:10	8+ V
9/22/67	*Murray the K in New York,* WPIX-TV, New York, NY People Are Strange (several takes), Light My Fire.	TV	0:20	8 V
9/30/67	Family Dog, Denver, CO (DU) Light My Fire. Note: The exact date of this recording is uncertain.	Sbd	0:09	8–
10/11/67	Danbury High School Auditorium, Danbury, CT Moonlight Drive » Horse Latitudes » Moonlight Drive, Money, Break on Through, Back Door Man, People Are Strange, Crystal Ship, Wake Up! » Light My Fire, The End.	Sbd	1:00	4
12/16/67	San Bernardino Swing Auditorium, San Bernardino, CA When the Music's Over, Horse Latitudes » Break on Through, Alabama Song, Light My Fire.	Aud	0:30	8
12/26/67	Winterland Arena, San Francisco, CA Back Door Man, Break on Through, When the Music's Over, Close to You » Mannish Boy, Light My Fire.	Aud	0:45	6
12/27/67	*Jonathan Winters Show,* CBS TV Studios (Conclusion of "Horse Latitudes" on tape ») Moonlight Drive, Light My Fire.	TV	0:10	7+ V
12/28/67	Winterland Arena, San Francisco, CA Alabama Song » Back Door Man, You're Lost Little Girl . . . Love Me Two Times, Wake Up! » Light My Fire, The Unknown Soldier.	Aud	0:35	8

3/7/68	Steve Paul's Scene, New York, NY	Sbd 0:55 9

Jim Morrison, Jimi Hendrix, Paul Caruso and others. Red House, I'm Gonna Leave This Town » Everything's Going to Be All Right [aka Woke Up This Morning & Found Myself Dead] » Bleeding Heart » "Morrison's Lament" » Uranus Rock » Tomorrow Never Knows » Outside Woman Blues » Sunshine of Your Love.

3/17/68 L	Back Bay Theatre, Boston, MA	Aud 1:00 7

Late Show: When the Music's Over, Back Door Man » Five to One » Back Door Man, Break on Through, Love Me Two Times, You're Lost Little Girl, Light My Fire, The End.

5/10/68	Chicago Coliseum, Chicago, IL	Aud 0:55 5

Soul Kitchen » Running Blue » Soul Kitchen, Break on Through, Alabama Song » Back Door Man » Five to One, When the Music's Over, Crystal Ship, Wake Up! » Light Fire.

7/5/68	Hollywood Bowl, Hollywood, CA	Aud 1:00 9 V

1) Audience Copy: (qlty. 6): When the Music's Over, Alabama Song » Back Door Man » Five to One, Hello I Love You,* Moonlight Drive » Horse Latitudes » Moonlight Drive, A Little Game » The Hill Dwellers » Spanish Caravan, Wake Up! » Light My Fire, The Unknown Soldier, The End. (*Not on video)
2) Video Copy: When the Music's Over, Alabama Song » Back Door Man » Five to One, Moonlight Drive » Horse Latitudes » Moonlight Drive, A Little Game » The Hill Dwellers » Spanish Caravan, The Unknown Soldier, Wake Up! » Light My Fire, The End.

7/9/68	Dallas Memorial Auditorium, Dallas, TX	Aud 1:00 8+

Soul Kitchen, Back Door Man » Five to One, Break on Through, Crystal Ship, Texas Radio » Hello I Love You » Moonlight Drive » Money, When The Music's Over, Wake Up! » Light My Fire.

7/68	Unknown Soldier / We Could Be So Good Together	Rec 0:10 9

Single (different mix)

8/2/68	Singer Bowl, Flushing Meadows, Queens, NY	Aud 0:45 7

Back Door Man » Five to One, Break on Through, When the Music's Over, Wild Child, Wake Up » Light My Fire. Note: "The End" is missing.

9/6/68 L	The Roundhouse, London, England	Aud 1:15 7 V

1) Late show: Audience Copy: Five to One, Break on Through, When the Music's Over, Alabama Song » Back Door Man » Crawlin' King Snake » Back Door Man, Spanish Caravan, Love Me Two Times, Light My Fire, Unknown Soldier, Soul Kitchen, Celebration of the Lizard, Hello I Love You, Moonlight Drive » Horse Latitudes » Moonlight Drive » Money.
2) Late Show: *Doors Are Open* Soundtrack. An incomplete television show (see Oct. 4, 1968).

9/7/68 E	The Roundhouse, London, England	Aud 0:45 7–

Early show: Five to One, Break on Through, When the Music's Over, Wake Up! » Light My Fire, The End. Note: On many tapes there is an additional "When the Music's Over" that may be from the late show.

9/14/68 E	Kongresshalle, Frankfurt, W. Germany	Aud 0:45 5

Early show: Break on Through, Alabama Song » Back Door Man, When the Music's Over, Texas Radio and the Big Beat » Hello I Love You, Light My Fire, Unknown Soldier.

9/14/68 L	Kongresshalle, Frankfurt, W. Germany	TV 0:05 8–

Late show: . . . Light My Fire . . . Five To One. Recording from a TV report that only included fragments of these two songs.

9/15/68 L	Concertgebouw, Amsterdam, Holland, Netherlands	Aud 0:45 5

Late show (probably): Break on Through, Soul Kitchen, Alabama Song » Back Door Man, Hello I Love You, Light My Fire. A unique performance without Jim Morrison.

9/18/68	Copenhagen TV—Byen, Copenhagen, Denmark	TV 0:30 8 V

Alabama Song » Back Door Man, Texas Radio and the Big Beat, Love Me Two Times, When the Music's Over, The Unknown Soldier. Circulates in video as well.

9/20/68 E   Konserthuset, Stockholm, Sweden   FM   0:45 9–
Early show: Five to One, Love Street, Love Me Two Times, When the Music's Over, A Little Game » The Hill Dwellers » Light My Fire, The Unknown Soldier.

9/20/68 L   Konserthuset, Stockholm, Sweden   FM   1:15 9–
Late show: Five to One, Mack the Knife » Alabama Song » Back Door Man, You're Lost Little Girl, Love Me Two Times, When the Music's Over, Wild Child, Money » Wake Up! » Light My Fire, The End (encore).

10/4/68   *The Doors Are Open* Soundtrack, Granada TV, U.K.   Vid   1:00 8   V
(Introduction), When the Music's Over, Five to One, Spanish Caravan, (ICA Press Conference), Hello I Love You (from soundcheck with Manzarek on vocals), (interviews), Back Door Man » Crawlin' King Snake » Back Door Man, (interview with Jim Morrison), Wake Up! » Light My Fire, Unknown Soldier, (conclusion).

12/14/68   Los Angeles Forum, Inglewood, CA.   Aud   1:10 7
Tell All the People, Love Me Two Times, Who Scared You, Spanish Caravan, Crystal Ship, Wild Child, Touch Me, Light My Fire, Celebration of the Lizard. Three different tapes are circulating.

12/15/68   *Smothers Brothers Comedy Hour*, CBS Studios, L.A.   TV   0:10 9– V
Wild Child, Touch Me.

2/25/69   Sunset Sound Recorders, Hollywood, CA   Brd   1:20 8–
Rock Is Dead, Albinoni's Adagio in "G" minor.
When I Was Back in Seminary School #1; When I Was Back in Seminary School #2 » Whiskey, Mystics & Men (with musical accompaniment); Love Me Tender; Rock Is Dead (Pt. 1); The Devil Is a Woman; Rock Is Dead (Pt. 2) ("Are You Ready?!") [» "Listen, I don't want to hear no talk about revolution..." » "We're Gonna Have A Good Time! Let's Roll!" » "I'm Talkin' About the Death of Rock 'n' Roll" » "Rock and Roll Woman" » "Baby, Love Me" ("The Queen of the Magazine") (slow blues)]; Pipeline; Rock Me Improvisation » Mystery Train » When I Got Home; Rock Is Dead » My Eyes Have Seen You Jam » Rock Is Dead! (conclusion) Additional tracks: 1) The "Roadhouse Blues Interlude" often appears at the start of recordings of this session but is actually from sessions for *Morrison Hotel*. 2) The Albinoni's Adagio in G minor is not from this date, but is from the sessions around this time period. The Doors recorded "Adagio" with a full orchestra in the studio.

3/1/69   Miami Dinner Key Auditorium, Miami, FL   Aud   1:05 8+
Break on Through jam » dialogue » Back Door Man » dialogue » Five to One » Touch Me (halts abruptly) » dialogue » Love Me Two Times » When the Music's Over » dialogue » Away in India » When the Music's Over, Wake Up!! » Light My Fire, dialogue (tape cuts at 1:05).

3/69   Sunset Sound Recorders, Hollywood, CA   Brd   0:45 8–
Poetry Session (Jim Morrison)

3/69   *Feast Of Friends* documentary.   Film 0:45 8+ V
Produced by the Doors; circulates in video.

3/69   *HWY* soundtrack   Aud   0:52 8+
Circulating tape is a recording made during a screening of the film.

4/28/69   *Critique*, PBS—WNET TV   TV   0:35 8
(Channel 13) Studios, New York, NY
Critique (musical portions): Tell All the People, Alabama Song » Back Door Man, Wishful Sinful, Build Me a Woman, The Soft Parade. Note: Richard Goldstein's interview was conducted the following day. The panel discussion was done at a later date.

6/25/69   *Critique*, broadcast, PBS—WNET TV   TV   1:00 8   V
(Channel 13), New York, NY
Critique (complete program): Five to One, [introduction by Richard Goldstein], Tell All the People, Alabama Song » Back Door Man, Wishful Sinful, Build Me a Woman, [panel discussion and interview with the Doors], The Soft Parade. Note: Music portion is the same as April 28, 1969; circulates in video as well.

| 9/13/69 | Varsity Stadium, Toronto, Ontario, Canada | Aud 1:00 7 |

When the Music's Over, Break on Through, Back Door Man » (Maggie M'Gill » Roadhouse Blues) » Back Door Man » Crystal Ship, Wake Up! » Light My Fire, The End.

| 1/17/70 L | Felt Forum (in Madison Square Garden), New York, NY | Aud 1:15 8 |

Late show: Roadhouse Blues, Break on Through, Ship of Fools, Alabama Song » Back Door Man » Five to One, Crawlin' King Snake, Build Me a Woman, (portion of show missing), "Bring out Your Dead" » The End.
Note: Peace Frog and Lizard, frequently on this tape, are from January 18.

| 1/18/70 E | Felt Forum (in Madison Square Garden), New York, NY | Aud 1:30 8+ |

Early show: Roadhouse Blues, Ship of Fools, Break on Through, Universal Mind, Alabama Song » Back Door Man » Five to One, Moonlight Drive » Horse Latitudes » Moonlight Drive, Who Do You Love, Money, Light My Fire, When the Music's Over.

| 1/18/70 L | Felt Forum (in Madison Square Garden), New York, NY | Aud 2:15 9– |

Late show: Roadhouse Blues, Peace Frog, Alabama Song » Back Door Man » Five to One, Celebration of the Lizard, Build Me a Woman, When the Music's Over, Soul Kitchen, Back in Seminary School » Light My Fire, Rock Me* » Close to You,* Ship of Fools, Goin' to New York,** Maggie M'Gill,** Gloria » Coda Queen » My Eyes Have Seen You. (*With John Sebastian) (**With John Sebastian and Dallas Taylor)

| 2/6/70 | Winterland Arena, San Francisco, CA | Aud 0:10 8 |

Carol, Rock Me.

| 2/7/70 | Long Beach Sports Arena, Long Beach, CA | Aud 1:40 7 |

Roadhouse Blues, Alabama Song » Back Door Man » Five to One, Ship of Fools, When the Music's Over, Spy in the House of Love, Break on Through, Peace Frog (cuts), (Universal Mind and Gloria are missing), Blue Sunday, Back In Seminary School » Light My Fire » Summertime » Fever » Light My Fire, Soul Kitchen, Love Me Two Times, Maggie M'Gill, (conclusion of show missing).

| 4/10/70 | Boston Arena, Boston, MA | Aud 1:35 7 |

Early show: Rock Me (a cappella introduction) » Roadhouse Blues, Ship of Fools, Alabama Song » Back Door Man » Five to One, When the Music's Over, Rock Me, People Get Ready » Mystery Train » Away in India » Crossroads, Wake Up! » Light My Fire.

| 6/5/70 | Seattle Center Coliseum, Seattle, WA | Sbd 1:15 6 |

Back Door Man » Love Hides » Back Door Man, "Adolf Hitler Is Still Alive," Roadhouse Blues, When the Music's Over, People Get Ready » Mystery Train (instrumental) » Baby Please Don't Go, Mystery Train » Away in India (instrumental) » Crossroads, Break on Through, Someday Soon, Five To One, (conclusion missing).

| 6/6/70 | PNE Coliseum, Vancouver, British Columbia, Canada | Sbd 1:40 6 |

Roadhouse Blues, Alabama Song » Back Door Man » Five to One, When the Music's Over, Love Me Two Times, Little Red Rooster,* Money,* Rock Me,* Who Do You Love,* "Back In Seminary School" » Light My Fire » Fever » Summertime » St. James Infirmary Blues » Fever » "There You Sit" » Light My Fire, The End » Across the Sea » Ensenada » The End. (* With Albert King)

| 8/22/70 | International Sports Arena, San Diego, CA | Aud 0:40 6 |

"Poetic improvisation" » Carol! » Louie, Louie » Lions in the Street and Roaming » Wake Up! » A Little Game » The Hill Dwellers » Wait, There's Been a Slaughter Here » Not to Touch the Earth » Names of the Kingdom » Heartbreak Hotel » Light My Fire » Fever » Summertime » St. James Infirmary Blues » Easy Ride » St. James Infirmary Blues » Fever » Light My Fire.

| 8/29/70 | "Isle of Wight" Festival, Isle Of Wight, England | Aud 1:00 7+ V |

(Audience copy): Back Door Man » Break on Through, When the Music's Over, Ship of Fools, Light My Fire, The End » Across the Sea » Away in India » Crossroads » Wake Up! » The End.
(Video copy): When the Music's Over, The End (edited).

| 12/8/70 | Note: Poetry session attributed to this date from the Village Recorders in Los Angeles is actually from March 1969. |

12/11/70 E State Fair Music Hall, Dallas, TX   Aud 1:00 5
Early show: Love Her Madly » Jam » Mack the Knife » Back Door Man, Ship of
Fools, The Changeling » L.A. Woman » When the Music's Over.

1970   *Absolutely Live* Outtakes   Sbd 0:35 8+
Roadhouse Blues, Money, Ship of Fools, "People Get Ready Jam" (People Get
Ready » Mystery Train » Away in India » Crossroads), Someday Soon. The
source of this recording is most likely an *Absolutely Live* or "Alive She
Cried" work tape, and the suggested origins for these cuts are very ques-
tionable. The Doors didn't play "Roadhouse Blues" and "Money" at the
Aquarius shows, and Bakersfield and Baltimore shows were not even
recorded for *Absolutely Live*. Note: The sources for the songs were attributed
as follows: Roadhouse Blues (Aquarius Theater, July 21, 1969), Money
(Aquarius Theater, July 22, 1969), Ship of Fools (Cobo Arena, May 8, 1970),
"People Get Ready Jam" (Bakersfield, August 21, 1970), Someday Soon (Baltimore, May 5, 1970).

MID 6/71   Paris Studio, Paris, France   Brd 0:15 9
Painfully awkward attempts at recording "Orange County Suite."
Note: The source of this tape has yet to be verified.

1967–1971 Rough mixes from several albums   Sbd 0:40 9
Hello I Love You, People Are Strange, Love Her Madly, Love Me Two Times,
Riders on the Storm, Touch Me, Soul Kitchen, Light My Fire, Take It As It
Comes, Moonlight Drive. These rough mixes are certainly inferior to the
released versions, but interesting just the same. Note: These songs suspi-
ciously correspond with the quadraphonic LP *Best of the Doors*, and may
simply be two tracks out of the four, which would definitely sound like a
different mix.

Post-Morrison Unreleased Recordings

The list shows date of show, location of show, source (e.g., Rec), length (e.g., 0:17), quality (e.g., 9–), and whether it is available in video (V).

11/23/71   Carnegie Hall, New York, NY   Aud 1:15 5
Tightrope Ride, Variety Is the Spice of Life, In the Eye of the Sun, I'm Horny I'm Stoned, Hang on to Your Life, Love Me Two Times, Down on the Farm, Close to You, Ships with Sails, Good Rockin',* Light My Fire, Hoochie Coochie Man.* (* With Tony Glover)

11/26/71   Hollywood Palladium, Hollywood, CA   Aud 1:15 7
Tightrope Ride, Variety Is the Spice of Life, In the Eye of the Sun, I'm Horny I'm Stoned, Hang on to Your Life, Love Me Two Times, Down on the Farm, Close to You, Ships with Sails, Hoochie Coochie Man.

12/2/71   Berkeley Community Theatre, Berkeley, CA   Aud 0:10 8+
Light My Fire (finale)

3/3/72   Painters Mill Music Theatre, Owings Mill, MD   Aud 1:05 8+
Tightrope Ride, Variety Is the Spice of Life, "Mosquito" (instrumental), In the Eye of the Sun, I'm Horny I'm Stoned, Love Me Two Times, Ships with Sails, Good Rockin', Light My Fire.

5/1/72   Olympia Theater, Paris, France   Aud 0:55 7+
In the Eye of the Sun, I'm Horny I'm Stoned, Love Me Two Times, Verdillac, Close To You, Ships With Sails, Good Rockin', Light My Fire, Hoochie Coochie Man.

5/3/72   *Beat Club*, Radio Bremen TV, West Germany   FM 0:50 8+ V
Good Rockin, Tightrope Ride, In the Eye of the Sun, I'm Horny I'm Stoned, Love Me Two Times, Verdillac, ("Ships with Sails" false start), Ships with Sails. Note: Broadcast on May 27; also circulates in video.

5/12/72   Imperial College Great Hall, London, England   Aud 0:30 7+
Tightrope Ride, In the Eye of the Sun, I'm Horny I'm Stoned, Love Me Two Times, (portion of show missing), Hoochie Coochie Man (encore).

7/21/72   Aragon Ballroom, Chicago, IL   FM 1:00 8+
In the Eye of the Sun, I'm Horny I'm Stoned, Verdillac, Love Me Two Times, Mosquito, Ships with Sails, Good Rockin', Light My Fire. Note: Broadcast on WGLD-FM.

8/13/72   San Diego Sports Arena, San Diego, CA   Aud 1:20 7+
Tightrope Ride, In the Eye of the Sun, I'm Horny I'm Stoned, Love Me Two times, Verdillac, Close to You, Mosquito, Ships with Sails, Good Rockin', Light My Fire.

8/21/72   Wollman Memorial Rink, Central Park, New York, NY   Aud 1:15 7+
Tightrope Ride, In the Eye of the Sun, Mosquito, Love Me Two Times, Verdillac (with Charles Lloyd), I'm Horny I'm Stoned, Good Rockin', Ships with Sails, Light My Fire, Close to You.

9/10/72   Hollywood Bowl, Hollywood, CA   Aud 1:00 8
The Doors' final performance. Tightrope Ride, In the Eye of the Sun, Mosquito, Love Me Two Times, Piano Bird, Verdillac, I'm Horny I'm Stoned, Ships with Sails, Light My Fire.

1/12/93   Century Plaza Hotel, Los Angeles, CA   Sbd 1:15 9
The "Rock 'n' Roll Hall of Fame" induction ceremonies. Rehearsals plus performance, which featured Roadhouse Blues, Break on Through, Light My Fire.

Videos

1/1/67   *Shebang*, KTLA TV-5, Los Angeles, CA (DU)   TV 0:02 8 V
Break on Through (only the first half of the song, then the tape cuts).

7/22/67   *American Bandstand*, ABC Studios, Hollywood, CA   TV 0:10 7 V
The Crystal Ship, Light My Fire

| 9/17/67 | *Ed Sullivan Show,* Ed Sullivan Theater, New York, NY | TV | 0:10 | 8+ | V |

People Are Strange, Light My Fire.

| 9/22/67 | *Murray the K in New York,* WPIX-TV, New York, NY | TV | 0:20 | 8 | V |

People Are Strange (several takes), Light My Fire.

| 10/16/67 | *The Rock Scene—Like It Is,* CBC, Toronto, Canada | TV | 0:10 | 9– | V |

Wake Up » The End.
Recorded September 14, 1967, and broadcast on CBC-TV on this date. The Doors' portion was also later broadcast in New York on August 1, 1970, on the *Now Explosion.*

| 12/27/67 | *Jonathan Winters Show,* CBS-TV Studios | TV | 0:10 | 7+ | V |

(Conclusion of "Horse Latitudes" on tape) » Moonlight Drive, Light My Fire.

| 9/18/68 | Copenhagen TV—Byen, Copenhagen, Denmark | TV | 0:30 | 8 | V |

Alabama Song » Back Door Man, Texas Radio and the Big Beat, Love Me Two Times, When the Music's Over, The Unknown Soldier.

| 10/4/68 | *The Doors Are Open* soundtrack, Granada TV, U.K. | TV | 1:00 | 8 | V |

(Introduction), When the Music's Over, Five to One, Spanish Caravan, (ICA press conference), Hello I Love You (from soundcheck with Manzarek on vocals), (interviews), Back Door Man » Crawlin' King Snake » Back Door Man, (interview with Jim Morrison), Wake Up! » Light My Fire, Unknown Soldier, (conclusion). Note: Now available commercially.

| 12/15/68 | *Smothers Brothers Comedy Hour,* CBS Studios, L.A. | TV | 0:10 | 9– | V |

Wild Child, Touch Me.

| 3/69 | *Feast Of Friends* documentary (produced by the Doors) | Film | 0:45 | 8+ | V |

| 6/25/69 | *Critique* broadcast, PBS—WNET-TV, NY, NY | TV | 1:00 | 8 | V |

Critique (complete program): Five to One, (introduction by Richard Goldstein), Tell All the People, Alabama Song » Back Door Man, Wishful Sinful, Build Me a Woman, (Panel discussion and interview with the Doors), The Soft Parade. Note: Music portion is the same as April 28, 1969. This is the original New York broadcast date of the show. Music portions recorded on April 28, interview on April 29, and panel discussion around mid-May.

| 8/29/70 | *Isle of Wight* Festival, Isle of Wight, England | Aud | 0:20 | 9– | V |

When the Music's Over, The End (edited).

| 5/3/72 | *Beat Club,* Radio Bremen TV, West Germany | FM | 0:50 | 8+ | V |

Good Rockin, Tightrope Ride, In the Eye of the Sun, I'm Horny I'm Stoned, Love Me Two Times, Verdillac, ("Ships with Sails" false start), Ships with Sails. Note: Broadcast on May 27.

Performance Locations

Arizona

5/6/67	Tucson, Hi-Corbett Stadium (DU)
5/24/68	Tucson, Hi-Corbett Stadium
7/29-31/66	Phoenix, 5th Estate (DU)
2/17/68	Phoenix Memorial Coliseum
11/7/68	Phoenix Memorial Coliseum

California

6/8/68	Bakersfield Civic Auditorium
8/21/70	Bakersfield Civic Auditorium
4/5/67	Fresno Fairgrounds (DU)
6/7/68	Fresno Fairgrounds

Los Angeles Vicinity

07-22-67	ABC Studios, *American Bandstand*
08-25-67	ABC, *Malibu U.*
7/15/67	Anaheim Convention Center
7/21–22/69	Aquarius Theater, Hollywood
5/19/66	Betty's Music Shop (DU)
6/7/67	Beverly Hills High School (DU)
9/15-18/66	Bido Lito's, Sunset Strip (DU)
5/12–14/66	Brave New World (DU)
5/20/67	Birmingham Stadium
10/6/67	California State, Los Angeles
10/27/67	California State, San Luis Obispo
12/1/67	California State, Long Beach
1/19–20/68	Carousel Theater, West Covina
12/27/67	CBS Studios, "Jonathan Winters"
12/04/68	CBS Studios, "Smothers Brothers" (rec)
12/15/68	CBS Studios, "Smothers Brothers" (b'cast)
1/12/93	Century Plaza Hotel
4/9/67	Cheetah, Venice
5/14/67	Cheetah, Venice
8/27/67	Cheetah, Venice
7/16/67	Devonshire Meadows
1/31/67	Gazzarri's
2/1–2/67	Gazzarri's
2/21/67	Gazzarri's
2/23–28/67	Gazzarri's
3/2/67	Gazzarri's
2/25/67	Griffith Park
7/5/68	Hollywood Bowl
9/10/72	Hollywood Bowl
11/26/71	Hollywood Palladium
11/19/65	Hughes Union Dance (DU)
5/30/66	Hullabaloo
2/18/67	Hullabaloo (DU)
2/25/67	Hullabaloo
4/30/67	Hullabaloo (Doors poss. didn't perform)
6/8/67	Hullabaloo
4/21–23/67	Kaleidoscope
3/29/68	Kaleidoscope
4/11/68	Kaleidoscope
4/24/68	Kaleidoscope
7/6/68	Kaleidoscope
1/1/67	KTLA TV Studios, Shebang (DU)
2/7/70	Long Beach Arena
2/66–5/7?/66	London Fog (DU)
12/14/68	Forum, Inglewood
6/2/67	*Cancelled:* Pasadena Civic Center
11/5/65	Pioneer Boat Club (DU)
12/31/65	Private Party [Krieger's]
12/31/66	Private Party, Montecito
1/66	Private Party, Marvin
7/3/67	Santa Monica Civic Center
12/9–10/66	Seawitch
12/16–17/66	Seawitch (DU)
12/22–23/67	Shrine Exposition Hall
4/20/67	Taft High School (DU)
12/10–11/65	UCLA Royce Hall
2/22/67	Valley Music Theater, Woodland Hills
5/7/67	Valley Music Theater, Woodland Hills (DU)
5/6–7/66	Warner Playhouse
5/13–14/66	Warner Playhouse
5/9/66	Whisky A Go Go (DU)
5/23–7/27/66	Whisky A Go Go (DU)
8/1–4/66	Whisky A Go Go
8/7–21/66	Whisky A Go Go (DU)
5/1/67 (?)	Whisky A Go Go (Show may not have occurred)
5/16–21/67	Whisky A Go Go
5/3/69	Whisky A Go Go (JM) (DU)
5/19–22/69	*Cancelled:* Whisky A Go Go
7/5/67	Lowell High School, La Habra
4/23/66	Will Rogers State Park
9/2/65	World Pacific Studios
2/11/66	Van Nuys Teen Center (DU)
4/7/67	Merced Legion Hall
4/12/68	Merced Fairgrounds
4/6/67	Modesto Skating Arena (DU)
7/28/66	Oxnard, Starlight Ballroom
8/5/66	Oxnard, Starlight Ballroom
1/7/72	Palm Springs Tramway Lodge
1/29/66	Redlands, Prospect Park (DU)
4/17/68	Riverside Auditorium
7/14/67	Sacramento State Fairgrounds
12/15/67	*Cancelled:* Sacramento Memorial Auditorium
6/15/68	Sacramento Memorial Auditorium
5/1/69	Sacramento, Sacramento SC Gallery (Jim Morrison with McClure)
12/16/67	San Bernardino Swing Auditorium
7/8/67	San Diego, Balboa Stadium
11/4/67	San Diego Community Concourse
6/29/68	San Diego Community Concourse
10/26/69	*Cancelled:* San Diego Balboa Stadium
8/22/70	San Diego International Sports Arena
8/13/72	San Diego Balboa Stadium
7/28/66	Santa Barbara, Earl Warren
8/6/66	Santa Barbara, Earl Warren
4/29/67	Santa Barbara, Earl Warren
5/27/67	Santa Barbara, Earl Warren
8/5/67	Santa Barbara, Earl Warren
10/29/67	Santa Barbara, University of California Robertson Gym
6/28/68	Santa Barbara, La Playa Stadium
7/9/67	Santa Clara, Continental Ballroom (DU)
5/19/68	Santa Clara Fairgrounds Folk Festival
4/13/68	Santa Rosa Fairgrounds
4/8/67	Turlock Fairgrounds

San Francisco Bay Area

3/3–4/67	Avalon Ballroom
4/14–15/67	Avalon Ballroom
5/12–13/67	Avalon Ballroom
6/3–4/67	Avalon Ballroom
10/15/67	Berkeley Community Theater
2/10/68	Berkeley Community Theater
12/2/71	Berkeley Community Theater
7/25/69	Cow Palace (Daly City)
1/6–8/67	Fillmore Auditorium
1/13/67?	Fillmore Auditorium (DU)
1/14–15/67	Fillmore Auditorium
6/9–10/67	Fillmore Auditorium
7/28–30/67	Fillmore Auditorium
11/16/67	Fillmore Auditorium
6/10/67	Mt. Tamalpais Amphitheater (Marin County)
3/7–11/67	Matrix
7/13/67	Oakland Auditorium
11/17–18/67	Winterland
12/26–28/67	Winterland
2/5–6/70	Winterland
2/14–15/67	Whisky A Go Go, S.F. (DU)

Colorado

9/29/67	Denver University Student Union
9/30/67	Denver, Family Dog
12/29–31/67	Denver, Family Dog
4/12/70	Denver, University Arena
10/21/67	Colo. Springs, Broadmoor Hotel

Connecticut

9/21/67	Westport, Staples High School
9/24/67	Wallingford, Oakdale Theater
10/11/67	Danbury High School
11/26/67	Hartford, Bushnell Auditorium
12/9/67	New Haven Arena
8/1/68	Bridgeport, JFK Stadium
5/9/70	Cancelled: Fairfield University
8/18/72	Hartford, Dillon Stadium

Florida

3/1/69	Miami, Dinner Key Auditorium
8/14/70	Miami, Hump, Marco Polo (JM)
3/9/69	Cancelled: Jacksonville Sports Coliseum
3/10/72	Dania, Pirate's World
3/11/72	Tallahassee Stadium, FSU
3/12/72	Tampa, Ft. Hesterly Armory

Georgia

3/9/72	Cancelled: Atlanta Municipal Auditorium
8/25/72	Cancelled: Atlanta Municipal Auditorium

Hawaii, Honolulu

7/20/68	Honolulu, HIC Arena
7/3–4/69	Cancelled: Honolulu, HIC Arena
1/25/70	Cancelled: Honolulu, HIC Arena
4/18/70	Honolulu, HIC Arena

Illinois

5/10/68	Chicago Coliseum
11/3/68	Chicago Coliseum
6/14/69	Chicago, Auditorium Theater
2/15/70	Chicago, Auditorium Theater
7/21/72	Chicago, Aragon Ballroom

Indiana

9/4/72	Cancelled: Bull Island "Erie Canal Festival"

Iowa

9/27/67	Des Moines, KRNT Theater

Kentucky

10/31/68	Louisville, Freedom Hall

Louisiana

6/24/69	New Orleans, The Roach (LU) (DU) (JM)
12/12/70	New Orleans Warehouse
9/2/72	New Orleans City Auditorium

Massachusetts

8/10–11/67	Brighton, Crosstown Bus Club
10/12/67	Nantasket Beach Surf Club
10/21/67	Williamstown, Williams College
3/17/68	Boston, Back Bay Theater
4/25/69	Cancelled: Boston Garden
4/10/70	Boston Arena
11/22/71	Boston Music Hall
8/16/72	Boston, Boston Common

Maryland

8/18/67	Annapolis Bard Armory
10/13/67	Baltimore, Lyric Theater
5/10/70	Baltimore Civic Center
8/30/68	Columbia, Merriweather Post.
3/3/72	Owings Mill, Painter's Mill Theater

Michigan

10/22/67	Ann Arbor, I.M.Building
5/11/68	Detroit, Cobo Arena
3/28/69	Cancelled: Olympia Stadium
5/8/70	Detroit, Cobo Arena
11/20/71	Detroit, East Towne Theater
8/14/72	Cancelled: Detroit, Cobo Arena
9/3/72	Detroit, Michigan Palace

Minnesota

11/10/68	Minneapolis Concert Hall
6/15/69	Minneapolis Convention Center
11/13/71	Minneapolis, Augsberg College

Missouri

11/9/68	St. Louis, Kiel Auditorium
6/13/69	Cancelled: St. Louis, Kiel Auditorium

Nebraska

5/26/68	Lincoln, Pershing Auditorium (probably cancelled)
11/12/71	Lincoln, Pershing Auditorium

New York State

4/26/69	Cancelled: Buffalo Memorial Auditorium
11/18/71	Buffalo, Peace Bridge Center
3/2/72	Greenvale, CW Post Dome
3/15/68	Hamilton, Colgate University
9/11/67	Oswego, State University NY
3/16/68	Rochester, Eastman Theater

9/1/68	Saratoga Performing Arts Center
12/8/67	Troy, Rensselaer Polytechnic Institute
9/1/68	Schenectady, Aerodrome (JM)
11/19/71	Cancelled: Schenectady, The Carousel
9/23/67	Stony Brook, State University of New York
4/27/69	Cancelled: Syracuse, Onondaga Memorial Auditorium

New York Metropolitan Area

11/8/67	ABC TV, Bruce Morrow's Music Power
8/25/72	ABC Studios Dick Cavett Show
6/16–17/67	Action House, Long Beach, LI
11/23/71	Carnegie Hall
8/21/72	Central Park, Wollman Rink
8/8/69	Cancelled: Electric Circus (never scheduled!)
1/17–18/70	Felt Forum, Madison Square Garden
3/22–23/68	Fillmore East
8/12/67	Forest Hills Stadium, Queens
11/24/67	Hunter College
1/24/69	Madison Square Garden
11/1–30/67	Ondine (early dates DU)
1/19–29/67	Ondine (26–29 DU)
3/13–4/2/67	Ondine
4/28–29/69	PBS Studios, Critique (recording)
6/25/69	PBS Studios, Critique (broadcast)
8/15/72	Ritz Theater, Staten Island
8/23/72	Ritz Theater, Staten Island
8/2/68	Singer Bowl, Queens
6/12–15/67	Steve Paul's Scene
6/19–7/1/67	Steve Paul's Scene
10/1–5/67	Steve Paul's Scene
10/9–10/67	Steve Paul's Scene
10/16–19/67	Steve Paul's Scene (16–19 DU)
3/7/68	Steve Paul's Scene (JM) (DU)
9/17/67	Ed Sullivan Theater
6/11/67	Village Theater
9/9/67	Village Theater
5/11/70	Village Gate (JM) (Uncertain if JM read)
4/19/68	Westbury Music Fair, LI
9/22/67	WPIX-TV, Murray the K in New York

Nevada

8/25/67	Las Vegas Convention Center
11/1/69	Las Vegas Ice Palace

New Hampshire

8/9/67	Hampton Beach Casino

New Jersey

9/2/67	Asbury Park Convention Center
8/31/68	Asbury Park Convention Center
9/20/67	Scotch Plains, Union Catholic High School (DU)

Oklahoma

10/8/67	Tulsa Civic Assembly Center

Oregon

11/11/67	Corvallis, Oregon State University
11/12/67	Eugene, University of Oregon (DU)
6/30/68	Eugene, MacArthur Court (DU)
7/26/69	Eugene Pop, University of Oregon
7/26/67	Portland Masonic Temple
12/2/67	Portland Civic Auditorium

Ohio

8/3/68	Cleveland Public Auditorium
3/29/69	Cancelled: Cleveland Public Auditorium
2/13–14/70	Cleveland, Allen Theater
11/2/68	Columbus Memorial Hall
5/9/70	Columbus Memorial Auditorium
3/30/69	Cancelled: Cincinnati Music Hall
3/23/69	Cancelled: Kent State University (DU)
9/21/69	Cancelled: University of Toledo Fieldhouse
9/14/67	Warrensville, Music Carnival

Pennsylvania

6/18/67	Philadelphia, Town Hall (Note: August 13 and December 10, 1967 were apparently never scheduled.)
8/4/68	Philadelphia Arena
3/18/69	Cancelled: Philadelphia Spectrum
3/19/69	Cancelled: Philadelphia Convention Center
9/19/69	Cancelled: Philadelphia Spectrum (relocated)
9/19/69	Philadelphia Arena
5/1/70	Philadelphia Spectrum
11/24/71	Irvine Auditorium, University of Pennsylvania
5/2/68	Pittsburgh Arena
3/17/69	Cancelled: Pittsburgh Electric Theater
3/22/69	Cancelled: Pittsburgh Arena
9/20/69	Pittsburgh Civic Arena
5/2/70	Pittsburgh Arena
10/14/67	Selinsgrove, Susquehanna University

Rhode Island

9/22/67	Providence, Brown University
3/20/69	Cancelled: Providence RI Auditorium
8/19/72	Providence, Loew's Theater

South Carolina

3/5/72	Charleston County Auditorium
3/8/72	Columbia USC Carolina Coliseum

Tennessee

8/27/72	Memphis County Music Hall

Texas

9/3/67	Fort Worth, Will Rogers Exhibit
7/9/68	Dallas Memorial Coliseum
4/4/69	Cancelled: Dallas Memorial Auditorium
12/11/70	Dallas State Fair Music Hall
9/1/72	Dallas Majestic Theater
7/10/68	Houston Coliseum
4/5/69	Cancelled: Houston Coliseum

Utah

9/8/67	Farmington, Lagoon Park
5/25/68	Farmington, Lagoon Park
4/11/70	Cancelled: Salt Lake Salt Palace

Virginia

8/18/67	Alexandria, Roller Rink
3/4/72	Williamsburg, William and Mary Hall
8/24/72	Norfolk City Hall

Washington, D.C. Area
9/15–16/67	Ambassador Theatre (possibly cancelled)
11/25/67	Hilton International Hotel Ballroom
8/18/67	Annapolis Bard Armory (National Guard)
8/20/72	Constitution Hall

Washington State
7/23–24/67	Seattle, Eagles Auditorium
11/10/67	Seattle, Eagles Auditorium
12/3/67	Seattle, Eagles Auditorium (DU)
7/12/68	Seattle Center Arena
7/5/69	Cancelled: Seattle, Sicks Stadium
7/27/69	Seattle Pop Festival
6/5/70	Seattle Center Coliseum

Wisconsin
11/8/68	Madison, Dane County Coliseum
11/1/68	Milwaukee Arena
7/23/72	Milwaukee, "Summerfest"

Canada

Ottawa, Ontario
11/17/71	Ottawa Civic Center

Toronto, Ontario
9/14/67	CBC-TV Studios, "Rock Scene" (rec)
10/16/67	CBC-TV "Rock Scene" (broadcast)
5/12/68	Canadian National Exhibition
3/21/69	Cancelled: Toronto Maple Leaf Gardens
9/13/69	Varsity Stadium
11/14/71	St. Lawrence Market

Montreal, Quebec
9/14/69	Montreal Forum

Vancouver, British Columbia
6/2/67	Victoria Arena (near Vancouver)
7/20/67	Victoria Arena (near Vancouver)
7/21–22/67	Dante's Inferno
7/13/68	PNE Coliseum
6/6/70	PNE Coliseum

Europe

Denmark
9/17/68	Copenhagen, Falkoner Centret
9/18/68	Copenhagen, TV—Byen
9/2/70	Cancelled: K.B. Hallen
4/27/72	Copenhagen, Tivoli Koncertsall

England
9/5/68	London, BBC Studios
9/6–7/68	London, Roundhouse
10/4/68	London BBC Doors Are Open (broadcast)
9/19/69	Cancelled: London, Royal Albert Hall
8/29/70	Isle of Wight Festival
5/9/72	London, "Old Gray Whistle Test"
5/10/72	Newcastle City Hall
5/11/72	Birmingham, Kinetic Circus
5/12/72	London, Imperial College
5/13/72	Reading University
5/14/72	Guildford City Hall

France
9/14/70	Cancelled: Olympia, Paris
Early 5/71	Paris, Astroquet (JM with Clinic) (DU)
5/1/72	Paris, Olympia Theater
12/8/78	Paris, Palais Club

Holland, Netherlands
9/15/68	Amsterdam Concertgebouw
5/6/72	Rotterdam, De Doelen
5/7/72	Amsterdam, Carre

Italy
9/11/70	Cancelled: Rome
9/12/70	Cancelled: Milan

Sweden
9/20/68	Stockholm, Konserthuset

Switzerland
8/31/70	Cancelled: Montreux Festival
4/30/72	Montreux Jazz Festival

West Germany
9/13/68	Frankfurt, Romer Square TV
9/14/68	Frankfurt, Kongresshalle
9/10/70	Cancelled: Bremen
4/28/72	Munchen, Circus Krone
4/29/72	Frankfurt, Jahrhunderthalle
5/3/72	Bremen, Beat Club (recording)
5/27/72	Bremen, Beat Club (broadcast)

Mexico
6/27–30/69	Mexico City, Forum

Poetry Readings
3/69	Elektra Studios, L.A.
5/1/69	SacSC Gallery (Jim Morrison with Michael McClure)
5/30–31/69	Cinematheque, Hollywood
3/27/70	Cancelled: Queen Elizabeth/Orpheum Theatre, Vancouver, Canada
5/11/70	Village Gate, New York, NY (uncertain if Jim Morrison read)
12/8/70	Village Recorders, L.A.

Television Broadcasts
1/1/67	Shebang (DU)
7/22/67	American Bandstand (ABC)
8/25/67	Malibu U. (ABC)
9/14/67	Toronto CBC, "Rock Scene" (recording)
9/17/67	Ed Sullivan Show (CBS)
9/22/67	"Murray The K in New York" (WPIX-NY)
10/16/67	Toronto CBC, "Rock Scene" (broadcast)
11/8/67	Bruce Morrow's Music Power (ABC)
12/27/67	Jonathan Winters Show (CBS)
7/7/68	Ed Sullivan Show (9/17/67 rebroadcast)
9/14/68	Frankfurt, West Germany TV
9/18/68	Danish TV Studio, Copenhagen
10/4/68	London BBC Doors Are Open

12/4/68	*Smothers Brothers Comedy Hour* recording (CBS)
12/15/68	*Smothers Brothers Comedy Hour* broadcast (CBS)
4/28–29/69	NDT/PBS-NY *Critique* (recording)
6/25/69	NDT/PBS—NY *Critique* (broadcast)
7/19/69	KCET—LA Broadcast of *Critique*
8/1/70	*Now Explosion* (WPIX-NY)
5/3/72	Bremen TV *Beat Club* (recording)
5/9/72	London, *Old Gray Whistle Test* (BBC)
5/27/72	Bremen TV *Beat Club* (broadcast)
8/25/72	*Dick Cavett Show*

Post Doors

6/4/74	*Midnight Special* (Butts Band) (ABC)

Radio Broadcasts

9/5/68	London BBC *Top of the Pops*
9/20/68	Konserthuset, Stockholm, Sweden (early and late shows)
3/10/72	Pirate's World, Miami (WBUS-FM)
7/21/72	Aragon Ballroom, Chicago (WGLD-FM)

Post Doors

5/13/74	January Sound Studios, Dallas, Texas (Ray Manzarek)
Circa 6/74	Chicago (Ray Manzarek)
6/11/74	My Father's Place, Roslyn, NY (WLIR-FM) (Ray Manzarek)

Film Festivals – Feast of Friends

5/30–31/69	Cinematheque 16, Hollywood
6/6–8/69	Cinematheque 16, Hollywood
6/8/69	Vancouver Film Festival
6/19/69	PNE Garden "Free Press Benefit"
6/20/69	Atlanta Film Festival
8/18/69	Solomon Theater, CAC Campus
8/31/69	Edinburgh, Scotland
9/29/69	Lincoln Center (7th) NY Film Festival
10/17/69	Santa Cruz Film Festival (DU)
10/31/69	San Francisco Film Festival
9/6/69	Varsity Arena, Canada
3/27/70	Queen Elizabeth/Orpheum, Vancouver